Government and

Social Welfare

Roles of Federal, State, and Local Governments
in Administering Welfare Services

WAYNE VASEY

Graduate School of Social Work
Rutgers · The State University

HENRY HOLT AND COMPANY · NEW YORK

Preface

Social welfare programs, like other features of life in today's world, are likely to be swept along in the swift current of social change. Even while this book has been in preparation, one of the more dramatic of these changes has occurred. The condition of the economy has shifted from an ascending level of production and employment to one of reduced production and a higher rate of unemployment. By the time the book reaches the classroom or the shelves of libraries, the economy may or may not have resumed its upward climb.

In a sense, however, this development highlights the way in which governmental provision for social welfare has become a basic part of our national life, a point stated in the book. It would be difficult to overstate the value many of these measures of social welfare have in mitigating the hardships which accompany such dips in the economy, and in slowing down the rate of decline.

The dominant theme in *Government and Social Welfare* is the respective roles of federal, state, and local governments in the provision of welfare services. It would be of little use to describe roles, however, without some description of the services themselves, or to describe either without consideration of the philosophy which underlies them both. In treating all aspects of the subject, I have tried to stress the impact these services have on our lives. I have written from a background of direct personal experience in local, state, and federal welfare administration, as well as of teaching this subject in a school of social work.

In this book I have stressed the importance of leadership in the administration of programs. My conviction on this point derives from experience for several years in a federal program under the leadership of Arthur J. Altmeyer, then Chairman of the Social Security Board, and Jane Hoey, then Director of the Bureau of Public Assistance in which I was employed at the time. In the years since then, I have more and more come to appreciate the influence these two and their associates, through their vision and strength of conviction, had on the programs which today mean so much to the national community. I owe them much for this experience.

iii

It would be next to impossible to make a complete acknowledgment of my indebtedness to those who have assisted me in so many ways, but I hope that those whom limited space prevents my mentioning will be completely aware of how keenly I appreciate their aid and encouragement. They include members of the staffs of the following federal agencies: the Children's Bureau, the Bureau of Old-Age and Survivors Insurance, the Bureau of Public Assistance of the Social Security Administration, and the Office of Vocational Rehabilitation, all parts of the Department of Health, Education, and Welfare; the Veterans Administration; the Department of Labor's Bureau of Labor Standards and Bureau of Employment Security. Thanks are also due my friends in local and state offices who provided me so much indispensable material, in particular Dr. Ellen Winston, Commissioner of the Board of Public Welfare, North Carolina, George Wyman, Director, and members of the staff of the California State Department of Social Welfare, and to Edward F. Hann, Jr., of the New Jersey Board of Child Welfare, for reviewing portions of the book. George Bigge, Special Assistant on Federal-State Problems, Department of Health, Education, and Welfare, certainly deserves my gratitude for his thorough and expeditious review of one of the most complex portions of the manuscript.

My old friend, Robert W. Beasley, has earned my thanks not only for his review of some of the chapters, but also for his reminder that a book can contain facts and still express a point of view. I want to include also my Rutgers colleagues, Jack Chernick, of the Rutgers Institute of Management and Labor Relations, and members of the staff of the Graduate School of Social Work, in my expression of appreciation. Certainly I should be seriously remiss and ungrateful if I failed to mention the assistance and the encouragement of my wife, Margaret, in the completion of this task.

W. V.

New Brunswick, N. J.
March 3, 1958

Contents

v

PART III

Part I

The Background

In a world in which news headlines almost daily proclaim technological advances of vast and dramatic importance, it is easy to
overlook the tremendous changes which have occurred in the
social and political spheres. But it would be difficult to overesti-
mate the extent to which some of these changes have altered the
way we live, and our whole pattern of social relationships.

In the past quarter of a century the role the government has
assumed in the provision of welfare services to the American people would have been unthinkable in 1930. Perhaps it would be
more accurate to say that the people themselves have sought to
provide these services through the agency of government, since in
a democracy the people do have this choice. During these past
twenty-five years governmentally administered social welfare has
grown from being a meager program of aid to an impoverished
few to be a major resource for virtually the entire people. Through
these programs of social welfare, the people have come to rely on
public services for protection against many hazards and contingencies which once were considered strictly the province of the
individual and his family.

Many facts could be cited to underscore the importance of
social welfare today. One could point to the number of services, to

the money which they require, to the people whose needs are met, to the effect on family life, and to the many other aspects of life currently affected by social welfare programs. One could dwell on the fact that programs now so customary as to be commonplace only a few years ago would have been considered, if they were proposed at all, to be the fantastic dream of some bemused radical.

Now, however, governmentally sponsored and administered social welfare is very much with us and even continues to increase its scope and volume of service. Let us look briefly at some of its major features.

For one thing, the programs are large and require an expenditure second only to national defense as a major cost of government. For example, in 1955-56, about 22 billion dollars were spent by federal, state, and local authorities on public welfare programs of social insurance, public assistance, health and medical care, vocational rehabilitation, child welfare, veterans' services, and institutional care.

Development of these tax-supported services has had an important effect on the apportionment of responsibilities among federal, state, and local governments. This is significant in itself, for any major change in this relationship reaches beyond the immediate program and has an effect upon the entire political structure of the nation. Social welfare measures have widely enlarged the area of intergovernmental relations, and new patterns of operation have emerged among and within the three levels of government.

The growth of public social services in the past twenty-five years also has affected privately-supported philanthropic programs. Greater assumption of responsibility by government has absorbed some and led to a realignment of others of the responsibilities formerly assumed by voluntary agencies. As one result these agencies have adjusted their programs so that they relate appropriately to the growing publicly-supported welfare enterprise.

While all this is important, perhaps most significant (certainly from a social scientist's viewpoint) is the change in the relationship of government to the individual. Conditions which underlie this development have compelled a thoughtful reconsideration of the responsibility of government to the individual. It has become more and more necessary to reconcile the demands and needs of a complex interdependent society with the tradition of personal responsibility which has been one of this country's basic characteristics. The struggle toward this reconciliation has been difficult and at times painful.

It has seemed an anomaly to some that in the midst of an unprecedented level of prosperity a flourishing welfare enterprise should have to exist. This in itself is indicative of the extent of the change. Through industrialization and standardization, large organizations controlling the means of production and of distribution have become the norm, indeed one outstanding characteristic, of our daily life. The organization of welfare programs is no exception to this norm. There is relatively little support today for any movement to return to the "good old days" by curtailing the government-supported social welfare programs, although as we shall see later, criticism and opposition to them are not unknown. More to the point today is argument over how to make them work better, and how far they should be extended. On such issues, the controversies are far from settled. It is vital that we work out a rationale which will determine how the personal responsibility of the individual for the care of himself and his family is related to the obligation of government and to the organized private resources of business, labor, and philanthropy.

In a democracy in which the people themselves make or support the decisions on public policy and programs, it is important that they be informed, especially when their lives are affected as directly as they are by social welfare. Yet social welfare is not so well understood; there are in fact many indications that it is one of the least comprehended of all of our government's functions. This lack of general information can be damaging, as the decisions it leads to are occasionally based on prejudice rather than knowledge. Such lack of information or misinformation has more than once resulted in action not only damaging to the people directly affected but also indirectly harmful to the whole community. The field of social welfare, like many others, has had its share of witch hunts and of other attacks based on misunderstanding.

This book has been written in the hope that it will shed some light on the subject of the respective roles of federal, state, and local government in this area of service. It has been prepared primarily for the undergraduate student in the social sciences, and for the undergraduate and graduate students in social welfare. It does not purport to be an exhaustive treatise on the theory underlying governmental support for and provision of welfare services; it is intended instead to be a descriptive text of current social welfare programs and of the measures which have been developed, the nature of the needs they meet, and the network of organizations which has been established to administer all these services.

Part I describes the nature and scope of contemporary tax-supported social welfare, its historical development, some of the most vital conflicts in views about social welfare, and the relations between governmental and voluntary social services. In Part II, the programs themselves will be considered, with special emphasis on the conditions—the eligibility requirements—under which people may receive welfare services from governmental programs, on the specific goals and major features of such programs as old age, survivors and disability insurance, unemployment benefits, workmen's compensation, public assistance, child welfare, mental health, and vocational rehabilitation, to name just a few. The organization and administration of welfare services, in federal, state, and local arms of government is the subject of Part III; the division of responsibility among these governmental areas has led in some programs to division of functions, in others it has led to shared administrative operations. In this section, the importance of the personnel and the methods of public welfare work are given due emphasis, for it is through these—through individuals dealing with each other face-to-face—that the people and the programs meet.

1

The Scope of Needs and Services

WHAT IS NEED?

People have many needs—social, biological, emotional, and spiritual. They represent a level of wants which are socially as well as individually determined. As a society increases its productive capacity, the wants of its members increase. Food which meets nutritional standards, clothing which presents certain attributes of appearance, and shelter which presents comfort and psychic satisfaction as well as protection against the elements, become essentials. Conveniences and appliances are thought of as necessities rather than luxuries. Needs are measured as much in terms of material standards as in terms of biological necessity.

In relation to social services, needs are said to exist when what the individual family is able to provide through the efforts of its members fails to meet an implicit or explicit standard considered to be a minimum for health and decency. This might be called the concept of minimum adequacy.

But needs cannot be measured entirely in terms of material well-being. In a society which stresses the dignity of the individual, other values are applied to depict the range of human

6

need. The need to feel secure against the hazards of daily living is important for the head of the household and for members of his family. The effects of unsatisfied material needs are not entirely material; according to the fact-finding report of the Mid-Century White House Conference on Children and Youth, low or insecure income may affect the growth of personality in the child.

> It [low income] may handicap physical development and efficiency of biological functioning. It may create tensions in interpersonal relationships, especially within the family but also in the child's relations with peers and others. It may handicap for social and cultural reasons, both because it may put the child in a disadvantaged social class and because it may make him feel that he has been deprived of his rightful heritage of equality of opportunity.[1]

Assurance of a place to sleep and food and clothing does not cover the range of needs of the older person either. The need for self-respect and for dignity and security in old age is recognized as important. Today, emphasis on the mental health of older people and on social acceptance of the status of old age are increasingly recognized as the proportion of senior citizens in the population continues to grow.

The insecurity of dependent old age is not confined to those who already have reached that stage in life. It is a real factor in the lives of the middle-aged, and even those who are younger. The words of one of the pioneers of social legislation for protection against insecurity in old age, I. M. Rubinow, still ring true. He wrote two decades ago that:

> The fear of approaching old age, not only of the failure of strength and health and power of enjoying life, . . . [is] also the fear of the economic problem which insecure old age must face. Go to Middletown, talk to the men in the fifties or even in the forties, sitting on the porch after dinner, smoking their pipes.

[1] Helen Leland Witmer and Ruth Kotinsky, eds., *Personality in the Making*, The Fact-Finding Report of the Mid-Century White House Conference on Children and Youth (New York, 1952), p. 105.

Talk particularly to their aging wives. And if you could read their thoughts, perhaps the one thought which is most responsible for the gloomy silence of the after-dinner siesta: "Well, how long can I hold on to this job? How long can my man hold on to this job? It is the younger men who get all the chances nowadays. And what will happen if . . ."[2]

Unemployment is a cause of fear even to a young man during his productive working years. Interruption of income is serious in economic terms alone but it has additional meaning to the jobholder in terms of dignity. The job means status. It is the worker's passport to a self-respecting place in the society of his fellows, a kind of social enfranchisement. It has vital meaning in terms of his place in the circle of his family.

A crippling injury, whether resulting from accident or from some other cause, may hit the family of the worker with double-barrelled force. Not only is he deprived of the means of livelihood, but he also must face the problem of meeting the costs of hospitalization for which he may be inadequately prepared. He may suffer from an illness of a chronic nature, or a member of the family may become ill or injured and consequently require care beyond his means. Here again, more than the loss of material goods is involved. As in other cases of interruption of income, fixed obligations perhaps cannot be met, and the family may lose a home or other possessions representing years of savings and self-denial, or the children may be denied educational opportunities. Without dramatizing the situation, one must realize that this kind of catastrophe has meaning far beyond the loss of minimum essentials.

Such examples of need could be multiplied. Thus far, most of those presented have illustrated misfortunes which are readily recognized as representing external experiences or perils. There is another type of problem, however, which is not so easily recognized but which has just as much real meaning in our society. Some problems are intrapsychic in their origin. They arise out of failure of the personality, sometimes even under favorable economic circumstances. They take their toll in terms of interpersonal

[2] I. M. Rubinow, *The Quest for Security* (New York, 1934), p. 227.

relations, both within the family and outside. The need for counselling and for treatment is just as real as the need for maintaining minimum income.

When problems are catalogued in this way, they may seem to be separate and classifiable. Yet more often than not they are interlocking. The ostensible or apparent problem may not be the real one. Unemployment may arise out of inability to hold a job, which in turn may stem from inability to get along with one's fellows. People are not always able to uproot this inability by themselves. Illness may be created by the tensions of daily living. The industrial accident may result from fatigue brought on by an excessive desire to meet the needs of a family and to live up to a high standard. Neglect of a child may be the act of defeated parents. It is frequently hard to determine exactly where these problems start and what the real difficulty is.

The social order even at its best produces its crop of difficulties and problems. As a former Commissioner of Social Security has noted,

> Even though we achieve the goal of full employment and full production, it is still necessary in a system of private enterprise such as ours to have a program designed to eliminate want, because the working people of this country will still be confronted with the great economic hazards of sickness, physical disability, want, old age and death, as well as intermittent unemployment. All of these hazards mean interruption of income to the individual family, and still spell want in a land of plenty.[3]

WHAT DO WE MEAN BY SOCIAL WELFARE?

Sometimes a definition is a most elusive thing. This is especially true when the term to be defined is as broad in its potential meaning as is this one. Such a term could encompass practically the entire range of social activity on behalf of people. It could refer to measures in support of agriculture, of public housing, of public

[3] Arthur J. Altmeyer, "Statement Before the Advisory Council on Social Security," Dec. 4, 1947, United States Senate Finance Committee.

safety, and in fact, to almost anything done by government, on the premise that in a democracy all government actions are performed for the general welfare.

Such a wide definition would be meaningless. Social welfare has a specific meaning in current terminology, in spite of the difficulty of precisely defining the phrase.

Friedlander has suggested the following definition: "Social welfare is the organized system of welfare services and institutions, designed to aid individuals and groups to attain satisfying standards of life and health. It aims at personal and social relationships which permit individuals the development of their full capacities and the promotion of their well-being in harmony with the needs of the community."[4]

This definition is comprehensive and emphasizes the fact that welfare services are organized services. It stresses a level of social aspiration for the individual and the family. It recognizes the meaning of social welfare in terms of providing conditions which permit the individual to develop his potentialities. Yet this could not be considered an exact definition, for it does not necessarily exclude certain services which generally might not be considered classifiable as social welfare.

A government agency, the Social Security Administration, has offered this definition, in relation to the kinds of services rendered: "The concept of social welfare in the United States of America is not constant but rather it alters with changing conditions. Most recently, social welfare has been defined as encompassing the development and administration of (1) Social Insurance, (2) Social Assistance, and (3) other social services designed to strengthen family life and to provide care and protection for special groups such as children, the aged, and mentally, socially, or physically handicapped persons."[5]

4 Walter A. Friedlander, *Introduction to Social Welfare* (New York, 1955), p. 4.
5 "Social Welfare Administration in the United States of America," Social Security Administration, June, 1950; a report prepared at the request of the United Nations for incorporation in its international study of social welfare administration, p. 1.

In these and other definitions of social welfare, two characteristics stand out: (1) the utilization of welfare measures to support or strengthen the family as a basic social institution through which needs are met. Even those programs designed to aid the victims of broken homes or untenable family situations attempt to find the best possible substitute pending the return to or development of a good family situation. (2) The intent to strengthen the individual's capacity to cope with his life situation.

What is meant by governmental social welfare? Governmental social welfare programs are those which are tax-supported and administered by agencies of government—federal, state, or local —or any combination thereof. Throughout this book, the terms "governmental social welfare" and "public welfare" will be used interchangeably to refer to this classification of programs. This choice is dictated by the cumbrousness of the term "governmental social welfare" and by the fact that "public welfare" is the more common usage. Voluntary social welfare denotes those organized services supported by gifts from individuals, corporations, and other groups.

Another and related term which has become prominent during the past quarter century is "social security." This term is indigenous to the United States. Many people erroneously use it with reference only to one particular form of service, old age insurance. Actually, as Dr. Eveline Burns has pointed out, social security may have a variety of meanings for different people. To some, notes Dr. Burns, it connotes "income security." To others it refers to a single program of income security. In some other countries, Dr. Burns further states, the meaning is indeed broad, including measures like wage legislation and housing.[6]

In a statement which emphasizes social security as an affirmative and broad program of social action, Mr. Altmeyer offers the following:[7]

---

[6] Eveline M. Burns, *The American Social Security System* (Boston, 1949), p. 4.
[7] Arthur J. Altmeyer, "The People and Their Government," in *New Directions in Social Work*, Cora Kasius, ed. (New York, 1954), p. 59.

. . . . Social Security is one of those magic terms which can mean as much or as little as the person using it chooses it to mean. It is now in general use throughout the world, although we, in America, can rightly claim credit for coining this term during the early thirties. Sometimes it is used to encompass all the good things of life. But in this country we use it to describe a specific governmental program designed to eliminate want by preventing the total loss of current income and by spreading the economic burden caused by various hazards to which large numbers of the people are subjected. Fortunately, to an increasing extent we are including in the term not only income maintenance programs but also constructive social services for the purpose of minimizing or eliminating the hazards which cause loss of income or other undesirable results and for the purpose of affirmatively promoting the well-being of the individual and family.

Social welfare is an action program, justified on the basis of its action on behalf of people, as well as on its underlying purpose. Let us turn to some instances which are representative of problems which might be met through the operation of public welfare programs.

FURTHER EXAMPLES OF NEED

We have already cited some of the problems which might call for the use of welfare services. Our individual circumstances are so varied that it would be close to impossible to more than generally indicate the circumstances which welfare programs are designed to cover. For illustrative purposes, however, the following abbreviated case histories are presented to show the relatedness of public welfare to our everyday lives. As these examples indicate, the problems which lead people to the doors of the offices administering public welfare are not remote from any of us, not bizarre experiences of strange people about which we read in our evening papers. These problems are close to the daily lives of ordinary people—to your life as well as to that of your neighbor.

Mr. B., a semiskilled factory worker, has been laid off. He may not count on re-employment at the plant. He knows that in the process of retooling the factory may install changes in production methods which will not call for his particular part in the process. On the other hand, he has every assurance that he has not been forgotten and that in time he may again find a place in the plant. He is married and has three children. His earnings have been matched by his family obligations, and he has not been able to pile up substantial savings. Fortunately, he is covered by unemployment insurance. Since he is involuntarily separated from his job, and is available for work, and other factors relating to wage experience and benefit period are favorable, he qualifies for unemployment compensation. He draws a check which, while not equal to his wages, provides him a measure of security against destitution and crushing debt. He registers regularly with the public employment service. Should his joblessness extend over too many weeks, he would be hard put to make ends meet. If he should still be unemployed after the maximum period for which benefits can be paid, he would have to seek aid from the local welfare agency.

Mr. Y. is not covered by unemployment insurance. He has been supporting himself and his family of five by working for different farmers in his community. When crops are poor, he finds himself without work. After vainly seeking employment sufficient to support himself and his family, he contemplates trying his luck in another community. This would mean leaving his home and local associations for what at best would be a most uncertain prospect. He decides to stay, and applies to the local welfare office for general assistance. The chances are that he will receive an amount far from sufficient to sustain his family with any great degree of comfort. For a period, however, he will be able to get by unless he has some large unanticipated emergency. How adequate or otherwise his general assistance would be varies greatly from state to state and in most instances, from locality to locality within the same state. It is possible also that his aid will consist only of a series of direct orders to be filled—humiliatingly—at local stores.

Mr. L. contemplates retirement. In many respects he epito-
mizes the familiar picture of the faithful office worker whose
value to the organization has been his steadiness rather than
any particular brilliance or originality. He is sixty-seven, and
has been permitted to postpone his retirement from the firm,
even though he could have qualified for old-age insurance two
years earlier. Now his wife has also reached the age where she
also may receive a monthly check from the federal government.
In addition, the company has a supplementary retirement plan
which permits him a respectable income. This man and wife
will live out their remaining years in the comparative comfort
afforded by the checks from his company and from the government.

Mr. L.'s brother finds himself unable to meet the demands of
making a living. The infirmities of age have caught up with
him at sixty-nine. For years he has operated a one-man repair
shop. While he has been quite successful, the needs first of a
growing family, and later the illness of his wife, have exhausted his personal cash reserves. He has not elected voluntary coverage under social security. His children have responsibilities of their own and cannot support him and his
wife. He applies to the county welfare department for old age
assistance. His wife files a concurrent separate application.
His lack of income and other resources and the fact that he has
lived in the state for many more than the number of years
required, qualify him for assistance. He and his wife will receive separate monthly checks. Their amount will depend on
the state in which he lives, since there is a wide disparity
among the states.

Mrs. N. and her four children have been deserted by the husband and father. They are penniless. The children, all under
twelve years of age, are totally dependent. While the mother
has had some work experience, she does not feel readily qualified for the kind of work necessary to support the family.
Uncertain about what to do, she goes to the welfare department to discuss her problem. Here, a caseworker helps her to
consider alternative courses of action. Mrs. N. decides that she
must stay home. Work would require her absence at a time
when the children need her presence, and would also demand

expenditure for care of the children. She decides to apply for aid to dependent children, which will give her a monthly check barely adequate for her needs, if she plans carefully.

Mrs. P., who also finds herself with sole responsibility for her family of four, is in a different set of circumstances. Her husband has died. He had worked in a job covered by old-age and survivors' insurance. Her children are all young, and the family qualifies for survivors' benefits. These will be paid for each child until he or she reaches the maximum age, and for the mother until all of the children have exceeded that age. Also the benefits paid on the death of the breadwinner will enable her to receive a lump sum payment.

The foregoing are representative of just a few of the many situations which might lead a family to seek help from a welfare agency of the government. All are examples of "income maintenance" programs, that is, aid which is available because of need arising out of the loss of family income. One essential feature of income maintenance is its provision of resources to the family to enable it to purchase goods and services. It is meant to provide at least a minimum level of income and to provide against major disruptions in the family economy when the regular source of earnings is lost.

The possibilities of expanding this list of examples are infinite. The range of human problems has no limits. The shattering effect on a family, for instance, when one member suffers from a long-term illness, is both dramatic in its effect and commonplace in its frequency of occurrence. The exact number of people who find their resources strained to the breaking point by the costs of medical care is not readily available but is nonetheless important. The head of the household who finds his earnings ample for the daily costs of food, shelter, clothing, and recreation, is likely to find himself "medically indigent," if such a disease as rheumatic fever, with its long period of treatment and convalescence, strikes one of his children, or when a member of the family is stricken with such a long-term illness as tuberculosis.

Nor do the preceding examples convey more than a hint of the emotional factors which may accompany dependency. The meaning of the loss of a job with its concomitant decline in status, the effects of economic deprivation on children, the erosion of the personality which results from struggle without hope, all these are as real as our economic want. As Charlotte Towle has noted,

> It may seem a far cry from the malnourished infant of today to the dictator or asocial citizen of tomorrow. To child welfare workers and all those versed in basic essentials in child development, however, there seems to be a logical cause-and-effect relationship. Likewise, illness and physical handicap may become decisive factors in the formation of personality . . . Just as the passing mood of any one of us may be created by a state of hunger, physical fatigue, or our general health condition, so persistent hunger, fatigue, and bodily suffering may shape the personality to their own ends.[8]

Programs of income maintenance serve the purpose of strengthening family life by providing a cushion against the hardship of loss of regular sources of employment.

The income maintenance programs by no means represent the limits of governmental participation in social welfare. Other services quite comprehensive in character are performed by governmental welfare agencies and, lacking a better term of classification, these might be called "direct services" in distinction to programs of income maintenance. The difference is that under direct services programs the service is given by the public agency. In income maintenance programs the funds are provided so that the family may purchase its own services.

Direct services

The following are examples of direct services.

> A child may be having difficulties of adjustment in his own home—perhaps to a new brother, a new step-parent, an illness or death in his family, or to any one of many other situations. His behavior may be creating serious problems for himself and

[8] Charlotte Towle, *Common Human Needs* (New York, American Association of Social Workers, 1953), p. 4.

for his family. The family may be solvent financially—or even comfortably more than solvent. The public agency may provide the services of a skilled child welfare worker to assist the family in helping the child to a better adjustment, or it may be necessary in some instances to find and use a foster home as a temporary means of meeting the situation.

A boy or girl may be in trouble with the law. Frequently, rather than reformatory or other correctional institution, helpful counselling and rehabilitative service are called for. Through such services, and with understanding and insight into his problem, the juvenile offender may have a chance to grow into self-respecting, responsible adulthood. The juvenile court may assign a child to the custody of a probation officer whose kindly but firm combination of authority and understanding may succeed where harsher treatment would fail.

A community may awaken to the magnitude of the problem of mental illness within its own population. Early diagnosis and treatment of the mentally ill person may forestall months or years of hospitalization for him. Through the use of public funds, a clinic may be established, with staff of psychiatrist, psychologist, and social worker to diagnose and treat the mentally ill.

An accident or a crippling disease may destroy a man's ability to earn his living at his accustomed trade. Physical restoration may be the first step. Counselling will be of crucial importance as the individual seeks to reorder his mode of life. Such counselling may help to direct him toward the acquisition of new skills, and toward what may be a totally different type of career. This often involves re-education or new training. During this period his family may be assisted by one of the public assistance programs. Following the physical treatment, the counselling, and the retraining will come the task of job placement. The rescue of a man and his family from a life of dependency often results from such services as these.

Classification of programs

Welfare programs may be classified according to: (1) the clientele; (2) the kind of service; or (3) the arrangement among the levels of government. Since public welfare programs represent a mixture of all these various classifications, we will look at some of the major ones.

By clientele.

The aged
Dependent or neglected children
The delinquent
The criminal
The unemployed
The emotionally disturbed children
The physically handicapped
The mentally retarded
The mentally ill
The veterans
The railroad workers
The wards of the national government

The above categories are not all mutually exclusive. The veteran, for example, also might be physically handicapped, unemployed, or suffering from the infirmities of old age; the fact that he is a veteran of military service does not exempt him from the other problems represented in this series. Yet because of a special and generally recognized obligation to veterans, they have the status of a special clientele. Similarly, other classifications also overlap, as for example the railroad worker also might be a veteran, and he might have a child with a serious problem. Historically, as social welfare programs developed, railroad workers have been recognized as a particular clientele. (See Part II.) The aged person may be dependent because of physical or mental handicap, rather than because of chronological age. Clientele, obviously, is a variable basis for classification.

By nature of service. As already suggested, the foregoing categories of clients may be served either by income maintenance or by other types of programs. In reviewing the classification by nature of service, one must remember that, like the listing by clientele, these are not exact, definitive, or mutually exclusive classifications. These are groupings of services, rather than precise categories.

Income maintenance

    Social insurance:
        Old-age, survivors and disability insurance[9]
        Unemployment insurance
        Workmen's compensation
        Disability insurance
        Retirement, disability, and unemployment insurance
        for railroad workers;
    Public assistance:
        Old-age assistance
        Aid to the blind
        Aid to dependent children
        Aid to the permanently and totally disabled
        General assistance
    Other income-maintenance programs including payments
    to veterans

Direct services

    Child welfare services
    Maternal and child health programs
    Crippled children's services
    Mental health
    Vocational rehabilitation
    Services to veterans
    Probation
    Parole
    Rehabilitation in correctional institutions

Certainly there are elements of direct service in such income maintenance programs as public assistance, and reciprocally, features of income maintenance in such programs as vocational rehabilitation; one classification must not be used to exclude another.

By level of government responsible for administration. Some of these programs are administered directly by the federal government, some by cooperative arrangements between federal and

[9] Until 1956 this program was known as Old-Age and Survivors' Insurance. The disability feature was added by a 1956 amendment to the Social Security Act.

state governments, while some are state, state-and-local, or entirely local programs.

Federally-administered programs
>   Old-age, survivors and disability insurance
>   Railroad workers' insurance
>   Services to veterans
>   Services to wards of government
>   Federal probation and parole
>   Administration of federal prisons

Federal-State Programs
>   Old age assistance
>   Aid to the blind
>   Aid to dependent children
>   Aid to the disabled
>   Unemployment compensation
>   Vocational rehabilitation
>   Mental health services
>   Crippled children's services
>   Child welfare services
>   Maternal and child health

State, State-Local and Local Programs
>   Workmen's compensation
>   Disability insurance[10]
>   General assistance
>   Local probation
>   Parole
>   State and local prisons and reformatories

These listings exclude many measures which many might classify as public welfare. It does not, for example, include social work in schools, which is in a sense a publicly supported social welfare program. Nor does it embrace a wide range of public health services. It excludes certain classes of dependents of the federal government, and does not take into consideration the retirement pro-

---

[10] This program exists only in four states: New Jersey, Rhode Island, California, and New York, and in the federal program for railroad workers.

visions in the federal, state, or local civil service. It would be difficult to present a consistent or convincing argument for excluding some of these programs; the author's choice, however, has generally followed professionally sanctioned practice. School social services, for example, have been omitted because they are part of educational programs, and to encompass them would require a description of the complex interrelationships between education and social welfare. Health, similarly, is an independently recognized area, but part of it—crippled children and maternal and child health measures—is generally included in social welfare or related services, and has been so classified in the federal administration by assigning responsibility for it to the Children's Bureau, a unit of the Social Security Administration. The problem of classification is a broad one, practically as well as theoretically. Federal and state governments alike have struggled with the problem of how to classify and apportion responsibility for welfare and related programs.

Summary

People have many needs. In essence, these needs represent a level of wants which are determined by the standards of the society as well as by the biological existence requirements of the individual. Need in relation to social services may be said to exist when what the family is able to provide through its own efforts is inadequate to meet what society considers to be a minimum standard.

These needs are assessed in relation both to material well-being and to the needs of the personality. The damaging effects of long-term deprivation on the lives of members of the family are too well known to require elaboration. The personality needs to feel secure against hazards to welfare which are beyond personal control, and which threaten a person's sense of dignity as a member of a social order.

Varying problems lead people to seek help from social agencies. Some arise out of external conditions, such as large-scale shutdowns of industry. Others result from casualties occurring in our system of production—such as injuries or illnesses which are work-connected or the human reactions to the results of a policy of laying off older workers. Others are personal catastrophes, such as death of the breadwinner or the expense of an illness which overtaxes the resources of the family. Some problems are intra-psychic in nature, that is, the result of the personality's failure to function adequately. Actually, these problems are interlocking. The ostensible or obvious problem may not be the basic one. At any rate, even the best social orders seem to produce an impressive crop of human problems.

Social welfare, as a field containing a group of measures to meet these problems, is difficult to define precisely. The essence of the definitions offered here is the characteristic of support for the family's own efforts to provide for its needs. Governmental social welfare programs are those which are tax-supported and administered by federal, state, or local government, or by any combination of the three. Voluntary social welfare programs are those which are supported through gifts from various nongovernmental sources.

Looking further at the kinds of problems which social welfare programs are designed to meet, a series of abridged case histories illustrated the kinds of situations which give rise to the need for financial and other forms of aid. Such situations could arise in any family; they are intimately related to the familiar circumstances of everyday life.

Welfare programs may be classified in several ways: by clientele, by the nature of the service, or by the level of government responsible for administration. These are not precise bases for classification, but are useful groupings of the various services. In the succeeding pages, attention will be devoted to the major programs which are readily identified with social welfare, and to those which are most closely related to those programs.

Selected References

1. Altmeyer, A. J., "The People and Their Government," *New Directions in Social Work*, Edited by Cora Kasius. New York, Harper & Brothers, 1954.

2. Burns, Eveline M., *The American Social Security System*. Boston, Houghton Mifflin Company, 1949. Part One.
3. Clague, Ewan, "The Economic Context of Social Work," in *Social Work Year Book, 1957*. New York, National Association of Social Workers, 1957.
4. Fink, Arthur, et al., *The Field of Social Work*. New York, Henry Holt and Company, 1955, Chapter One, "Problems People Present."
5. Friedlander, Walter, *Introduction to Social Welfare*. New York, Prentice-Hall, Inc., 1955.
6. Leyendecker, Hilary, *Problems and Policy in Public Assistance*. New York, Harper and Brothers, 1955, Chapter I.
7. Miles, Arthur P., *An Introduction to Public Welfare*. Boston, D. C. Heath and Company, 1949, Chapter I, "The Meaning of Public Welfare."
8. Towle, Charlotte, *Common Human Needs*. New York, American Association of Social Workers, 1953.

2

A Changing Philosophy of Governmental Responsibility

Helping the distressed is a practice at least as old as civilization. It was general in ancient societies, even though not necessarily on a formal, organized basis. Ancient China had refuges for the aged and for the sick poor, and other provisions for distributing clothing and feeding the unfortunate. Both Greece and Rome had the xenodochia, or buildings for the custody and care of various classes of unfortunates. The act of almsgiving has been recognized by many religions as a duty, and many of them have considered acts of charity to be among the noblest expressions of sacred practices. It is true that almsgiving and other early forms of charity were, in some religions, means of obtaining grace for the giver rather than expressions of a personal desire to help the distressed, but the fact remains that since the days of antiquity the needy in society have been cared for in some fashion, however inadequate that care may seem by later standards.

Welfare as a secular enterprise was developed chiefly in England and in the countries of northern Europe, and was transported

24

to America by the early colonists. Actually, the English Poor Law, brought here by the colonists from England, remained the basis for public welfare theory and practice until the depression of the 1930's. Up to that time, such principles of the Poor Law as local responsibility for care of the needy, the obligation of relatives to take care of their own, and settlement laws designed to discourage the indigent traveler, survived the changing conditions of life, which were the consequences of economic and social progress. These principles, developed during the late sixteenth and the seventeenth centuries, were important and in those times quite progressive expressions of social responsibility. The very idea of secular responsibility for the needy was in itself a significant development, and it also was an important part of the social and political philosophy carried here by English colonists.

An exhaustive history of the development of public welfare is outside the scope of this book. That task has been performed ably by others. What is intended in this chapter is a brief review of the major steps in this historical development, and of the political, social, and economic conditions which accompanied it.

In the American colonies the conditions of life were favorable to the nurture and development of the system of poor relief which was imported from England. The comparative isolation and self-containment of the colonial settlements were a sufficient rationale for local assumption of responsibility for the needy. Communal life, which was fostered by the need of people in a sparsely settled land to pool their efforts, meant that every hand was required in some form of labor and this led to an attitude of strong disapprobation of idleness, especially when aggravated by vagabondage. In other aspects of life, access to the virtually unlimited resources of a raw, undeveloped land and the hardships of wresting a livelihood on or from it fostered individualism. With few changes in philosophy of treatment, the substance of the Poor Law remained the basis for public welfare in this country throughout the nineteenth century. Josephine C. Brown has summarized the prevailing methods of care by the end of the nineteenth century as follows:

1. Outdoor relief, given to "paupers" in their homes. 2. Farming out to the lowest bidder, who undertook to care for a single "pauper". 3. Contract, usually with the lowest bidder, for the care of all the "paupers" of a given locality. 4. Care in an almshouse which was under the direct control of the public officials. 5. Indenture or "binding out," a form of apprenticeship.[1]

As Miss Brown further points out, the tendency in our earlier history was increasingly to rely on the almshouse or indoor relief as the preferred method of meeting needs. The two features of the almshouse which were especially appealing were the lower cost, as compared with outdoor relief, and the opportunity it provided for greater control over the behavior of the inmates—or in more current wording, of the recipients of aid. The almshouse was likely to house many classes of indigents without any separation between them according to the cause of the condition, the age group, or the nature of the individual's needs: small children, so-called vagabonds, mentally ill people and criminals all lived under the same roof, subject to the more or less tender mercies of the superintendent, then often called an "overseer of the poor."

The second step was the development of public institutional programs for special groups. These programs were designed to remove some groups of inmates from the undifferentiated misery of incarceration in the local almshouse, and indicated a recognition of a special claim these persons had on the sympathies of the community. Early in the nineteenth century special institutions were founded for orphans, for the deaf, the blind, and the mentally ill, all special classes of paupers. This in effect removed people with these special classes of problems from completely local control, for state as well as local institutions were developed.

In the third major development, state departments of charities and corrections were created to supervise the administration of institutional care. The first of these state agencies was established in Massachusetts in 1863. In the ensuing years, most of the states followed suit. The powers of some states' departments were

[1] Josephine C. Brown. *Public Relief, 1929-1939* (New York, 1940), p. 8.

merely visitorial and inspectional, while those of others also included administrative authority over local and state institutions. This authority included the power (1) to recommend institutional changes to the legislature, and (2) to compel the institutions to carry out the intent of the relevant statutes as interpreted by the state agency.

The early part of the twentieth century saw a fourth important step, and the beginning of one current practice, that of aiding the needy without institutionalizing them.[2] To meet the needs of special groups of people, special measures were enacted. The first was in Illinois in 1903 when a system was set up which provided pensions be given to the blind. In 1911 Missouri pioneered by enacting mothers' aid legislation, or as it became known in some states, widows' compensation. The present program of old age security had its humble beginnings in 1912 when Alaska enacted an old age pension measure which was later declared unconstitutional. The first such provision to survive the test of constitutionality was in a law passed in Montana in 1923.[3]

The welfare pattern throughout the nation on the eve of the Great Depression was a patchwork consisting of local, county, state, and private activities. In spite of the development of private or voluntary social services, about three fourths of all the aid to the indigent was provided under public measures. The public services so provided were limited in scope and inadequate in amount. The programs were scattered and the administration of them tended to be desultory, dependent, as they were, on the administrative guidance of county or municipal governing bodies even though the programs were operated under state laws. They were based on tax measures far from adequate to support them. They were in a real sense simply a preferential form of poor relief. The almshouse still existed. Poor relief generally was administered harshly and meagerly to all the people who were not in any of the few special categories. The poor had no clearly dis-

[2] See Hilary M. Leyendecker, *Problems and Policy in Public Assistance* (New York, 1954), Chapters 1 and 2.

[3] *Ibid.*, page 54.

tinguishable "right" to relief of their distress[4] and the harshness of the laws themselves reflected a tendency to regard the poor as beyond hope of redemption.

The inadequacies of the state programs of special assistance in 1934—just before the passage of the Social Security Act—were summarized by the Social Security Board in part as follows:[5]

1) only thirty of the fifty-one jurisdictions (states and territories) had legislation permitting or providing old-age assistance;

2) within this thirty, one third of the counties did not provide old age assistance;

3) in most of the counties where assistance was provided, the qualification requirements were highly restrictive and lack of funds resulted in long waiting lists;

4) forty-five states authorized aid to dependent children, but it was provided in less than half of the local units in these states; and

5) in the 24 states with laws for public pensions to the blind, only two thirds of the counties participated in these programs.

To appreciate this picture of welfare patterns, it is helpful to reconsider the formerly prevailing attitude toward dependent groups in general. This attitude is revealed in the historical development of treatment of poor children. In the past the child of the poor has been regarded with a mixture of compassion and contempt. Some most noble phrases concerning children as inheritors of the future have been enunciated but they have rarely been expressed through action and never consistently. Sometimes, moreover, the most righteously expressed sentiment conceals the most ruthless of views. The child, more than is generally realized, has been an involuntary legatee of prejudice. Exemplifying this,

---

[4] See Edith Abbott, "Is There a Legal Right to Relief." in *Public Assistance, American Principles and Policies* (Chicago, 1940), Volume 1, pp. 7-12.

[5] *First Annual Report*, Social Security Board to the 75th Congress, 1st Session, page 9. When this report was issued, Puerto Rico and the Virgin Islands were not included among the jurisdictions because they had no federally-aided assistance programs.

part of our English heritage was expressed in a document in the Annual Register of England dated 1775, and is worth citing here. Called a "Project for the Employment of Female Infants, Especially of the Poor," it notes that the numbers of persons whose children were too numerous to receive maintenance, much less an education, led to concern about the daughters in these families. The document set forth this proposal:

> Poor and ignorant as they are, and encompassed with every temptation, they are too often driven to destruction long before their passions can have any share in their guilt; and that principally, if not entirely, for want of employment suitable to their tender age; so as to become in time both in body and in mind the most wretched parts of the community; and all the while a heartbreak and a disgrace to their wretched families. To remedy these evils, and if possible prevent them, to encourage industry by employing a number of female infants, especially of the poor; and to save so considerable a remittance to France amounting to about 400,000 pounds a year, is the intent of the present plan.

Such a project would scarcely have been seriously proposed in later times. Yet it is only a slightly exaggerated expression of the mixture of exploitation of children and concern for their well-being which found implementation in the indenture (binding out) of children and in the forms of institutional care which prevailed for years.

For other classes of dependents, the special institutions which developed before 1930 were probably as much a means of removing the sufferer from public sight as of helping restore him to social living. Yet, despite all of the limitations, these provisions manifested a growing sense of public responsibility.

The 1930's

The depression which began with the stock market crash in October, 1929, hit the nation with a jarring impact. While this was not the first nation-wide economic depression, it came at a time when there was no easy escape into beckoning frontiers. Millions of unemployed had no place to go from their home communities, except to others similarly afflicted. Mass destitution was a fact which had to be faced.

Welfare services were ill prepared for such a contingency. Mutual aid or neighborly help could not be relied upon as a major resource, especially when the neighbors themselves were likely to be suffering from one or another degree of deprivation. Personal savings in the form of bank accounts, and insurance, were pitifully meager for confronting the prolonged loss of regular earnings. The huddled figure shuffling despondently in the breadline or in front of the soup kitchen could find little hope for the future in this kind of temporary help. Private agencies soon found the requirements of the large number of needy far beyond their means.

Public action to meet the emergency of large-scale unemployment did not come easily. Millions of unemployed were not regarded at first as a problem demanding national action. Efforts were made in the early days of the depression to encourage re-employment, and to rely on traditional local resources for aid, or upon public subsidies from local government to voluntary agencies. Committees were organized in 1930 and 1931 by the President, but were strictly advisory in nature, and confined their activities to encouraging local enterprise. But with the exception of some federal and state disaster aid to drought sufferers, no action of consequence was taken until September 1931. On that date, the state of New York led the way for state action with the enactment of the Temporary Emergency Relief Administration. Most of the states followed with similar action.[6]

The first break in the opposition to federal aid came with the passage of the Emergency Relief and Construction Act in July 1932. This Act empowered the Reconstruction Finance Corporation, which had been established chiefly for the purpose of assisting industry and agriculture, to provide funds to states for relief work. These funds were labelled advances or loans, rather than

---

[6] See Josephine Brown, *op. cit.*, also, Leyendecker, *op. cit.* Chapter 3, "The Emergence of Public Assistance."

grants. The real development of federal responsibility, however, occurred in the period between 1933 and 1935. In March 1933 the Civilian Conservation Corps was established by Act of Congress, to provide work opportunities for young men in the conservation of natural resources.

The most significant of the succession of measures was the Federal Emergency Relief Act of 1933, which provided for grants to states for relief of unemployment. This grant of $500 million marked the entry of the national government into cooperative relations with the states, and required the setting up of administrative organizations in the states to administer the services. It was an important acceptance of national responsibility in an area in which it had been consistently and staunchly repudiated up to that time.

Other important measures of that period included the Wagner-Peyser Act of 1933, which established a nation-wide public employment service, the National Recovery Act, under which a program of public works was developed, and the Civil Works Administration, which was a short-lived program of public works.

Aid under the Federal Emergency Relief Administration (F.E.R.A.) included both direct relief, or assistance to people in their own homes, and work relief. The latter really paved the way for the development of the Works Progress Administration (later known as the Work Projects Administration) in December 1935, after the liquidation of the F.E.R.A. This was a large-scale program of relief through employment on publicly sponsored projects. Eligibility to work on such projects was based on the need of the individual and family. Actually, the advent of the WPA coincided with the effort to limit federal aid to the employable persons, with the exception of those who suffered from contingencies covered by the Social Security Act, and to return the unemployables to the relief programs of the states and localities.

Other important measures of this period were the Rural Resettlement Administration, later the Farm Security Administration, with its grants and loans to needy farmers, and the National Youth Administration, which was established within the Works

Progress Administration to provide relief, work relief, and employment to needy youths between the ages of sixteen and twenty-five. The program also provided aid to students.

This is one of the fascinating periods in the history of public social welfare. The struggles which went on in the halls of government before these emergency welfare programs were actually enacted were not without considerable intensity. Years of traditional thinking did not yield readily, even to the flood of human destitution. These wholesale beginnings of state and federal aid might be designated as the fifth step in the historical development of governmental responsibility for social welfare.

All of these measures, however, were clearly labelled "emergency" devices. There was the implicit and in some cases the explicit assumption that they brought the government into "this business of relief" only for the duration of the crisis. Yet the effect of this emergency was to bring about continuing state and federal roles quite different from those which had prevailed in the past.

In 1934, by executive order President Roosevelt created a Committee on Economic Security. This committee was authorized to recommend a program to provide what he himself had termed "safeguards against misfortunes which cannot be wholly eliminated in this man-made world of ours."[7]

The report of this Committee, transmitted to the President on January 15, 1935, presented recommendations for a comprehensive program of protection against these various misfortunes. Among the major features were public works, as a part of employment assurance; unemployment compensation; "non-contributory old-age pensions, compulsory contributory annuities, and voluntary contributory annuities;" "aid to fatherless children," a system of local services for the protection and care of "homeless, neglected and delinquent children, and for child and maternal health services, especially in rural areas;" health insurance, and grants to states for public health.

The recommendations did not suggest that the federal govern-

---

[7] As quoted in *Report to the President,* Committee on Economic Security (Washington, 1935), p. v.

ment assume responsibility for all forms of welfare aid. The report, instead, acknowledged the continuing responsibility of states and of localities for their traditional forms of aid through general assistance programs. Nor did it, for example, include any provisions for the blind, although subsequently such aid was included in the Social Security Act.

The report, however, did not entirely neglect the areas which federal aid would not cover. It stated: "We believe that if these measures are adopted, the residual relief problem will have diminished to a point where it will be possible to return primary responsibility for the care of people who cannot work to the State and local governments." The report then went on to recommend:

> To prevent such a step from resulting in less humane and less intelligent treatment of unfortunate fellow-citizens, we strongly recommend that the States substitute for their ancient, out-moded poor laws modernized public assistance laws, and replace their traditional poor-law administrations by unified and efficient State and local public welfare departments, such as exist in some States and for which there is a nucleus in all States in the Federal Emergency Relief Organization.[8]

The immediate outcome of this report and series of recommendations was the Social Security Act, the provisions of which will be discussed in more detail in later chapters. The important fact to note here is that this Act established a new and revolutionary alignment of responsibilities among the levels of government in the welfare function. It changed the emphasis from limited aid to a few needy persons to a comprehensive system for the entire population. It brought much broader resources to bear upon the problems of social welfare. It marked a sixth stage in the development of governmental responsibility for social welfare.

The Social Security Act became effective on August 14, 1935. It provided for the following programs: grants to states to aid them in providing assistance to aged people, dependent children, and the blind; a federal-state system of unemployment insurance; a federal system of old age insurance; grants to states to enable them to improve their services in maternal and child health, in

[8] *Ibid.*, p. 7.

crippled children's services, and in child welfare; grants to states for public health services; and grants to states for vocational rehabilitation. (The last two have since been removed from the Social Security Act and have been incorporated in other laws.)

The combination of modern social insurance and assistance legislation with the conventional style of poor relief led Miss Edith Abbott to remark in 1937 that: "Public assistance, in the second quarter of the twentieth century, is a strange assortment of things old and new, often with threads and patches underneath, and then some grand and quite new outside garment; the old pauper laws of the state underneath, and the new social security program shining with glittering promises for the top layer."[9]

Miss Abbott's comment regarding the concurrent existence of the old and the new underscores an important fact in the historical development of governmental social welfare. History does not progress from one orderly stage to another; rather, the stages tend to overlap. The old system of poor relief, with its restrictions and cruelties, is still with us in many places. Institutions for special groups, such as the handicapped, the mentally ill, or the lawbreakers, are far from being idealized expressions of modern enlightenment throughout the nation. These institutions, despite many a devoted staff, all too often reflect inadequate appropriations, overcrowding, poor facilities, and overworked personnel. The local almshouse or county poor farm still stands in some places as a bleak and sometimes inhabited monument to the past. In many cases, however, its functions have changed and it now cares for handicapped persons.

WHY GOVERNMENTAL RESPONSIBILITY HAS GROWN

Changes in methods of social welfare have reflected and accompanied changes in our thinking about social welfare. Changes in both and the reasons for these changes have come about through the combination of many factors. These factors explain

---

[9] *Proceedings* of the National Conference of Social Work, 1937 (Chicago, 1937), p. 3.

why, on most of the social welfare issues today, the major political parties differ chiefly on details rather than on general principles.

What are the explanations? The first set of reasons for this expansion of social welfare programs is to be found in the basic changes in our national society. They arise out of an expanding population, increasing urbanization, industrialization, and greater dependence upon the job for a living.

In a familiar American idyll, the frontiersman-hero might be standing in the clearing in a forest, surveying his recently planted crops. Perhaps he could barely see smoke from the chimney of his neighbor's house, a mile or so away. Inside his rudely constructed cabin, his wife would be preparing the evening meal, following a busy day of cooking, spinning, weaving, and sewing, with the help of the elder daughter. The man would be looking forward to the day when his sons would assist him in the many tasks of farming the land, in planting, in cultivating, and in harvesting. A family was in essence an almost complete unit of economic production. The head of the household could easily supplement the family larder by an occasional hunting trip or, if the crops failed, by a job which would provide cash to permit him to recoup whatever losses he thereby suffered. When disaster struck, the neighbors pitched in to help.

Today we live longer, enjoy greater comfort, and in general consider ourselves better off. But, in the words of one writer, "life is safer, but living less secure.[10] The Great Depression dramatized a pre-existing fact—our interdependence as a people.

This interdependence, however, is not a local one. It exists in a national (and even an international) sense. As Justice Cardozo stated in an oft-quoted opinion relative to Titles II and VIII of the Social Security Act.

> Needs that were narrow or parochial a century ago may be interwoven in our day with the well-being of the nation . . . Spreading from state to state, unemployment is an ill not

[10] Mary Ross, "Why Social Security," in William Haber and Wilbur Cohen, *Readings in Social Security* (New York, 1948), p. 8.

particular but general which may be checked if Congress so determines, by the resources of the nation. But the ill is all one, or at least not greatly different, whether men are thrown out of work because there is no longer work to do, or because the disabilities of age make them incapable of doing it. Preventing want in old age is plainly national in area and in dimension.[11]

Few problems of any magnitude can be localized today. The improvement in ease of communication together with reliance upon a commerce which recognizes no state boundaries make isolation of troubles well-nigh impossible. The fact of interdependence must be accepted, both locally and nationally.

Students of the problem of poverty and dependency in this country had noted the implications of changed living conditions on the needs for social welfare long before they were recognized by the general public. As long ago as 1879, speaking to the National Conference of Charities and Corrections, Frederick B. Sanborn, a prominent welfare leader observed:

> At present, however, from the facility of communication between one section and another, and from the immense development of manufacturing and commercial industry . . . the conditions of pauperism and crime which prevail in one part of the country are shared and equalized with other parts of the country to an extent never known before the Civil War. In popular belief, and, to a considerable extent in fact, the tramp is a person who thus equalizes and distributes the wretchedness and vice of one community to the people of another.[12]

Isaac M. Rubinow, called attention in the 1920's and early 1930's to the probability that in itself our growing reliance on machinery as a means of producing an increasing flow of economic goods created perils over which the individual could have little control and which added to the burden of insecurity. This quite possibly was true, noted Mr. Rubinow, not only because of the threat of disablement by the machine, but also as the result of livelihood

---

[11] Helvering *v.* Davis, 301 U. S. 619.

[12] "The Year's Work in Administration and Legislation," *Proceedings* of the National Conference of Charities and Corrections, 1879, p. 25.

coming increasingly to depend upon the continuing operation of the machine.[13]

But the increased interdependence of people and the greater hazards to their livelihoods do not entirely explain the present dimension of welfare service. Under the most favorable economic conditions, welfare services have continued to expand through various successive state and federal legislative enactments. The trend has been consistently toward liberalization.

This reflects an important fact. Today, welfare programs are more an expression of aspiration than of desperation. They constitute a level or a floor of living below which no one should be allowed to fall. As a society's productivity rises, so is there a rise in the minimum level of living.

This rising level of aspiration is reflected in many services. Certainly better care and protective services are provided children than ever before in the history of the country. A greater obligation has been assumed for the care and restoration of the handicapped than would once have been considered appropriate or desirable. The conscience of the community continually stirs and sometimes precipitates action with reference to institutions which are below standards of decency. These facts serve to demonstrate the importance of regarding public social welfare in the context of continuing social, political, and economic progress of the national community.

CONFLICT OF VIEWS

Perhaps it would be well at this point to note that the development of social welfare has not been a pageant of constant beneficence on the part of an unreservedly benevolent people. Instead, its history has featured considerable conflict of views; many of these conflicts persist. It is of course well known that values and attitudes have a tendency to outlive the context within which they developed. Deeply-rooted social attitudes became ingrained and

---

[13] Isaac M. Rubinow, *The Quest for Security* (New York, 1934), Chapter 5, "The Industrial Juggernaut."

have worked against as well as for the growth of welfare services. These attitudes and conflicts perhaps provide some explanations for the apparent anomalies of social welfare today—the co-existence of relatively adequate provisions along with other overly restrictive ones.

Certainly the pride in personal responsibility for well-being is prominent among the attitudes which militate against the uncritical acceptance of bigger and better welfare programs offered without stint and promising a limitless future. Dependence upon others has been and to a measure still is considered a mark of failure, with consequent loss of dignity and self-respect.

A persistent social attitude, then, has been disapprobation toward the poor as a counterpart of approbation toward successful outcome of a self-reliant struggle. Benjamin Franklin could look with complete disapproval upon a poor law which compelled the rich to maintain the poor. Nathaniel Ware, an early social philosopher, could allege in the early nineteenth century, that the unemployed lacked pride; that the man who begged or relied upon the bounty of others, was beyond redeeming and should be considered as having sunk to the "level of a mere eating brute." He stated further that "humanity aside, it would be to the interest of society to kill all such drones."[14] Examples of the mixture of pity and abhorrence with which the poor were regarded abound in our literature.

Sometimes the disapproval has been rooted in anxiety. The protean fears of the Malthusians and the neo-Malthusians may have led to fears that propagation by those they consider unfit would threaten the food supply of the rest of the population.[15]

Certainly the Social Darwinists tend to disapprove of any measures designed to help the weak survive the economic struggle. In this country, the exigencies of a pioneer society which required production by every member reinforced this attitude.

This view, of course, is in direct conflict with the humanitarian

---

[14] Joseph Dorfman, *History of Economic Thought in the U. S.*, Vol I (New York, 1946), p. 943.

[15] Amos G. Warner, in his *American Charities*, has noted that Malthus himself was not opposed to charity, and even assigned to it a broader field than did Herbert Spencer, (New York, 1908), p. 11.

impulses which are an integral part of our religious and democratic philosophy. Throughout the history of the nineteenth century, many voices were raised in defense of the needy. Leaders in
philanthropy, in their attempt to find the root causes of poverty,
acted on the assumption that the individual was not necessarily
defective in character because of his poverty, and advanced the
possibility that he might have been the victim of circumstances
beyond his control. At other times, prominent welfare leaders have
insisted that the problem was basically one of social justice, and
advocated the removal of bad environmental conditions as the
soundest approach to the alleviation or elimination of poverty.
The belief that improvement of working conditions through labor
legislation could reduce the need for any kind of relief appears in
the writings of some nineteenth-century philanthropists and leaders in social welfare. In 1899 at the National Conference of Charities and Corrections, Professor S. McCune Lindsay stressed the
following causes of poverty:[16]

A. Within the family: disregard of family ties; intemperance,
   licentiousness, dishonesty or other moral defect; lack of
   fiscal judgment; physical or mental defects; sickness or accident or death.
B. Outside the family: unemployment not due to employee;
   defective sanitation; degrading surroundings; unwise philanthropy; public calamity.
C. Unclassified.

This viewpoint presents an interesting amalgam of personal and
social responsibility and significantly acknowledges the fact that
some problems defy classification.

Fear of government has been another prominently displayed
viewpoint which has worked in opposition to the growth of public
social services. Leaders in social welfare have themselves at times
expressed disapproval of some government welfare programs. A
society which traditionally has operated on the premise that that
government is best which governs least could be expected to resist large-scale governmental activity in such a field as social welfare. It is scarcely surprising that people in the field of welfare

---

[16] *Proceedings* of the National Conference of Charities and Corrections, 1899.

itself might have thought tax-supported services, in their early development, were a threat to voluntary services.

This factor has had particular force as the amount of federal welfare activity has grown. Such scare phrases as "The Welfare State" have been used by opponents of welfare enterprise. Fears have been expressed that the tools of benevolence may be converted into the instruments of tyranny, or that citizens are surrendering their birthrights of freedom for a mess of pottage called security. The specter of the leviathan state has haunted the dreams of more than one political and social philosopher.

Another conflict has arisen with respect to alleged interference with the division of responsibilities among the three levels of government—federal, state, and local. Some critics fear that the national level has usurped powers constitutionally assigned to state authority and responsibility. One might argue, on the other hand, that in the exercise of this particular responsibility state and local governments have flourished only since they began to receive aid on a large scale from the national government. For some people the fear remains that the constitutionally-determined division of authority has been undermined, and that the federal government, using money and control as tools, has invaded the area of state authority. This argument will be considered in more detail in a later chapter.

A closely related conflict has been in the area of the fear of disturbing the structure of taxation. Some have averred that the federal government practice of taxing inhabitants of the states, and then returning money in the form of grants-in-aid, has been both costly and inequitable. It has been argued that it is unfair to expect the wealthy states to share the local burden of those with a smaller amount of taxable wealth.

On the other hand, the acceptance of the fact of interdependence, of an economy which cuts across state lines, operates in opposition to this view. Significant, also, is the ability of the federal government to tap sources of taxation which are not all available to the states. The assumption that the same dollar is involved in either case is highly questionable.

As social welfare measures have become the largest of the nonmilitary expenses, the burden of taxation has resulted in a critical attitude toward further expansion of these activities. While no exact measure has yet been devised to determine the exact danger point of such taxation, there nevertheless is a definite fear that a point may be reached when the general welfare itself is threatened by this growing tax load, some of which is attributable to social welfare. Naturally, people who fear the costs are inclined to disapprove the services, although frequently disapproval of costs and approval of programs are bedfellows, logically incompatible ones, in some people's minds.

Another area of conflict relates to the feeling that some people have about the assignment of something so personal as welfare to the expert. Organized services tend to arouse fear that the spontaneity of the act of giving and helping will be lost in official procedures. The fear that the giver loses his identity in relation to the beneficiary, and the belief that the services are relatively impersonal, have both had some effect on the attitudes toward the services themselves.

On the other hand, it has been argued that public welfare service, with its emphasis upon the right of the individual to receive the benefits, promotes personal dignity and has a desirable effect.

There are undoubtedly other areas of conflict. Every hope has its counterpart in anxiety. These have operated sometimes to slow the pace of development but in recent years they have not had much apparent effect in reducing or curtailing activities.

Government welfare programs have been evolved in terms of specific needs for specific categories of problems. Special programs, such as those of Social Security, Veterans Services, Vocational Rehabilitation, and others, have represented a response to a particularized object of sympathy or concern. In no sense has there been a master plan or design for the extension of these services or for the growth of new ones. This is probably the inevitable method of development in a democracy.

Summary

Today's large governmental welfare enterprise is comparatively young. Social security, for example, has been in existence in this country for less than twenty-five years. Prior to the Great Depression of the 1930's, public social welfare was comparatively small in scope. A niggardly, grudging, poor relief was the earliest form of social welfare offered under governmental auspices in this country. Later, institutions were built for special classes of dependents but throughout most of the 19th century the almshouse or the meager dole were the basic forms of welfare aid. In the earlier part of this century, special provisions were made for pensions to special classes of needy, the aged person, the blind, or widows and their children. These programs were spotty and inadequate, however, and the almshouse and the special institution continued as the major types of social welfare.

The depression brought with it large-scale federal aid to states and localities and resulted in a major change in the philosophy of governmental responsibility for social welfare. A national catastrophe required national action. The reality of millions of unemployed persons, all needing aid, refuted the belief that poverty and depravity were inevitably associated. Throughout the earlier years of the decade a succession of measures devised to meet the emergency brought about an apparently irreversible trend toward increasing governmental participation in social welfare, culminating in the Social Security Act.

The depression dramatized an already existing fact—our interdependence as a people, and our interlocking fortunes. The changing philosophy of governmental responsibility is a reflection of the changed conditions of life. Problems of wide scope demand remedies of equal scope. Events since the depression have confirmed and strengthened the fact of our interdependence. At the same time, welfare measures express a higher level of aspiration as well as the greater hazards of modern living.

Public social welfare has not developed without engendering some major conflicts in values. Subjects of some of these conflicts have been: deep disapproval of dependency and a glorification of self-reliance; distrust of government as a source of personal aid; disapproval of the changing roles of federal, state, and local governments; the growing tax burden; distrust of the official agency in dealing with anything so directly personal as family welfare.

Continuing growth, caution, and uncertainty regarding the nature of such growth, along with a willingness to meet problems when they cry out for solution, are characteristics of this democratic society which are reflected in the development of governmental social welfare.

Selected References

1. Abbott, Edith, *Public Assistance*. Chicago, University of Chicago Press, 1940.
2. Brown, Josephine C., *Public Relief, 1929-39*. New York, Henry Holt and Company, 1940.
3. De Schweinitz, Karl, "The Development of Governmental Responsibility for Human Welfare," in *Social Work As Human Relations,* Anniversary Papers of the New York School of Social Work and the Community Service Society of New York. New York, Columbia University Press, 1949.
4. Fink, Arthur, et al., *The Field of Social Work*. New York, Henry Holt and Company, rev. ed. 1955, Chapter Three, "The Social Services in America—From the Almshouse to Social Security."
5. Howard, Donald S., *The WPA and Federal Relief Policy*. New York, Russell Sage Foundation, 1943.
6. Leyendecker, Hilary M., *Problems and Policy in Public Assistance*. New York, Harper & Brothers, 1955, Chapter Three, "The Emergence of Public Assistance."
7. Miles, Arthur P., *An Introduction to Public Welfare*. Boston, D. C. Heath and Company, 1949, Chapter Four, "American Poor Law History."
8. Rubinow, Isaac M., *The Quest for Security*. New York, Henry Holt and Company, 1934, Chapter 5, "The Industrial Juggernaut."
9. Schneider, David M., *The History of Public Welfare in New York*. Chicago, University of Chicago Press, 1938.
10. Stroup, Herbert, "The Cultural Context of Social Work," in *The Social Work Year Book, 1957*. New York, The National Association of Social Workers, 1957.
11. Warner, Amos G., *American Charities*. New York, Thomas Y. Crowell and Company, 1908.
12. Williams, E. A., *Federal Aid for Relief*. New York, Columbia University Press, 1939.

3

The Voluntary Agency
in Social Welfare

BACKGROUND

It may seem strange that a book on governmental programs and organization should devote even a short chapter to the voluntary agency. The term "voluntary," as we employ it, refers to those agencies which have been organized by private initiative, and which are for the most part financed by private gifts. We shall deal later in this chapter with the chief characteristics of the voluntary agencies.

It does not seem so strange to include material on this form of social welfare, however, when it is realized that the two types of agencies, governmental and voluntary, so influence each other that an attempt to describe one without some attention to the other would be futile. Throughout their respective histories, this has been true. Voluntary social welfare grew essentially out of the dissatisfaction of enlightened and concerned people with the negligence, and general harshness, of poor-law administration, the misery and degradation of the almshouses, and the failure of poor-law authorities to attempt in any way to help the people under their care to improve their lot, or even to recognize any hope for such improvement.

Many features of modern public programs owe their origin to discoveries made by the voluntary agencies. It would be difficult to enumerate them all but as Fink has noted, much of modern public welfare practice began in the voluntary services.[1] He calls attention to the fact that during the hundred years preceding the Social Security Act, it was the private societies that developed the basis for our present welfare programs of individualized services. He notes many other influences of voluntary services on present-day public welfare, including the development of the bases for social group work services of today, community organization practices, and many of the techniques for securing social action on welfare needs. It was private initiative that established the earliest of the special institutions for the handicapped. Social work as a profession developed through voluntary social welfare.

Throughout the nineteenth century and early part of the twentieth, the voluntary agency played an important role in the relief of destitution, particularly in the larger cities. This does not, however, mean that the poor law was dead. In fact, on the eve of the great depression, in 1929, in most areas a good part of aid to the needy, and in rural communities, just about all the aid was provided by public agencies.

The depression of the 1930's was a decisive period for the voluntary as well as for the tax-supported welfare services. According to Josephine Brown, private agencies through the community chest organizations had used relief needs as "the easiest way to reach the community pocketbook."[2] Miss Brown further notes: "Having failed to give to their contributors an understanding and appreciation of the non-relief functions of their member agencies, the chests now saw in the growing recognition of the responsibility of government for relief, not only the loss of their most productive money-raising appeal, but a threat to their very existence."[3]

When compelled by the pressure of need to call for government measures to relieve destitution, leaders of voluntary agencies may have begun to fear the demise of their services. Indeed, some of

---

[1] Arthur Fink *et al.*, *The Field of Social Work* (New York, rev. 1955), p. 74.
[2] *Public Relief, 1929-39* (New York, 1940), p. 78.
[3] *Ibid.*

them did predict that public aid would engulf private social welfare, and result in a virtual government monopoly of this field. These leaders faced the loss of their most popularly understood service, that of giving relief. They saw many of their best staff members recruited into the government service. They saw their resources constricted during the depression, for with the drop in national income the total of contributions from private donors dwindled.

That voluntary social welfare did not "go under" during the 1930's is due to at least three factors. The first, as Miss Brown has stated, is that voluntary agencies had already developed many services other than relief-giving, many of which were not in any way tied to people's financial needs. Family casework, group activities, camping, adoption services, and many others had become increasingly dominant in the private agency's practice.

The second factor contributing to the survival of the voluntary agency and service is the nature of the public services, for these are limited in their range, and they are provided only under statutory authorization. There may be many conditions which have not so aroused the public as to result in a statute providing for the meeting of certain needs. There have been and are many problems unmet by the public social services, more than enough to engage the efforts of voluntary agencies for an indefinite future. In a sense, the private agencies' loss of the relief-giving function may have been a blessing in disguise, for it freed them for further development of the kinds of services which already were becoming their most promising activities.

The capacity to adapt their work to the changes in their clients' needs is the third reason for the survival and continued health of voluntary social welfare. One of the strengths of the American society has been its genius for serving itself through a variety of social institutions. For a great many people, the voluntary agency offers a means of expressing civic and social responsibility. To stop up this outlet and to direct all welfare through governmental channels would stifle what for many people is a most creative form of self-expression.

These are among the reasons why voluntary services, instead of dying out, have grown. The fact of multibillion dollar support of voluntary health and welfare services itself is ample evidence that the private agency has a continuing and essential role to play in social welfare.

SOME CHARACTERISTICS OF VOLUNTARY SOCIAL WELFARE

Today, the private social agency continues to play an important part in community life. Family and children's services, neighborhood or community centers, health agencies, youth-serving activities, and many others exist side by side with public social welfare. Casework, group work, recreation leadership, psychiatric and other types of medical care are among the services offered. They are designed to meet needs of people in all the different age groups. Such contemporary and serious community problems as juvenile delinquency, or such growing needs as those of the many elderly people, may engage special attention, as the voluntary organizations continue to play their historic role of reaching out to and developing new areas of social service.

These services may be either sectarian or nonsectarian. Church-supported social welfare dates from colonial times in America, and some of the earliest facilities for institutional care were provided by churches. Today, Catholic, Jewish, and Protestant organizations just about encompass the range of private social services.[4]

Since, as we have said, we do not propose to give a history of social welfare, we shall but mention two voluntary organizations in the nineteenth century which had considerable influence in the development of modern social welfare. One was the Association for Improving the Condition of the Poor, organized first in New York City in 1843, the other the Charity Organization Society which first appeared in this country in Buffalo in 1877. The AICP was formed by a citizens' group which sought to combine necessary

---

[4] See *Social Work Yearbook, 1957* (New York, National Association of Social Workers, 1957), chapters on Catholic, Jewish, and Protestant social services, respectively.

material relief-giving with efforts through friendly encouragement to persuade the poor to attempt to improve their lot and station. The COS movement was not established originally as a relief giving society but sought, instead, to provide improved organization of existing charities. Its founders were convinced that voluntary charity was superior to public relief, but as the COS expanded beyond its original purposes, it had a profound effect on the development of professional practices which today are features of public welfare.

Another feature of the voluntary agency, both sectarian and nonsectarian, is the way in which it engages substantial numbers of people in the communities as volunteers. These people work with professional staff members in performing a variety of tasks. They serve on advisory, policy-making, and fund-raising boards, help with public relations, give expert advice on such matters as finances, and perform tasks which do not demand the particular professional attention and skill of the trained staff member. These volunteers serve for many reasons, among which civic interest, moral and religious convictions, and a personal commitment to serve their community in some way—is a notably frequent concern of many people today.

The agencies are financed by gifts from individuals, corporations, and other organizations. Some have continuing sources of support in community chests, charitable foundations, and endowments in the form of property holdings.[5] Some have membership dues or fees which defray a part of their operating costs. Some agencies have developed the practice of charging varying fees based on the clients' ability to pay; these fees do not pay the costs of service and are not intended to be a major source of the agency's income.

Fund-raising, independent and federated

The annual fund-raising campaign is a familiar part of community life today. These campaigns appeal for funds by organized

[5] See Eleanor K. Taylor, *Public Accountability of Foundations and Charitable Trusts* (New York, 1953); also F. Emerson Andrews, *Philanthropic Giving* (New York, 1950).

solicitation of homes, offices, industries, schools, in fact often of the entire population. The drives are carefully planned, combining the efforts of professional and volunteer, and utilizing the most modern methods of public relations to interpret their services, hoping thereby to establish a wide base of informed donors. A major value of the campaigns, besides their primary money-raising objective, the social agencies consider, is the fact that they acquaint the public with the nature of the services the agencies provide. In a society with so much competition for the individual's attention, the stimulus of an organized activity such as this is perhaps necessary to engage the attention of many, although the professional community organization leader will testify that behind the campaign must be a year-round program of public information and service.

Some organizations conduct their own individual drives. Many pool their major campaigns in a federated effort. The federated organization may be a community chest, which includes in its membership local agencies, and local branches of state and national organizations. The united fund, a development since the 1950's, is an extension of the community chest concept to include some of the major or large national agencies which had hitherto refused to join the community chest organization.

In spite of its growth—federated fund raising is today the rule in more than 2,000 American communities, and the idea has spread to foreign countries[6]—the concept and practice are still controversial among voluntary health and welfare agencies. The Federation for Charity and Philanthropy, organized in Cleveland in 1913, is considered to be the first community chest organization.[7] In the years since then, some of the largest of the national voluntary agencies have adhered to their practice of independent fund raising. Arguments for and against the federated appeal

---

[6] See Wayne McMillen, "Financing Social Welfare Services," *Social Work Year Book, 1957* (New York, National Association of Social Workers), pp. 260-266.

[7] Some people credit Denver with having the first cooperative appeal, for in that city in 1887 the Charity Organization Society was founded to unite the appeals of several agencies for funds. The Cleveland Federation, however, was the first to incorporate the practice of budgeting, a basic feature of the community chest.

arise frequently. Proponents point to the jungle of confusion which antedated the federated method, when competition for the giver's dollar and the great number of independent drives for funds often confused the donors into complete irritation (and sometimes into the refusal to contribute what they otherwise might have). Proponents point also to an important function of the federated organization, the allocation to the member agencies of the funds raised by the campaign. They contend that requiring the organizations to submit carefully planned budgets has a salutary effect on agency operation, and that the community chest or united fund usually makes a more equitable allocation of money, in terms of the effectiveness of the services provided, than results when potential donors are besieged by a multitude of agencies all campaigning separately for funds.

Opponents of the federated method of financing have their arguments also. They contend that they get less money from the federated effort than they could raise independently, that their needs are lost in the larger mass of needs confronting the central organization, and that they cannot afford to accept what they consider the dictation of the allocating group. They insist that they have more freedom for experimentation and innovation if they are independent of any united fund.

It is not easy to assess the respective merits of these two points of view, nor, for this book, is it necessary. What is important to the study of governmental services is the fact that voluntary services continue to be substantial and growing. While voluntary health and welfare services raise and spend less than one-fourth the amount spent by tax-supported welfare services, their importance is undeniable in terms of the kinds of services they provide.

Modern voluntary social welfare draws its financial support from a large part of the population. This was not always true. Over sixty years ago, one writer stated that "In scanning the contributors' list of a number of societies, it becomes apparent that the burden of voluntary charity falls on a very small number of givers and that there is a large portion of the public able to give, whose names do not appear . . ."[8] Today, fortunately, the service formerly existing as the pet charity of a family or small group of wealthy people has given way to the organization with community-wide support. The slogan, "Everybody benefits—everybody gives" is descriptive of the intent of voluntary services to universalize in their communities their sources of support as well as the groups and individuals they serve.

Organization

Planning is essential to social welfare. Coordinated organization of services is an essential counterpart to organized fund raising and financial planning. That this be done on a community-wide basis is recognized by social welfare leadership when reference is made to "community-mindedness" rather than "agency-mindedness." Most communities with substantial numbers of voluntary and governmental health and welfare agencies have councils of social agencies, sometimes called community welfare councils or councils of social planning. The phrase "community-mindedness" denotes a consistent habit of thinking broadly in terms of the needs of the public rather than narrowly in terms of exclusive preoccupation with a single clientele or sponsoring group. The community welfare council provides a means for cooperative or coordinated thinking that will promote the total community's well-being.

Such councils include in their membership representatives of both public and private agencies. Public agencies are members of the council even if it is affiliated with the federated fund-raising organization. The councils usually are supported financially by community chests or united funds and in some places, particularly in the smaller cities, the chest and council director may be the same person. Nevertheless, the two have related but distinct functions.

Representatives from the agencies include both volunteers and professional staff members. Frequently an individual may join simply because he has a personal interest in the work of the coun-

---

[8] Amos G. Warner, *American Charities* (New York, 1894), p. 384.

cil. Such groups as parent-teachers' associations, service clubs, and civic organizations may also participate in the council. The obvious purpose of the organization is to make it as representative as possible of the range of community interests.

In Newark, New Jersey, a community of more than half a million people, the Council of Social Agencies membership consists of 87 nonprofit voluntary agencies, 43 government agencies, 3 community groups and 15 members at large.[9] According to the 1957 report of this council, in 1955 its activities included the participation of 511 laymen in the following classifications:[10]

Employers, businessmen, executives	156
Professionals in medicine, law, dentistry, education, the ministry	149
Housewives	177
Wage earners or representatives of organized labor	21
Other occupations, not classified	8

No claim can be made that in all communities an equally large proportion of the public participates in the work of the council, or that these proportions of occupational classifications are typical of citizens participating elsewhere. Communities differ too much to permit any such assertion. Yet the fact of participation by persons from so many different areas of community life most probably is typical, and the association of such people with the professional staffs of the agencies is one major source of the councils' strengths.

What is the function of a community council? The pattern varies from place to place, but according to one report,[11] offering a succinct and comprehensive summary of the nature, purpose, and function of such organizations,

> The most vital part of a community council's job is to study problems and needs, and to plan cooperatively to meet them. It does this by:

9 "The Council of Social Agencies Is a Vital Part of the New Newark," a summary of a citizen study (Newark, New Jersey, Council of Social Agencies, May 1957), p. 8.

10 *Ibid.*, p. 9.

11 *Teamwork in the Community,* a pamphlet prepared under the auspices of the Wisconsin Community Organization Committee (July, 1951). See also Robert McRae, "Community Welfare Councils," in the *Social Work Year Book, 1957.*

1. Encouraging informed citizen participation.
2. Fact-finding.
3. Developing public understanding and support.
4. Coordinating community activities and services.
5. Cooperative action.

This report summarizes fairly well the functions of the councils. It is of course true that volumes could be written about each of them, about how citizen participation is enlisted, or how research is organized for fact-finding purposes. Developing public support is in itself worthy of a treatise, as is concerted organization and central planning, without which the spontaneous growth of services by the agencies might lead to utter confusion.

Thus far the term "community" has been used to indicate a locality, or more particularly, a municipality. The term, however, has wider application. In the first place, such designations as "greater metropolis" indicate that the central fund-raising and planning agencies have had to reach out to include the suburban area. In some places the area included has been the county. In general, this reflects the need to take into account the fact that people do not necessarily live and work in the same city, and that the need for services in the outlying areas may exceed the capacities of the services such areas are able to provide.

The importance of the state in the organization of voluntary social welfare should not be overlooked. All states have conferences of social welfare, many of which have paid executive staff. Some agencies, notably in the child welfare and adoption field, operate on a state-wide basis. Some of the large national voluntary agencies have state affiliates. For the most part, the state organizations hold conferences and perform other functions. Many states have associations of local community chests and councils. Some have state-wide federated fund raising, although this is still in an early and developing stage. In some, state-wide citizens groups have formed to stimulate social legislation and planning for welfare services. (Such organizations operate in Pennsylvania, New York, Massachusetts, New Jersey, and Ohio.)

In the *Social Work Year Book, 1957,* more than 350 national voluntary health and welfare agencies are listed.[12] Many of them, like the American Red Cross, or the National Travelers' Aid Association, have local chapters or affiliates. The organization called the United Community Funds and Councils of America claims membership of 2000 community chests, united funds, and welfare councils in the United States and Canada. Such organizations as the Child Welfare League of America and the Family Service Association of America have memberships consisting of both voluntary and public agencies. These are but some of the many national agencies whose functions include the development of standards for services, large-scale research, publication of technical journals, consultation to state and local services, creation of a professional literature, recruitment of personnel, the further development of public understanding, and cooperation with governmental agencies.

No mention of national agencies should exclude the National Conference on Social Welfare (formerly the National Conference of Social Work). Organized in 1874, and known in its earlier years as the National Conference on Charities and Corrections, this agency has served as the forum for the discussion of major social issues. Although the Conference eschews any direct participation in social action, from the speakers' platforms of successive annual forums have come many ideas and principles later embodied in the most important social policies.[13]

Of particular interest to public welfare is the American Public Welfare Association, a national organization primarily devoted to the field of governmental social welfare. While its membership is open to anyone interested in public welfare, the bulk of participation in its activities comes from national, state, and local public agencies. Through its biennial "round tables" or national meetings, and its annual regional conferences, this agency provides

---

12 See George Rabinoff, "National Organization in Social Welfare," in *Social Work Year Book, 1957* (National Association of Social Workers, New York, 1957), pp. 383-393.

13 For a history of this organization see Frank Bruno, *Trends in Social Work* (New York, 1948). Mr. Bruno's book shows with clarity the influence of this forum on the development of social welfare.

an opportunity for presentation and discussion of the most important issues in public welfare, and for exchange of information on developments in practices and policies in the field. Consultation and advisory services are available from the Association to its member agencies and individuals. It conducts or sponsors special studies to increase knowledge of the field, and to test and evaluate standards and practices. This organization has had a most important role in the shaping of public welfare legislation, and in educating the national community to public welfare needs. Through its journal, it has provided a medium of information and knowledge of social welfare practice. Its constituent national councils of state public welfare administrators, local administrators, field representatives, and public welfare board members give people at these respective levels of administration opportunity to communicate with each other on their common problems. Its emphasis on the need for professional training has made this organization a telling influence on the quality of service in public social welfare.

Another national voluntary organization of particular interest is the National Social Welfare Assembly. In a sense, this is a national council of social agencies. It includes individuals nominated by affiliated organizations, and some elected at large by the membership. Its affiliates include both voluntary and governmental national agencies. As an agency concerned with national planning, this organization has a wide range of activities, including fact-finding; studying major social issues; coordinating planning among national agencies; improving communication among national agencies and between national and local services; relating American public welfare theories, practice, and goals, to those of foreign countries; providing forums for discussion and study of social problems; and other functions stemming from its over-all one of study, planning, and the dissemination of information for improved public understanding of social welfare.

This is but a hint of the size and importance of the national voluntary agency. As Rabinoff suggests, it is difficult to fit them into any neat classification, although one may distinguish between those that are organized around a widespread problem, and those which exist chiefly to serve local agencies and local needs.

By now it should be clear that public and voluntary agencies cannot be considered in isolation from each other. Their interests overlap, they are constantly modifying their programs in relation to each other, and both are ultimately accountable to the same public. With the universalizing of giving in the communities, it is increasingly true to say that both are supported by exactly the same public. The donor and the taxpayer are the same person. It is also true that the distinction between voluntary and governmental is not absolute; and the voluntary agency is accorded certain privileges such as tax exemption in recognition of the fact that it serves a useful public purpose. It is, as we shall see, subject to regulation by the public through various branches of government. On the other hand, the governmental agency is served by many devoted volunteers, who are members of boards of the public organizations, and who act in volunteer capacities similar to those others have in the voluntary service organizations.

HOW GOVERNMENTAL AND VOLUNTARY
SERVICES ARE RELATED

Some of the forms of association between governmental and voluntary agencies in social welfare have already been mentioned, including joint participation in community welfare councils, in social planning at all levels of government, in various kinds of forums and conferences, and in research and study. With these many kinds of association, it is hard to draw clear-cut distinction between their basic roles.

The traditional delineations of these roles were embodied in the "extension ladder" theory of Sidney Webb, and the "parallel bars" theory of Benjamin Kirkman Gray.[14] The former held that the public agency would not relinquish all responsibility to the private but would provide a minimum or "floor" of assistance in all

[14] For a description of these two theories, see Wayne McMillen, *Community Organization for Social Welfare* (Chicago, 1945), pp. 95-99.

cases. The latter theory held that while the private agency would set the standards and lead the way for the public agency, it also would carry complete responsibility for all cases it accepted, and provide all the services in those cases. In both theories, the standard-setting and improvement role was assigned exclusively to the private agency.

The development of the governmental social services during the past several years has largely dispelled the idea that the public agency is incapable of discovery and innovation, and that it must always look to its privately financed and operated counterpart for new ideas and methods. In fact in many of the major national programs such as mental health, child welfare, and certainly vocational rehabilitation, leadership in standard-setting is shared between the public and voluntary services. This does not mean that the governmental agency is about to take over the entire field. The voluntary agency will continue its historic role of service, research, and discovery so long as it retains its vitality of purpose.

Andrews has suggested a contemporary division of function along the following lines:[15]

> In broad generalization, public agencies undertake to meet, more or less adequately, basic economic, health, and educational needs; in some cases for the whole population, in others for only certain specific classes of the disadvantaged. To voluntary agencies remain the important tasks of filling in gaps and inadequacies in these fields, of establishing standards and checking the work of public agencies, of covering many additional needs not now met by government, and of doing most of the exploratory, experimental and research work in building that important fence of prevention above the dangerous cliff.

One may question whether, in the light of developments in public services during the past five or six years, it still is true that "most" of the exploratory experimental and research work is being done by the voluntary agencies. This question suggests not a

[15] Andrews, *op. cit.*, p. 112.

diminution of their work but rather an increase in governmental activity.

Two of the more tangible areas of relationship have scarcely been mentioned thus far in this volume. These are the areas of governmental supervision and regulation of voluntary services, and the subsidization by government of voluntary services.

State welfare departments have exercised the function of supervising certain types of voluntary services since the first State authorities were created in the 1860's. Supervision deemed necessary for the public interest has been exercised with respect to such voluntary services as child-placement and adoption, maternity homes, homes for the aged, and other types of institutions and agencies through such devices and powers as licensing, incorporation requirements, determining standards and issuing regulations, regular inspection of facilities, and by requiring reports on agency operations. Many nonprofit organizations operate under charters approved by the states. In exchange, in recognition of the public interest in and nature of their work, they are accorded tax exemption and other important privileges, as already indicated.

Such a relationship is prone to misunderstanding and conflict unless it is properly maintained. With respect to one form of voluntary organization, the foundation and charitable trust, there is an important distinction between accountability and control. As Andrews states, "Society has the clear right to define broadly the social goals within which tax exemption and other special privileges may be granted. It also has power to impose controls, but could do so only at heavy cost."[16] The regulating and supervising authority which applied too heavy a hand to its task would create conflict, and would stultify the voluntary service by smothering it in excessively detailed control. It would also raise serious questions regarding the limits of control. Fortunately, there is little evidence that many serious conflicts have arisen in this area of relationships.

In an earlier period when governmental services were meager,

16 F. Emerson Andrews, in "Introduction" to *Public Accountability of Foundations and Charitable Trusts*, by Eleanor K. Taylor (New York, 1953), pp. 5 and 6.

and in many instances nonexistent, public funds were used extensively to subsidize voluntary agencies rendering needed services. In some instances these payments were in the form of lump sums, as a subsidy to help cover the cost of its operations, in others they were payments for specific services rendered or for individuals receiving care. Donald S. Howard has referred to such wholesale subsidization as "the earlier easy-going ladling out of public funds to private welfare agencies."[17] There of course are occasions for the purchase of services from voluntary agencies and institutions by the government, but for most public services, the government relies and undoubtedly will continue to rely on the governmental welfare agencies. The principle that public control should be exercised over public funds has a fundamental and historical validity in social welfare.

IMPORTANCE OF A COOPERATIVE APPROACH

The quality of the relationship between governmental and voluntary welfare agencies is of great importance to both types of agencies and to the public which both serve. As McMillen has noted: "In some places the relationship between public and private agencies is characterized by antagonism and a spirit of criticism. To some extent this is a tradition inherited from the past, which may be further accentuated by wide differences in professional standards. Where this situation exists, the community organization activities of the social agency group as a whole fall short of desirable standards of effectiveness."[18] He goes on to point out that the most promising approach is at the level of treatment, which offers the opportunity to cooperate at the day-by-day job, but he further notes that antagonism frequently arises over responsibility for cases. He suggests that it is imperative that all professionals involved in treating any one case arrive at agreement through the method of conference.

[17] Donald S. Howard, "Changing Roles of Public and Private Social Welfare Agencies," *Proceedings* of the National Conference of Social Work (New York, 1952), p. 232.

[18] McMillen, *op. cit.*, p. 93.

What he says is all too frequently true, and the public has the right to insist that energies of staff of all agencies be deployed to something more fruitful for the community interest than jurisdictional disputes. It is imperative for the voluntary agency and its public counterpart to communicate effectively and to work harmoniously. The voluntary agency must realize that the governmental services today are not the last step on the road to degradation for the client, and that innovation is possible and desirable in the public service. Similarly, hostility and suspicion of the voluntary agency must not be characteristic of the attitude of the representatives of the governmental service.

In a Utopia, there would be few if any problems requiring the help of a welfare agency. But a member of such a society might find that removing outer pressures merely intensifies inner stresses, and might need help in resolving these. If the society had a perfectly organized social welfare system, the troubled person would have no trouble finding the voluntary or public agency to meet his need. Each type of service would be fully engaged in doing that for which it was best equipped, and all of the services would be functioning in perfect harmony, without bickerings or disabling differences.

While, as McMillen has pointed out, such perfection does not exist, there are impressive examples of cooperation in the public interest. Much of this has been in the promotion of improved laws and other support for needed public services. One such example is provided by the National Travelers Aid Association, which is working to abolish harsh settlement laws which deny many people public aid they very much need. From its own experience with impoverished travelers, members of local offices and of the national organization have perceived the essential inhumanity of these vestigial measures, carried over, as we have seen, from an earlier day when the self-sufficient local community discouraged movement of people from one community to another. Throughout the country today, board members and professional staffs are working to secure changes in state legislation on this point.

On occasions when public assistance is under unfair and un-warranted attack, voluntary services have helped to convey more accurate information to the public. Unfortunately, this has not happened often enough during attacks in recent years on the defenseless recipient of aid (see Chapter 5). Today, national organizations, both public and voluntary, are working to establish a closer bond through better communication and through unity in the common cause of social justice in social welfare. The volun-tary agencies' membership and especially their boards are gen-erally broadly representative of various groups in community life. These citizen participants in social welfare can often be more effective as spokesmen for improved public measures than can the public officials directly engaged in administering the service.

This does not mean that the voluntary agency should not criti-cize bad public practice. There are occasions when criticism is needed, and harmony should not be purchased at the price of disregarding standards. In discussing the future role of voluntary agencies in relation to the public social welfare programs, Lester Granger, the Executive Director of the National Urban League, has this to say:[19]

> For some time to come, voluntary agencies will continue to assume, as they have in the past few decades, oddly contra-dictory roles in relation to public welfare programs. By con-viction they must support a high quality of public service and must interpret public welfare to the citizen body and defend it against unfair attack. They must throw their influence on the side of adequate budgets for the administration of public services, with respectable salaries for staff members, and on the side of protection of public administrators from political pressures and reprisals. These duties must be assumed by vol-untary social work in order to safeguard the welfare of indi-viduals who can be adequately served only through the re-sources of the government. On the other hand, there may be occasions when the voluntary agency will be called upon to oppose what it considers inadequate administration or unwise

[19] Lester B. Granger, "The Changing Functions of Voluntary Agencies," in *New Directions in Social Work*, edited by Cora Kasius (New York, 1954), pp. 71-72.

planning in governmental programs. In a sense, the voluntary agency is a spokesman for the beneficiaries of the social services, and it may be called upon to be critical of particular operations at the same time that it is defending principles.

In any consideration of the future of the relationships between voluntary and governmental welfare programs, it should be emphasized that the voluntary agency must find its role in the context of community need rather than in the inadequacy of its tax-supported associate. Each type of service will have its distinctive contribution to make in the light of its structure, purpose, and support, and each can learn from the other. The basis for the future relationship will be most sound in proportion to the extent to which it is complementary and cooperative rather than competitive. With the continuing growth of public social welfare, the voluntary agency will have the opportunity, if it possesses the imagination, to be increasingly selective in its services, with growing emphasis on research and discovery. In this way, and in its continuing interest in public policy, it may serve best as a force stimulating and supporting the enlightened conscience of the community.

Thus we can look forward to a continuation of the historic role of voluntary social welfare with respect to the public services. We have noted the profound influence of such agencies as the Charity Organization society and its successors on the development of social work. We would be remiss if we failed to mention also the role of the social settlements in the development of public response to human need. Organized near the close of the nineteenth century, the settlement houses furnished such champions of better social conditions as Jane Addams, Octavia Hill, Edward T. Devine, and others. Many of the leaders recruited into the public field during the rapid development of the 1930's had been influenced by the philosophy of human welfare of the social settlement.

Summary

The depression of the 1930's resulted in a profound change in the relationships between public and private agencies. The latter, by the pressure of needs which their resources could not meet, were compelled to surrender their functions of giving large scale relief. With the advent of large public agencies, voluntary organizations began to emphasize other types of service. The transition was successfully achieved. In fact, even before the depression, the voluntary agency had tended more and more to offer services not necessarily tied to financial need. The depression was in a sense a blessing in disguise to the private agencies, as they gained new vitality in broader areas of service to the total community.

Voluntary agencies are supported by gifts from individuals, corporations, and other organizations, and by foundations and charitable trusts. Some are heavily endowed, while others are not so fortunate. Many agencies secure support through federated fund raising, *i.e.*, community chests, and united funds. Others conduct annual independent campaigns for funds.

The counterpart of fund-raising is social planning. The community welfare council is the central body for agency cooperation, coordination of services, fact-finding, and dissemination of information to the public. These councils engage the participation of both professional and volunteer workers in the agencies, and their membership includes both public and private agencies.

Voluntary services are organized on state and national as well as local levels. Fund-raising, coordination of local services, and study of welfare problems and needs are functions all levels of welfare agencies perform.

In order to understand the relationship between public and private agencies, it is important to discard some earlier ideas now discredited by experience. One is that the public agency cannot render individualized, sensitive service. Another is that only the private agency is capable of discovery and innovation. In today's world of social welfare, there is plenty of room for research and discovery by any organization capable of it.

The private agency today may perform its historic mission of arousing the conscience of the community to deal with unmet needs. Greater cooperation between public and private agencies for this purpose is necessary. More effective communication and cooperation are essential. The rationale is found in the fact that public and private agencies in a society as flexible as this must be complementary rather than competitive.

Selected References

1. Andrews, F. Emerson, *Philanthropic Giving*. New York, Russell Sage Foundation, 1950.
2. Howard, Donald S., "Changing Roles of Public and Private Social Agencies," in *Proceedings* of the National Conference of Social Work, 1952, New York: Columbia University Press, 1953.
3. Kasius, Cora, ed., *New Directions in Social Work*. New York, Harper & Brothers, 1954.
4. McMillen, Wayne, *Community Organization for Social Welfare*. Chicago, University of Chicago Press, 1945.
5. ———, "Financing Social Welfare Services," in *Social Work Year Book, 1957*. New York, National Association of Social Workers, 1957.
6. Murphy, Campbell, *Community Organization Practice*. Boston, Houghton Mifflin Co., 1955.
7. Rabinoff, George, "National Agencies in Social Work," *Social Work Year Book, 1957*.
8. Rich, Margaret E., *A Belief in People, A History of Family Social Work*, New York, Family Service Association of America, 1956.
9. Taylor, Eleanor K., *Public Accountability of Foundations and Charitable Trusts*. New York, Russell Sage Foundation, 1953.

Part II

The Programs

The next three chapters will present briefly the programs of social welfare provided through agencies of government. These chapters are concerned with the description of services, how they have developed, and apparent trends in coverage and scope. Some attention will also be devoted to evaluating the adequacy of the programs—to how well they actually meet the needs they are intended to meet—although no exhaustive analysis of the sufficiency of the various measures can be given here.

With reference to adequacy, one should remember that the programs must be considered in relation to a dynamic society in which the standards of living for the total population are constantly changing. As the reader will recall, it has already been pointed out that services in social welfare are measured against economic and social goals. As the level of living of the society changes, so does the standard for social welfare. During the years since 1935, the date of enactment of the Social Security Act, the change in American standards of living has been generally and steadily upward. In this sense, welfare programs must also be improved. So rapid in recent years have been the developments in productivity through great strides in the technology of production that welfare programs are in danger of becoming obsolete almost from the date of their inception. This is especially true because legislation for welfare does not anticipate general increases in standards of living, but rather is responsive to them.

In the world of today, it would be next to impossible to have a static program of social welfare. The American public is too far committed to a level of service which is related to a standard of decency. It would be extremely unlikely that social conditions would permit public social welfare to undergo so little change as it did in the eighteenth, nineteenth, and early twentieth centuries. Throughout this two-and-a-half-century period, as we have seen, the broad outlines of public welfare services remained the same.

In actual fact, many changes have been made since 1935 when the Social Security Act was passed. New programs have been added, and amendments to existing measures have added to the scope and the liberality of their provisions. Whether these changes have been commensurate with the rise in the general living standard, however, is open to question, at least in some of the programs. We have experienced a spectacular rise in the production of goods and services, or what is termed the Gross National Product. As Dr. Eveline Burns reminds us, the increase has been from $91.1 billions in 1930, to $360.5 billions in 1954, and the rate has continued to rise.[1] Dr. Burns further notes that the growth has been unevenly distributed throughout the population, with the result that there are "pockets of poverty in the midst of increasing plenty." In such a situation, it is possible that relatively speaking, some people may be in a relatively worse condition as general standards rise, particularly when there is an accompanying increase in prices. In brief, progress in social welfare cannot be exclusively measured against provisions of money or services in previous years; they must also be related to contemporary standards. A case could be made for the contention that some welfare measures, when considered in this light, are less adequate than they were several years ago, although, as we shall see, substantial progress has been made in bringing others up to date.

It is true that social welfare programs, like other governmental

[1] Eveline M. Burns, "High Productivity and People's Social Needs," in *Public Welfare*, Vol. 14, No. 3 (July, 1956), pp. 154-155. The Gross National Product has shown a consistent increase. The amount was $434 billion in 1957, according to the President's Economic Report to Congress.

programs do not have an unlimited scope, but are the official expression of a social purpose. It would be difficult to defend any claim that they are meant, in contemporary society, to underwrite a cradle-to-the-grave system of complete protection by the government against all the major hazards to personal and family well-being. Social welfare programs are designed to support, not to supplant, the efforts of the family to meet its needs. The basic resources are still those which the family provides through employment, personal savings, and other personal efforts. However, in its social welfare programs, society, through the agency of government, has expressly undertaken to equalize the opportunities for self-maintenance through measures which mitigate the burden of misfortune and (through income security and other provisions) offer protection against hazards beyond individual control. Public social welfare programs provide a floor of well-being, and it is against that purpose that they should be considered.

These programs are varied. They include the income security programs of social insurance and public assistance, as well as direct services such as child-welfare, services to veterans of armed conflict, mental health, and others. What are the general characteristics which are common to all these services?

First, is the fact that all are established under laws which define the nature of the services which are provided and also the conditions of eligibility which determine who shall receive them. This may seem on casual reading to be so obvious that it is scarcely worth mentioning. In an area of service as individual and personal as social welfare has traditionally been, it would be difficult to overstate this point; it is important because a problem may be met by a public social welfare program only if the nature of it has been included in the statute which governs the service. No matter how acute the problem may be to the individual experiencing it, the governmental agency must be sure that it is within the provisions of the law before any aid may be extended. Furthermore, even if the applicant for service has a problem so covered, he must meet specified conditions of eligibility.

A second characteristic is that the program must be applied

impartially, for all persons are presumed to be equal before the law. Putting it in the negative, if discrimination is practiced against anyone in need of and eligible for public welfare assistance, it is a violation of the principle embodied in the law. The fact that someone working in an agency may dislike the person seeking assistance, or disapprove of something he has done, does not give him the right to deny the service. The governmental agency also does not have the freedom of choice that a voluntary agency has in the selection of clientele, although it must be noted that the latter have only relatively greater and not complete freedom of selection.

Governmental programs vary in the extent to which they objectify the conditions of eligibility. Of all the programs, the social insurance ones have the most explicit specifications of the terms of eligibility or "entitlement," although public assistance programs also have quite explicit specifications. This comparison should be made with caution, however. Any measure dealing with human affairs, whether unemployment insurance, aid to dependent children, or vocational rehabilitation, must reckon with the infinite variability of human circumstances. On this point, we like especially the following statements by Karl De Schweinitz:[2]

> On first sight any comprehensive and well-organized statute appears to state precisely and in detail just what the body which made the law intended. An act of the legislature seems to consist of a succession of exact instructions setting forth who shall be served, what shall be done, who shall do it, and to contain exhaustive definitions of rights and requirements, of conditions and exceptions. The paragraphs follow one another in a cumulating mass of prescription that baffles the unaccustomed reader.
>
> Once, however, one has passed the initial barrier of this kind of extensive specification, he finds that the statute does not contain nearly enough to clarify for him what, in every particular, was intended. . . .

[2] Karl De Schweinitz, *People and Process in Social Security* (Washington, American Council on Education, 1948), pp. 22-23.

The contingencies that can arise in the lives of human beings
are almost infinite. How possibly can the law state precisely
what must be done under each set of circumstances? If the
Congress had undertaken to include in the Social Security Act
all that every individual would want to know, it would have
been able to accomplish little beyond this one piece of legislation.

Thus, it should be clear that the processes of determining eligibility, and of offering service, are far from being cut-and-dried mechanical operations, or simple and automatic matching of the
conditions of eligibility with the circumstances of the person seeking help. Involved in the process is a careful and exacting, and
certainly a human task of evaluating the circumstances of the
individual in relation to the program.

A third characteristic of these various programs is that they are
generally interrelated, as parts of a general scheme of social security and welfare. This does not imply that they have been
evolved logically through comprehensive planning as parts of a
calculated master-design. Social progress just doesn't come about
in that way. Their purposes and their provisions, however, make
them interrelated. As will be noted, public assistance certainly is
responsive to changes in social insurance. As coverage of the latter
increases, both the volume and character of the public assistance
clientele are altered. We shall give more attention to this later, as
well as to the effect such programs as disability insurance and
vocational rehabilitation have upon each other. This statement is
a logical corollary to one made earlier, that needs are interrelated.
It is natural, therefore, that the same is true of measures designed
to meet the needs.

4

Social Insurance

Although the United States has had social security legislation for more than twenty years, this country was far from being the first to institute national programs of social insurance. Germany was the first to develop such a program, when it adopted, in 1883, a system of compulsory insurance for sickness and maternity, and a short time later added to its original program provisions for protection against income loss due to invalidism, disabling injury, and old age as well. Following the German lead, the idea of social insurance took a firm hold in European countries, so that by the time our Social Security Act was passed, this form of protection was quite common throughout the western world.

The idea of joining in groups for protection against economic hazards had been expressed through the voluntary organization of "friendly societies" by working men as a means of escaping from the hated poor law in Europe, long before the advent of social insurance. The working people despised the poor law because of its humiliating conditions, and also because it required declaration of a level of destitution in order to qualify.

While voluntary mutual effort offered some protection, it had its limitations, too. As Dr. Maurice Stack has said, "The societies were supported only by the thriftier, more prosperous section of the workers. Even so, the contributions they could levy were insufficient to cover the risks they purported to assume; and their technical inadequacies and lack of authority prevented them from making the most effective use of such resources as they had."[1]

In this country, some state measures of social insurance antedate the national program of the Social Security Act. Workmen's Compensation had been in existence since 1911. Wisconsin had a program of unemployment compensation on its books but it was not being enforced. In general in this country social insurance on a nationwide scale really dates from 1935.

Social insurance has been defined by Wilbur Cohen as[2]

> a plan whereby funds are built up out of contributions made by or on behalf of an individual (a) to compensate for part of the loss he and his family suffers when he meets with the risk covered by the program—unemployment, sickness, disability, old age, or death, or (b) to provide medical services or compensate him for such services when he or his family is sick. Like other forms of insurance it spreads the costs or risks that relatively few people suffer in a given year, over large groups of persons, nearly all of whom are subject to the risk, and over periods of time.

Another way of describing social insurance is as "savings on a social basis."[3]

As Mr. Cohen has noted, an essential feature of social insurance is that of spreading the risk of such hazards as are included in these laws. The principle of insurance is familiar in this society. Many people protect themselves against income loss through private insurance covering death, accidents, and illness. Many kinds of retirement programs have been known for a long time. What social insurance has done has been to expand greatly coverage of

---

[1] Maurice Stack, "The Meaning of Social Security," in *Readings in Social Security,* ed. by William Haber and Wilbur J. Cohen (New York, 1948), p. 47.

[2] Wilbur J. Cohen, "Social Insurance," in *Social Work Year Book, 1957* (New York, National Association of Social Workers), p. 537.

[3] From *A Brief Explanation of the Social Security Act,* Social Security Administration (July, 1957), p. 3.

protection against certain hazards, many of which would be considered unprofitable and out of the question for commercial insurance companies to cover, and to work toward inclusion of the total population. What is new about this program is the role of government as the agency through which protection is afforded. This role has developed out of the virtual impossibility of today providing adequately through other means against major disruptions of earnings.

Social insurance programs in the United States include Unemployment Insurance, Old-Age, Survivors and Disability Insurance, Workmen's Compensation, coverage for railroad workers for disability, retirement, and unemployment (the most comprehensive of the social insurances currently in force), and some state measures of Temporary Disability Insurance. In addition, for years there have been retirement provisions for public employees in federal, state, county, and municipal employment. We shall not devote further space to the last-named programs, and only limited attention to the measures for railroad workers, since both provide only for a "closed group" of the population.

Eligibility for social insurance, and the amounts and duration of benefits are based for the most part on income experience. Generally, income experience comprises both the rate of earnings and the period over which income was received. The common requirement is membership in the labor force.

Both the social insurance and the public assistance programs are designed to protect people from complete loss of income. Social insurance is different from public assistance, however, in several important ways. In the first place, social insurance, based as it is on earnings experience, does not require an individual test of the applicant's need for benefits. Public assistance has such a requirement. In other words, in order to qualify for social insurance, the individual is not compelled to use up his personal resources to the point that he becomes "needy." In the second place, the social insurance programs in this country are "contributory," that is, they are financed by payments made directly on behalf of the individual, either by his employer, or by the individual and his employer together, or by himself if he is self-employed. Public assistance is noncontributory; that is, financed out of general revenues.

National programs of social insurance originated with the passage of the Social Security Act in 1935. It was clearly the intent of Congress in enacting this law that social insurance would be the keystone of the arch of social security for the population. Public assistance was seen as performing a supplementary and residual task. In the earlier years of the programs, however, the purpose of social insurance as the basic protection was not completely achieved. Limitations of coverage, of benefits, and of scope worked against complete fulfillment of the original intent. In later years and particularly during the past decade, successive liberalizing enactments have brought the goal nearer to realization, although substantial gaps still exist.

The following parts of this chapter concern the general features of eligibility requirements for social insurance, the nature of the benefits, some appraisal of their adequacy, and the methods of financing. This is a technical subject which could be analyzed and described exhaustively. Since this is not a treatise on social insurance as such, however, the purpose here is to convey some basic and general understanding of these programs' characteristics as part of the whole social welfare enterprise.

OLD-AGE, SURVIVORS AND DISABILITY INSURANCE

In a challenging and comprehensive study of the economic needs of older people in contemporary American society, Corson and McConnell describe public concern over old age and the aged persons in the population as expressed in dramatic headlines in the daily press and in magazines. They then present the problem of the aged in these words:[4]

4 John J. Corson and John W. McConnell, *Economic Needs of Older People* (New York, 1956), p. 3.

. . . The problem of the aged is also individual and intensely personal. It is the problem of each aged person who recognizes his declining physical strength, and the isolation he will suffer when he no longer can work. It haunts those who have aging parents with no prospect of support when they can no longer work. It crushes men and women in their fifties who lose a job and desperately seek another. It is the problem each individual faces who finds it hard to save for a rainy day. It is the problem of every family forced to choose between the support of a retired father and the better education of its children, of every household that finds Grandma increasingly "difficult" as she makes her annual "visit".

As these authors suggest, two factors underlie the problem. One is the relative increase in the number of old people in the population, and the other is the whole composite of changes in social conditions and attitudes which affect the status of the aged. From today's proportion of one of every twelve persons in the population being over sixty-five, the relative number of older persons is expected to increase still further as medical science and social conditions continue to lengthen the average life span.[5]

But as these same authors indicate, population change is only part of the picture. While life is lengthened, the opportunities for employment tend to be constricted. Actually, this problem of employability begins to be acute when a worker reaches the age of forty-five. As another writer has noted:[6]

Whatever the justification, the older worker is disadvantaged in his search for a job. The difficulty starts with the age restriction on the job specification. Implementation of employer policy is reflected in hiring records which demonstrate the bias against older workers. The effect on older jobseekers is immediately apparent; once unemployed they have greater difficulty in finding a job and have longer spells of joblessness.

[5] *Ibid.*, p. 4.

[6] Norman Medvin, "Employment Problems of Older Workers," *Social Security Bulletin*, Vol. 20, No. 4 (April, 1957), p. 14.

In this situation, according to one student of the problem, who bases his observation on a study of employers' attitudes toward older workers, the choice is as follows: "Unless we choose the prospect of an ever-increasing number of unemployed older workers dependent upon tax support, we must find profitable employment for all persons who are willing and able to work."[7]

It is true that, for the aged, income loss may be accompanied by such problems as chronic illness, loneliness, and poor housing, among others. But the need for reasonably adequate income maintenance for the person unable to work or unable to secure employment is vitally important. Relatively few persons have accumulated resources sufficient to see them through however many years remain to them after sixty-five and it is the rare person who would choose a life of dependency, either upon his own family or upon others. Anxiety over the fate of his survivors troubles the working man during his productive years. The disabled person beyond the optimum working age finds the difficulties of securing work because of his age further compounded by his disability. These are all factors which are taken into account in the present program of old-age, survivors, and disability insurance.

In its 1935 report to the President, the Committee on Economic Security stated: "It is only through a compulsory, contributory system of old-age annuities that the burden upon future generations of the support of the aged can be lightened."[8] The Committee then went on to recommend enactment of a compulsory system to cover all manual workers and all nonmanual workers earning less than $250 per month, with exceptions for those covered under Railroad Retirement measures, or governmental ones. The exclusions in the original Social Security Act that same year were such that the measure was far from being as comprehensive in coverage as had been recommended. Large excluded groups such as farm and domestic workers, employees of nonprofit corporations, the

---

[7] Jack F. Culley, "It's Good Business to Hire Older Workers," *Iowa Business Digest,* Spring, 1957 (Iowa City, Iowa, Bureau of Business and Economic Research, College of Commerce, State University of Iowa).

[8] *Report to the President* of the Committee on Economic Security, 1935, p. 29.

self-employed, in addition to the individuals who were disqualified because of insufficient wage experience, added up to a substantial part of the population. It should be noted, however, that the workers covered by the law were not limited to those earning more than $250 a month (although only the first $3000 of earnings a year was covered).

In 1939, old-age insurance became old-age and survivors insurance, with the addition of benefits for the families of deceased or aged workers who had been employed in industries covered. In 1950, 1954, and 1956, classes of survivors entitled to benefits were added, the range of employment covered was greatly increased—most self-employed persons were brought under the program, including farm operators, certain state and local government employees, and farm and domestic employees, and so forth—and benefit formulas were liberalized. Among the most important of the recent additions are the inclusion (through the 1956 amendments) of severely disabled persons fifty years or over, and the lowering of the age at which women may qualify from 65 to 62, and the coverage of the armed services on a contributory basis.[9] The result is that today more than ninety percent of all the paid civilian jobs in the country are covered. According to a recent appraisal, the proportion of jobs not covered by this or by some other public retirement system is only about seven percent.[10]

Benefits, paid monthly, are based upon average earnings and the length of covered employment. In September, 1957, there were more than ten and one-half million beneficiaries of Old-Age, Survivors and Disability Insurance, known as O. A. S. D. I. The following table shows the number of beneficiaries, the total monthly amounts of benefits paid, and the average payments.[11]

[9] See Wilbur J. Cohen and Fedele F. Fauri, "The Social Security Amendments of 1956," in *Public Welfare,* Vol. 14, No. 4 (October, 1956). Also Phillip Schiff, "Twenty Years of Social Security," in *Social Casework,* October, 1955.

[10] Irwin Wolkstein, "Elective Coverage Under Old-Age, Survivors, and Disability Insurance," in Social Security *Bulletin,* Vol. 20, No. 5 (May, 1957).

[11] Adapted from "Current Social Security Program Operations," September, 1957, Division of Program Research, Social Security Administration.

Old-Age, Survivors and Disability Insurance	*September, 1957*
Beneficiaries	10,792,000
Aged (62 and over)	8,892,000
Young survivors and dependents	1,780,000
Disabled (aged 50-64)	120,000
Monthly benefit payments:	$584,000,000
Aged (62 and over)	504,000,000
Young survivors and dependents	71,000,000
Disabled (aged 50-64)	9,000,000
Average old-age (retired worker) benefit	64.31
Average old-age benefit awarded in month	69.12

It is evident from these figures that not only is a large part of the population now covered under the system, but also that a substantial proportion of those now of retirement age are receiving benefit payments. It should be borne in mind that the intent of the program is to provide a basic floor of protection. Benefits under this program may be received concurrently with payments from private retirement plans. In addition there are state and local pension programs for public employees who now may be included under old-age survivors and disability insurance. In some instances, public assistance supplements the insurance benefit.

Let us look next at the chief features of this program, reviewing first the general characteristics, and then examining the 1957 eligibility requirements, the method of computing benefits, and financing. These are, of course, subject to change from time to time by amendment to the Social Security Act.

The purpose of the program is to provide monthly benefits to make up a portion of income lost by men over sixty-five and women over sixty-two who have retired from employment and to their dependents, persons between fifty and sixty-five who are disabled to the extent of being unable to perform substantial work, or survivors of deceased workers.

The program now includes nine out of ten of the gainfully employed, but excludes state and local government groups which have not been brought under the program by voluntary agreement between the individual states and the federal government; non-profit organizations which have not elected coverage; most federal civilian employees who are under another retirement system; self-employed persons not netting $400 a year or more; self-employed doctors of medicine; clergymen, members of religious orders; and Christian Science practitioners who have not elected to come under the system as self-employed individuals.

O. A. S. D. I. is federally administered by the Social Security Administration, a part of the Department of Health, Education, and Welfare. Services in connection with the filing and payment of claims, with information on coverage and entitlement, and with general interpretation of the program are offered through a nation-wide system of district offices.

The program is financed by contributions paid by employers and employees or by payments directly from self-employed people into the trust funds maintained by the United States Treasury Department, and managed by a Board of Trustees which includes the Secretary of the Treasury, the Secretary of Health, Education, and Welfare, and the Secretary of Labor. The Commissioner of Social Security acts as Secretary to the Board of Trustees.

These are in general some of the chief characteristics or features. Let us now examine the program in more detail.

Eligibility

With respect to work experience in covered employment or self-employment, there are two classes of eligibility. The first of these is called "fully insured" status. A person is fully insured if at death, or upon reaching retirement age (65 in the case of men, 62 for women) or more, he has had a number of quarters of coverage equal to at least half the quarters after 1950, or after the quarter in which he reached the age of twenty-one (if that is after 1950), and up to the quarter in which he dies or reaches retirement age. He must have had at least six calendar quarters of coverage in order to have this status. When he has forty quarters, or the equivalent of ten years of coverage, he is fully insured for life. All types of old-age and survivors benefits (except benefits for dependent husbands or widowers of insured women) are payable on the basis of fully insured status alone. Persons newly covered by the Social Security Amendments of 1954 and 1956, who have not had the opportunity to acquire the number of quarters of coverage described above, may qualify for a fully insured status under special statutory conditions.

In order to be "currently insured," a worker must have at least six quarters of coverage within the three years preceding his eligibility to a retirement claim, beginning of disability, or death. Only the lump-sum death payment, and monthly benefits to surviving children and their mothers, can be paid on the basis of currently insured status alone. Benefits can be paid to dependent husbands and widowers only if the wife is both fully insured and currently insured.

The phrase "a quarter of coverage" means any calendar quarter (a 3-month period beginning with January, April, July, or October) in which a worker is paid wages (except for farm work) of $50 or more, or for which he is credited with net earnings from self-employment of $100 or more, or is credited with wages of $100 or more from farm work.

Under the 1956 Amendments, farm operators compute their earnings for old-age and survivors insurance purposes (as part of their tax return) on an annual basis of net income or an amount figured under an optional method. If gross earnings from farming are not more than $1800, the farm operator may figure his net earnings from farming either as the actual net amount, or as two thirds of his gross. If the gross farm earnings exceed $1800, and net farm earnings are less than $1200, the farm operator is permitted to choose between actual net earnings or $1200 as the basis for computing his taxable income. If gross earnings are greater than $1800 and the net exceeds $1200, the actual net earnings must be figured.

Farm laborers too have a separate basis for computing earnings required to qualify for coverage under the old-age and survivors insurance program. They are covered if paid $150 or more in cash by a single employer during the calendar year, or if engaged in farm work for an employer on 20 or more days during the year for cash wages figured on a time basis.

Under the 1956 amendments to the Social Security Act, members of the armed services were covered, and their base pay now counts toward insured status. Deductions from servicemen's pay have been made since January 1, 1957. Previously, service between September 15, 1940, and December 31, 1956, had been "blanketed in," and wage credits allowed at the rate of $160 per month, unless other federal benefits based on the same period of service were available to a serviceman. Payments from the Veterans' Administration do not affect this entitlement. For coverage of service previous to 1957, no deductions are made from the serviceman's pay. Servicemen under contributory coverage after December, 1956, may be granted wage credits for active military or naval service performed after 1950 and before 1957 even though such service counts toward retirement benefits under a military staff retirement system.

Because earnings are related to covered earnings, eligibility for or the amount of benefits is seriously affected by periods of unemployment or reduced earnings. Recognition of this fact has led to special consideration for those unable to work because of some severe disabling condition. This is the so-called "disability freeze," which provides that the periods of such disability are treated as nonexistent, *i.e.,* as periods of employment, so far as the earnings and employment record for O. A. S. D. I. is concerned. This provision has been in effect since January, 1955.

Age is another of the qualifying conditions. The retirement age for men is sixty-five, and for women sixty-two. For the dependents of the retired worker, following are the requirements:

The wife is eligible when she is sixty-two, the dependent husband when he is sixty-five, provided he has been receiving half or

more than half of his support from his wife when she becomes
entitled to benefits, and provided proof of support is filed within
two years of the date on which she becomes entitled to retirement
benefits. If there are no children, benefits are payable only if the
marriage is three years old or more, and the dependent spouse is
living with the worker when the application is filed.

Unmarried children of the retired worker are eligible, if the
children are under eighteen, or an unmarried child of any age if
severely disabled before reaching the age of eighteen.

A wife at any age is eligible, provided she has in her care a child
of the worker who is entitled to benefits, and provided she is living with her husband when the application is filed.

Survivorship is another of the conditions of entitlement. The
following survivors of a fully insured person are eligible for
monthly benefits.[12]

> Unmarried dependent children under 18 or dependent un-
> married children of any age totally disabled before age 18.
>
> A widow of any age while she has in her care children who
> are entitled to benefits, providing she was living with the
> husband at the time of his death.
>
> A widow when she reaches the age of 62 if she has not re-
> married, and she was living with the husband at the time of
> his death.
>
> A former wife divorced—of any age—if she has in her care a
> child entitled to benefits, and she was receiving (pursuant to
> agreement or court order) at least one-half her support from
> the worker at the time of his death.
>
> A dependent widower when he reaches the age of 65 if he has
> not remarried, his wife was both fully and currently insured,
> and he filed proof of support within two years of the time of
> her death.
>
> Dependent parents (aged 62 for mothers, 65 for fathers) if
> the worker leaves no widow, dependent widower, or child who
> could ever become entitled to benefits and the parents filed

12 From *A Brief Explanation of the Social Security Act*. Social Security Administration, July, 1957, p. 18.

proof of dependency on the insured person within two years
of his or her death.

There are other provisions relating to survivors, among them,
that the dependent spouse may receive benefits if the couple had
been married three or more years or if they had a child. In determining the eligibility of the widow or dependent widower for
benefits, the marriage must have been in effect for at least one
year, unless the couple had a natural child or adopted a child
before he was eighteen.

Disability as a condition of eligibility for this program is defined
as inability to engage in any substantial gainful activity because of
a medically determinable physical or mental impairment which is
expected to result in death or to be of long-continued and indefinite duration. This form of benefit is available to disabled persons
between the ages of fifty and sixty-five. The worker in order to
qualify under this provision must be both fully and currently
insured. He must have twenty quarters of coverage in the forty
before the beginning date of disability, including six of the twelve
immediately preceding the established beginning date of the disability. To establish the fact of disability the individual must
present medical evidence of a disabling physical or mental condition causing inability to engage in gainful work. The provisions
of the Social Security Act stipulate that the disability must have
been of at least six months' duration, and that it is expected to last
indefinitely. The claimant must accept treatment and training
designed to restore him to gainful employment. Furthermore, the
Social Security disability benefit must be reduced by the amount
of any other periodic federal benefit (except compensation paid
to a veteran by the Veterans Administration for service-connected
disability) or workmen's compensation benefit paid on account of
disability.

If the individual receiving disability benefits becomes able to
engage in work of a substantial nature before he reaches the age
of sixty-five, disability benefits are discontinued. An exception
may be made for work undertaken as part of a plan of vocational

rehabilitation (see chap. 6). As much as a year of disability benefit payments may be permitted under that circumstance.

Payments under the disability feature of the program began
July 1, 1957. The task of determining the degree and extent of
disability has been assigned to the state vocational rehabilitation
agencies or to other designated state services. This is one of the
most difficult of the tasks of administration. Judgment must be
rendered not only on the medically determined condition of impairment, but also on its relation to ability to perform gainful
work. This is one further example of a fact already noted, that
while the law establishes conditions of eligibility in the social insurances on as objective a basis as possible, it still requires administrative and highly technical judgment to apply the program
to individuals.

Since retirement from gainful employment is an eligibility condition, limits are placed on the amount which a person may earn
and still continue to receive benefits. These limits apply to non-
covered as well as to covered employment. The maximum amount
which may be earned in employment is $1200 per year. After the
insured has reached the age of seventy-two, he may earn any
amount without having it affect his benefit payments.

This brief summary of eligibility is meant to give an idea of
the character of eligibility factors in this program. These provisions are constantly being changed, as the enactments of the past
few years have demonstrated. There is every reason to anticipate
further broadening of the Act from a government which has by
now a firmly established commitment to a comprehensive pattern
of protection under this program.

Amount of benefits (as of October, 1957)

The maximum monthly payment to a retired person is $108.50,
the minimum $30. The most which can be paid monthly to the
insured and his family is $200; the minimum is $45. The minimum
benefit to a single survivor is $30 per month.

Computing the monthly benefit payments

The monthly benefit payments are based on average earnings during the period of work in covered employment. In general, the earnings are averaged over periods beginning with 1937, 1951, or the year in which the worker attains age 22 and ending with the year before the worker reaches retirement age, retires, or dies. The maximum amount of earnings which may be counted in a year is the same as the maximum amount of earnings subject to the social security tax. The maximum amount which may be included in the computation is $4200 per year. After the worker's earnings in the calendar year have reached that amount, the excess is not computed. In order to minimize the effect of periods of low earnings the law provides that up to five years of the lowest earnings may be omitted from the determination of the average.

The amount of the individual payment is computed as follows: on the average monthly earnings, 55 percent of the first $110 and 20 percent of the next $240 are allowed. This is the primary insurance benefit.

The wife or the dependent husband, if sixty-five years or over, is entitled to half the amount of the primary insurance benefit. The widow, the dependent widower, the dependent parent, or single surviving dependent child may be paid three-fourths the amount of the primary benefit.

In addition to the benefits in the form of monthly payments, a lump sum may be claimed by the widow or widower on the death of the wage earner. If no eligible widow or widower survives, the lump sum may be paid to the person or persons who pay the burial expenses. The amount of this lump sum is three times the monthly primary insurance benefit, up to a maximum of $255.

The wife of an insured worker may elect to apply at the age of sixty-two rather than waiting until she becomes sixty-five. If she decides to do this, she will receive only three-fourths as much as she would have each month if she had waited the three additional years.

The following table shows the relationship of different amounts of average earnings to benefits:

Examples of Social Security Benefits

(The amount of a worker's benefit is 55% of the first $110 of average monthly earnings plus 20% of the next $240.)	*Average monthly earnings after 1950**						
	$50	$100	$150	$200	$250	$300	$350
RETIREMENT AND DISABILITY INSURANCE PAYMENTS:							
Monthly retirement benefit at 65 or later, or disability benefit at 50	$30.00	$55.00	$68.50	$78.50	$88.50	$98.50	$108.50
Monthly retirement benefit for woman worker, starting at:**							
62	24.00	44.00	54.80	62.80	70.80	78.80	86.86
63	26.00	47.70	59.40	68.10	76.70	85.40	94.10
64	28.00	51.40	64.00	73.30	82.60	92.00	101.30
Monthly retirement benefit for couple, man 65 or over, wife starting at:**							
62	41.30	75.70	94.30	108.00	121.80	135.50	149.30
63	42.50	78.00	97.10	111.30	125.50	139.60	153.80
64	43.80	80.30	100.00	114.60	129.20	143.70	158.30
65	45.00	82.50	102.80	117.80	132.80	147.80	162.80
SURVIVORS INSURANCE PAYMENTS:							
Widow, widower, child, or parent (monthly)	30.00	41.30	51.40	58.90	66.40	73.90	81.40
Widow and 1 child (monthly)	45.00	82.60	102.80	117.80	132.80	147.80	162.80
Widow and 2 children (monthly)	50.20	82.60	120.00	157.10	177.20	197.10	200.00
Lump sum death payment	90.00	165.00	205.50	235.50	255.00	255.00	255.00

* In figuring your average monthly earnings after 1950, you may omit
    As many as 5 years in which you had low earnings.
    Any period in which your earnings record was frozen because you were disabled.

** Payments to women workers and wives are permanently reduced if started before age 65.

Source: Reprinted from "A Brief Explanation of the Social Security Act," Social Security Administration, p. 23.

Financing the O. A. S. D. I. payments

As has already been noted, O. A. S. D. I. is financed by a tax on earnings. In the case of the wage earner, the employer and employee each pay an equal amount every month. The current rate is 2.25 percent of earnings up to a maximum wage or salary of $4200 per year. In other words, the tax is collected monthly until the employee's earnings from a single employer have reached $4200. All income in excess of that amount in the calendar year is exempt from the tax. Since the self-employed individual carries total responsibility for his retirement program, his tax is set at a higher rate, 3.375 percent, of the first $4200 earned in the calendar year.

The excess over the costs of benefits and administration is invested in interest-bearing United States Government securities. It has been known since the inception of the program that the obligations would increase in number and amount throughout the years as more people qualified (through meeting the requirements of earnings in covered employment), and as the number of people reaching the age of sixty-five continued to increase. The liberalizing amendments have had the effect of accentuating the rate of increase in the obligations against the funds. Consequently the plan, anticipating the rising level of payments, has called for periodic increases in the contribution rate. The present rate represents an increase over the 1 percent which was originally required from both employer and employee and which was not raised until 1950. In 1960 the tax will be increased to 2.75 percent for the wage earner or salaried person, and 4.125 percent for the self-employed. According to the present law, the maximum will be reached in 1975, when employer and employee will each pay 4.25 percent, according to present schedules, and the self-employed will pay 6.375. (These tax rates are percentage equivalents to the rates listed in the following table.)

This table shows the present schedule of increases:

Summary of Effective Contribution Rates and Maximum Earnings Bases under Old-Age, Survivors, and Disability Insurance

Year(s)	Contribution rates (percent)			Maximum earnings base
	Employer	Employee	Self-employed	
1937-49	1	1	. .	$3000
1950	1½	1½	. .	3000
1951-53	1½	1½	2¼	3600
1954	2	2	3	3600
1955-56	2	2	3	4200
1957-59	2¼	2¼	3⅜	4200
1960-64	2¾	2¾	4⅛	4200
1965-69	3¼	3¼	4⅞	4200
1970-74	3¾	3¾	5⅝	4200
1975 and after	4¼	4¼	6⅜	4200

SOURCE: *Social Security Bulletin,* Vol. 20, No. 7 (July, 1957), p. 8.

Other important financial provisions affecting the O. A. S. D. I. program in the 1956 amendments to the Social Security Act, effective January 1, 1957, are as follows: Disability benefits are to be paid out of a special trust fund. From covered employment, the employers and employees each pay .25 percent, and the self-employed .375 percent. The wage credits allowed veterans who served in the armed forces between September 16, 1940, and December 31, 1956, are to be financed by reimbursement from the general revenue to the old-age and survivors trust fund. As mentioned earlier, veterans of military service during this period are automatically allowed wage credits of $160 per month.

Earlier reference was made to scheduled O. A. S. D. I. tax raises up to the year 1975. Under the 1956 amendments, each increase will be subject to review by an Advisory Council on Social Security Financing which will analyze the status of the trust funds in relation to their long-range obligations and commitments.

The financing of this program has been the subject of debate at various times. Some of this has stemmed from the feeling that the government, by collecting funds, investing them in its own securities, and charging interest on those securities, was engaging in double charging the public. As Wilbur Cohen has noted, however, the consensus among insurance, financial, and business experts is that "the investment policy of the OASI system is sound."[13]

General observations about O. A. S. D. I.

After a slow start, O. A. S. D. I. has come close to complete coverage of the population, thanks to the amendments of 1939, 1950, 1952, and 1956. It thus is becoming the chief public resource for income maintenance for those who have reached the age of retirement, for the families who are dependent upon them, and for the widows and children of the workers who die before reaching the age of sixty-five. The additions of the disability provisions, first the "freeze" in 1954, and later the benefits for disabled workers over fifty in 1956, have significantly enlarged the scope and social purpose of the program. Coverage does not mean the same as eligibility, however. Only half of those sixty-five or over now qualify, although the proportion will increase during the coming years.

There is another criterion by which the adequacy of the program should be measured, however, and it is important that this be done if any sound evaluation is to be made. This is the adequacy or inadequacy of the amounts of benefit payments. In this respect, the program has had its ups and downs, sometimes gaining in relation to the rise in the general standard of living, sometimes falling behind. Inflation of course has the effect of reducing a fixed amount of benefits through decreasing the purchasing power of each monthly payment.

In a recent analysis of the effect of consumer price changes on

[13] Cohen, *op. cit.,* in *Social Work Year Book, 1957,* p. 545. Also see Ida C. Merriam, *Social Security Financing,* Social Security Administration Bureau Report No. 17, Bureau of Research and Statistics, 1952, pp. 28-31.

the adequacy of social security benefits, the Social Security Administration has offered evidence that the position of average benefits under O. A. S. D. I. has improved relative to the general price structure. The rise in the wage level, the increase in the base of average earnings against which benefits are computed, the greater stability of employment in recent years, the provisions designed to give a more favorable earnings experience such as the disability freeze, and the exemption of periods of low earnings, all are calculated to improve the position of the beneficiary. Summarizing the situation, the Social Security Administration stated that, "Taking a longer view, it appears that a worker who retired in 1940 and received a benefit of $22.60—the average old-age benefit in December of that year—would, if still living, have been receiving $51.60 since the 1954 amendments to the Social Security Act became effective. In December, 1940 dollars, a benefit of this amount was worth $25.97 in May, 1957."[14]

The report states further that the improvement is more substantial for the average of all old-age benefits, since these reflect the improved wage level and other factors that are omitted in the adjusted figure for the benefits as paid in 1940. The average benefit has increased $9.56 per month, according to this report, or more than 40 percent. In relation to price levels for the whole population, the position of the beneficiary of this program is also favorable compared to that which he occupied prior to the amendments of the 1950's. According to the Bureau of Old-Age and Survivors Insurance, while the Consumer Price Index[15] rose 18 percent from 1950 to the end of 1957, the benefits paid for December 1956 to retired workers who began to receive benefits on or before December 1950 were about 31 percent higher, on the average, than the monthly benefits paid to all retired workers on the rolls at the end of 1950. In brief, these averages show that beneficiaries today generally receive more dollars and also have greater purchasing power than they did in 1940 or 1950.

14 "Impact of Changes in Consumer Prices on Social Security Benefits and Payments," Social Security Administration, Division of Program Research, Washington, July 31, 1957.
15 Prepared monthly by the Bureau of Labor Statistics.

A factor which may be important to the able-bodied person over sixty-five is his opportunity to work without forfeiting his benefit. The amount he may earn is higher now than it formerly was. On the other hand, when the list of industry not covered was much larger, the beneficiary had more opportunity to secure employment in which his earnings had no effect on his entitlement to O. A. S. D. I.

The retirement test is a feature of the law which has been subject to some dispute. Some people feel that no obstacles should be placed in the way of the older person who wishes to continue working, and advocate that he be permitted to earn any amount without having it limit his benefit. It is better for the older person to work, these people believe, and better for society to have the use of his skills. On the other hand, others point out, the essential purpose of the whole O. A. S. D. I. plan is to compensate for income loss, and payment to the person who continues to be fully employed would be a distortion, and a very expensive one, at that. The liberalization of the amount of earnings permitted without effect on the benefit, which amount has increased from $15 in 1935 to $100 per month in 1957, has seemed to be a reasonable adaptation to the principle of encouraging the older person to utilize his skills without altering the essential purpose of an income maintenance program.

By another yardstick, however, the present scale of benefits appears in a less favorable light. There is evidence that the average of workers' earnings has increased faster than has the Consumers' Price Index, so that even though the beneficiary under this system of social insurance may have more purchasing power than he did in earlier years, the amount he receives may be less than proportionate to what he would earn if he were employed.

Recent amendments to the program have recognized, according to Corson and McConnell, the principle of "social adequacy," which was absent from the measure in 1935. The benefits are less and less related strictly to individual contributions. As these authors state:[16]

16 *Op. cit.,* p. 198.

The single worker, the young worker who would be employed under the old-age insurance system for a long period of years, and the worker who died leaving no dependents would receive *less* in relation to the contributions they themselves had made than would the worker with a wife or children at the time of retirement, the worker already nearing retirement in 1939, and the worker who died and left survivors entitled to benefits. The employers' share would help finance the more costly benefits of the latter groups. Yet every worker contributing to the system would receive more protection than his own contributions would purchase from a private insurance carrier.

UNEMPLOYMENT INSURANCE

Unemployment is always with us. This is not a cheerful statement but its truth is supported by the number of people unemployed even during the times of highest national income, productivity, and prosperity. As of July 1957, there were more than three million people counted as unemployed out of a total labor force of more than seventy million. Throughout the most prosperous of the past several years of good business, the number of unemployed has been in the millions.

Why should this be true? During a business slump, we expect unemployment, but why are so many people out of work when business conditions are good? The answer lies in the nature of our dynamic economy, which is responsive to many sorts of influences. New technological discoveries may cause unemployment when they make the skills of some workers suddenly obsolete, while others are the victims of layoffs because a previously profitable process is now outmoded. In certain industries, re-tooling to produce new models of products causes at least temporary unemployment. Businesses fail, move to new locations, or merge with other business firms, all of which may mean joblessness to some former employees. Others work in seasonal industries and have weeks or months of joblessness during those industries' yearly slack periods. These and other factors, present even in prosperous times, account for the persistent and perhaps inescapable feature of unemployment in our economy.

Beginning with the fall of 1957, a business recession has increased unemployment. Although the condition was first reflected in unemployment at that time, as early as January 1957 economists had called attention to signs and portents of impending decline in business activity. A result of the recession has been a rise in the number of jobless to 4,494,000 by mid-January 1958, with insured unemployed under state programs totalling 2,895,000 as of January 25.

The fact that unemployment is one of the great hazards to the security of a family in an industrial society scarcely demands elaboration. The effect on a family of loss of employment income even for a relatively short time is often shattering. Fixed obligations will not wait, and the family with an unemployed able-bodied father is not in the most favorable position to apply for and receive public assistance.

The effect of joblessness on the individual and the family was stated quite graphically by Eric A. Johnston, then president of the United States Chamber of Commerce, in 1944, in these terms:[17]

> When a worker loses his job and wage, his monthly bills face him just as inevitably as when he is on the payroll. His rent, or his mortgage payments and property taxes, his installment contracts, his grocery bills and his public utility bills must be paid. Job and wage losses destroy *his* way of life. They disorganize his family and his family relationships. They destroy his standing in the community, his credit with his suppliers. Mass unemployment, I believe, must and can be substantially mitigated. That part of unemployment and wage losses which cannot be abolished can be provided for by means of individual thrift, by voluntary group programs of sharing and spreading the risks, and, where these two do not suffice, by social insurance.

[17] Quoted in "Twenty Years of Unemployment Insurance in the USA," *Employment Security Review*, Vol. 22, No. 8 (August, 1955), Bureau of Employment Security, U. S. Department of Labor, p. 4, "An Employer Speaks."

Today throughout the country, unemployment insurance is designated to provide a cushion against the shock of temporary joblessness. It operates in combination with the Public Employment Service. It is a federal-state program, operating under the Federal Unemployment Tax Act, the Social Security Act, the Wagner-Peyser Act, under which the Employment Service was established, the Veterans Readjustment Assistance Act of 1952, and state employment security laws.

Unemployment insurance in the United States really began with the passage of the Social Security Act in 1935. Before this Wisconsin had passed such a measure in 1932, and four other states also passed laws anticipating the federal one. The federal employment service, a related program of placement, however, also had been established before the enactment of the Social Security law, under the Wagner-Peyser Act in 1933. As an over-all system, unemployment insurance began in Great Britain in 1911 and by 1935 had spread to ten nations, while some other nations had programs providing financial support to voluntary insurance systems. In the United States, the great depression made the nation employment-conscious, and this formed part of the favorable climate for social legislation in the 1930's which made it possible to enact such a program here.

When the unemployment insurance program was proposed in this country, in its recommendations to the President, the Commission on Economic Security advocated a federally operated system of insurance. Congress, however, faced by questions of constitutionality, enacted this part of the Social Security Act to provide for a combined federal-state system of operation. The federal government levied an unemployment insurance tax (on the payroll) of 3 percent on employers, and provided for a tax credit, or "offset" to those states which enacted measures of their own, up to 2.7 per cent. The balance of .3 percent was to be retained by the federal government for paying the states' costs of administration of the Act. It was believed that the incentive to the states to derive the benefits themselves from the taxes being paid by businesses within their boundaries would lead to state legislation. Also, the effect of a nation-wide tax was to reduce or eliminate any advantage which businesses in states without this cost might have over competitors in states which had enacted such legislation.

In the ensuing years, the program has survived the test of constitutionality,[18] and has been adopted by all of the forty-eight states, by the District of Columbia, and by the territories of Alaska and Hawaii.

Currently, the federal tax extends to employers who have four or more employees during twenty or more weeks of the year. Federal requirements are not extensive and allow the states essential jurisdiction over their programs. The conditions prescribed by the federal government, in addition to those which apply to administration and financing, are that the state must provide to workers the opportunity to appeal decisions of the state agencies with respect to their claims; and that compensation shall not be denied the worker who refuses new employment if the employment is available as the result of a labor dispute, if the payment offered for work is substantially below the prevailing local rate for similar work, or if employment requires the worker to join a company union, or to resign from or to refrain from joining an established, legitimate labor organization. Also the federal government permits the exclusion of certain types of employment in addition to those which may be excluded under size of firm. The federal tax does not apply to certain types of services such as agricultural and domestic services and government employment. In general the states have tended to follow federal coverage provisions, although they are free to exclude employment subject to federal tax, and to cover those excluded by federal law. An example of the former practice is the New Jersey unemployment insurance law, which excludes national banks from coverage, even though the federal act has covered them since 1939.

The functions of unemployment insurance, as summarized by the Bureau of Employment Security of the United States Department of Labor, are as follows:[19]

[18] *Ibid.,* see p. 14.
[19] *Ibid.,* pp. 3-4.

To insured workers who are employed, unemployment insurance lends a feeling of security; they know that should they lose their jobs through no fault of their own, they will not be totally without income. For insured workers who are unemployed, it means cash to ease the crisis of loss of their jobs. These payments help workers buy food, housing, and other essentials for themselves and their families. Since the program requires registration at the public employment offices, it helps workers find new jobs—and suitable jobs.

Benefits between jobs help to conserve workers' skills. They reduce the pressure on jobless workers to take blind-alley jobs in which they would lose their skills and the status which goes with skills. At the same time unemployment insurance facilitates the free flow of workers between communities. When workers must leave a community because of industrial or community changes or for personal reasons, unemployment insurance helps sustain them until they find employment in other locations where their skills are needed.

Unemployment insurance serves employers by helping them maintain a trained labor force . . .

Unemployment insurance helps maintain purchasing power in a neighborhood, town, or region where workers have been laid off. By maintaining part of the purchasing power of the workers directly concerned, unemployment insurance helps prevent "secondary unemployment" of people who provide the goods and services that workers buy—for example, workers in stores and shops, restaurants, and laundries. Thus, unemployment insurance helps maintain confidence among workers, employers, and the communities in which they live. It helps prevent the contagion of fear which starts a downward spiral of curtailment of business.

The importance of a strong system of protection against the great hazard of unemployment would be difficult to overstate. How well the functions are performed, however, depends very much upon state action, upon the kinds of provisions made in the states under the federal-state system of operating the unemployment insurance program.

Subject to general federal provisions, the states have the authority to determine the conditions of coverage, the eligibility requirements, conditions of disqualification, and the rate of taxation. The states also have jurisdiction over the amount of benefit payments, and the length of time during which they may be paid. Variations among the states are considerable with respect to all features of the program, as the ensuing description will indicate.

Coverage and eligibility

The following summary[20] gives the general features of state plans as they relate to requirements which the worker must meet in order to qualify for unemployment insurance benefits:

1. He must register for work at a public employment office and file his claim for benefits.
2. He must have worked previously on a job covered by the State law. This usually includes jobs in factories, shops, mines, mills, stores, offices, or other places of private industry and commerce. In more than half the States the law applies only to employment in concerns that have four or more persons on the payroll during 20 weeks of the year. In the other States it applies also to jobs in smaller establishments.
3. He must have a certain amount of "wage credits"— which means he must have had a certain amount of pay for work in covered jobs in a specified "base period" during the year or two before he lost his job or was laid off.
4. He must be able to work. In general, unemployment insurance benefits are not payable to workers who are sick or *unable* to work for any other reason, although a few States pay benefits to workers who become ill after they are unemployed and continue paying the benefits, within the legal limits, if there are no suitable jobs to offer the individual. . . .
5. He must be available for work and must be ready and willing to take a suitable job if one is offered.

This succinct summary of the provisions conveys only a hint of the complexities of the laws as they are administered in the various states. However, these are the general features of the programs, so far as eligibility is concerned.

[20] From *A Brief Explanation of the Social Security Act, op. cit.*, pp. 8-9.

The worker may be disqualified for benefits under all state programs if he : (1) has quit his job without good cause or has caused the employer to discharge him because of some misconduct in relation to his work; (2) has refused to apply for or accept an offer of suitable work; (3) is unemployed because of work stoppage due to a labor dispute. Many states have additional disqualifying conditions, including those of persons who are unemployed while engaged in full time study, women unable to work because of pregnancy or who leave employment to take care of their homes.

When an unemployed person has been disqualified, if he later is again declared eligible, he may be compelled to wait a longer period than usual before his benefits begin, and in some states the amount of his benefit will also be reduced. In states with the most severe penalties, the worker who has been disqualified must start all over again to build wage credits in covered employment.

The size of the firm is an important factor in coverage. In some states whether or not the worker is covered depends on the number of people employed in the firm for which he works. In some states, the amount of wages paid during a specified period of time is a factor. In five states, coverage depends entirely upon the total amount of a firm's payroll, rather than upon the number of employees.

The federal tax now applies to firms which have employed four or more persons for at least twenty weeks of the year. Laws in twenty-eight of the states have the same provision for coverage. In others the coverage extends also to smaller firms, even to those with a single employee. Some states also are more liberal than required by federal law with respect to the number of weeks during which the firm must have had the specified number of employees.

The determination of whether a person is actually an employee is not so simple as it might appear at first glance. The object in state laws which stipulate that the worker be a *bona fide* employee is to exclude those who are in an independent contractual arrangement with the employer. States apply various tests to the relationship, including the fact of control by the employer over the conditions of the employee's work, whether the service is related to the usual course of the business for which it is performed, and whether the individual is customarily engaged in an independent trade, occupation, profession, or business and therefore only occasionally employed by the firm.

Location of employment is an important factor for those employed in firms which are engaged in interstate operations. Because an employee who worked in more than one state might find himself consequently ineligible for any program, all or most states have adopted a uniform provision which calls for coverage in the state in which the worker would most likely seek work if he lost his current job.

Coverage generally includes: "jobs in factories, shops, mines, mills, stores, offices, restaurants, laundries, banks, American ships, and other places of private industry or commerce." Generally excluded from state unemployment insurance laws are: "a. Railroad workers who are covered by the Federal Railroad Unemployment Insurance Act; b. Agricultural workers; c. Domestic workers; d. State and municipal workers; e. Workers in nonprofit educational, religious or charitable organizations; f. Casual labor, that is, occasional work not connected with the employer's regular business; and g. Service by one spouse for the other, by a parent for a child, or by a minor child for a parent."[21] For the most part, states permit the employers in firms not covered to elect coverage, subject to payment of the payroll tax.

Interpreting many of the provisions of all these laws frequently has led to controversy. All of the provisions, except that for the period of employment, have resulted in cases of dispute which have made unemployment insurance one of the most controversial of the income-maintenance programs. An individual who is unable to work because of illness or disability ordinarily would be excluded from a program designed to compensate for involuntary unemployment of the able-bodied. In practice this has presented

---

[21] *Federal Labor Laws and Agencies,* Bulletin 123 (rev.) of the Bureau of Labor Standards of the U. S. Dept. of Labor, pp. 81-82.

problems of adjudication, although not so many as has the provision relating to acceptance of "suitable" work. In effect, work is
generally deemed suitable if it is of the type that permits the
exercise of the worker's skill and training, if it offers wages comparable with those prevailing in the community for similar work,
and if it is reasonably accessible to him. If the worker refuses jobs
meeting such conditions he must show good cause, that is, something which seems to represent reasonable behavior. These and
other requirements in state programs are often complex to administer because they involve interpreting human behavior, and the
enormous variety of individual circumstances account for a growing body of administrative and court decisions based on appeals
from decisions on claims.

As to period of earnings, states generally specify a base period
during which the employee must have earned a certain number of
wage credits in covered employment. In all states the base period
is one year. In most states, that year must be the one immediately
preceding the date of application for benefits. In a few, however,
the base period is a calendar year and in some states this applies
to all workers, no matter when they apply for benefits. In these
states, for example, the eligibility of an employee who applied in
April of one year would depend on whether he had worked a sufficient period of time and earned a specified minimum amount
during the year ending on the previous December 31.

In some states eligibility always depends on the employee's
earning a specified minimum amount during the base period. Some
provide a formula such as the specification that he must have
earned as much as thirty times the weekly amount of the benefits
to which he would be entitled. Some stipulate a "high quarter"—
a three-months period during which he must have earned at least
a certain minimum amount—as a qualification in addition to that
relating to earnings during the whole base period. Some states
specify that the worker must have received wages in at least two
quarters.

There are many different methods in state laws relating to these matters, and many various combinations. An example of one combination is provided by the Indiana program. In that state, a flat amount of wages, $250, must have been earned during the year, and the worker must have earned $150 during the last two quarters (combined) of the base period. In New Hampshire the law merely specifies a flat amount of earnings, $400, in the base period. In Alabama the worker must have earned thirty-five times his weekly benefit amount during the base period, and at least $112 of this total in one "high quarter." The list of variations could be lengthened almost indefinitely. The important general feature is that all states relate eligibility to earnings in a recent period.

Amount and duration of benefits

Benefits are paid on a weekly basis.[22] In general, state laws specify that one half the total income loss should be covered by unemployment insurance, although such low maximum payment rates are set that in effect they completely defeat this purpose. These maximum rates vary from $25 per week to $41.[23] The tendency in recent years has been to use the three-month period when earnings were highest as the basis for computing benefits. In 1957 forty-one states used the average of this quarter as the basis rather than the average for the entire base period. In computing benefits this way, the state takes the total earnings during the thirteen weeks of highest earnings, and divides it by 26 (or whatever figure is stipulated in the law). The effect of this is to pay half the weekly wage at the highest point of the base period, subject of course to the maximum set forth in the law.

While the average benefits have increased over the years, they have not kept pace with the rise of wages. Because the maximum amounts stipulated in state laws are low when compared to wage rates, the unemployed in most of the states receive less than one half the weekly wage earned in their most recent job.

[22] In all but one state.
[23] In Alaska, however, the maximum weekly benefit for the worker without dependents is $45.

Maximum Weekly Benefit Amount as of October 1, 1957, and Ratio to 1956 Average Weekly Wages in Covered Employment

State	Maximum weekly benefit amount[1] Oct. 1, 1957	Average weekly wages in cov. emp't., 1956	Maximum as percent of weekly wages
Average, all States	..	$81.16	..
Alabama	$28	65.07	43.0
Alaska	45 (70)[2]	137.90	32.6 (50.8)
Arizona	30	81.32	36.9
Arkansas	26	55.27	47.0
California	40	89.54	44.7
Colorado	35 (44)	79.62	44.0 (55.3)
Connecticut	40 (60)	85.71	46.7 (70.0)
Delaware	35	90.37	38.7
Dist. of Columbia	30[1]	77.41	38.8
Florida	30	67.42	44.5
Georgia	30	62.77	47.8
Hawaii	35	61.58	56.8
Idaho	40	72.83	54.9
Illinois	30 (45)	90.32	33.2 (49.8)
Indiana	33	84.90	38.9
Iowa	30	74.03	40.5
Kansas	34	76.05	44.7
Kentucky	32	71.34	44.9
Louisiana	25	71.75	34.8
Maine	33	66.39	49.7
Maryland	35 (43)	73.99	47.3 (58.1)
Massachusetts	35[1]	74.57	46.9[1]
Michigan	30 (55)	97.26	30.8[1]
Minnesota	38	79.28	47.9
Mississippi	30	55.16	54.4
Missouri	33	77.86	42.4
Montana	32	75.33	42.5
Nebraska	32	70.48	45.4

State	Maximum weekly benefit amount[1] Oct. 1, 1957	Average weekly wages in cov. emp't., 1956	Maximum as percent of weekly wages
Nevada	37.50 (57.50)	86.15	43.5 (66.7)
New Hampshire	32	66.87	47.9
New Jersey	35	87.24	40.1
New Mexico	30	73.78	40.7
New York	36	88.50	40.7
North Carolina	32	59.65	53.6
North Dakota	26 (35)	68.16	38.1 (51.3)
Ohio	33 (39)	88.92	37.1 (43.9)
Oklahoma	28	75.74	37.0
Oregon	40	83.54	47.9
Pennsylvania	35	78.32	44.7
Rhode Island	30	69.65	43.1
South Carolina	26	58.14	44.7
South Dakota	28	66.98	41.8
Tennessee	30	66.29	45.3
Texas	28	75.32	37.2
Utah	37[3]	73.89	50.1
Vermont	28	68.09	41.1
Virginia	28	66.22	42.3
Washington	35	84.08	41.6
West Virginia	30	81.75	36.7
Wisconsin	38	83.37	45.6
Wyoming	41 (47)[3]	74.27	55.2 (63.3)

[1] Figures in parenthesis represent maximum including dependents' allowances, except in Colorado where the maximum is higher for claimants meeting certain requirements. The Dist. of Col. maximum is the same with or without dependents. Figure not shown for Mass. since weekly benefit plus allowance is limited by claimant's average weekly wage. Ratio is not shown for Michigan since wage higher than 1956 average is necessary to receive maximum.

[2] $25 for interstate claimants.

[3] Maximum computed annually as a specified percentage of Statewide average weekly wages in covered employment (50 percent in Utah, 55 percent in Wyoming). Difference from percentages in table due to rounding.

SOURCE: Bureau of Employment Security, U. S. Dept. of Labor, November 26, 1957.

In eleven states allowances additional to the benefits are provided for dependents of the beneficiary. These allowances make the maximum weekly benefit amount as high as $70 weekly. All states provide partial benefits to people not fully employed.

States use many different kinds of methods and formulae in the administration of unemployment insurance programs, and only the most general indication of how benefits are computed can be given here without going into great technical detail.

All states except Wisconsin limit the length of time that benefits may be paid in any year. All have what is called a "benefit year," a fifty-two-week period during which the individual may draw the benefits awarded him on his base period earnings. Limitations are established on the total amount of benefits which may be received in any benefit year. This limitation may be either a multiple of the weekly benefit amount, and a fraction of the earnings received over the base period, or a uniform multiple of the weekly benefit amount. The multiple of the weekly rate may be anywhere from sixteen to thirty, with twenty-six the most common. The most common portion of total base period earnings used to compute the maximum benefit which may be drawn in a benefit year is one-third. The result of this practice (of using a multiple of earnings rather than a flat amount) is an increase in the number of weeks a person may draw benefits, if, as the result of earnings during one week, his benefit for that week has been reduced.

When a claimant has received all the benefits to which he is entitled in a benefit year, he is said to have exhausted his benefit rights, and must wait until the end of the benefit year before he again may claim payments. When he files for a new benefit year, earnings received within the applicable base period are used to compute his benefit rights. Twelve states have additional wage or employment requirements to assure recent employment and to prevent payment of benefits in a second year without intervening employment.[24]

[24] For this material on payments during benefit year the writer is indebted to the staff of the Unemployment Insurance Service, Bureau of Employment Security, U. S. Dept. of Labor.

Most states provide a waiting period between the filing of the claim and the receipt of the first payment. In most states, the period is one week. Unlike workmen's compensation, there is no retroactive payment to cover this period. In general, the same waiting period applies to both partial and total unemployment.

Financing

Each State collects taxes on those wages which are subject to state law. The rate of this tax generally is 2.7 percent, though it is varied by experience-rating. The typical pattern among the states is to limit the amount of wages subject to this tax at $3000 per year, although in a few states the amount is $3600 per year. Normally, the state tax is collected quarterly by the states, and the amount is deposited to the state's account in the Unemployment Trust Fund of the United States Treasury. In three jurisdictions (Alaska, Alabama, and New Jersey) the employee also is taxed, but in all the others, only the employer is taxed. All the money deposited to the states' accounts in the Unemployment Trust Fund is used for the payment of benefits.

The federal tax is .3 percent of the payroll, and is collected annually by the federal government. This money is used to finance state administration of the program. Any surplus may be deposited in the Federal Loan Fund, and any surplus over the amount needed for loans is credited to the states for use in payment of benefits, or, in certain instances, for administrative expenditures.

The practice of experience or merit rating is common to all state unemployment insurance administration. This term refers to the practice of reducing the payroll tax on those employers who have records of steady employment—of whose employees only a small number have drawn unemployment insurance.

There are five ways of computing experience-rating, and they all are too technical for description here. They have in common the feature of giving the employer the advantage of periods of steady employment,[25] and they are intended to act as an incentive to the

[25] Those interested in studying this subject should see Ida C. Merriam, *Social Security Financing*, Social Security Administration, Division of Research and Statistics, Bureau Report No. 17, November 1952; also, Eveline M. Burns, *The American Social Security System* (New York, 1949). pp. 156-169.

employer to keep employment stable. Whether the device actually has had this result is highly debatable; for whether the employer has sufficient control over conditions of employment to accomplish this purpose is itself questionable, and if he does not, then merely his desire to keep people on the job cannot be a particularly important factor in reducing unemployment. Conditions which cause layoffs are in large part due to forces other than the employers' inclination. One effect of experience-rating is to reduce taxes during periods of prosperity, and to increase them during slack times when it is more difficult for employers to pay the tax increases. Employers who have seasonal work are penalized by the system of experience-rating, even though to alter the seasonal nature of the work is not within their power. It is possible, also, that their desire to keep the unemployment-insurance tax rate low may incline employers to challenge claims made by the unemployed for benefits, since most of these plans for experience-rating are based on actual payments of unemployment insurance.

The result of experience-rating has been a considerable reduction in the rates of taxes in the states, in some instances reducing them to an average of less than one percent. This is attributable to the past few years of prosperity and steady employment. In some states, employers, who by and large are strongly in favor of the system of experience-rating, can point to a substantial accumulated reserve in the unemployment-insurance trust fund.

A rationale for financing unemployment insurance was suggested by Lewis Meriam some years ago along these lines:

> The system in the United States is, moreover, not a substitute for public relief for unemployment but only a first line of defense, or, as it is often called, a cushion to absorb the first shock. Back of it must lie some form of public assistance. This fact should be frankly recognized, and, when a recession is on, payroll taxes—taxes on employment—should not be raised to safeguard the reserves. On the other hand, taxes should not be reduced automatically because good times have made the reserves climb . . .

Mr. Meriam then suggests that when the reserves become higher than seems necessary, adjustments should be made by legislative action in the light of experience, but that high rates should prevail when employment is up, and lower rates when employment is down.[26]

From time to time suggestions are made for extending the tax to employees as well as employers. Their proponents believe that a case could be made that this would strengthen the position of labor when its representatives appear before legislative bodies to present the need for more adequate measures, and would tend to make the beneficiaries more responsible in their requests than is the case when they are not directly involved in supporting the system.[27] It is hardly likely, however, that labor would fail to oppose such a development.

Coverage of special groups

Special programs of unemployment insurance are provided for veterans and for federal employees. Eligible veterans are those with ninety days or more continuous military service between June 27, 1950, and January 31, 1955. If the veteran is covered under another program, *i.e.,* state unemployment insurance or railroad workers unemployment insurance, he must exhaust those benefits before he is eligible for veterans benefits. An unemployed federal worker is entitled to benefits according to the provisions of the last state in which he worked as a federal employee or in subsequent private employment.

Some comments on unemployment insurance

The purposes of unemployment insurance are socially desirable and scarcely require defense. The objective of a system providing protection against involuntary joblessness is quite generally accepted. Nevertheless the program presents some vexing problems.

[26] Lewis Meriam, *Relief and Social Security* (Washington, The Brookings Institution, 1946), pp. 230-231.
[27] Burns, *op. cit.,* pp. 154-155.

Some phases of it require an exercise of administrative judgment in determining the facts relating to rights to receive benefits, since these may be rooted in the behavior of the individual, as well as in the circumstances of unemployment. Charges that people prefer receiving the "dole" to working are often made against recipients of unemployment insurance. Some of the criticisms are redolent of the worst ones hurled at the hapless person on WPA during the depression, but others reflect a genuine public perplexity over the nature and fundamental purpose of this program.

It is always wise, however, to ascertain whether criticism is based on rumor, or on fact. It is all too easy to generalize broadly from one or two known instances, and to assume that the behavior of one person is typical of all who receive benefits under this program. Myths are likely to develop, and to get wide circulation. In an article on this subject, an official of the Bureau of Employment Security has commented:[28]

> During the 20 years of unemployment insurance history in this country, various public impressions of the way the program operates have been widely circulated and widely accepted. While some of these are reasonably accurate, others have little, if any, factual support. Many of the latter are concerned with the extent to which benefits are paid to "chiselers" and "work dodgers." In a program protecting more than 40 million workers, some "chiselers" are bound to show up. But if we take account of benefit payments equaling as much as $2 billion a year, the amount of money going out in improper payments in comparison with proper payments is remarkably small. Neither the weekly amount of benefits nor the methods of administration make the system particularly inviting to chiselers.

In an excellent chapter on "Income Guarantees and Willingness to Work," Eveline Burns considers the measures which are employed in legislation and in administrative policy and method to keep the program related to continued involuntary unemploy-

28 Philip Booth, "Myths and Realities in Unemployment Insurance," *Employment Security Review,* December, 1955, p. 1.

ment.[29] She acknowledges the problem of marginal workers, whose low normal income makes benefit payments comparatively attractive, especially if work conditions are unpleasant, wants modest, or family responsibilities light. Dr. Burns mentions also "Certain categories of workers who do not have a firm attachment to the labor market" who "are also less likely to resist the temptation to prefer idleness on benefit to an earned income."[30] Irregularly employed laborers, married women who prefer to attend to family responsibilities (apparently the most numerous group in the category of the willingly involuntarily idle) and the small group who find the responsibility for maintaining self and family overwhelming, are other categories mentioned by Dr. Burns.

Various tests, some statutory, some administrative, are used to safeguard the uses of unemployment insurance. The limited amount of payment is designed to make the status less attractive than that of working for pay. Benefits are limited in duration. The test of regular attachment to the labor force is a part of all laws. Claimants are, as we have seen, required to present themselves regularly to the employment office to look for work, and the disqualifying conditions are a part of all states' laws.

But it is in the interpretation of some of these disqualifying conditions that difficulties arise. Availability for work can create many problems of interpretation. What is "suitable work"? How does one measure the genuineness of availability for work? How is effort to secure work determined or measured? The worker is required to take work available locally. What is a reasonable interpretation of "local"? How far may the worker be expected to travel? What are the circumstances that justify quitting a job? These and other parts of this program present baffling problems of administration, some possibilities for popular misunderstanding, and some opportunity for abuse.

Nevertheless, it is equally evident that the program continues to have great social utility. But it presents also, some serious defi-

---

[29] Eveline M. Burns, *Social Security and Public Policy* (New York, 1956), pp. 56-79. For a detailed discussion see Joseph M. Becker, *The Problem of Abuse in Unemployment Benefits* (New York, 1953).

[30] *Ibid.*, p. 57.

ciencies in adequacy and coverage. In his "Economic Report to the Congress," President Eisenhower early in 1957 pointed out some of the most necessary changes in these words:[31]

> Additional improvements are needed. First, benefits are still inadequate in relation to wages. It is again suggested that the States raise the dollar maximums so that the great majority of covered workers will be eligible for payments equal to at least half their regular earnings. Second, the duration of benefits is still inadequate in many states. It is again suggested that the States which have not yet done so lengthen the maximum term of benefits to 26 weeks for every person who qualifies and remains unemployed that long. Third, important classes of workers are still not covered. It is recommended that the Congress extend Unemployment Insurance to the 1.8 million employers with 1 to 3 persons on their payrolls who are still uncovered in many States. Also the States are urged to include the 4.5 million persons who work for them in their political subdivisions.

It is true that in the three years, 1954-57, many states moved to improve their programs, with thirty-eight raising their weekly benefits, according to the President's Report, twelve lengthening the potential duration of benefits, and four extending coverage to employers with fewer than four employees. Still the program needs further development in order to reach the goal of adequacy of protection against one of the most prevalent of economic hazards.

WORKMEN'S COMPENSATION[32]

People sometimes are injured on the job, or develop illness which is attributable to their work. They lose wages, and incur heavy medical costs. They may be crippled or die from injury or disease. To meet these contingencies, workmen's compensation

[31] *Economic Report of the President,* transmitted to Congress January 23, 1957, p. 67.

[32] For the material on workmen's compensation the writer is heavily indebted to the Bureau of Labor Standards of the U. S. Dept. of Labor, and especially to Mr. Paul Gurske, Director of the Bureau.

programs have been enacted which protect the worker and his beneficiaries against economic hardship due to occupational diseases or injuries connected with employment.

This was the earliest of the social insurances in the United States. The first law was passed by the federal government in 1908 and covered the civilian employees of the national government. The first state workmen's compensation laws were enacted in 1911, in ten of the states. After 1911, the states were generally quick to adopt and develop such a program and by 1930 all the states and territories had workmen's compensation laws. The numbers of workers now covered by these laws in the United States is estimated to be between 60 and 80 percent of the working population.

Prior to the development of these programs, the injured worker's only recourse was to the courts, where he could sue the employer for damages. He was subject to all the delays and expense attendant upon legal action, and in addition he had to prove the employer's responsibility. As a rule this was not an easy thing to do. Lacking the resources to bear the expenses of such action, he often did not even press his claim. If he did go to court, he had to establish his case subject to three common law defenses which worked against him: (1) the assumption of risk, which provided that he might voluntarily and knowingly have accepted the hazards of employment and was thereby responsible; (2) the fellow servant rule, which exempted the employer from obligation for any injury caused one worker by the carelessness of a fellow worker; and (3) contributory negligence, which meant that the employee must establish the fact that the accident which inflicted the injury was not caused by his own neglect of proper precaution.

By establishing this form of insurance, the states and the federal government have said in effect that the costs of work-incurred injury or disease are a part of the cost of production. Except in five states[33] workers are no longer compelled to go to court to secure redress. Costly delays and expensive counsel are not contemplated under this program, and exist only where there are

[33] Alabama, Louisiana, Tennessee, Wyoming, and New Mexico.

either inadequacies of administration or deficiencies in the law.

In the words of one authority, "The primary purposes of a workmen's compensation act are to provide benefit payments to an injured worker, to provide adequate and competent medical services, to rehabilitate the worker as promptly as possible for return to gainful employment, and to work for accident prevention."[34] Wide variation is found among the states in the various phases of their programs, including occupations and industries covered, size and duration of benefits, provisions for rulings of permanent total disability, inclusions of occupational diseases, and methods of insuring risks. These wide variations exist because this program is not federally administered or aided. Federal provisions extend mainly to longshoremen, harbor workers, private employees in the District of Columbia, and the national government's own civil employees.[35] As is frequently the case, the program which in its origin was a pioneering one, since then has been less responsive to the need for changes in it than have some of the newer measures, but substantial progress seems to have been made in the states' workmen's compensation programs in recent years.

Coverage and eligibility

Many factors operate against complete coverage of workers throughout the country, and against complete protection of those who are covered. One of the major limitations of coverage—unique to this alone of all the social insurance systems—is the provision in some states that it is elective rather than compulsory; either the employer or the employee has the power of election, if the work falls within the statutory definition. As of November 1955, twenty-nine of the fifty-four jurisdictions (the forty-eight states, the territories, and the federal government) had laws making coverage compulsory, while twenty-five provided for elective coverage. In most of the states with elective provisions, the em-

---

[34] Max D. Kossoris, "Workmen's Compensation in the United States—an Appraisal," in *Bulletin* No. 1149, Bureau of Labor Statistics, U. S. Dept. of Labor, pp. 2-3.

[35] These now include employees of the District of Columbia government, the Tennessee Valley Authority, the Virgin Islands Corporation, etc.

ployee is presumed to be covered unless he submits in writing his rejection of the plan. In general, and despite important exceptions, the majority of the employers in the twenty-five jurisdictions allowing choice have elected to come under the plan. In two states, the employees are allowed the right to elect coverage.[36]

There are variations of the compulsory features among the states which require coverage. As stated in the summary of state laws prepared by the Department of Labor's Bureau of Labor Standards: "In a few cases the laws are in part compulsory and in part elective. For instance, some are elective as they apply to private employers, but compulsory as to the State or other public employers. Some are elective for most employers but compulsory as to coal mining or other hazardous work." The summary adds that in most states,[37]

> the employments that are exempted from coverage may be brought under the law through the voluntary acceptance of the employer. Such coverage is called voluntary because the employer does not lose his common law rights or defenses if he does not accept. Thus, a compensation law in its application may be either compulsory or elective as to certain employments and voluntary as to others.

Another limitation of coverage is the exemption of employers who have fewer than a specified number of employees. Only twenty-three of the jurisdictions make no numerical exemptions. This specification varies, from fewer than two employees in Nevada and Oklahoma to fewer than fifteen employees in South Carolina. In this respect workmen's compensation laws resemble somewhat the unemployment insurance laws, which also tend to permit exemption of the small firm.

Some states provide coverage only to workers in especially hazardous occupations omitting coverage for all other workers. Other important areas of noncoverage are farm-workers (covered only in fourteen states and in Hawaii and Puerto Rico), domestic

[36] This information is taken from *States' Workmen's Compensation Laws*, Bulletin No. 161, issued in 1955 by the Bureau of Labor Standards of the U. S. Dept. of Labor, and the *Supplement to Bulletin 161.*
[37] *Ibid.*, p. 3.

workers (although steps have been taken in some states to bring in certain categories of domestic servants), and so-called "casual" or irregularly employed workers.

Contingencies covered by workmen's compensation laws include: temporary total disability, permanent total disability, permanent partial disability, dismemberment, loss of sight or hearing, and death. Obviously these are not all mutually exclusive. Temporary total disability is the most common of all the compensable conditions. A second most common compensable condition is permanent partial disability due to impairment of physical functioning or dismemberment sufficient to handicap the worker but not so severe as to incapacitate him completely for employment. In case of death from job-incurred injury or disease, the worker's dependents receive workmen's compensation benefits.

Such are the major eligibility requirements. They are definitely connected with and limited to the hazards of employment. They do not contemplate coverage of injuries or illnesses incurred off the job, and the limitations of coverage would refute any claim that comprehensive protection from economic loss on the job is provided to all workers.

Under workmen's compensation, benefits are of two main types: payment for medical and related expenses, and payment to compensate for loss or decrease in earnings and earnings ability.

Medical benefits are provided under all the states' laws. In the majority of the jurisdictions either the full cost of medical care is assumed, or the law sets a limit which the administrative authority has the discretionary power to disregard and to extend medical care without limit. Limitations on the period during which medical care may be provided, on the amounts which may be paid, or on both, are in effect in a minority of the states. According to the prevailing practice, the laws stipulate that the employer or the carrier of insurance shall choose the physician or surgeon to attend the worker, although in some jurisdictions the worker has the right to choose either from a panel or from all the available doctors.

Included under medical care is primary medical or surgical

treatment and post-operative and convalescent care. Increasing emphasis is being placed today upon rehabilitative medical treatment. In addition, allowance generally is made for the provision of prosthetic appliances and for training the individual in the use of such appliances. Thus, under the more advanced systems, and to an increasing degree throughout the country, medical care provisions include both treatment and physical rehabilitation.

Except in one state, Oregon, the laws provide for a waiting period before the injured worker may begin to draw his benefits. This waiting period may be a few days, or a week, but in most instances when the payments do start they are retroactive to the date of disability, provided it lasts for a certain minimum period of time. In North Carolina, for example, a worker must wait seven days before his payments start, so that actually he receives his first week's payment at the end of the second week, and if his disability lasted for twenty-eight days, not until the end of that period would he receive a check covering his first week. The purpose of this measure is to discourage workers from malingering in recuperation or from lodging trivial claims.

Payments to the worker to compensate for loss of income from total temporary disability generally are based on a percentage of his weekly wage at the time of injury. This percentage varies but the most common figure is two-thirds of the weekly wage. Both top and bottom limits are generally placed on weekly amounts, however, and in some jurisdictions maximum amounts are set on total dollar payments. In a few of the states, payments may be greater for the worker with a family or other dependents.

In general, the laws place limits on the duration of payment of benefits. This maximum varies from two to roughly ten years. Some states and the federal government, however, have no such limit, and pay during the entire period of disability.

Permanent partial disability may mean either classified or "schedule" injuries, or injuries of a less specific but crippling nature, such as an injury to the back. Examples of the former would be the loss of a limb, or the loss of sight or hearing. States differentiate between schedule and non-schedule injuries in their provision for a maximum period and amount of benefit. To pay a percentage of wages to compensate for wage loss, together with maximum weekly payments is characteristic of most measures for permanent partial disability, with maximum total amounts specified by law in most states.

Compensation for permanent total disability is paid for life in some states. In most jurisdictions, however, limits are placed on the length of time that benefit payments may be paid, as well as limits on the amount of money. The same pattern of percentage of wages and maximum weekly payments prevails in this as in the payments for other classifications of disability.

Death benefits to the survivors of the worker generally are in the form of weekly payments. In general, the average weekly wage of the worker is used as the basis for computing benefit amounts. In the majority of the states, the period of death benefit payments is limited. In some jurisdictions, payments continue for the surviving children until they are eighteen. Adjustments are made in some states in the weekly benefit payments on behalf of the dependent children.

Burial benefits are allowed in all programs except the Oklahoma one. In all instances where this form of benefit is paid, a maximum amount is set by law, and in some states, burial benefits are paid only in those cases in which there are dependents.

One of the ironies of social legislation is that it occasionally does harm to those it is intended to benefit. One true example of this is the worker suffering a permanent physical impairment. Because of workmen's compensation he has found the safety- and cost-conscious employers hesitant to hire him, fearing that his handicap might make him likely to injure himself again. In order to counteract this source of difficulty for the handicapped worker, many states have developed what is known as the "second injury fund," which in essence provides that the employer of a person who previously received an injury shall be liable only for a part of the cost of a second work-incurred injury or illness, with the balance paid from a second injury fund. The employee is paid the entire amount of the appropriate benefit, however, from the combination of sources. While limitations on the kinds of injuries recognized under second-injury measures mean that coverage is far from complete, the effect has been a broadening of opportunities for the handicapped. In the words of Paul E. Gurske, Director of the Bureau of Labor Standards of the United States Department of Labor, "Perhaps no other single form of legislation has done so much to open the doors of the Nation's factories, stores, and workshops to handicapped workers than the second-injury fund provisions that are found today in the workmen's compensation laws of forty-three states."[38]

Financing

There are three methods of financing workmen's compensation, used variously in the different jurisdictions. These are: self-insurance, insurance with a private carrier, and a state fund. In the first of these methods, the employer is required to furnish evidence of his ability to carry his own risk, and may be required to post bond or deposit securities.

In nineteen of the jurisdictions, state fund systems are provided, that is, the employer makes his payment for coverage to the state, which maintains a special insurance fund. In only eight of the jurisdictions are the employers required to use the state fund. In the other eleven, the systems are competitive, with the employer having the right to choose the state or a private insurance agency. In all of the others, insurance is carried either with a private carrier or by the method of self-insurance.

In general the employee does not contribute to the financing of workmen's compensation.[39] The cost is carried by the employer in line with the philosophy that this is one of the legitimate costs of production.

[38] Paul E. Gurske, "The Open Door to Jobs for the Handicapped," reprinted from the April, 1956, issue of *Performance*.

[39] In seven states (Arizona, Idaho, Mississippi, Montana, Nevada, Oregon, and Washington) the laws provide that the employee "shall" or "may" contribute. With the exception of Nevada, Oregon, and Mississippi, assessments on employees are limited to use for medical aid.

Handling of claims

The following description of how claims are administered sets forth the procedure with clarity.[40]

> In establishing a workmen's compensation system the principal objective was to provide a simple, convenient, and inexpensive method of settling claims of injured workers and their dependents. Full and prompt payment is the very essence of any workmen's compensation system. Few employees can afford to wait weeks or months for compensation for the time lost from their jobs.
>
> In uncontested cases the two main methods followed under workmen's compensation laws in effecting the payments due are the direct payment system and the agreement system.
>
> Under the direct payment system, the employer or his carrier takes the initiative and begins the payment of compensation to the worker or his dependents. The injured worker does not have to enter into an agreement and he is not required to sign any papers before compensation starts. The laws specify what a worker should get. If he fails to receive this, the administrative agency can step in, investigate the matter and correct any error. Laws which provide a direct payment system include those of Arkansas, Michigan, Mississippi, Wisconsin, the District of Columbia, and the Longshoremen and Harbor Workers' Act. New York has recently changed from a hearing system to a direct payment system.
>
> Under the agreement system, in effect in a majority of the States, the parties, that is, the employer or his carrier, and the worker agree upon a settlement before payment is made. In some cases the agreement must be approved by the administrative agency before payments start.
>
> In contested cases, most workmen's compensation laws provide for a hearing by a referee or hearing officer with an appeal from the decision of the referee or hearing officer to the Commission or Appeals Board and from there to the courts. In a State where the law is administered by a State administrative

[40] Bureau of Labor Standards, *State Workmen's Compensation Laws as of September 1954,* Bulletin 161, 1955, p. 56.

agency, this agency usually has exclusive jurisdiction over the determination of facts, with appeals to the courts limited to questions of law.

The responsibility for the above procedure is generally placed with an administrative body, rather than the courts. It is recognized that the purpose of this program is to eliminate costly and technical legal procedures. In only five of the states do the courts have responsibility. In the event of dissatisfaction with the findings of an administrative agency, however, recourse may be had to the courts.

General observations on workmen's compensation

As one authority has pointed out, the original programs were "based on an essentially static concept of disability."[41] With the improvement of the medical, vocational, and social aspects of rehabilitation, however, more stress is being laid on restoration of the worker to gainful employment. Under this concept, workmen's compensation becomes much more than a process of adjudication of claims. As Mr. Pollack notes, it seeks to attain the goal of "rehabilitation of the worker to optimal family, social, and economic life."[42]

The effect of this program on industrial safety precautions is a very important development. Many efforts and measures designed to lower the accident rate have been due at least in part to workmen's compensation.

The program has its faults. Critics point to the disparities among the states in many features of the program, although this criticism may hardly be confined to workmen's compensation laws alone. The disparities are perhaps greater than in some of the other income-maintenance measures because there is no federal participation in the workmen's compensation programs. Significant gaps in coverage still exist. In some places, administrative mishandling defeats the purpose of the program. Many states still

---

[41] Jerome Pollack, "Rehabilitation," in *Workmen's Compensation in the United States*, p. 40.
[42] *Ibid.*

do not provide for payments to the worker during his period of rehabilitation. In computing losses due to permanent handicap, systems do not generally take into account the degree of loss in terms of "working life expectancy"[43] nor give recognition to the factor of age at the time of injury, or to the meaning in terms of loss of ability to exercise a skill which has been developed through considerable investment of the worker's time.

One of the most severe criticisms of workmen's compensation in its present form is directed at the scale of benefits by organized labor groups, which characterize the present rates as "tragically low and limited."[44] Labor critics charge that low maximum benefits operate to reduce compensation below the proportion of wage loss they are intended to cover, that the benefits have not kept pace with wage increases so that today they fall far short of providing as high a portion of wage loss as they formerly did, that a large amount of occupational disease is still not acknowledged as occupational and consequently is uncompensated for, and that all too often the settlement of claims still takes on the character of a contest between employee and employer, with all the trappings of litigation.

These are undoubtedly significant gaps and defects. Another which might be cited is the lack of skilled social services to help the worker and his family to improve their capacity for self-care and self-maintenance.

SOCIAL INSURANCE FOR RAILROAD WORKERS

As Wilbur Cohen has observed, "The railroad social insurance system is the most comprehensive and most adequate social insurance system in the United States."[45] It covers the most contingencies, and it has the highest rate of contribution from both employer and employee.

Why is this the strongest social insurance system? According to

---

[43] Kossoris, *op. cit.*, p. 4.
[44] From *Labor's Economic Review*, Vol. 2, No. 2 (February, 1957), Department of Research, American Federation of Labor-Congress of Industrial Organizations.
[45] *Social Work Year Book, 1957*, p. 546.

Corson and McConnell, the origin and development of this independent insurance system "is partly attributable to the strength of the railroad brotherhoods, but also to a recognition of the railroad industry as affected with a national interest; existence of long-standing railroad pension plans when social security legislation reached congressional agenda; the concept of the Railroad Retirement System as a staff pension plan rather than as a part of an over-all program for the nation's aged; and the acute crisis of the railroad industry, including its labor force, in 1933-34."[46]

As it is, the system provides for compensation for wage loss due to old age, death, unemployment, sickness, disability, and maternity. The Railroad Retirement Board, a federal agency, is responsible for its administration.

Retirement provisions of these various measures extend to employees of railroads, express and sleeping car companies,[47]

> "and any company which may be directly or indirectly owned or controlled thereby or under common control therewith, and, which operates any equipment or facilities or performs any service (other than trucking service) in connection with the transportation of passengers or property by railroad, or the receipt, delivery, elevation, transfer in transit, refrigeration or icing, storage, or handling of property transported by railroad, and any receiver, trustee, or other individual or body, judicial or otherwise, when in possession of and operating the business of any such "carrier.""

The following statement summarizes eligibility for annuities for retirement due to old-age and permanent disability under the Railroad Retirement Act:[48]

> Workers in covered employment are eligible for retirement annuities if they are:
>
> a. Sixty-five years of age or over, and have 10 years of service, or

---

[46] Corson and McConnell, *op. cit.,* p. 273.

[47] Sec. 1a, Public Law 400, 74th Cong., Carriers' Taxing Law of 1935, passed August 20, 1935.

[48] *Federal Labor Laws and Agencies,* Bulletin 123 rev., Bureau of Labor Standards, U. S. Dept. of Labor, p. 69.

b. Between 60 and 65 years and have completed 30 years of service, except that if the worker is a man the benefit is reduced for each month that he is under age 65, or

c. Permanently disabled for all regular work and have completed 10 years of service, regardless of age, or

d. Permanently disabled for work at regular railroad occupation, currently connected with the railroad industry, and have completed 20 years of service, regardless of age, or

e. Permanently disabled for work at regular railroad occupation, currently connected with the railroad industry, between 60 and 65 years of age, and have completed 10 years of service.

(An employee is "currently connected with the railroad industry" if he worked in at least 12 out of the last 30 months before his annuity begins. Any other 30-month period may be used, if the employee had no regular non-railroad employment after such 30-month period.)

The tests of connection with the railroad industry are quite explicit; they are designed to limit eligibility only to those persons whose regular and full livelihood is derived from employment in the railroad industry.

The wife of a railroad worker may receive benefits at sixty-five years of age, or earlier if she is responsible for the care of a child of a railroad employee. A dependent husband of a railroad employee is entitled to benefits at age sixty-five.

A worker may not receive benefits while employed by a firm covered under the Act. Disabled workers become ineligible if their earnings from work in outside covered employment come to more than $100 per month.

Survivors benefits are also a part of this law, and are payable to families of workers who were "completely insured" at the time of their death. The "completely insured" clause refers to conditions which include: the worker's receipt of a retirement annuity from the Railroad Retirement Act program at the time of his death, and to his having worked in railroad employment for a specified number of years after 1936.

Provisions of eligibility for survivors resemble those in effect in the O.A.S.D.I. program under the Social Security Act. Eligible survivors include the widow or dependent widower at the age of sixty or over; dependent children (unmarried) under eighteen; children over eighteen if permanently and totally disabled before reaching that age; widows caring for a dependent child provided the child is otherwise eligible for an annuity; or, if there is no surviving spouse or eligible child, dependent parents of sixty or over.

Benefits to survivors of workers who are partially insured at death are payable to dependent children and to widows as stipulated above. The worker is "partially insured" when he has had ten years of railroad service, provided he has a current connection with the industry and has worked one-and-one-half years of the three immediately preceding the year of his death.

Benefits

The benefit structure is rather complicated; for our purposes some of its most technical details can and will be omitted. Benefits are calculated on the first $350 of monthly earnings (just as for O.A.S.D.I.). Under the law governing the present scale of benefits, the amounts eventually will reach $250 per month although they are not that high at present. The law guarantees that a worker's benefits will not be less than those which would have been payable to him under the Social Security Act, had his employment been in a job covered by that Act. If he has had more than twenty years of service, the probability is that he will receive larger rather than smaller benefits than would have been his under the Social Security Act (3.04 percent of the first $50 of average monthly earnings, 2.28 percent of the next $100, and 1.52 percent of the remaining amount up to the maximum set forth in the law). To figure the amount of the annuity, the sum given by adding the amounts yielded by these percentages is multiplied by the number of years of service. For a worker with a "current connection," a minimum formula may be applied.

If there are no other benefits payable under either the Railroad Retirement or the Social Security Act, the widow, widower, children or dependent parents may be paid what is known as a "residual lump sum."

This program is financed by a tax rate of 6.25 percent each on employer and employee, on earnings up to $350 per month.

Unemployment insurance for railroad workers

The Railroad Unemployment Insurance Act provides for both unemployment and sickness benefits. The latter includes maternity benefits. Under this Act, benefits are administered by the Railroad Retirement Board. The conditions of coverage are the same as those pertaining to the Railroad Retirement Act.

The worker may qualify if he has earned as much as $400 in the calendar year preceding his benefit year. The benefit year runs from July 1 to June 30. Compensation must have been derived from employment covered under the Act.

A railroad worker may be disqualified for unemployment benefits for any day in which he has received unemployment benefits under another plan; sickness benefits under this program; benefits from another social insurance program; any day of unemployment resulting from a strike which is in violation of the Railway Labor Act or the rules and practices of his union; for thirty days if he has left work voluntarily, has refused suitable work, or has failed to apply for work or to report to an employment office, if instructed to do so by the Railroad Retirement Board; or for seventy-five days if he is found guilty of false or fraudulent statements.

He may be disqualified for sickness benefits for the following reasons: failure to take required medical examinations, concurrent receipt of sickness benefits under another law, or any other social insurance benefits. He is also disqualified for ninety days if he knowingly makes false or fraudulent statements in order to qualify for benefits.

Unemployment benefits are claimed by registering with a claims agent of the Railroad Retirement Board. The claims agent is usually an employee of the railroad. The claimant must appear at the agent's office once each week. To secure sickness benefits he must present a statement of sickness, signed by an authorized person, within ten days of the first day claimed.

The costs of this program are met through a payroll tax paid by the carriers. The employee does not contribute. The rate of tax is computed on a sliding scale, with the amount depending on the size of the fund. The rate varies between .5 to 3 percent.

The benefit rate is computed on a daily basis, with the amount dependent on earnings during the base year. The benefit amounts range from a minimum of $3.50 per day to a maximum of $8.50 per day. The limit of the period of payments during the benefit year is 130 times the amount of his per day benefit, or the amount of the worker's earnings in the base year, whichever is less.

TEMPORARY DISABILITY INSURANCE

Sickness or injury incurred while off duty may temporarily incapacitate the worker. Such incapacity is not covered by workmen's compensation, which is based on work-connected disability, or by unemployment insurance which applies only to persons able to work. Under old age, survivors, and disability insurance, it will be recalled, only permanent and total disability is covered, and that only for persons over fifty. This adds up to a large gap in protection in the nation as a whole, since much loss of earnings is the result of sickness or injury which is not work-connected.

In addition to the railway employees, workers in four states are covered under temporary disability insurance programs. These states are Rhode Island, California, New Jersey, and New York. The laws cover persons who temporarily are unable to perform regular or customary work because of nonwork-connected sickness or injury.

Coverage in Rhode Island, California and New Jersey, is identical with the provisions in unemployment insurance. In New York the coverage is different. The programs in all four states are like those of unemployment insurance in its relationship of earnings to compensation, in payment of amounts which are a portion of the weekly earnings in the base period, and in the limitations on duration of payments. The programs require employee contributions. The 1956 amendments to the Social Security Act provided that the employee contributions to the unemployment insurance fund could be used to pay disability benefits. In 1956, all of the states which now have this program provided for employee payments into the unemployment insurance fund, except New York.

Each of the four states has different provisions relating to coverage, eligibility, benefit amounts and duration, and financing. The program is too limited to justify detailed description of all the programs, but the following briefly describes the measures in effect in California and New Jersey.

Coverage in California extends to employers of one or more persons, provided there has been a minimum amount of $100 in the quarterly payroll. In New Jersey, employers of four or more in a twenty-week period are covered.

Eligibility in California requires an annual wage of $750, or 30 times the weekly benefit amount, or $1\frac{1}{3}$ times the earnings in a high wage quarter, whichever is less. In no event will less than $350 of earnings qualify. New Jersey requires seventeen weeks of employment at a wage of $15 per week or more.

In California the benefit amount varies from $10 to $50 per week, and is based on a high quarter of earnings. The duration of benefits is twenty-six weeks. In New Jersey the benefit is two-thirds of the average weekly wage for benefit amounts up to a maximum of $30 per week, plus two-fifths the amount by which the average weekly wage exceeds $45, up to a maximum benefit of $35. The duration is three-fourths of the number of weeks of employment during the base year, to a maximum of twenty-six weeks.

California requires a 1 percent employee contribution. New Jersey provides under the state plan that the employee contribute .5 percent, the employer from .1 to .75 percent, depending on experience rating. Under a private plan in New Jersey the employees may pay up to .5 percent toward premiums.

In all four states except Rhode Island, the employer has the option of insuring under either a state plan or a private plan. The laws all provide that under any private plan, the benefits must be equal to those established in the state law.

In California, hospital benefits are also provided.

It may seem surprising that other states have been slow to follow the lead of these four in developing temporary disability insurance. It seems that elsewhere proposals so far presented generally have foundered in disputes over the method of insurance, with labor groups wanting insurance under state systems, and other groups, notably professional medical organizations and employers, preferring insurance under private plans. At present this seems to be the impasse which accounts for virtually no action in the field since 1949, plus the fact that this program has not been given the impetus of any federal action.

RELATION OF SOCIAL INSURANCE TO PRIVATE PLANS

One of the most important of recent developments in the field of income security is the number of private plans which are being "meshed" with public measures of social insurance. In a sense, this relationship is a reversal of the earlier philosophy of social insurance, which held that governmental programs should supplement private provision. Under these newer programs, the opposite is true; the private plans supplement the social insurances.

One of the clearest examples of such a situation is the plan of supplemental unemployment benefits. Under this type of program, benefits are paid in an amount which represents the difference between that for which the worker qualifies under unemployment insurance, and an agreed-upon total amount. This total amount is generally 60 to 65 percent of the worker's take-home pay. In order to qualify for supplemental benefits the worker must be entitled to unemployment insurance. These programs, while relatively new, and far from complete in their coverage of employees, are expected to grow quite rapidly among employees of larger enterprises. Of longer standing but less significant in size and coverage is the guaranteed annual wage. This program provides for a guarantee of a stipulated amount of work or wages over an agreed-upon period of time. This has been the subject of some negotiation in collective bargaining, but still is limited to relatively few companies. The guaranteed wage differs from unemployment insurance in the sense that it implies a final obligation[49] rather than a supplement which depends upon the volume of employment and the size of individual earnings.

Retirement is another area of importance in the relations between social insurance and private plans. This is particularly true since the coverage of O. A. S. D. I. has been extended to many categories of employers which had previously been covered under other programs. The inclusion by their own choice of many state and local employees, and of nonprofit enterprises has brought the social insurance measures into the combined plans in many organizations. Also, business organizations have related their programs of retirement to O. A. S. D. I., providing for supplementation of the public benefits.

Further employee-benefit plans of significance are programs of life insurance, disability protection, hospital, medical, and surgical benefits.

Consideration of various company medical plans for group coverage under prepaid medical care programs, and others, could much prolong this discussion.[50] Perhaps the relationship of these public programs to private systems of protection is best symbolized by the approach of many of the life insurance companies. Today, when a representative discusses an insurance program with the head of the family, he charts the protection required throughout the years in relation to the public social insurance protection as a family asset, thus helping them to choose an over-all plan which combines private life insurance with the provisions of public programs.

The significance of social insurance as a family resource is in-

[49] For a description of the guaranteed wage see Jack Chernick, *A Guide to the Guaranteed Wage,* Bulletin No. 4, 1955, Institute of Management and Labor Relations, Rutgers University, New Brunswick, New Jersey.

[50] For a description of prepaid medical care programs, see Oscar N. Serbein, *Paying for Medical Care in the United States* (New York, 1953).

terestingly brought out in the following statement written with reference to O. A. S. D. I.:[51]

> On the more positive side the bulk of the population is becoming aware of its great financial stake in the system. For example: in the case of an insured worker aged 35, earning $4000 per year, with a wife of the same age and three children, aged 10, 8, and 3, a not untypical pattern, the survivor benefits to the family, should he die this year, would come to approximately $44,000; should he and his wife live to 65 the capital value of their old age retirement insurance would represent about $20,000. The financial value of the insurance protection now available under OASDI is about the same as the aggregate in force with all private insurance companies in the country. Nobody has attempted to keep such information confidential and if at times an average worker looks at the social insurance structure in approximately the same spirit that a broker examines the stock market, it may not be wholly surprising. There is also steadily increasing acceptance of social insurance by the business community, which has effectively built it into a more productive system of industrial relations and also looks to it as an important source of economic stability.

The relationship between voluntary programs of protection against income loss and the social insurances, is certain to increase in the next few years. But at best, it is sure to be spotty, and confined to the larger firms. There will remain millions of workers whose protection will continue to be their own individual savings, their personal insurance programs, and other resources of their own in combination with the social insurances.

CURRENT ISSUES IN SOCIAL INSURANCE

In the preceding discussion of social insurance, some of the questions relating to gaps in coverage and adequacy were pre-

---

[51] Herman M. and Anne R. Somers, *Trends and Current Issues In Social Insurance,* Institute of Industrial Relations, University of California (at Berkeley), Reprinted from the *Proceedings* of the Ninth Annual Meeting, Industrial Relations Research Association, 1957, pp. 2-3.

sented as they have appeared in the administration of the different programs. There are other gaps in protection, however, which are over-all in nature.

One of these is the lack of any comprehensive provision for medical care. This is one of the most controversial and explosive issues in the whole field of protection through social means. The very mention of "socialized medicine" is enough to arouse vehement opposition among many, who see it as a threat to the basic quality of medical care. The rapid growth of group plans during the past few years had represented a response to the challenge. Still, coverage under these plans is far from universal, and leaves many without protection, or with incomplete coverage.

Proposals for a national system have been made, both by Truman and Eisenhower administrations. The former presented a plan which aroused the most violent opposition, with a provision for medical care to be financed by compulsory contributions in the form of taxes, and to be administered by public agencies. The Eisenhower administration's proposals were for government reinsurance of private plans. This proposal also failed to make much headway. Meanwhile, medical care has become an increasing part of the public assistance programs, which find numbers of people "medically indigent" even though able to meet their other needs. Also, there is currently under way a national health survey to present a factual analysis of health needs in relation to existing resources.

Income loss due to permanent disability presents another serious gap. The present O. A. S. D. I. law, as we have seen, covers only those fifty years of age and older. The Somers' point out the probability that need for such protection is actually greater for those who are under fifty. The younger person is more likely, they note, to have family responsibilities, to offer possibilities for rehabilitation to gainful employment, and to have more years of productive work ahead.[52]

Extension of temporary disability benefits to people in more states has been hampered by disputes over the method of insur-

[52] Somers and Somers, *op. cit.*, p. 7.

ance, *i.e.*, whether by exclusively state or by optional state or private plans. Yet this program, which has remained at a standstill since 1949, is one of the most seriously needed, in terms of wage loss and persons affected.

Plans in many other countries include "family allowances" or "children's allowances" as they are variously called. These programs provide cash payments to families in relation to the numbers of children under the maximum age established in the law. This system is designed to equalize opportunities for health, education, etc., for members of large families. Whether such a program is desirable in this country is open to debate. It has not up to this time been seriously proposed in the United States, for here a relatively (although not a universally) high standard of living has militated against even the introduction of such a proposal.

One feature of social insurance which is important, however, is the closest possible coordination among the programs, and between the insurances and other welfare measures. We have seen how important it is to accompany disability payments with measures for physical, mental, social, and vocational rehabilitation. In this country, with our tendency to achieve results through what the Somers' refer to as pluralistic measures, programs lose their effectiveness to some extent unless there are determined efforts to keep them coordinated.

Moreover, in a changing society it is necessary to keep such measures in step with the times. Without continuing study and evaluation, social inventions rapidly become obsolete.

Summary

Social insurance really began on a large scale in the United States with the enactment of the Social Security Act in 1935. This Act provided for old age insurance and unemployment insurance. In addition, at that time a program of social insurance was enacted for railroad workers.

It was intended that social insurance would be the basic form of income security under the Social Security Act, with public assistance performing a supplementary and residual role. For many years, or really until the 1950's, the fulfillment of this purpose was thwarted by the inadequacies of the social insurance measures.

Social insurance is a form of shared provision against the risk of loss of income from certain causes. It differs from public assistance in the sense that it is related to work and earnings rather than to need, and is contributory, that is, financed by contributions from the employer, or the employer and employee combined, to a fund. Public assistance on the other hand is not contributory.

We see the necessity for old age, survivors, and disability insurance in the growing needs of the older population. More people are living to an old age, and find that their opportunities for employment become narrower. Important amendments to the Social Security Act in 1939, 1950, 1954, and 1956 have materially improved the program. The original measure of old age insurance was broadened in 1939 to include survivors of deceased covered employees, while coverage was increased by successive amendments, and permanently disabled persons fifty or over were added in 1956.

Coverage under this program now extends to more than nine-tenths of the population. In July 1957, ten-and-one-half million beneficiaries together received more than $.5 billion. The program is administered federally by the Social Security Administration in the Department of Health, Education, and Welfare. It is financed by payments from employers and employees into trust funds. Eligibility is determined by employment in covered industry, earnings in a certain number of quarters during the period of employment, age or disability, the fact of retirement, or conditions of survivorship. The maximum monthly benefit which may be paid to a retired person is $108.50 per month, the minimum $30. The most that can be paid per month as a family benefit is $200, or 80 percent of the actual wage, whichever is less, while the minimum is $50 or one and one-half the benefit amount, whichever is the greater. In addition to monthly benefits, a lump sum may be claimed by the survivors on the death of the wage earner. The contribution rate is now 2.25 percent of earnings up to $4200 per year from the employee and the same for the employer. The self-employed rate is 3.375 percent of earnings up to the same amount. The rate of these taxes is scheduled to increase until 1975, when it will reach 4.25 percent for employer and employee and 6.375 percent for the self-employed.

Involuntary unemployment is one of the great hazards of an industrial society. In recognition of this fact, this country enacted a federal-state system of unemployment insurance as part of the Social Security Act in 1935. The federal government levies a 3 percent payroll tax on all employers who have four or more persons working for them during twenty or more weeks of the year. The states may "offset" up to 90 percent of this tax by enacting a state program. In other words, the state is credited with the amount it levies on employment subject to federal tax up to 90 percent of the amount of federal tax. The portion retained by the federal government is used to pay the costs of state administration.

The states have the authority to determine the conditions of coverage, of eligibility, and the rate of taxation. The states also decide the amount and duration of benefit payments. As one might expect, wide variations are found among the states in relation to all factors of the programs. In general, qualifications include the requirement that the worker register and apply for work at the employment office, that he must have worked in covered employment, that he has built up sufficient wage credits, and that he is able to work and available for suitable employment. He may be disqualified if he has quit his job without good cause, has refused to apply for or accept suitable work, or is unemployed because of a work stoppage resulting from a labor dispute. In general the conditions of qualification and disqualification are designed to test the involuntary nature of unemployment, and the fact of attachment to the labor force. Benefits are paid on a weekly basis, and in amounts generally intended to equal half the wage loss. The present practice of imposing maximum limits considerably below half of the usual rate, however, has made the actual portion much less. There are limits on the length of time that the benefits may be paid.

Workmen's compensation is designed to protect workers against hardship resulting from work-connected disability. This was the first social insurance adopted in the United States. Before workmen's compensation, the employee seeking maintenance during disability connected with employment was compelled to seek redress through the court, where his claim was subject to certain common law defenses which were difficult to overcome. These programs are designed to help compensate for income loss and to provide medical services to aid in rehabilitating disabled workers. These programs are exclusively state ones, with no federal aid, although the federal government does carry workmen's compensation insurance for its own employees. In some states, coverage is elective as far as the employer is concerned, in others coverage is compulsory, while in some the program is part elective and part compulsory. There are wide variations in conditions of coverage, adequacy of benefits, and methods of administration. Some states include second-injury funds, to protect the worker who has suffered a previous disability. Benefits in all programs include medical care. Payments for temporary disability are based on a proportion of the average wage, with both top and bottom limits placed on weekly amounts. States also specify the maximum period over which benefits may be paid for temporary disability. The program also includes payments for partial disability, for permanent total disability, death and burial benefit payments. Insurance under workmen's compensation may be financed by the employer himself, by insurance with a private carrier, or by a state fund. In general, the cost is carried by the employer. The insurance program for railroad workers provides the most comprehensive coverage of all. They are protected against wage loss due to unemployment, sickness, old age, disability, maternity and death. Responsibility for administration is carried by the Railroad Retirement Board, a federal agency.

Only four of the states have temporary disability insurance. These are California, New Jersey, New York and Rhode Island. These programs provide for compensation for wage loss due to temporary nonwork-connected disability.

It is increasingly important to consider public and private protection as they relate to each other. The development of supplemental unemployment benefits, of the guaranteed annual wage, of company retirement plans, among others, underscores this relationship.

The programs of social insurance in this country leave significant gaps, which show that protection against economic hardship from causes beyond individual control is far from complete. Nevertheless, this form of enterprise is contributing significantly to the reduction of hardship, and to increasing stabilization of the economy. But continuing study and careful analysis of social conditions are necessary if social insurance is to continue its useful role in a dynamic economy.

Selected References

1. Burns, Eveline M., *The American Social Security System*. New York, Houghton Mifflin Company, 1949.
2. Burns, Eveline M., *Social Security and Public Policy*. New York, McGraw-Hill Book Company, 1956.
3. Burns, Eveline M., High Productivity and People's Social Needs," *Public Welfare*, Vol. 14, No. 3 (July, 1956).
4. Cohen, Wilbur J., "Social Insurance," *Social Work Year Book, 1957*. New York, National Association of Social Workers, 1957.
5. Cohen, Wilbur J., and Fauri, Fidele, "The Social Security Amendments of 1956," *Public Welfare*, Vol. 14, No. 4 (October, 1956).
6. Corson, John J., and McConnell, John W., *Economic Needs of Older People*. New York, Twentieth Century Fund, 1956.
7. Epstein, Abraham, *Insecurity, A Challenge to America*. New York, Random House, Inc., 1938.
8. Gurske, Paul E., "The Open Door to the Handicapped," *Performance*, April, 1956.
9. Haber, William, and Cohen, Wilbur J., *Readings in Social Security*. New York, Prentice-Hall, 1948.
10. Hogan, John D., and Ianni, Francis A., *American Social Legislation*. New York, Harper and Brothers, 1956.
11. Kossoris, Max E., *Workmen's Compensation in the United States, An Appraisal*, Bulletin No. 1149, Bureau of Labor Statistics, Department of Labor.

12. Medvin, Norman, "Employment Problems of Older Workers," *Social Security Bulletin*, Volume 20, No. 4 (April, 1957).

13. Merriam, Ida C., *Social Security Financing*, Bureau Report No. 17 (1952), Bureau of Research and Statistics, Social Security Administration.

14. Rubinow, I. M., *The Quest for Security*. New York, Henry Holt and Company, 1934.

15. *A Brief Explanation of the Social Security Act*, Social Security Administration, July, 1957.

16. *Employment Security Review*, Vol. 22, No. 8 (August, 1955), Bureau of Employment Security, U. S. Department of Labor.

17. *Federal Labor Laws and Agencies*, Bulletin 123 rev., Bureau of Labor Standards, U. S. Department of Labor.

18. *State Workmen's Compensation Laws*, Bulletin 161 and Supplement to Bulletin 161, Bureau of Labor Standards, U. S. Department of Labor.

19. *Compilation of Social Security Laws, Including the Social Security Act as Amended, and Related Enactments*, Social Security Administration.

5

Public Assistance

Even under the best laid plans for social insurance, public assistance and other welfare services would still be required. With the gaps which were pointed out in the preceding chapter, the need is even greater than it might otherwise be. As we have seen, many people now sixty-five lack eligibility for O. A. S. D. I. The permanently and totally disabled under fifty are not included. Social insurance in those programs which specify maximum periods for receipt of benefits may expire before the need for it does. These and other problems continue to require measures of public assistance.

What is the relationship of the two types of programs to each other? When the Social Security Act was passed, it was recognized that there would be certain needs not covered by the social insurances, although the latter were conceived to be the basic form of protection. Public assistance was foreseen as playing a residual role in relation to the social insurances, with that role diminishing as the insurance programs matured. The contingencies which were included in the public assistance provisions of the Social Security Act were old age, dependent childhood, and blindness (under, respectively, Titles I, IV, and X. A "Title" is a division of a law). In 1950 a fourth category, aid to the permanently and totally disabled, was added (under Title XIV). These are federal-state programs, with the federal government providing financial aid to the states, to assist them to provide more adequately for assistance to the needy.

During the first years of the social security program, it seemed that the anticipated relationship between public assistance and social insurance would be reversed. Slowness of action to improve old-age and unemployment insurance, combined with the rapid expansion of public assistance by the states under the impetus of federal aid, for the initial fifteen years threatened to make public assistance the primary rather than the secondary program of income security. With the passage of amendments in the 1950's, however, the goal of primary reliance upon social insurance has come much closer to realization. The increasing number of persons receiving old-age, survivors, or disability benefits has reduced the loads in the respective public assistance programs, at least in the proportion of recipients to the total population.

Despite all that, the public assistance programs continue to be substantial in terms both of numbers of people who receive aid, and of amounts of money paid in assistance grants. The following table shows the number, as of July, 1957, of recipients of the public assistance programs.[1]

Recipients	*July, 1957*
Old-age assistance	2,501,000
Aid to dependent children—children	1,827,000
families	644,000
total recipients	2,391,000
Aid to the blind	109,000
Aid to the permanently and totally disabled	286,000
General assistance—cases	290,000
persons	674,000

In the calendar year ending December 31, 1956, the total expenditure for public assistance and for administration of the

[1] Based on a table in *Current Social Security Program Operations, July, 1957,* Division of Program Research of the Social Security Administration, September 13, 1957.

programs was $3,101,975,000. This is a substantial figure even in these days of multibillion-dollar thinking.

Left to administration by the states and/or the local governments is the residual program of aid, called "general assistance." Thus has the social security program continued the practice noted earlier (in Chapter 2), that of removing special classes from the undifferentiated group of needy persons.

What are the characteristics of public assistance? How do these programs compare with social insurance? How do they differ from poor relief?

Public assistance has been defined by Leyendecker as "Financial aid extended to needy people in their own homes or places of residence."[2] Its purpose, as stated by the Bureau of Public Assistance, is as follows:[3]

> As part of the social security system of the United States, the primary purpose of the public assistance programs is to provide needy persons with income to supplement their own resources to enable them to secure the necessities of life, and to help them achieve the greatest economic and personal independence possible to them.

The similarities and dissimilarities between public assistance and social insurance have been considered briefly in the preceding chapter, but it will be helpful to recapitulate them here. While both types of programs provide for cash payments to individuals, social insurance payments under the Social Security Act are based on earnings, while public assistance payments are based on needs of the individual or family. In the social insurances, wage and work experience is the determinant of eligibility, while in public assistance the factor is need, or the inability of the recipient to support or otherwise provide for himself. Social insurances are contributory, that is, they are financed by payments made directly by employers and in some instances also by employees.

[2] Hilary M. Leyendecker, *Problems and Policy in Public Assistance* (New York, 1955), p. 2.

[3] *Public Assistance Under the Social Security Act,* Bureau of Public Assistance, Social Security Administration, August, 1957, p. 3.

Public assistance is financed by taxes levied on the general public.

But if public assistance is different in many respects from social insurance, it also is unlike poor relief, even though the latter too is based on need. The standard of need is much higher under public assistance. As the Director of the Bureau of Public Assistance has stated:[4]

> In contrast with earlier poor relief where the needy person had to be actually destitute, without food, shelter, or other basic essentials, today a needy person is ordinarily considered one whose own resources are too small to provide what the state has set as the minimum amount required to purchase his basic maintenance needs. In most instances, assistance is given in an amount to supplement any resources the applicant possesses, to bring them up to this standard. Generally, the possession of a modest home, a small amount of cash assets for such purposes as illness and burial, and household and personal effects do not render an individual ineligible for assistance insofar as his need is concerned. . . .

These are important differences. In essence, they mean that public assistance places much more emphasis on the dignity and rights of the individual recipients than did the poor law, and attaches more importance to how people are treated and assisted. In four out of the five public assistance programs, this is true, but of the fifth, the general assistance program, this claim cannot be made without serious reservation. The Committee on Economic Security foresaw the dangers of inadequate treatment of those whose needs did not fall within the categories of assistance which were to be federally aided, and recommended that the states substitute for their "ancient, outmoded poor laws" the preferred "modernized public assistance laws."[5] It cannot be said that this recommendation has been the basis for much of the general assistance legislation among the states. In many states, townships and municipalities bear the burden of general assistance with their

---

[4] Jay Roney, "Public Assistance," in *Social Work Year Book, 1957* (New York, 1957), p. 444.

[5] *Report* of the Committee on Econmic Security, transmitted to the President, January 15, 1935, p. 7.

limited tax resources, and in many cases, with state aid only if local support funds are grossly inadequate. In other states, the county is financially and administratively responsible. In many places, "voucher relief" or direct orders on vendors instead of cash is given to help the individual and family pay for food, shelter, and clothing. This humiliating method of rendering assistance is in marked contrast to the insistence in the categorical aid programs on cash rather than voucher payments. In many states, general assistance falls far short of the other forms of assistance in the adequacy of amounts granted, and no clear-cut conditions of eligibility protect the individual from arbitrary decisions. This general category of aid may be said to reflect the surviving prejudices toward the poor, as well as the financial stringencies of local governments.

In the federally aided, or categorical programs, federal requirements have had an important bearing on the conditions of eligibility and the standards of service by the state and local agencies. These requirements are ones that the states must meet in order to receive federal funds to aid them in financing their programs. The states are free, in principle, to accept or to reject both the funds and the conditions.

The three federal requirements most directly related to the treatment of people are the following: First, information relating to people applying for or receiving assistance must be confidential, that is, use or disclosure of such information is limited to purposes directly connected with the administration of the program. In 1951 Congress modified this provision somewhat by passing a law which permitted the states to make the names of recipients and the amounts received matters of public record. The states were required, however, to safeguard against the use of these items for political and commercial purposes.

Second, all state public assistance programs for which federal funds are received must provide the opportunity to applicants or recipients for appeal and a fair hearing. Persons who feel that their cases were not fairly or adequately handled may appeal to the state welfare authority, and the state must have established procedures which guarantee a fair and impartial hearing. Such a grievance might be the denial of a request for assistance, what the applicant considers an unreasonably long delay by the administrative office in taking action, or other complaint.

Third, a further protection to the rights of people under the public assistance laws is the provision in the Social Security Act that anyone shall have the right to apply for assistance and to have action taken promptly on his application. The importance of this measure is obvious. Delay may have just as much of an effect on the denial of the individual's rights as would an adverse decision.

Federal prescription of eligibility provisions are minimal and tend to set limits for states within which considerable variation is possible. For example, the maximum periods of residence which state law may require are specified in the federal statute. In old-age assistance, aid to the totally and permanently disabled, and aid to the blind, no state may demand residence in the state of more than five years out of the nine preceding the date of application for assistance, with one of the five the year immediately before the date of application. In aid to dependent children the maximum residence which a state may require is one year. States may specify shorter periods of residence than these, but may not demand longer ones for those programs for which they receive federal aid. Another federal provision stipulates that the state shall not impose any citizenship requirement which bars a citizen of the United States whose eligibility is otherwise clearly established. This is designed to prevent discrimination against any United States citizen, but it does not prohibit the state from requiring that all recipients be citizens, as some of the state programs do.

One of the most influential of the federal requirements has been the stipulation that federal aid to states[6] is provided for "money payments" to the needy. The effect of this requirement has been

---

[6] "States," so far as public assistance is concerned, includes the jurisdictions of the District of Columbia, Alaska, Hawaii, Puerto Rico, and the Virgin Islands.

to make cash payments rather than voucher relief or direct distribution of commodities the prevailing form of public categorical assistance payments. As a result, the recipient of assistance is enabled to take his money to the market and purchase groceries, to the store to buy clothes, or to pay his rent with it as anyone else does. He is not set apart from others by having to take an "order" to a store designated by an agency, perhaps with a stipulated list of items which he may purchase, or by having to go to a "commodity depot" or warehouse operated by a county or municipal agency to receive whatever may be doled out. This again is in marked distinction from the poor law, past and present, even though in many places it has been changed in name to the more modern term "general assistance," though the change has not always been reflected in practice. The poor law was administered in accordance with the belief that the recipient must not be considered competent to manage his own affairs. The intent of the money payment has been construed by the federal authority to mean that the recipient receives a check but, like anyone else, he is free to decide for himself how he shall spend it.

If the individual is legally declared incompetent, and a guardian is appointed to manage his affairs, payments may be made to the guardian. This exception to the requirement that payment be made directly to the needy individual has been in effect since the programs first began. Another more recent exception has been made with respect to medical care, and direct payments to "vendors" of medical service are now permitted under federal requirements.

A further federal requirement stipulates that the state must consider a person's total income and resources when it determines need and the amount of assistance. This means that there may be no automatic exemption of earned income, except for the blind, who are allowed to earn up to $50 per month without this affecting the amount of assistance granted. The requirement that all income and resources be considered reflects an intent to assist only "needy" individuals.

Other requirements relating to eligibility and method and amount of payment will be presented separately in descriptions of each of the public assistance categories in this chapter. Those requirements which relate to administration and organization will be presented in Part III of this volume.

OLD-AGE ASSISTANCE

According to the Bureau of Public Assistance of the Social Security Administration, the basic purpose of the old-age assistance title is "to encourage States to provide financial assistance to aged needy individuals and to help them attain the maximum degree of economic and personal independence, of which they are capable, with special emphasis in relation to self-care."[7] Furthermore, the Bureau declares, "The States' old-age assistance programs, with Federal participation, should enable older people to remain in their own homes as long as possible, to participate in the life of the community, and to plan more easily for sheltered care when such care is required because of illness or infirmity."[8]

Eligibility

Each of the states has certain definite eligibility requirements for old-age assistance. In general, they include the factors of age, residence, need, and property and income limitations, although they may vary in the nature of these requirements. Some states require United States citizenship and some few have special requirements, such as Iowa, which forbids old-age assistance to anyone convicted of desertion or nonsupport of his family within ten years preceding his application, or Nebraska, which includes a special requirement that no assistance may be paid a person who is able to work and not needed in the home, when a job is available for which the administrators of the program deem the applicant suitable.

[7] *Handbook of Public Assistance,* Part I, Sec. 3200, Bureau of Public Assistance, Social Security Administration (undated).
[8] *Ibid.*

To take one state, California, as an example, the following are the eligibility requirements there:[9]

The aged person must apply and meet the following requirements:

1. Is 65 years of age or over.
2. Is a citizen of the United States or was a resident of the United States continuously for 25 years and was prohibited from applying for citizenship because of race or national origin prior to December 24, 1952.
3. Lived in California for five of the last nine years, the last year of which immediately preceded the date of application.
4. Is not an inmate of a public institution for tuberculosis or mental disease, or because of a diagnosis of psychosis or tuberculosis, or of a custodial, penal, or correctional character, or one which is operated by the United States Government.

   Any person excluded above may apply for aid but must leave institution on receipt of first check.
5. Assessed valuation of real property less encumbrances of record of applicant and spouse does not exceed $3500. Separate property of spouse excluded if living apart.
6. Value of personal property less encumbrances of record does not exceed $1200. Limit is $2000 for married couple living together if both on aid.
7. Has not transferred property for the purpose of qualifying for aid.
8. Is not receiving adequate support from responsible relative.

All of the states and other jurisdictions set the age requirement at sixty-five, with the exception of Colorado. In that state, there are two programs of old-age assistance: one is for those sixty-five years of age and over, and the other for persons sixty to sixty-

[9] The material on comparative eligibility provisions is taken from *Characteristics of State Public Assistance Plans,* Public Assistance Report No. 27, Bureau of Public Assistance, Social Security Administration, Washington, 1956, brought up to date by later information from the Bureau of Public Assistance. The information on California is taken from "Public Assistance and Welfare Service in California," State of California, Department of Social Welfare, 1956, p. 4.

four. In the latter a residence requirement of thirty-five continuous years in the state, as compared with five out of nine for people sixty-five or over, confines this program to a small number of recipients.

The second of the California requirements, United States citizenship, is not general. In fact, thirty-four of the fifty-three jurisdictions have no citizenship requirement. Among those which do demand citizenship as a qualifying condition, the alternative of a certain number of years in residence in the country may be offered.

With respect to residence, all states require that the person be a resident of the state at the time of application. Like California, twenty-one other states set the period at five of the nine years preceding the date of application, the maximum number of years permitted under federal participation. At the other end of the scale, New York, Rhode Island, and the territories of Alaska, Puerto Rico, and the Virgin Islands do not specify any duration of residence prior to applying. The other twenty-seven states require residence periods of three years of the preceding ten (Vermont), three of the seven (Kentucky), three of the nine in Massachusetts, and simply of one year in each of twenty-four other states.

"Residence," as pertaining to public assistance, is not, as Leyendecker has noted, to be confused with "settlement" under the old poor law. Leyendecker defines a person's place of residence as "where he is actually residing and what he considers his permanent home. His place of settlement, however, is that civil subdivision responsible for the cost of his care should he become a public charge."[10] One could, as Leyendecker further notes, be in residence in one place, and have settlement in another.

The federal law excludes grants to states for inmates in public institutions (except hospitals or other medical institutions), patients in institutions for tuberculosis and mental diseases, or in any medical institution because of a diagnosis of tuberculosis or

10 Hilary M. Leyendecker, *Problems and Policy in Public Assistance* (New York, 1955), p. 87.

psychosis. The emphasis in old-age assistance on aid to persons in their own homes has led to the limitations on the use of old-age assistance to defray the costs of maintenance in public institutions. In a real sense, too, this measure still reflects the earlier emphasis on eliminating the almshouse or comparable public facility. All the states have followed the federal lead in this respect, and have comparable restrictions on people residing in institutions.

A common method of defining need in old-age assistance is "an amount necessary to maintain a standard of decency and health." Anyone otherwise eligible who lacked the means to maintain such a standard would be considered as qualifying for old-age assistance. Actually, however, the states generally do not use only this broad definition. Most state laws have provisions similar to those in California, in which the maximum value of real estate which a recipient may own is specified. Similar maximums govern the amount of personal property permitted the individual without disqualifying him for assistance. In general, the intent is to avoid penalizing the aged person for the ownership of a home or personal effects. Also, it is recognized that property ownership tends to reduce need. The amounts vary widely from state to state, and frequently there are accompanying provisions which prohibit the transfer of any property for the purpose of qualifying for assistance. In other words, a person who had owned too much property, and who had transferred it without receiving an adequate return, perhaps shortly before applying for old-age assistance might be adjudged to have deliberately given away his property in order that he might receive aid.

In thirty-two of the states, the District of Columbia, and in Alaska and Hawaii, the amount of assistance paid becomes a claim in the form of a lien on property against the person receiving it, and is enforceable against his estate. Most generally, however, this measure is accompanied by a specification that the claim is not to be enforced during the lifetime of the surviving spouse. There are many variations of this provision, but in general the intent is to reimburse the state rather than surviving relatives who did not support the recipient during his lifetime.

Another major eligibility factor is income. The federal statute requires that states consider all income as well as other resources available to the person seeking or receiving assistance. This does not mean that the federal government instructs the states on how much income shall disqualify anyone from receiving assistance, but it does prohibit the states from generally exempting any particular kinds of earnings. The usual practice in state programs is to determine a standard of need against which any income available to the individual is measured. If the income is less than the amount of this standard, the person is determined to be in need. The way in which the states work out this method of determining the extent of need will be considered more fully in a succeeding section. The income may be derived from property, from stocks, bonds or other securities, or from any of the common sources of earnings. Regular support from relatives is also counted as income.

In many states, certain relatives are held legally responsible for support, provided they are deemed financially able. These relatives include husband, wife, and children. Where such laws are in effect, the administering authority may sue for the amount of support which has been determined to be within the relative's capability. This type of law is a direct carry-over from many which were on the state statutes as poor law measures. The administrative agency is expected to make a reasonable determination of fact, and generally, the enforcement is much less harsh than it was under the old poor law. Most states with such laws have some standardized measurement of ability of relatives to contribute, with a consideration of the size of the relative's family and income, and with provision for review of special circumstances or hardship situations.

Such are the major eligibility requirements for old-age assistance. Some states have miscellaneous other provisions, such as prohibiting aid to anyone serving sentence for a felony, receiving other assistance, or absent without leave from a tuberculosis hospital, and, in Arizona, the law includes a provision that the older person must not have refused work except under justifiable circumstances (a far cry from the depression days when old-age assistance came into being, and when all the pressure was on the older person to give up his job to the younger worker). These are not particularly significant, however, and probably have relatively little effect on the general character of the program.

Amount of assistance

In the fiscal year 1957, the total amount expended for old-age assistance was $1,723,362,000.[11] Of this amount, more than $161,-000,000 were paid to "vendors" of medical care.

The states show a wide variation in the average amounts of assistance per month to each recipient. In October 1957, the average payments ranged from a high of $94.95 in New York to a low of $28.49 in Mississippi.[12] The national average for payments was $60.67 for that month. The amount of assistance which a person may receive certainly depends in large part on where he lives, judging by these differences in the average amounts of individual grants.

In general, the amount of assistance to be received by an individual is ascertained by determining a standard of minimum needs for food, shelter, clothing, utilities, fuel, and other items (this is called a quantity-quality cost budget), and by computing the cost of providing these essentials. Periodic reviews are the prevailing method of keeping costs current with changing prices (in a period of inflation, it is highly doubtful whether even with the best of intentions, the agency can keep the standards current). The amount of assistance then equals this figure minus any deductible income.

Most states specify the maximum amount which may be paid. This may come to less than the amount reached through the budgeting process just described. The state may set this maxi-

---

[11] "Source of Funds," advance release of statistics, Division of Program Statistics and Analysis, Bureau of Public Assistance, Social Security Administration, October 24, 1957.

[12] "Advance Release of Statistics," Bureau of Public Assistance, December 6, 1957. These are figures only for the states. Puerto Rico and the Virgin Islands had much lower average payments.

mum by law, or it may be administratively determined by the state welfare agency. Colorado has a statutory minimum payment, with no maximum except as required by limited funds. A few other states have no specified maximum amounts. Illinois and California have unique provisions. In Illinois, the legal maximum is subject to adjustment up or down in the amount of $1 per month for each three points of change in the Consumer's Price Index of the Bureau of Labor Statistics. In California, while the legal maximum is $85 per month, this is considered as "basic maintenance." Special needs, such as those arising out of sickness, may be considered over and above the amount allowed for maintenance.

One of the knottiest problems for state and local welfare staff has been that of paying for medical care. In the past, the practice of including the medical need in the grant was not satisfactory since this payment is always ex post facto with reference to the need. Frequently, the amounts included in the individual's budgeted medical expense grant were used to pay for other items. The recent amendments to the Social Security Act have permitted the federal government to grant the states funds for the direct payment of medical care. As the result, since 1950 the doctor, the druggist, or the hospital may now receive payments directly from the administering authority. This has been possible also because the federal legislation exempted this particular type of payment from the requirement that the recipient must be paid in cash. The same kind of provision for direct payments to vendors has been made for the other categories of assistance.

In a study conducted in 1953, the Social Security Administration found that while allowances for basic requirements of food, clothing, personal incidentals, and household operating expenses, tended to be fairly uniform among various areas within each state, there were wide variations among the states. It was noted that these differences among the states seemed to be far greater than variations in living costs would warrant. The study also found that most of the states made some allowance for special needs, such as special diets, medical care, transportation for medical treatment, and laundry service when required.[13]

AID TO DEPENDENT CHILDREN

By 1934, programs of financial aid for the care of children in their own homes were in effect in 41 states, and in Alaska, the District of Columbia, Hawaii, and Puerto Rico. These programs were variously styled "mother's aid," "mother's allowances," "widow's pensions," etc. Like the state measures for "old age pensions," however, the coverage was spotty, and the aid was meager. Also, the contingencies covered were limited, by and large, to loss of the father by death.

Inclusion of aid to dependent children as one of the state-federal programs in the Social Security Act has had the effect of stimulating the states to make more adequate provisions for children in their own homes by providing for federal aid to the states for financing the programs, and by encouraging standards of assistance more nearly designed to meet the needs of families. One characteristic of the program has been its consistent emphasis on services designed to strengthen the family's ability to provide the child with an opportunity to realize to the full his potentialities for growth and development.

In its "Handbook of Public Assistance Administration," the federal agency defines the purpose of aid to dependent children as follows:[14]

> The purpose of the program for aid to dependent children is to enable needy children who are deprived of parental support or care to have the economic support and services they need for health and development, to assure for them an opportunity to grow up in the setting of their own family relationships, to receive an education that will help them to realize their capacities, and to share in the life of the neighborhood

[13] Charles E. Hawkins, "Recipients of Old-Age Assistance: Their Requirements," Social Security *Bulletin,* Vol. 20, No. 2 (February, 1957).

[14] Social Security Administration, Bureau of Public Assistance, "Handbook of Public Assistance Administration," Sec. 3300.

and the community. In these ways the program for aid to dependent children supports and strengthens family life in the United States.

An increasing proportion of the children receiving aid under this program are in need because of family instability, including desertion of the father, or divorce, separation, or unwed parenthood. According to the Commissioner of Social Security, Charles Schottland, these conditions are the basis of dependency for about half the children currently receiving this form of aid. This does not necessarily mean that the incidence of these kinds of family problems is increasing. It does indicate the extent to which the survivors provisions in old age and survivors insurance has taken over the function, formerly that of the aid to dependent children program, of meeting the needs of children deprived of care by the death of the breadwinner.

In October 1957, 651,479 families were receiving aid to dependent children in the states, the territories, and the District of Columbia. The families receiving assistance included over 1,800,-000 children, and more than 500,000 adult "caretakers," relatives receiving aid as persons responsible for the care of the dependent children. More than $65 million were paid as assistance to these families during the month.[15]

Providing conditions favorable to the development of children deprived through no fault of their own of the normal opportunity for growth would seem to be a generally acceptable objective. It might well be supposed that few would find any fault with such a purpose. Yet, this has been the most generally controversial of the federally aided public assistance measures. From time to time in many areas public criticism has reached serious proportions. In the words of one local welfare director, Robert Rippeto of the St. Louis, Missouri, City Welfare Office, "The Aid to Dependent Children program is probably the least understood and one of the most criticized of the assistance programs. These misunderstandings usually arise from the observation of a few cases, which are

15 "Advance Release of Statistics on Public Assistance," December 6, 1957, Bureau of Public Assistance, Social Security Administration.

then applied to the entire caseload. The belief that certain women are having children in order to increase their grants is one of the frequent indictments of this type of assistance. Another misconception that people often express regarding the aid to dependent children program is that once a family is added to the rolls, they remain there until all the children have reached the maximum age of sixteen years."[16] The City Welfare Administration in St. Louis made some studies of the program and found that charge to be unjustified.[17] Nationally, it has been found that the average family receiving aid under this program does so for about two-and-a-half years.

These are only some of the charges levelled against the program. Others include the claim that this form of assistance encourages desertion by the parent, fosters family breakdown, or that it tends to increase the incidence of unwed motherhood. Such beliefs probably have their root causes in social disapproval of the parental acts which have led to dependency, and literally reflect a tendency to visit the so-called sins of the parents upon the children. In a sense, prejudices against the parents are extended to the children who of course are in no way responsible for the socially disapproved behavior of their parents. Whereas the plight of the orphan is easily understood and arouses sympathy and concern, this is not always true of these other circumstances. The problem in aid to dependent children has been especially pronounced since the growth of old-age and survivors insurance has removed many orphaned children from the assistance programs.

A companion attitude to the disapproval of the program is the belief that the families who receive its aid do not live according to community standards of behavior, and that they are rearing children destined to be problems to society. In 1952 a comprehensive study, published by the American Public Welfare Association, factually refuted such opinion. This study was undertaken by Gordon W. Blackwell and Raymond F. Gould of the

---

[16] "Finding Answers to Criticism of ADC," *Public Welfare*, Vol. 14, No. 3, a brief summary of a series of studies undertaken by the St. Louis City Welfare Office, July, 1956, p. 168.

[17] *Ibid.*

Institute for Social Research, University of North Carolina (and was financed by a grant from the Field Foundation). Through their study of the actual circumstances of families receiving aid to dependent children in thirty-eight states, the authors found that the facts refuted the suspicion and censure directed against the families receiving this type of assistance. In their summary they reported that "We have been impressed with the evidence that the great preponderance of ADC families have been functioning relatively well under a heavy weight of hardship. The scholastic, vocational, and other achievements of ADC children seem remarkable in some instances. Delinquency, crime, child neglect, and children born out of wedlock occur less frequently than one would expect in such a stress-ridden group."[18]

These authors, as many others, have noted the importance of the program of aid to dependent children in carrying out the purpose assigned to it in the Social Security Act, that of enabling children to remain with their mothers. Blackwell and Gould estimated that in 91 percent of the families they studied, the program had made this possible, and expressed the belief that without such assistance many of the families would have disintegrated, causing permanent detriment to the children.

Despite all the suspicion which finds frequent expression, however, the laws continue to strengthen the support of services to the families. Without popular belief in the success of such services, this support would not be forthcoming. Unless there is some conviction that the families have the strength to respond to services, there can be little enthusiasm for financing activities on their behalf.

Eligibility

The chief factors of eligibility in this program are age, residence, reason for dependency, and need. In addition, all state laws specify the degree of relationship to the person with whom the child must be living in order to qualify.

18 Gordon W. Blackwell, and Raymond F. Gould, "Future Citizens All" (Chicago, American Public Welfare Association, 1952), p. xxiii.

As it does for old-age assistance, the Social Security Act includes a general definition of eligibility for aid to dependent children. This definition specifies those conditions which must be present in order that the state may receive federal funds to match its expenditures for the recipient of aid. The federal law defines an eligible person as a needy child under the age of eighteen, "who has been deprived of parental support or care by reason of the death, continued absence from the home, or physical or mental incapacity of a parent . . ."[19] The relatives specified in the federal law are: father, mother, grandfather, grandmother, brother, sister, stepfather, stepmother, stepbrother, stepsister, uncle or aunt, and (only since 1956) first cousins, nephews or nieces.

Before the 1956 amendments changed the age requirement, the federal law stipulated that the child for whom federal funds were received must be under sixteen, or under eighteen if regularly attending school. The amendments eliminated the provision relating to school attendance from the federal law, and set the requirement simply at under eighteen years of age. Prior to this action, the District of Columbia, North Dakota, Hawaii, Rhode Island and Wyoming had no provision on school attendance, while Wisconsin had set the maximum age at twenty-one (which is beyond the limits of the federal law). Of course, for the children over the maximum specified in the Social Security Act, the federal government does not provide funds. North Dakota, likewise, had set the age requirement higher than the federal maximum, at eighteen with no school attendance stipulated, or twenty-one if in a licensed institution or foster home, or if incapacitated. Minnesota had allowed for some conditions that might excuse school attendance for the child sixteen or over and under eighteen. Some states have set age limits lower than those for which federal aid is available. Georgia, Nebraska, and Nevada, have set the limit at sixteen years of age, and Texas at fourteen. By and large, however, the majority of the states have followed the national government's lead in this matter. As of November 1, 1957, the qualifying age

[19] Social Security Act, Sec. 406 *(a)*.

in twenty-three states is under eighteen without any qualifications for school attendance.

The federal law sets the maximum period of residence which the state may require if it is to receive federal funds at one year preceding the date of applying for aid for the child or, for the child less than one year old, at the time of application. If the child is under one year old the state may require that the relatives have resided in the state for one year preceding the child's birth. Most of the states have modeled their laws on this specification, although some have shorter or no periods of residence demanded.

Unlike old-age assistance, the aid to dependent children program does demand a cause of dependency as one of its qualifying conditions. In the program for the aged, it will be recalled, the legislation is unrelated to how the person had come to be in need. In aid to dependent children, however, the reason for dependency is part of the purpose of the program, which is designed for children in certain particular kinds of circumstances. All of the conditions—death, continued absence from the home, or physical or mental incapacity—of this requirement refer to the parent and are related to family situations on which the law is based.

Such qualifications as physical or mental incapacity do not permit precise formulations. There is the presumption that an impairment is so disabling that it deprives the breadwinner of the ability to earn a living. This requires the administering authority to secure the necessary medical information on which to base a decision as to whether the parent is actually incapable of working, and inevitably involves personality factors as well as medical facts.

Similarly, continued absence from the home is not necessarily a simple fact to determine. The agency may find itself confronted with a question as to whether the desertion by the parent is permanent or temporary. Some states attempt to meet the situation by specifying the period of absence which must have elapsed before the family can qualify, which has the effect of denying aid for some time to families which have been deserted. Currently, laws specify that law enforcement officials must be notified without delay when assistance is paid on behalf of a child who has been deserted or abandoned by a parent.

The standard on which the determination of need is based is expressed generally as one which is compatible with decency and health. The child is deemed to be in need when he lacks adequate means of support. The practice generally is to specify a maximum monetary amount of real and personal property owned by the family. In some instances, certain resources may be classified as not disqualifying the family for the receipt of assistance. Such resources may be the home in which the family resides. In this as in the other state-federal assistance programs, the wide variation among the states makes any general description of standards of need difficult.

The practice generally is to establish a budget for the measurement of need. This budget specifies those items, with the monetary amounts to be allowed, which are deemed necessary to provide an adequate standard of living for the family. Available income is then compared to the total amount of this budget, and if there is a deficit, need is considered to exist.

Most states have followed the federal requirement in determining policy with respect to the relatives with whom the child may live, although in some states the definition has been broadened beyond the federal limits.

Other miscellaneous eligibility measures appear in the jurisdictions. A few states specify that the person caring for the child must be mentally, morally, and physically fit to rear the child, or that the home be "suitable." A rather frequent specification is that the parent physically able to work must not refuse a reasonable job offer. This requirement may be accompanied by an insistence that the incapacitated parent accept vocational rehabilitation whenever it is deemed feasible. In cases of desertion the state may, like California, require that the parent having custody of the child shall provide "reasonable assistance" to the law enforcement officer in locating the absent parent and in securing his support.

These provisions further reflect the latitude which the states have in determining eligibility conditions within the limits established by the federal government. Still, in general, the requirements follow the pattern of emphasizing the importance of promoting the quality of family life. Some of the specifications listed above might be said to reflect the mixture of compassion and severity with which this welfare clientele is regarded.

Amount of assistance

The amount of assistance in aid to dependent children programs is the total need as determined by the use of a budgetary standard less the income available to the family (to the exent that state maxima permit). The needs of all eligible children may be included, in addition to those of the relative with whom the child lives, provided that relative also is needy. Not all states include the relative's individual needs, although these needs might be computed in the budget for the total family.

The Social Security Act sets maxima for federal financial participation in individual payments. For the first child in the family, federal funds are available for a proportion up to $32 per month, and for each additional child up to $23. The maximum monthly amount in which the federal government will participate for the relative is $32. (See Chapter 7.) These amounts have been changed from time to time by law, and in fact have been substantially increased over the years as the cost of living has risen.

In addition, the federal government participates directly in the costs of medical care, as it does in the other forms of categorical public assistance. This participation permits "vendor payments," *i.e.*, direct payments to the persons rendering the services. All other payments, so far as federal participation is concerned, must be made in cash to the child's guardian.

Some of the states have no maximum payment, and consequently accept all responsibility for payments above the limits of federal participation, either through the use of state funds or a combination of state and local funds. The majority do specify a maximum, generally equal to or more than the federal figure. Also, a number of the states which set maximum figures for assistance provide for larger amounts in cases of special needs such as medical care or particular hardship.

Variation in the size of monthly payments appears in this program from state to state, as it does in the others. In their study of aid to dependent children Blackwell and Gould called attention to regional differences from 1938 to 1951 in the average sizes of state payments for aid to dependent children.[20] Their figures indicated that the highest payments tend to be in the Far Western states, with the Southeastern and Southwestern states consistently having the lowest average payments.

As of October 1957, the national average monthly payment per family in the aid to dependent children program was $100.10, and the average per individual was $26.80. Among the states there was a wide range both with respect to individual and to family payments, from an average per family of $28.22 in Mississippi to $157.14 in Wisconsin, while per individual the two states at the bottom and top of the range respectively, were Mississippi with average payments of $7.54, and Massachusetts with $45.52. These are not absolute comparisons, since the size of payments is conditioned by the number in the family, and by the amount of income available to the family.[21] Nevertheless, the disparities among the states at the high and low extremes of payment are not accounted for by these factors nor by state or regional differences in living costs.

AID TO THE BLIND

Assistance to the blind is a form of special assistance which antedated the Social Security Act. As Fink has noted, "Because the blind are frequently at a disadvantage in the labor market and less likely to earn sufficient money for self-maintenance, the movement for allowances from public funds got under way, long before public aid to dependent children or the aged."[22] The first measure of special assistance was enacted by the state of Illinois in 1903. By 1935, the year when the Social Security Act was passed, twenty-seven states had special measures on their books. These

[20] *Op. cit.,* p. 13.
[21] *Advance Release of Statistics on Public Assistance,* October, 1957, Bureau of Public Assistance, December 6, 1957. Social Security Administration, Table 3.
[22] Arthur Fink et al., *The Field of Social Work* (New York, rev. 1955), p. 47.

measures, however, generally had the same features of inadequacy which characterized the provisions for children and for the aged—meager amounts of aid, spottiness of coverage even within the states, and limited emphasis on services.

Aid to the blind was incorporated in Title X of the Social Security Act in 1935. It had not been among the programs recommended in the Report of the President's Committee on Economic Security but a strong organization of blind people and others concerned with the problem of blindness successfully put the needs of this group before Congress. Today, programs of aid to the blind are in effect in fifty-three jurisdictions—in all the states, the District of Columbia, Alaska, Hawaii, Puerto Rico, and the Virgin Islands.

The purpose of this program, according to the Social Security Administration's "Handbook of Public Assistance Administration," is to enable "needy blind individuals to secure the essentials of living and to provide them with the opportunity to continue to participate in the life of the community."[23] The federal statement notes that the federal insurance measures contain no special provisions for the blind, so that public assistance is the major resource "for blind persons whose other resources are insufficient to obtain the essentials of living." The document also calls attention to the fact that "The great majority of the people who are blind are dependent upon others for support. It is, therefore, desirable that there be a dual approach to their economic problem, providing necessary financial assistance to the needy blind, and encouraging and assisting them to become self-supporting in whole or in part."

In October 1957, persons receiving aid to the blind in the states and other jurisdictions numbered 108,450. Expenditures for this program amounted to slightly more than $7 million for the month.[24] This is the smallest of all the public assistance programs both in persons served and amounts expended.

[23] *Handbook of Public Assistance Administration,* Social Security Administration, Sec. 3400.

[24] *Advance Release of Statistics on Public Assistance,* October, 1957, Bureau of Public Assistance, Social Security Administration, December 6, 1957.

In addition to the program of care provided under the Social Security Act, one state, California, has, besides, a nonfederally-aided program called "Aid to Partially Self-Supporting Blind." This measure is more liberal in its provisions relating to how much a person can earn or own, and is designed for those blind persons who present evidence of a plan for some self-support. Pennsylvania and Missouri also provide pensions to the blind.

Aid to the blind programs throughout the country maintain a strong emphasis on services designed to help the individual to become self-supporting. Income-maintenance provisions are closely related to services for the restoration of sight, and to vocational training and placement. The development of this program has come a long way since the days when the dependent blind person whose family could not maintain him faced the prospect of institutional care, or work of a narrowly prescribed character which could not bring out the full potentialities many blind people nevertheless have for useful and satisfying lives.

Eligibility

The general provision in the public assistance titles of the Social Security Act barring the imposition of any discriminatory legislation against an otherwise eligible citizen applies to this category of assistance, as well as to the others. Besides this, the major eligibility requirements for aid to the blind programs in the states include age (minimum rather than maximum), residence, citizenship, blindness to a degree considered as rendering the individual unable to earn a living, need, and residence outside public institutions except for the purpose of receiving medical or surgical care.

Some of the states have no age requirement for aid to the blind. In those that do, the minimum age is sixteen, eighteen, or—in a few states—even higher. This is based on the principle of relating the program to "economic blindness"—that degree of blindness which incapacitates a person for earning a livelihood—and consequently of establishing a requirement at the age at which an individual might be expected to earn his own living.

The degree of blindness sometimes is expressed in medical

terms, such as "20/200 or less vision in the better eye with correcting lenses," and sometimes in addition specifies the range of field of vision which may accompany this degree of impairment of visual acuity. Such measures are common, as the states attempt either through law or administrative policy to seek some objective measure of what could otherwise be very difficult to determine. The usual practice is to base the decision on blindness on the recommendation of a medical expert, such as a state supervising ophthalmologist.

Required periods of state residence for aid to the blind are quite similar to those in old-age assistance programs. In some states no residence is required. Other states specify the maximum permissible under federal requirements—five years of the nine preceding the date of application. In still others the requirements are somewhere between these two extremes. It is common in those states which require periods of residence to specify a shorter period for those who have become blind while state residents.

Provisions relating to need are similar to those for old-age assistance except for the factor of income. The states are required to exempt the first $50 of a recipient's earned income from consideration by the administering authority. The blind person, secure in the realization that some earnings will not be deducted from the grant, is encouraged to secure employment. This is an important part of a program which deals with persons so disadvantaged as the blind are in the labor market, and which lays such heavy stress on assisting the individual to attain self-maintenance.

All of the states make some provision limiting the value of real and personal property a recipient may own. Here too the pattern is very similar to that of the old-age assistance programs. This type of assistance also makes a special effort to avoid penalizing the individual for the ownership of a home or for a reasonable amount of cash or insurance or securities as a cushion against emergencies which may not be covered by assistance programs. Even more fundamental, perhaps, is the recognition of the meaning to the individual person of having some things which he owns, and which contribute to his sense of personal security. As noted in discussing the old-age-assistance programs, ownership tends to reduce need for aid. In some states liens enforceable against the estate of the recipient are required, although in fewer instances than under old-age assistance programs.

The interest in promoting self-maintenance on the part of the blind is reflected in some states' provisions that the blind person becomes ineligible if he refuses corrective treatment, or, in some states, any training which might contribute to his capacity for self-maintenance.

In cases of aid to the blind, as in other forms of aid, relatives may be held legally responsible for support. This is a common but not universal requirement among the states.[25] As Leyendecker has noted, no federal pressure is exerted on the states to include such a requirement in this or other forms of categorical assistance.

Amount of assistance

Federal matching of assistance payments is available to states up to a maximum of $60 for any one individual. States may set the maximum amount of aid at a higher figure for the individual. The maximum amount under state laws as of December, 1956, tended to equal or exceed the amount matchable by the federal government in most states, with further provision in some for payments above the specified maximum for persons with certain special medical requirements. In some states maximum amounts of assistance were stipulated for the family of the recipient to cover all types of public aid to the family.[26] In twenty-two of the fifty-three jurisdictions with aid to the blind programs, no maximum amounts are stated.

As in other types of public assistance, need is determined by computing costs through the use of a standard individual or family budget. Any amount of income received by the individual, except the exempted $50 of earnings, is deducted from this amount.

In October 1957, the average payment nationally was $66.21.

---

[25] For a discussion of this feature of public assistance, see Leyendecker, *op. cit.*, pp. 215-235.

[26] "Effect of the Public Assistance Amendments of 1956," statistical summary by the Bureau of Public Assistance, Division of Program Statistics and Analysis.

States, again as in old-age assistance and aid to dependent children programs, showed a wide range in average individual payments. This range extended from a high of $113.35 in (the state of) Washington to a low of $37.77 in West Virginia.[27] These figures do not include Puerto Rico or the Virgin Islands.

AID TO THE PERMANENTLY AND TOTALLY DISABLED

This is the newest of the categorical public assistance programs. The program establishing federal aid was set up in 1950, by amendment to the Social Security Act. Disabled persons, other than the blind, who were too old to receive aid under the dependent-children provisions, too young for old-age assistance, and who because of their loss of function had not been able to build up wage experience for social insurance, could look only to general assistance for help. Local assistance standards were inadequate and the disabled were considered a serious drain on the resources of local and state government.

The addition of this aid to the rest of the federal public welfare program was a continuation of the historical practice of treating special groups separately, according to their special needs. The objective, in addition to providing maintenance, was to encourage the states to help needy disabled persons to attain "self-support or self-care."[28] The objectives of this program are closely related to those of vocational rehabilitation efforts (see Chapter 7), and in achieving them state and local welfare offices are encouraged to work closely with the agency administering the vocational rehabilitation program.

The response of the states to this new federal program was prompt. Within two years after its enactment, thirty-nine of the fifty-three jurisdictions had passed legislation setting up programs of aid to the disabled. Currently, except for four of the states plus

27 Advance Release of Statistics in Public Assistance, Bureau of Public Assistance, October, 1957, December 6, 1957.
28 Social Security Act, Title XIV, Section 1401.

Alaska, all the jurisdictions have such a program in operation.[29] In October 1957, 287,373 persons were receiving this form of assistance throughout the country.

In addition to this measure, other legislation for the disabled has been enacted in old-age and survivors insurance, it will be recalled, providing for first a disability "freeze" on eligibility for the person who becomes injured prior to retirement age, and since 1956, for benefits to disabled people of fifty or over.[30] Further, as will be noted in succeeding chapters, extension and strengthening of vocational rehabilitation services have been important in providing increased opportunities for restoring handicapped people to productive work.

Eligibility

Like the other forms of categorical assistance, aid to the permanently and totally disabled has qualifications relating to age, residence, need, institutional status, and in a few instances, citizenship. The condition of eligibility for this type of assistance is disability. As the title of the program suggests, it is meant to provide for the person whose impairment incapacitates him for gainful employment. As in the case of blindness, the test is economic as well as medical. The fact of such impairment is related to the competence of the individual, *i.e.*, disability to perform work of which he would otherwise be capable.

Federal requirements relating to maximum periods of residence and prohibition of discrimination against citizens are the same as for old-age assistance and aid to the blind—five of the nine years preceding application for the aid. As in all other categories of assistance, the federal law requires that states whose plans provide for payments to people living in institutions shall empower a designated state authority to establish and maintain good institutional standards.

The minimum age for qualifying for this form of assistance is eighteen. Many states also set a maximum age of sixty-five, on the

[29] The states are Arizona, Indiana, Iowa, and Nevada.
[30] See preceding chapter.

assumption that people that age or over are eligible for aid under the O.A.S.D.I. program, or for old-age assistance.

Residence qualifications are in force in most states. In this type of assistance, as in the others, the minimum residence requirement varies among the states. At present, thirty-one of the jurisdictions providing this form of assistance require one year of residence, seven have no residence requirement, and only eight demand the maximum permitted by federal law.[31]

The definition of disability in New York State is typical of that in other states' laws. This definition reads:[32]

> A person is considered disabled when he is between 18 and 65 years of age and a diagnosis and medical findings and a report of his social situation show him to have continuing impairments, disease or defects that substantially prevent him from engaging in a useful occupation such as working at a job within his competence or, in the case of a woman homemaker, prevents her from performing the usual activities in the care of the home. Disability is determined in accordance with standards, established by the State Department of Social Welfare, which include review of the medical findings of the examining physician and the report of the social conditions made by the local public welfare agency. Temporary illness or partial disability will not meet the eligibility requirements for aid to the disabled.

The elements of this definition are: degree of impairment, its relatedness to ability to work, and a method of determining these factors. Such a definition, including both physical and mental impairment, is common to the other states' disability laws.

The requirement of need is not particularly different from those in the other categorical assistance programs. Need is determined by the same method as in the other categories of aid. The federal provisions do not permit exemption of income in this category as they do in aid to the blind, and all income resources must be

---

[31] Bureau of Public Assistance (letter to author, Dec. 3, 1957).

[32] "Questions and Answers: Aid to the Disabled," New York State Department of Social Welfare, November, 1955.

considered by the state and local agencies administering the assistance.

Other eligibility provisions found in some states, but not in all, are stipulations that the individual must accept corrective treatment or vocational rehabilitation, must not have certain types of disease, such as tuberculosis or mental illness, and must be ineligible to receive other types of assistance.[33]

The average national payment for aid to the disabled was $59.53 in October 1957. Among the states the payments ranged from a high average of $124.32 per recipient in Wisconsin to a low of $19.04 in Mississippi.[34]

The federal government participates in individual payments up to a maximum of $60 per month. (See Chapter 7 for the formula determining the degree of participation.) In this as in the other categories the states in many instances have provided for maximum payments in excess of that amount, and in others have no maximum. In a number of states the maximum corresponds to the federal amount, although in some of these the state may allow more to those with special needs or hardships. In a few states the maximum payment is less than the $60 federal limit.

GENERAL ASSISTANCE

This is the residual program of assistance. It is operated for those persons who are in need but who for one reason or other do not qualify for any of the categorical assistance programs. It is not federally aided, and is financed entirely by states and localities, by the states, or in many instances by localities alone. The patterns of state and local responsibilities are so diverse that any attempt at classification is futile. In some states, the counties are responsible for operating general assistance programs. In others

[33] "Characteristics of State Public Assistance Plans," *Public Assistance Report No. 27*, 1956, Bureau of Public Assistance, Social Security Administration.

[34] *Advance Release of Public Assistance Statistics,* October, 1957, Bureau of Public Assistance, Social Security Administration. This range does not include Puerto Rico or the Virgin Islands, where the situation is not comparable with respect to federal provisions of general standards of living.

the task belongs to the towns or townships. In still others any one of several local units may be responsible. In some states the same staff administers general and the other categorical assistance programs. In others, staff in separate offices are responsible. The generalization which the facts do justify is that this is the form of assistance program which carries on the tradition of local responsibility of the poor law.

Fink calls general assistance a "modern euphemism for what used to be termed poor relief."[35] Many of the features of general assistance justify this rather unflattering designation. In many places, assistance is given in kind, *i.e.*, in the form of orders on stores or landlords. As has been previously noted, this is humiliating to the individuals who must identify themselves as recipients. Settlement rather than residence governs eligibility in many states.[36] In most states the standards for determining need for general assistance are much lower than those for the categorical assistance programs. An exception is New York, where the same standard is used for what is termed "home relief" and for the categorical assistance programs. In other places, throughout the country, this is not the rule, and one of the essential differences between categorical assistance and general assistance is that in the former the conditions of eligibility are more specific, and that in the latter, there is less emphasis on the right of the individual to receive aid. More often than not, however, general assistance is a meager form of aid, grudgingly given, and financed by limited local funds.

Nevertheless, in October 1957 there were 297,000 cases of general assistance. (Case refers to family or to individual recipients.) For the past few years of general prosperity, when income-maintenance provisions of the social insurances and other public assistance programs have been broadened, this figure would also be representative. It slightly exceeds the monthly total of permanently and totally disabled cases, and is considerably larger than the number of blind recipients of aid.

---

[35] *Op. cit.*, p. 150.
[36] See p. 146 for the difference between "settlement" and "residence."

As this figure indicates, general assistance is still a significant program. It must mean that there are still a number of contingencies outside the coverage of the social insurances or the other programs of public assistance. Indeed, general assistance caseloads certainly indicate this fact. The family breadwinner may become ill, for example, and not be permanently and totally disabled within the definition of that category, nor incapacitated in the sense the term is employed in aid programs for dependent children, nor eligible for either workmen's compensation or unemployment insurance. Or able employable people may be out of work for a length of time which exceeds the maximum benefit period under unemployment insurance. Or a member of the family may become ill and require medical care beyond the family's financial capacity.

Innumerable examples of problems which fall within this "catchall" program could be given. In some states general assistance funds are used to pay the costs of child care in foster homes, that is, in homes of nonrelatives, and therefore outside the coverage of aid to dependent children. In many areas general assistance programs finance those of local public medical care. These funds may be used, for example, to send a child to a state-operated clinic for speech correction, or for orthopedic treatment, where crippled children's funds do not cover maintenance of the child while it is receiving treatment.

That this program has a distinct social utility, despite all its limitations, is unquestionable. Its use to meet emergency situations or situations arising out of conditions not covered by the formal provisions of other programs makes it an important part of the welfare program. From time to time proposals have been made to incorporate general assistance into an additional category, but instead the pattern of reducing the scope of this form of assistance by making other allowances for special groups has continued.

In October 1957 a total of $17,152,000 was expended by general assistance programs in the United States. The average payment per case for the month was $57.66, with variations among the average payments in different states. The average amount per case was lower than for any of the other forms of assistance, which reflects in a general way the lower standards which prevail in this program, although because the kinds of assistance provided in this program are so different from those the categorical assistance measures provide that any meaningful comparison is difficult. For one thing, general assistance payments may be made directly to the person providing a specific service and may not cover all of a family's or individual's needs. For another, the assistance may be given to meet an emergency period, even one shorter than a month. Still, such differences do not explain away the fact that quite generally, the standards for this are lower than those of any other type of assistance, or that, to be eligible for general assistance, one must be closer to a level of destitution than eligibility conditions require in the categorical aids. It would be a rare instance in which the applicant for general assistance would be declared eligible if he possesses even the level of personal resources that is allowed under the categorical assistance programs.

FINANCING PUBLIC ASSISTANCE

Federal support for the public assistance program comes out of the general revenues of the United States, through appropriations by Congress. This is in contrast both to O.A.S.D.I., which is financed through taxes levied specifically against the employer and the employee, and to unemployment insurance, which levies a payroll tax on employers as the means of financing the federal share of the payments.

Most of the state support of public assistance comes from the general revenues of the states. According to a Social Security Administration report, almost 80 percent of the more than $1 billion of state funds expended in assistance payments in 1955 came from general revenues.[37] This means that most of the state support did not come from funds from any particular source of revenue earmarked specifically for public assistance expenditures. The tendency to use general rather than earmarked sources of funds has grown in the past years.

[37] "Sources of Revenue for the State Share of Public Assistance—Fiscal Years 1953-55," Social Security Administration.

This is a good and an important tendency, for the practice of earmarking certain kinds of revenue, such as all or part of income from general sales taxes, license and privilege taxes, or taxes on liquor, tobacco, amusements, or public utilities, to name just a few, ties the fate of the welfare program to that of the industry or activity being taxed. It might be argued that if the source were a profitable one this would be advantageous. It seems, though, that welfare as a general responsibility should be financed on the basis of the ability of the state as a whole to support the service. Some students of government also have noted from time to time the questionable soundness of tying the support of the needy to direct taxes, to a general sales tax which, if there is such a tax of 2 percent, means that rich, poor and middle-income members of society alike all will pay 2 cents in tax on a $1 purchase. This results in taxing the needy to support themselves. The argument on this issue goes beyond the scope of this book, but the fact worth noting here is that the social utility of a program definitely is affected by the way in which its financial support is obtained.

In some states (as will be described in more detail in Part III, following, which deals with intergovernmental relations), local participation is required in one or more of the categorical assistance programs. In the general assistance programs, however, the prevailing pattern is one of local support alone, or of joint local-state support. Usually, the local share comes from general tax funds of the local governmental unit, although in some large municipalities certain taxes are earmarked for the financing of assistance programs.

SOCIAL SERVICES IN PUBLIC ASSISTANCE

Almost any conceivable human problem sooner or later is likely to appear among those of the clientele of public assistance programs.[38] At first, this may seem like a pretty strong statement, particularly because we may be inclined to think that need for public assistance stems strictly from loss of income. As we take a further look at the program, however, we soon perceive the many

[38] As this author learned some years ago when he was the director of a county department of public welfare.

needs that lead to, are caused by, or at least accompany, loss of financial means. To attempt to reduce the problem of need for financial aid to any single factor is a gross oversimplification. The nature of these needs is such that logically they must be viewed as interlocking problems—some causing, and others aggravating or being aggravated by economic hardship.

Recently the Federal Bureau of Public Assistance compiled a list of the major problem areas in public assistance. It is a relatively long list, but we are including it here because it is important to any adequate comprehension of the scope of public assistance and pertinent to recent public assistance legislation. The list also helps explain the later sections of this book which describe the organizational and administrative patterns in public welfare.[39]

1. Financial need:

    a. Difficulties in maintaining health, home life, family, social and community relationships on marginal or inadequate income,

    b. Problems of parents unable to provide for family,

    c. Problems of material deprivation for individual children,

    d. Effects of economic dependency upon self-esteem of individual and family,

    e. Readjustment to lowered standard of living,

    f. Problems resulting from long-time economic deprivation or dependency.

2. Physical or mental illness or handicap—acute or chronic:

    a. Problem of personal and family adjustment to illness or handicap, and to necessary treatment and care,

    b. Conditions requiring immediate arrangements for care,

    c. Conditions requiring long-time planning, treatment and care,

    d. Conditions requiring protective measures for other members of the family,

    e. Problems resulting from nutritional deficiencies,

[39] The list was compiled by the Bureau of Public Assistance, Social Security Administration, and dated April 8, 1957.

    f. Conditions needing special appliances, special home facilities and/or retraining for self-care,

    g. Problems of mental deficiency of adult or child—in family life, community relationships, employment, training, etc.,

    h. Special problems of blindness—reorientation, and extent of dependence on others,

    i. Special problems of alcoholism and drug addiction.

3. Broken family (illness, death, divorce, desertion, incarceration):

    a. Difficulties for individual family members in dealing with trauma of the experience,

    b. Lack of normal relationships for remaining spouse, for individual children,

    c. Difficulties for remaining parent in carrying total responsibility for maintenance of home and rearing of children.

4. Problems in family relationships, marital, parent-child, and other relatives:

    a. Conflict around support arrangements, inadequate support or nonsupport,

    b. Conflict around children's visiting absent parent in cases of divorce or separation, and visiting relatives,

    c. Conflict between or among family members because of change in family roles (changes in role of wage earner, homemaker, working child, aged person, etc.),

    d. Conflict resulting from lowered self-esteem or regard for other family member (as in case of illness, desertion, separation, loss of job, etc.),

    e. Conflict among family members resulting in failure to meet children's needs for love, affection and security,

    f. Conflict between family members resulting in using child as tool against another family member, or forcing child to take sides.

5. Problems in relation to children's opportunity for education, recreation and maintenance of health:

    a. Lack of recognition on part of parent or child of need for and value of appropriate education and/or vocational training, preventive health measures and recreation,

   b. Lack of knowledge of available resources suited to needs of child,

   c. Difficulties in family planning or individual use of appropriate resources,

   d. Conflicting attitudes on part of child or other family members in using resources,

   e. Lack of appropriate resources for education, recreation and health.

6. Employment problems:

   a. Lack of vocational skills or experience,

   b. Handicaps requiring special training or placement,

   c. Personal attitudes that affect employment,

   d. Attitudes and problems within the family affecting employment,

   e. Difficulties in finding and lack of opportunity for employment suitable to physical and mental capacity, skills and interests, or family responsibilities.

7. Inadequate housing, furnishings or undesirable neighborhood:

   a. Problems of inadequate space in relation to number, ages, and sex of family members,

   b. Conditions requiring improvements or repairs,

   c. Lack of necessary furniture and household equipment,

   d. Unwholesome neighborhood influences.

8. Problems in carrying excessive responsibility (economic, physical, emotional) for adult or child over prolonged period:

   a. Problems in carrying both homemaker and wage earner role,

   b. Problems for child carrying adult or other responsibilities that limit his opportunity for healthy growth and development.

9. Social isolation:

   a. Lack of opportunity for satisfying relationships with peer group, relatives, etc.,

    b. Lack of opportunity to participate in community life.

10. Difficulties in interpersonal relationships outside family group (withdrawal, inability to participate in social activities, conflict with others).

11. Behavior problems of adults or children:

    a. Stealing, lying,
    b. Assaultive, aggressive, or destructive behavior,
    c. Sexual problem, such as deviate sexual practices, or promiscuity,
    d. Eating, sleeping, speech difficulties, enuresis, etc.,
    e. Truancy and running away.

12. Serious personality or character defect:

    a. Consistent inability to carry normal responsibility, *e.g.*, employment, home management, care of children, etc.,
    b. Inability to carry sustained relationships with other persons.

13. Problems resulting from adverse community attitudes (religious, racial, cultural, etc.).

14. Unmarried parenthood:

    a. Problems for the mother—both immediate and long-time (medical, economic, family and community attitudes, need for special living arrangements or care; conflicting feelings in making decision about child, feelings about the child and its father; legal problems, etc.),
    b. Problems for the father (economic, legal, family and community attitudes, conflicting feelings toward the mother and child, problems in providing continuing support, etc.),
    c. Problems for child (lack of normal family relationships; family and community attitudes; legal status—immediate and long-time; need for special care or living arrangements when family care is not possible or desirable; maternal deprivation in temporary separations or frequent changes in living arrangements; conflicting feelings of child about himself, his parents and his family),
    d. Problems for siblings (economic, feelings toward the child,

the mother and child's father; family and community attitudes),

e. Special problems in cases of repeated illegitimate births—
for mother, children and other members of family (economic, personal and social).

15. Special problems of aging:

a. Personal and family attitudes affecting continued role in
family and community,
b. Problems for individual and family of personal and financial dependency upon children and/or others,
c. Restriction in normal activities because of physical limitations, lack of confidence or lack of opportunities,
d. Difficulties in remaining in own home because of personal,
family and community attitudes, unsuitable physical set-up
of home, or lack of home aid resources,
e. Need for special care outside of own home suited to current health and social needs,
f. Difficulties in management of personal and financial affairs.

16. Need for social protection:

a. Neglect, abuse or exploitation of adult or child,
b. Lack of family or interested persons to provide needed
planning and attention for individuals unable to assume
these responsibilities.

17. Lack of legal protection (such as need for guardianship, legal
residence, etc.):

a. Problem of mentally incompetent adult, requiring legal
guardian,
b. Problem of child without legal guardian (as in cases of
orphan, children whose parents' whereabouts are unknown,
or who have no known legally responsible adult),
c. Person lacking legal status due to failure to restore legal
rights following release from penal or mental commitment.

Such a list of needs would seem to call for an equally comprehensive program of social services, manned by skilled workers,
and designed to promote to the full the innate capacities of people

to work through their problems. There is an authoritative definition of social services in public assistance in the following statement, prepared by the Committee on Social Work Education and Personnel of the American Public Welfare Association,[40]

> Social Services are essential in public assistance. Among their purposes are: (1) providing financial assistance based on a sound and constructive determination of eligibility and the extent of need; (2) making appropriate referrals to other agencies when the clients wish to use them; (3) assisting clients to become self-supporting whenever this is possible; (4) aiding clients, within the limits of defined agency functions, in assuming the maximum extent of their capacity, their normal responsibilities and privileges as members of the family group and the community, and (5) obtaining protective services for clients who are in situations which are detrimental to their well-being or that of the community. This refers especially to children and others unable to help themselves. It may involve securing appropriate help for them through relatives, friends, other social agencies or legal action in the interest of the individual and the public.

From the beginning of the public assistance programs in 1935 the emphasis on social services designed to assist the individual to utilize to the full his capacity for self-maintenance has been an integral part of administration. State and federal policy has featured this emphasis in programs which, in contrast to the poor law of former times, were based on the assumption that people receiving public aid had the capacity to improve their lot. Funds for training personnel have been provided in order to improve the abilities of staff members to help their clients toward self-maintenance. Recently the 1956 Social Security Act amendments have furthered this emphasis by providing more federal support for administrative services intended, as the statement of purpose in the law declares, "to promote the well-being of the Nation by encouraging the States to place greater emphasis on helping to strengthen family life and helping needy families and individuals

[40] "The Public Assistance Worker," a pamphlet, issued April 19, 1952.

attain the maximum economic and personal independence of which they are capable."[41] Its further purpose is "to assist in improving the administration of public assistance programs

> (1) through making grants and contracts, and entering into jointly financed cooperative arrangements, for research and demonstration projects and
>
> (2) through Federal-State programs of grants to institutions and traineeships and fellowships so as to provide training of public welfare personnel, thereby securing more adequately trained personnel . . .

Similarly, state laws also generally contain expressions of intent which stress respect for the dignity of the person served and standards for a level of health and decency. More often than not they specifically mention the obligation of the administering authority to work toward the preservation of family life and the strengthening of the individual recipient's capacity for self-sufficiency.[42]

A fairly typical statement is found in "Article I: General Provisions—Definitions" of the Public Assistance Code of Illinois. It reads as follows:[43]

> Sec. 1-1. (Public Responsibility—Aims in Providing Assistance) Assistance and services for persons who are unable to provide themselves with a minimum standard of living compatible with decency and health is hereby declared to be a special matter of public concern and a necessity in promoting the public health and welfare. The principal aim in providing assistance and services shall be to aid those persons, who can be so helped, to become self-supporting, and to adopt such standards that those persons who cannot become self-supporting may have the opportunity to maintain a decent and healthful standard of living.

[41] Social Security Amendments of 1956, Public Law 880, Title III, Sec. 300, 84th Cong., 2nd Ses.

[42] See Leyendecker, *op. cit.*, Chap. 4, "The Legislative Framework of Public Assistance," pp. 82 to 108.

[43] Chap. 23, paragraphs 436-1 through 444-3, *Illinois Revised Statutes, 1953*, reprinted in *Public Aid in Illinois*, April, 1954, bulletin of the Illinois Public Aid Commission.

Toward achieving these goals, however, variations among the states in performance are pronounced. Large caseloads, under-trained staffs, and the sheer volume of administrative detail have militated against a comprehensive approach to social services. It is also true that the technical processes of determining eligibility have been so demanding that some welfare workers may have derived satisfaction from preoccupation with the technical details of eligibility—to the extent that the client is forgotten. The federal government has recognized the importance of doing more than a minimal technical job, by its provision of funds to assist the states to perform a range of service wider than the technical determination of eligibility. The law calling for the grant of money to state agencies for training personnel was not followed by an actual appropriation of money to finance this training, either by the 84th or 85th Congress, but it is probable or at least possible that action will be taken one day to provide funds for this purpose.

The comparative reduction in volume of public assistance as the result of the extension of coverage in the social insurances may have a considerable effect on the range of services public assistance programs provide. More time should be available for social services beyond that required for the granting of financial aid. It is likely that the case load will increasingly be dominated by people with personal problems requiring intensive and skilled help. The present pattern indicates a trend toward developing the local public assistance agency into a comprehensive family welfare service for the needy, with greater stress on cooperation with such other services as vocational rehabilitation, public health, and child welfare, as well as with voluntary social agencies.

Summary

Public assistance was intended, from the outset of the social security programs, to be the supplementary and residual program of income security. In the first years of experience, however, the slowness of development of the social insurances plus the rapid growth of the public assistance programs threatened to reverse these intended roles. With the broadening of the insurance measures, however, the intended relationship now is nearer realization.

Public assistance includes the federal-state programs of old-age assistance, aid to dependent children, aid to the blind, and aid to the permanently and totally disabled. In addition, throughout the country there are the state-local or local programs of general assistance.

Public assistance has been defined as financial aid to needy people in their own homes or places of residence. Public assistance differs from social insurance in being based on need, and in being noncontributory.

It also differs from the poor law in major concept. It places more stress on the dignity and rights of the individual than did the poor law, offering higher standards of aid, and providing certain safeguards against invasion of the rights or impairment of the dignity of the individual. This must be said with reservations, however, with reference to general assistance, which in many places still is characterized by the philosophy and practice of the poor law.

As a condition of granting funds to the states to assist them in providing programs of financial aid to the needy, the federal government, in the Social Security Act, imposes certain requirements, including some relating to administration. These include requirements that states prevent the use or disclosure of information concerning applicants and recipients, that state programs provide a system of appeals and fair hearings, that any person shall have the right to apply and to have his application acted upon with reasonable promptness, and certain other stipulations relating to the nature of eligibility provisions. In addition, the federal provisions require that all income and resources be "considered," except in aid-to-the-blind programs.

Each of the four categorical assistance programs contains eligibility requirements. In old-age assistance, these include age, residence, need, and property and income limitations. The states vary in these requirements, since in this and all the other assistance programs, the federal law leaves considerable latitude. Some states require citizenship as a condition of eligibility. Many have provisions for requiring help from legally responsible relatives of the recipients. Certain conditions are imposed with reference to persons residing in public institutions, with the exceptions of hospitals and other medical institutions. Another condition is, in some states, that liens may be put on the property of recipients of old-age assistance.

States vary widely in the amounts of old-age assistance paid per individual. The amount is determined by measuring needs in accordance with an administratively determined standard. Many states stipulate the maximum amount which may be paid any individual, even though his need may be for more than that figure will provide.

Aid to dependent children is designed to keep children in their own homes, to avoid removal of the child from his family and home for economic reasons. Eligibility requirements include age, reason for dependency, need, and residence in the home of a relative whose degree of relationship to the child is one specified as acceptable in the law. Reasons for dependency which are specified are death, continued absence from the home, physical or mental incapacity of the parent. In addition to the child, in some states the needs of the guardian with whom the child lives are included in computing the amount of financial aid to be granted.

In this program, also, the states show wide variations. Some states have maximum payments, while others do not. In many states, eligibility is broader than the provisions of the federal law require.

The blind were among the first to claim the attention of the public in the form of special measures of assistance. Pensions for the blind were first granted in the state of Illinois. In this program today, there is a strong emphasis throughout the country on aiding the blind person to become self-supporting. Income-security provisions are closely related to services for the restoration of sight, and to vocational training and placement. In addition to requirements of residence, need, and limitations of aid to people residing in public institutions, state aid-to-the-blind laws specify a degree of blindness, calculated on the basis of the degree that disables a person to support himself. Some states have age requirements.

One feature of this program is its provision that earnings, up to a specified amount, do not prevent a person from receiving a grant of aid. Another is the practice in some states of requiring the blind to accept corrective treatment or services designed to help them achieve a self-supporting status.

The newest of the federally-aided programs of public assistance is aid to the permanently and totally disabled. This is closely related to vocational rehabilitation, and the agencies offering one or the other are encouraged to work closely together. The particular feature of eligibility in this program which distinguishes it from the others relates to the condition of impairment which is deemed to constitute disability. Disability is related to extent of impairment of function, and to how much such impairment affects the person's ability to perform gainful work. Both physical and mental impairment are included in the definitions. In order to qualify, in some states the needy disabled person must agree to accept corrective treatment. Some states exclude certain types of disease from coverage, and further stipulate that this form of aid may be paid only if the individual is ineligible to receive other forms of assistance.

General assistance is the residual form of assistance. It is operated for those needy persons who for one reason or another do not qualify for any other category of federally-aided assistance. In many respects, this kind of assistance carries on the practices of the poor law, although in some areas, the methods have been improved and now represent the more modern concept of public assistance.

In some states the counties are responsible for general assistance programs, in others the townships or the towns. In many places, assistance is still given in the form of vouchers for goods. Standards of amounts of aid are lower generally than those in other types of assistance, with some notable exceptions. Also, the requirements relating to need tend to be more restrictive.

Support for public assistance comes in most states from general taxes. In some states the practice is to earmark certain sources of revenue for this purpose, but this practice is becoming less common.

Public assistance clients, like other people, have a wide range of problems. These may require help in addition to that provided by financial aid. From the inception of the public assistance programs under the Social Security Act, other nonfinancial services have been emphasized. In fact, the earlier leaders in this program recognized public assistance as a means of strengthening family life, and of helping people to live more satisfying and productive lives. The 1956 amendments to the Social Security Act gave further impetus to this philosophy by expressing a statement of purpose which emphasized "helping to strengthen family life and helping needy families and individuals attain the maximum personal independence of which they are capable." Many state programs carry similar expressions of intent.

Variations in ability to carry out such purposes are quite marked. Lack of staff sufficient in numbers, qualifications, or both, the sheer volume of administrative detail, and fiscal limitations have militated against the achievement of such a broad purpose. But the trend is toward the development of agency services focussed on family welfare, even by many agencies which are the only full-time welfare organizations in their communities.

Selected References

1. Abbott, Edith, *Public Assistance* (Vols. I, II). Chicago, University of Chicago Press, 1940.
2. American Public Welfare Association, *The Public Assistance Worker*, April, 1952.
3. Blackwell, Gordon W., and Gould, Raymond F., *Future Citizens All*. Chicago, American Public Welfare Association, 1952.
4. *Public Assistance Under the Social Security Act*, Social Security Administration, 1957.
5. Feldman, Frances Lomas, *The Family in a Money World*. New York, Family Service Association of America, 1957.
6. Hawkins, Charles E., "Recipients of Old-Age Assistance: Their Requirements," *Social Security Bulletin*, Vol. 20, No. 2 (February, 1957).
7. Hoey, Jane M., "The Lack of Money: Its Cost In Human Values," *Social Casework*, Vol. XXXVIII, No. 8 (October, 1957).

8. Hogan, John D., and Ianni, Francis A., *American Social Legislation.* New York, Harper & Brothers, 1956, esp. Chap. 16, "The Social Security Act: Assistance Features."

9. Leyendecker, Hilary M., *Problems and Policy In Public Assistance.* New York, Harper & Brothers, 1955.

10. Martz, Helen E., "The Contribution of Social Work to the Administration of Public Assistance," *Social Casework,* Vol. XXXVII, No. 2 (February, 1956).

11. Miles, Arthur P., *An Introduction to Public Welfare.* Boston, D. C. Heath and Company, 1949.

12. Roney, Jay, "Public Assistance," *Social Work Year Book, 1957.* New York, National Association of Social Workers, 1957.

13. Smith, A. Delafield, *The Right to Life.* Chapel Hill, University of North Carolina Press, 1956.

14. Towle, Charlotte, *Common Human Needs.* New York, National Association of Social Workers, 1945.

15. Wiltse, Kermit T., "Social Casework Services in the ADC Program," *Social Service Review,* June, 1954.

6

The Growing Scope of Public Social Welfare

In this chapter attention will be devoted to programs which feature direct services by the government to the individual or family, as distinguished from income maintenance services, which are based upon the provision of money permitting the individual to purchase goods and services. These are by no means pure classifications. In workmen's compensation, for example, direct payments are made for surgical or other medical service. Even in such a basically income-maintenance program as public assistance, vendor payments directly to the provider of medical care are an exception to the rule of money payments to the individual. In the programs described in this chapter, there are some features of income maintenance. This is certainly true of some of the veterans' allowances, of vocational rehabilitation, where there are subsistence payments during training, and of child welfare services. The classification of the programs, therefore, must rest on the prevailing rather than the absolute character of the services. As previously noted, veterans services include a large measure of income maintenance.

As is true of social insurance and public assistance, these programs have developed to their present size and significance largely during the past quarter century. Although some of them antedate the 1930's, their present nature is a product of recent times. They are still developing. Veterans' programs, which of course are always products of wars, have come into their own in the past fifteen years. Slight tendency is evident that these programs are diminishing, and therefore any study of social welfare must include them as important and growing parts of our national life.

A point which has been made, but which can stand reiteration, is the interrelatedness of welfare services. The reader should keep in mind that one individual may receive services from more than one program, even concurrently. Later in this chapter a case will be presented showing how public assistance, vocational rehabilitation, and employment service agencies work together on one individual's problem. Attention has already been directed to the relationship between workmen's compensation and vocational rehabilitation. A child may be receiving survivors benefits from O. A. S. D. I., and if the amount of social insurance is insufficient, may receive aid under the dependent-children program, and in addition may receive treatment for behavior problems from a child welfare service or for physical restoration from a crippled-children's service. Many services, which share the purpose of improving the status and life situation of the aged person, are being established and improved. Income maintenance through one or both of the public assistance and social insurance programs for the aged, vocational rehabilitation and training, research by the public health services into the causes of physical and mental deterioration in old age, and the encouragement of the development of community services for the older age group, among others, are all parts of the over-all picture.

The succeeding descriptions of these separate services are necessarily brief. The person interested in any one of them would find it a rewarding field for special, detailed study.

SERVICES TO CHILDREN

If a society neglects its children, it threatens itself. This is evident. Our concern for children is rooted in the realization of the importance of providing decent opportunities for them which will nurture their growth and provide them with every chance to make the most of their physical and mental endowments. It is in the interest of society that we give the child a chance for full self-development.)

Children have a special claim on the community. As Fink has stated, without having applied for admission, they enter a world in which the rules are laid down by others, and in which they have little to say about how they will live during their first years of existence.[1] They are dependent on others for the opportunity to grow, and to develop into the kinds of adults who will contribute to society. Enough is known about the forces that shape or distort the personality structure to tell us which features of the environment must be modified and strengthened if the earlier years of life are to be periods of productive growth rather than of unhappy portent.

It is natural to raise the question of where the responsibility rests for insuring this kind of opportunity for children. Generally, the family is considered to have the primary role in meeting the needs of the child. A recent Children's Bureau publication includes this statement,[2] which expresses simply but effectively the role of the family in the nurture of children:

> Children grow and develop in the favorable climate of warm, human relationships, and the nourishing soil of good social conditions. In our society parents have the primary responsibility for providing the care and guidance of their children. Children need good, stable families, capable of providing them with a haven of security in a changing, uncertain world and the incentive to move from one stage of development to another.

The family, it would seem, is the social institution with the obligation to provide the child the protection he needs, and the opportunity to learn to adapt his behavior to the rights and needs of others. If the child receives from the family the security, the

[1] Arthur Fink, *et al., The Field of Social Work* (New York, 1955), p. 183.
[2] *Child Welfare Services—How They Help Children and Their Parents,* Publication No. 359, Children's Bureau, Social Security Administration, 1957, p. 1.

love, and the encouragement he needs, if he is provided the firm but kindly discipline he requires, his chances for a normal life are good.

But the family is not the only resource for the child. He spends many of his waking hours outside the home, especially as he becomes older. As the same publication further stated, the parents' role must be "reenforced by adequate community resources." Among these are: education, recreation, health protection, and social services.

But the family may fail the child. The parents may be unwilling or unable to meet his needs. He may be in danger of being neglected, exploited, abandoned, or abused. Or he may not have any parental care. All or any of these things can and do happen, and this is where the role of government becomes clear. It becomes the responsibility of governmental social welfare services to support the efforts of the family to meet the needs of the child, to meet special needs when the parents cannot meet them, to protect the child from the consequences of harsh treatment, and to provide other facilities, such as foster home or institutional care when the home is unavailable or when it has been adjudged (by the proper authorities) necessary to remove the child from the home.

As was briefly noted in Chapter 3, early public treatment of children who needed care reflected little understanding of their needs or concern for their welfare. In the almshouse with the companionship of the criminal, the mentally ill, and others who bore the weight of community disapproval, the child was scarcely likely to find conditions conducive to wholesome growth. Apprenticeship and indenture, while intended to offer a chance to develop skills, was often characterized by exploitation and by use of the child more for purposes of profit to the master than of good to the child. Exploitation in factories during our early industrial development was far from unknown.

Leadership for better care for children was exercised by voluntary organizations in the nineteenth century. The pioneer work of Charles Loring Brace, in establishing in 1853 the first Children's Aid Society, and the growth of this children's program in many of the larger cities, started the movement for foster home care in this country, and took many children out of institutions. The somewhat later growth of voluntary state-wide services was another landmark, and an important antecedent to present-day programs for children. With the encouragement of movements of this kind in the voluntary field, some states began to provide, in the late nineteenth century, publicly sponsored foster home placement for children who had been in public institutions.[3]

Other public services to children prior to 1900 included the establishment of special institutions for the care of the handicapped—the deaf, the blind, or the mentally retarded. While these institutions, by present-day standards, were far from ideal or even adequate, in most cases they were an improvement over the almshouse. Another development was the special institution for the juvenile offender. Throughout the country in the nineteenth century, states began to provide separate facilities for juvenile lawbreakers. Another important step was the development of the juvenile court.

The present system of tax-supported welfare services for children is a development of the twentieth century. Emma Lundberg, in recognition of this fact, has called this the "century of the child."[4] The early part of the century saw the establishment of the first mother's aid laws for economic assistance. This measure, by giving expression to the philosophy that the child should not be forced to leave his home because of poverty, had great importance.

National leadership in child welfare work began in 1909 when the first White House Conference for Children was called by President Theodore Roosevelt. This was followed by the establishment of the U. S. Children's Bureau in 1912. This Bureau was given the responsibility to investigate and to report upon "all matters pertaining to the welfare of children and child life among all classes of our people," and especially to investigate "the questions of

---

[3] Fink *et al., op. cit.,* Chap. 8, "Welfare Services for Children."
[4] *Unto the Least of These* (New York, 1947), Chap. 6, "The Century of Promise."

infant mortality, the birthrate, orphanage, juvenile courts, desertions, dangerous occupations, accidents and the diseases of children; employment legislation affecting children in the several States and Territories."[5] Investigation, fact-finding, and reporting, developed into activities which had a considerable impact upon national knowledge and understanding of children's problems. Throughout the years the research of the Bureau into problems of child life has had the effect of influencing programs for the child through a succession of reports and studies. Standards of care evolved by the Bureau have had an immeasurable influence on child-care practices, state, local, public and voluntary. While the federal bureau has had no police power or authority to compel action, nor, until much later, any funds to influence state or local activity, the power of facts and knowledge has been demonstrated repeatedly by the response to information provided by the Bureau staff.

Successive White House Conferences have continued to provide springboards to social action for the child. These have been called in 1919, 1930, 1940, and 1950. Each has had a general theme of vital import to child welfare and that theme has been presented in a program which has had consequences in improvement of services to children.

Programs administered by the Children's Bureau prior to the Social Security Act were the Owen-Keating Act of 1916, providing for enforcement of laws against child labor in interstate commerce, and the Sheppard-Towner or Maternity and Infancy Act in 1921. The former was declared unconstitutional in 1918, and the latter, which provided for grants to the states for the improvement of health services, was allowed to expire in 1929.

Meanwhile, in the 1920's, some state and county action was taking place in the child-welfare field. Three states, Missouri, Virginia, and Alabama, developed county programs of child welfare. In other states also, county social service agencies were established and began programs of social service to families. As Miss Lundberg has stated, however, "Although these early pro-

[5] *Act* establishing the Children's Bureau, 37 Stat. 79, approved April 9, 1912.

grams of county boards of child welfare and county boards of public welfare focused attention upon the need for constructive social service upon a county-wide basis, the plan fell short of its promises in most states."[6] Too little money and too little community education about children's needs were blamed for the shortcomings of these services.

Another important development was the establishment of the Child Welfare League of America in 1920. This organization, with its membership of both voluntary and public services, has played an important part in providing nation-wide standards, and in the education of the public about children's needs and the services necessary to meet them.

The current state-federal system of programs for children dates from 1935, with the inclusion of three areas of children's services in Title V of the Social Security Act. The three programs established by this title were those of Maternal and Child Health, Crippled Children's Services, and Child Welfare Services. Federal responsibility for these programs was vested in the U. S. Children's Bureau.

This measure was enacted during a time when acute economic distress was having an extremely damaging effect upon the lives of children. During the Great Depression problems were acute for virtually everyone, and the result was a special perceptiveness of human needs, and a willingness to enact sweeping measures to meet these needs. The times were described by Dr. Martha M. Eliot, formerly Chief of the Children's Bureau, in these words:[7]

> The dark, grim days of the depression were taking their toll in the well-being of children. Many children were not getting the health services or medical care they needed because of financial distress of the family or community. Many children were undernourished. State and local maternal and child health services and medical and hospital care and services for crippled children were being curtailed. Adolescents, unable to

[6] Lundberg, *op. cit.*, p. 143.

[7] "Twenty Years of Progress for Children," *Social Security Bulletin*, Vol. 18, No. 8 (August, 1955), p. 23.

meet the problems arising from unemployment and depleted family resources, roamed the country. Destitute and neglected children were going without needed care and protection as a result of the reduction in State and local appropriations and voluntary contributions for child care services. In some communities, agencies had lists of children living in their own homes under conditions of serious neglect for whom foster care was not available.

One of the programs, that of aid to dependent children, established under Title IV (of the Social Security Act) has been described in the preceding chapter. Let us now look at those for child welfare, crippled children's, and maternal and child health services.

One might ask what place such programs as these have in a social security program. Usually, we think of social security as providing income maintenance rather than direct health or welfare services. On the other hand, security in its more comprehensive meaning may well connote those services designed to strengthen the capacity of people to cope with their environment, and to redress those inequities which are the result of disadvantage due to personal handicaps or inadequate social opportunities.

CHILD WELFARE SERVICES

This program is designed for children who are dependent, neglected, or in danger of becoming delinquent. As part of this responsibility, the federal government provides grants to states to assist them in improving their services to children in these conditions, especially in rural or other areas where special needs exist. This program has made an excellent record of achievement since its enactment. All the states, the District of Columbia, Hawaii, Puerto Rico, Alaska, and the Virgin Islands are now participating in public programs of child welfare. As of 1955, more than half the counties of the nation, representing three-fourths of the country's children. were served by child welfare staffs, even though in some places this consisted of the services of a single worker. Although federal aid has had a profound influence on the scope and nature of services, state and local funds have been used extensively to enlarge child welfare services, and to extend them both to new localities and to new types of service.

As expressed in a statement by the American Public Welfare Association,[8] the objectives of the child-welfare services programs are:

> to help children in attaining the benefits of wholesome growth and development and the responsibilities of adult citizenship, and to protect them from those social, economic, and emotional hazards to which their immaturity renders them especially vulnerable. Because of the inter-relatedness of all aspects of public welfare, the responsibilities for extending help and protection to children are best carried out as an integrated part of the broad range of public welfare services . . .

As this statement suggests, such objectives are best fulfilled within a sound legal framework. Matters of child welfare operate in a complex legal framework in such areas as family relations in the sense of parental responsibility as it relates to children's rights, and need to be continually responsive to constantly changing social conditions. The statement just quoted continues:[9]

> A public child welfare program depends not only upon the organic law which defines its purpose and structure, but also upon related substantive law which determines the status, rights, responsibilities, and relationships of children and their parents; upon the laws which establish other services and procedures affecting children, such as adoption, custody and guardianship, termination of the parent-child relationship, and the licensing of child-caring and placing agencies; and upon the laws on delinquency, dependency, and neglect. Similarly, the relationships between public agencies and other agencies serving children, such as juvenile courts, schools, health agen-

---

[8] *Essentials of Public Child Welfare Services,* Committee on Services to Children, American Public Welfare Association, approved by the Board of Directors, July 9, 1955, p. 3.

[9] *Ibid.*

cies, veterans' agencies, and social insurance, are in their broad
outlines defined by legislation. Thus the legal setting of public
child welfare services consists of a large body of laws which
bear both directly and indirectly upon the child-serving agencies, all of which contribute significantly to the effectiveness
of the program. Moreover, a sound legal base for a public child
welfare program must be fortified with financial support commensurate with the responsibilities and functions which are
legislatively established.

To expand this statement somewhat, the responsibilities of
public child welfare programs require the performance of certain
quite definite functions. These include the development, maintenance and enforcement of standards for the care and protection
of children, the supervision of local public child welfare services,
and the licensing and regulation of voluntary services. Encouraging legislation for the improvement of child welfare services, providing consultation and leadership, maintaining personnel standards, compiling and publishing reports regarding the operation
of the program, research into needs for change in existing programs, maintaining specialized services which are not feasible
for local agencies themselves to offer, developing liaison with
other state agencies serving children, and being the point of
contact and channel of communication with federal services,
should be essential features of every state program, according to
the American Public Welfare Association.[10]

What kinds of services are given by the local agency, the point
where the services are directly provided? Local agency refers
variously to a country or municipal office, or to a district or other
subdivision office of a state agency. The major purpose of child
welfare services is the support and strengthening of the "natural" family. This is the task of the staff person who works with
the child, the parents, and with other members of the family
when there are problems of behavior or neglect. Every effort is
made to keep the child in the home, and to avoid removal or
placement unless it is considered essential and unavoidable.

[10] *Ibid.*

These are situations in which more drastic action is required for the protection of the child. As Edwin F. Hann, Jr., Deputy Director of the New Jersey State Board of Child Welfare declared:[11]

Agencies frequently face family situations where the available services for children are not used. These are instances where, for example, children are being abused, are receiving inadequate food, shelter, supervision, have specific physical or emotional health needs which are not receiving attention and where, on the other hand, the parent or guardian wilfully or through ignorance or incompetence refuses to take necessary steps to correct inadequate care of his child. In such instances, some community group with authority, actual or implied, is required to get necessary action under way, but it should be emphasized that this is not authority in the usual "police" sense, but must be authority combined with the skill of the experienced caseworker.

In such instances, the state must move without the consent of the parents if necessary. Such action is taken only after a complaint of neglect or of mistreatment, and then only after careful study has found no evident possibility of improving the home situation. Then the agency may apply to a court for permission to act on behalf of the child to correct the situation. This comes under the name of protective services for children.

The range of services in child welfare is suggested by the following list from the North Carolina State Board of Public Welfare:[12]

1. Financial assistance under the program of Aid to Dependent Children.
2. Adoption services both to children in need of adoption placement and to applicants wishing to adopt a child.
3. Services to children with behavior difficulties.
4. Services to determine a child's maximum ability, includ-

[11] In a lecture on "Social Welfare Organization," Graduate School of Social Work, Rutgers University, New Brunswick, New Jersey, delivered Nov. 18, 1956.
[12] "Public Welfare Services Available to Children in North Carolina," Information *Bulletin No. 21,* State Board of Public Welfare, Raleigh, North Carolina.

ing psychological services, as well as referral to mental
health clinics, child guidance clinics, and others.

5. Services to children with physical or mental handicaps.
6. Preparation of applications for admission to State schools
   for deaf and blind.
7. Preparation of applications for admission to State institutions for children who are mentally handicapped.
8. Referral to local and other medical resources.
9. Referral to licensed day care facilities in the community.
10. Certification of children for services through other pro-
    grams, including school-health program, cerebral palsy
    hospital, crippled children's program, etc.
11. Cooperative services with schools on special problems in-
    cluding attendance and other school behavior problems.
12. Services to children in need of care as result of neglect or
    dependency.
13. Social studies for courts as an aid in determining custody
    or guardianship of children.
14. Services to juvenile courts and State training schools, in-
    cluding social studies of children referred by the courts
    and supervisory services to children on probation to the
    court or on conditional release from State training schools.
15. Locating and studying foster homes for children for
    licensing.
16. Placement of children away from their homes, when nec-
    essary, in foster homes, child caring institutions, etc.
17. Social studies and supervisory services to children placed
    for foster care across state lines, in accordance with inter-
    state placement statutes.
18. Services to unmarried mothers.
19. Legal responsibility for approval of plans for separating
    a child under six months of age from the mother when the
    placement is with a nonrelative.
20. Issuance of work permits to minors under regulations of
    the State Department of Labor.

In providing services to children in their own homes, the child
welfare worker frequently works through other people to render
the service. He works with the parents, and may deal with the

parents' own personal problems, while helping them to function more effectively in meeting the child's needs. Similarly, one writer notes, "in protective services, the child welfare worker strives to preserve the child's home for him. He does this, however, by helping the parent change his way of behaving so that the welfare of his child is assured."[13]

As the above list indicates, services, including those supporting the child's own family life, and those relating to foster care, must cover a wide range of physical, emotional, and social needs. The placement of children in institutions, the selection of foster homes and the placement of children in them, and the responsibility of working with foster parents, are all most important functions. In the institutions, the modern emphasis is placed on social services designed to help the child develop his ability to live with others.

Other services for children generally include homemaker service, which provides to families temporarily bereft of the care of the mother (because of illness, separation or desertion or divorce, or some other reason), the help of a person who comes into the home to give the care normally provided by the mother.

In addition, the responsibilities of a public child welfare program entail the provision of leadership and guidance in the improvement of all community services available to the child. The American Public Welfare Association defines this kind of state responsibility as follows:[14]

> The state agency should also have authority and responsibility for regulation and standard setting in order to assure minimum levels of service throughout the state whether under public or private auspices. This should include licensing and standard setting for the care and placement of children.
>
> In addition, the state agency, generally, should perform those functions which are necessary to the operation of an effective public child welfare program throughout the state, and which local agencies are, for practical purposes, less able to perform. These functions include: providing technical and professional

---

[13] Helen R. Hagen, "Distinctive Aspects of Child Welfare," *Child Welfare,* Vol. XXXVI, No. 7, Bulletin of the Child Welfare League of America (July, 1957), p. 4.
[14] *Op. cit.,* pp. 4 and 5.

consultation to both public and private agencies; maintaining personnel standards; conducting programs and providing leadership and materials for the improvement of skills and abilities of agency personnel; compiling and publishing reports regarding the operation of the public child welfare program; conducting research to determine the need for modifying the existing services or initiating new services; maintaining specialized services which are needed by children throughout the state and which cannot feasibly be provided by local agencies; developing liaison with other state-wide agencies and organizations which have a relationship to public child welfare services, and with public child welfare agencies of other states; and serving as the state channel of communication with related federal child welfare services.

This statement highlights the function of the state agency in helping to raise the general standards of child care through cooperation with federal and local child-serving agencies, and through working with voluntary services. It also demonstrates the over-all concern of the state for the level of all child care within its boundaries. One other point important to an adequate appreciation of the nature of state responsibility relates to the state's obligation to take leadership in informing the community of special areas of children's needs, and for stimulating necessary action. Like the Children's Bureau on the national scene, the state agencies are expected to study and report on virtually all matters pertaining to child life. This might mean acting on behalf of children with such special problems as emotional disturbance, or calling the attention of the public to inadequacies in provisions for care and treatment of retarded children, or working toward the improvement of the quality of probation and parole. In these and other matters, "Public child welfare services must . . . have the vitality and the leadership not only to keep abreast of changing times but also to serve as an agent of constructive change."[15]

An important area of the public agency's service, from the

[15] *Ibid.*, p. 6.

standpoint both of direct service and of improving standards, is the field of adoptions. This is one of the most publicized problem areas in all child welfare work. It has also been one of the more controversial, as magazine articles, newspaper stories, and radio and television programs often feature accounts of childless couples, abandoned or orphaned children, exploitation of adoption rings throughout the country, and accusations that agency procedures are slow and unproductive, along with other features which attest to the human interest in the whole problem. The child of the unwed mother, or the child in another untenable family situation, may need adoption as the only means of assuring him an adequate opportunity for a healthy start in life. The process of placement and adoption, for which authority rests in the courts, is a painstaking procedure, in which, as Fink notes, "there are actually three basic considerations: the needs of the child, of the own parent (or parents), and of the adoptive parent."[16] There is the child who is difficult to place.

Many adoptions are made independently; that is, without the services of an authorized agency. In fact, the majority at present are made in this way, although as Delli Quadri states, there is an encouraging growth in the number who are placed through agencies, voluntary and public.[17] In a few states, the majority of adoptions are now being made through agencies, which means that the needs of the child are given primacy, and that safeguards are provided against unfortunate mismatching of child and adoptive parents to the detriment of both. Here is a field for productive cooperation at all levels of government, between public agencies and such national voluntary organizations as the Child Welfare League of America, and between state-wide and local private organizations.

When the parents cannot provide the home conditions a child needs, care outside the home may be required.[18] This may be

16 Fink *et al., op. cit.,* p. 212.

17 Fred Delli Quadri, "Child Welfare," *Social Work Year Book, 1957,* p. 152; and see Clyde Getz, "Adoptions," *Ibid.,* pp. 82-87.

18 See Helen R. Hagen, "Foster Care for Children," *Social Work Year Book, 1957.*

necessary either because of inadequacies of the home, because the child has special needs which require a particular kind of facility, or it may be the result of a child being without a home. The foster care facility may be used for the child awaiting adoption, or awaiting a court hearing. There are many factors in this process which require the exercise of skill, understanding, and sound professional judgment. The temporary home must be one which will meet the needs of the child, needs which are individual and almost infinitely varied. Whether the problem is illness, emotional disturbance, physical handicap, delinquent behavior, parental neglect or abuse, or any other of the many problems that children have, foster care requires a study both of the child's needs and the factors in the foster care facility which will meet those needs.

Foster care is a subject worth study in itself. It may refer to homes, to day care centers, or to institutions. They may be operated under either a public or a voluntary organization. If the latter, the agency or institution is subject to licensing by the public authority, usually the state welfare department.

Another of the important areas of service in child welfare is the study, care, and treatment of the child who manifests delinquent behavior, whom we shall deal with in more detail in a following section on Corrections.

Thus far, the discussion in this description of child welfare services has indicated the roles of federal and state agencies. This should not lead to overlooking the importance of the local agencies which perform the functions of direct services to children, of co-operation with local voluntary organizations, and of community leadership in the improvement of standards, within the areas these agencies serve. Variations in local needs, and problems, and in the facilities for meeting them demand the same kinds of competence and concern as those which are demanded of state and federal government agencies.

These are among the problems and services in child welfare. The programs have grown during the years since the first White House Conference in 1909, but much of the development in the size and importance of public services for children has come since the enactment of the Social Security Act.

In the Social Security Act (under Title V), federal aid was earmarked for rural areas. This was done in recognition of the relative paucity of services in rural areas as compared with those in urban ones. The latter were presumed to have voluntary services, as well as public agencies, much better equipped to meet the needs of children. Later the definition under the federal law was broadened to include "areas of special need." The federal influence has been strong, however, on child welfare in all areas of the states. The continuance of the Children's Bureau's traditional role of study, consultation, and reporting, and its influence on standards of child care have done much to shape the character of state and local services to children.

Child welfare services require competent personnel. They demand workers with knowledge, with insight, understanding, and skill. The meaning to the child welfare worker of the responsibility these services entail has been expressed in one state document as follows: "There can be no greater social trust than this responsibility to protect the welfare of a child. It means that at times you as a child welfare worker will have to stand in the place of the parents; you will have to resolve the whole complex of rights and responsibilities and needs of parents, children and other persons; you will have to make decisions which will directly affect the lives of children—and others—for years to come."[19]

Because of the importance of the quality of personnel to the success of the program, a large part of funds for child welfare work have been devoted more to the provision and the improvement of personnel. Much of the money granted to the states from Washington has been used for the education of social workers and others who provide technical skills. State funds, too, have been used for this purpose. In some states child welfare funds are used for payments for foster care. The number of persons who have received professional training for child welfare work is now in the thousands. In 1956 there were 4,829 fulltime professional persons working in public child welfare programs.[20]

[19] "Foreword" to New York *Child Welfare Manual,* New York State Department of Social Welfare.

[20] *Staff in Public Child Welfare Programs, 1956,* Statistical Series No. 41, Children's Bureau, Social Security Administration, 1957.

The professional classifications covered in this number are those of directors, consultants, supervisors, specialists, attorneys, psychologists, statisticians, and case-workers. As of December 1, 1955, child welfare services from public agencies were being received by a total of 282,506 children. This has become a program of major proportions.

The foregoing description of child welfare services should not convey the impression that they are completely adequate, and served by a nation-wide system of people with all the skill and the time necessary to doing a good job. The record of public child welfare services is one of progress rather than of completed achievement. Further research into the needs of the child and the origin of his difficulties, better mobilization of community resources, more complete community education, and more intensive recruitment and training of child welfare staffs are necessary before the performance can match the need.[21]

CRIPPLED CHILDREN'S SERVICES

In Title V, Part 2 of the Social Security Act, the purpose of grants to the states for crippled children's services is stated as follows: "To extend and improve (especially in rural areas and in areas suffering from severe economic distress) services for locating crippled children, and for providing medical, surgical, corrective, and other services and care, and facilities for diagnosis, hospitalization and after-care for children who are crippled or who are suffering from conditions which lead to crippling."

The definition of the exact physical condition which crippled children's services may treat is left to each of the states. All states have programs for children under twenty-one years of age with some degree of handicap. The coverage is much broader than the mere provision of orthopedic care. It includes children who have many forms of handicap, such as defects which lead to problems of locomotion, hearing, sight, speech, muscle coordination, and heart damage. Among the conditions included under these general

[21] For a description of the qualifications needed by a child welfare worker, see Helen R. Hagen, *op. cit.*

classifications are: cleft palate, club feet, deformities of bones and tuberculosis of bone and joint, cerebral palsy, rheumatic fever or other cardiac conditions, damage from severe burns, and deformities which impair the child's appearance. The age maximum for care under the state programs is twenty-one years.

This program, too, is designated especially for rural areas and areas of special need. Again, as in child welfare services, this provision is based on the assumption that larger urban centers have more adequate facilities without state-federal help.

If it were not for crippled children's services, many children would be doomed for life to all the physical and social consequences of their handicaps. Many families able to provide the normal economic requirements of daily living cannot, without severe hardship, take on the expense either of long-time care of many of these conditions or of correcting them. Many of the children in rural areas are remote from the centers of treatment and care. Others have undiagnosed problems. It would be difficult to estimate the numbers who have, for example, some heart damage from undetected rheumatic fever.

The Children's Bureau has given the following estimates of the numbers of children who need various services: [22]

1. 7,500,000 school children need eye care.
2. 2,000,000 children have speech disorders of such severity as to interfere with their social and emotional growth.
3. 1,000,000 children are completely or partially deaf.
4. 1,000,000 children have orthopedic defects sufficiently severe to justify referral to a physician.
5. 600,000 children have or have had rheumatic fever.
6. 245,000 children have cerebral palsy.
7. 240,000 children have epilepsy.

The publication from which these figures are taken states that no one knows how many of these children receive the treatment they need, or how many receive treatment beyond the acute stage of an illness or injury.

What kinds of services are provided in this program? First,

[22] "Services for Crippled Children," Children's Bureau *Folder No. 38,* rev. 1955, Children's Bureau, Social Security Administration, pp. 10-11.

clinical diagnoses are made, in clinics staffed by specialists—by orthopedists, pediatricians, otologists, laryngologists—or other specialties as required. This does not mean that each clinic has all these specialists on its permanent staff, but they do generally have the services available. In addition, the staff may include public health nurses, medical social workers, nutritionists, speech therapists, physical therapists, and others who are skilled in particular areas of the treatment program. These diagnostic clinics are supported by the state-federal programs, and do not charge fees. Various other consultants assist in the process of diagnosis, including a nutritionist who advises on the dietary needs for different kinds of conditions. The foregoing describes the better or more complete clinics. Some, however, operate with only a doctor and a nurse.

Many states, in addition to diagnostic clinical facilities, provide resources for clinical treatment, and other treatment needed by the child. This may include corrective, convalescent, and restorative services. The state agency may help the family by locating the needed treatment facilities, or in many instances, by assuming all or part of the financial costs.

This treatment may be provided either at a publicly financed clinic or hospital, or under contract with a voluntary hospital or a convalescent home.

Crippled children's services generally assume also the responsibility for providing needed prosthetic appliances, such as hearing aids, braces, artificial limbs, etc.

Crippled children's programs have recognized the importance of helping the family with the child's adjustment to his condition, to family life, and to the community. The public health nurse through her assistance with health guidance, and the social worker, through help with social and emotional as well as financial problems, have an important part to play in this program. Frequently it involves extensive co-operation with other public or with voluntary services. It may include an educational program for the handicapped child. It means a working relationship with such agencies as the National Foundation for Infantile Paralysis, with the American Heart Association, the Society for Crippled Children and Adults, the United Cerebral Palsy Association, and many others.

Also important is the task of educating the community to the needs of handicapped children. This means a program of information about the importance of detecting the handicapping conditions, many of which are not always clearly evident.

In 1955, 278,000 children received some kind of physician's service under this program.[23] Of these, 221,000 were seen in clinics, while others were seen in home or office visits. About 48,000 received hospital care, and 3800 convalescent home care.

MATERNAL AND CHILD HEALTH SERVICES

This was the first of the federal-state programs to be established —in the Sheppard-Towner Act—under the Children's Bureau. Even though the act expired in 1929, it is probable that the experience with its provisions had much to do with the development of Title V of the Social Security Act. Under this title, the maternal and child health program is designed to provide or strengthen such services for mothers and children as pre-natal care clinics, well child clinics, health services for school children, dental hygiene and dental care, licensing and inspection of maternity homes, assistance to hospitals through advice on care of the maternity patient or the newborn child, education in nutrition for the mother and child, and related services. The purpose is primarily to prevent natal and neonatal difficulty.

In addition to prevention of pre- and postnatal problems, some states provide medical care facilities. This may include medical and hospital care for premature infants, treatment and hospital care for mothers whose pregnancies have complications, and dental care. Provision of these facilities, however, varies widely among the states.

Much emphasis has been placed upon the education of physi-

[23] *Social Security Bulletin,* Annual Statistical Supplement, 1955, Social Security Administration, Table 85, p. 62.

cians, nurses, and nutritionists. Through the maternal and child health program, funds are made available for in-service training and institutes, as well as for postgraduate training of physicians, nurses and nutritionists. This training may include the payment of tuition in universities in specified amounts for maintenance while in school.

In this program, also, funds are earmarked for rural areas and areas of special need. Here again this is a reflection of the relative lack of facilities in rural sections of the country, or at least the assumption of such a lack. Educating mothers in prenatal and maternity care has been an important function of the physician, the public health nurse, the social worker, and others in this program. Its importance in reducing the incidence of maternal and child death and of promoting good health conditions for newborn infants and their mothers would be difficult to assess. Certainly it has played a very important part in improving health conditions, and in lowering the maternal and infant death rate.

The number of people who have received maternity service or who have benefited by infant and preschool hygiene, by early immunization against infectious disease, by dental inspection, and other services, is literally in the millions. According to the former Chief of the Children's Bureau, Dr. Martha Eliot, state reports showed that in 1954, "under regular continuing programs administered or supervised by the State health agencies, 190,000 mothers attended prenatal clinics, and 432,000 infants and 569,000 preschool children attended well-child conferences, representing a total of 2.8 million visits." Besides this, Dr. Eliot reported, "There were also almost 4.4 million nursing visits for mothers, infants, and preschool children. In addition there were about 2.6 million examinations of school children and almost 2.9 million dental inspections of preschool and school children. About 4.1 million immunizations against diphtheria and smallpox were given."[24]

Achievements cited by Dr. Eliot include the reduction of maternal mortality by 91 percent, and infant mortality by 52 percent between 1935 and 1954. She attributes these reductions to many

24 *Op. cit.*, p. 26.

factors, among which are "the cumulative work of scientific research workers, educators, and the public health and medical professions."[25]

Despite all the improvements brought about in the care of mothers and infants through the state and local maternal and child health programs, authorities in this field hasten to point out the fact that the situation is still far from ideal. Less progress has been made in the reduction of infant mortality during the first month of life. Reduction in maternal mortality has been relative rather than complete. This program, like others, is one in which progress has been made, but in which much remains to be accomplished.

VOCATIONAL REHABILITATION SERVICES

Each year, according to the federal Office of Vocational Rehabilitation, about 250,000 persons come to need vocational rehabilitation. These are some of the people who through chronic illness or injury become unable to engage in remunerative employment. A fraction of these, as we have seen, through workmen's compensation are helped to maintain themselves for a temporary period and to get needed medical care. The extension of Old Age and Survivors Insurance to the permanently and totally disabled over fifty has helped to meet the economic problem for another portion of the disabled. Temporary disability insurance in four states and in the railroad retirement program provide some measure of help to some disabled people. The categories of public assistance, especially aid to the permanently and totally disabled and aid to the blind, give other income-maintenance aid which particularly helps the disabled.

But these by no means meet all the needs of the disabled person who is vocationally handicapped. Vocational rehabilitation is a program of human reclamation. Services are provided for the purpose of developing, preserving, or restoring the ability of disabled men and women to perform useful work. The injury or illness may have incapacitated him for his accustomed employment but some-

[25] *Ibid.*

times with help he can regain his ability to perform the task for which he is trained. Other workers need assistance in finding another kind of employment, and training which will enable them to perform and to establish themselves in new lines of work.

The disabled person, like others, needs to be engaged in productive enterprise, with the satisfaction of being a full-fledged member of society. The public recognition expressed by a program of government service, that disability does not necessarily doom the individual to a life of dependency, is an extremely important contribution to social welfare. In a culture in which employment is so important, the ability to secure and hold a job is to the individual a card of full, rather than associate, membership in society.

In the words of the rehabilitation consultant to the American Heart Association, "one more principle has been recognized: that man must be useful—that he must exercise his mind and body, or both deteriorate—that it is important, economically and socially, as well as psychologically, for a man to contribute to the best of his ability, no matter how small the offering, to the pool of community human resources."[26]

An authoritative estimate places the number of people, as of June, 1954, needing vocational rehabilitation in order to work, at more than two million.[27] This figure is divided as follows:

Group I	(persons 14 to 64 years of age with long-term disability, not in institutions)	1,250,000
Group II	(persons 14 to 64 years of age with long-term disability, in institutions)	190,000
Group III	(other persons 14 to 64 years of age with major chronic conditions not in institutions)	480,000
Group IV	(persons 65 years of age and over with chronic conditions in institutions and not in institutions)	100,000

26 Dr. Frederick A. Whitehouse, "Rehabilitation as a Concept in the Utilization of Human Resources in the Evolving Concept of Rehabilitation," Monograph 1 (Washington, The American Association of Medical Social Workers), July, 1955.

27 "Number of Disabled Persons in Need of Vocational Rehabilitation," Rehabilitation Service Series No. 274, Office of Vocational Rehabilitation, Division of Research and Statistics, Washington, June, 1954.

This figure does not represent the total number of persons who are suffering from some degree of disability. Some are restored to employment without help. Others have a degree of impairment which precludes the possibility of restoration to employment even with help. The two million cited are people who could resume employment if they were assisted by vocational rehabilitation services.

Vocational rehabilitation is the oldest of the modern state-federal programs of social welfare. The Vocational Rehabilitation Act of 1920 provided for grants to the states for services to the disabled, including training, guidance, and placement. This law was enacted for a four-year period, and was successively extended until the Social Security Act of 1935 was enacted. It was one of the programs included in the Social Security Act which substantially incorporated the provisions of the already existing law. The Barden-LaFollette Act (Public Law 113 of the 78th Congress, 1943), took vocational rehabilitation out of the Social Security Act and provided separate legislation.[28] Notable features of this law were the addition of physical restoration services and extension of the program to serve the mentally handicapped.

The Barden-LaFollette Act remained substantially unchanged until 1954, when Public Law 565 of the 83rd Congress provided some very significant amendments. According to a publication of the National Office of Vocational Rehabilitation, these 1954 amendments marked "a new era in the vocational rehabilitation of handicapped men and women."[29] It extended and improved the coverage, strengthened the ties between federal and state agencies, and provided a program of special grants for training and research designed to increase the knowledge and understanding of the problems of the disabled. This law was passed in recognition of the wide gap between the numbers served and the numbers in need of the service. Its objective was the expansion of services to

[28] For an excellent historical account of the history of the program between 1920 and 1944, see Mary E. MacDonald, *Federal Grants for Rehabilitation* (Chicago, 1944), p. 404.

[29] "New Hope for the Disabled," P. L. 565, "The Vocational Rehabilitation Amendments of 1954," Office of Vocational Rehabilitation, 1954.

the point where the number of people being rehabilitated will more nearly coincide with the number of those who could benefit by such service.

It is interesting to note the circumstances under which the various measures for vocational rehabilitation have been passed. The act of 1920 reflected the public concern that vocational rehabilitation of civilians who were injured in work accidents in war industries was fully as important as vocational rehabilitation of those injured in the armed forces. It was intended to stimulate the states to develop their own programs with the tacit assumption that in time the federal government would withdraw from this field. This of course did not happen. The need proved too great for this withdrawal as the provision of services revealed the extent of the problem. The incorporation of this program into the Social Security Act reflected an acceptance of the permanent nature of the federal government's responsibility, in cooperation with that of the states. It was an indication of the part which rehabilitation of the handicapped could be expected to play in a comprehensive approach to welfare. The vocational rehabilitation amendments of 1954, like those of 1956 to the Social Security program, were significant; the far-reaching program changes were an expression of public determination really to cope with the problem rather than simply and contentedly meeting only a portion of the need.

This is, as has been noted, a state-federal program. The states have the basic responsibility for providing the services. The federal government, in addition to administering the grants to the states, provides technical assistance and consultation, and national leadership.

According to the publication referred to earlier in this section, "By the end of 1955," one report stated, "852,000 handicapped men and women have been restored to useful occupations and better living through the public rehabilitation program—642,000 of them since 1943."[30] During the fiscal year 1956, it is reported that 65,640 were rehabilitated.

---

[30] *Ibid.*, p. 168.

Who may qualify for services?

The first requirement is a disability of a handicapping nature. As has been indicated, this might be the result either of disease or of injury. According to a national health survey, a majority of cases are the result of disease, or about 88 percent, with accidents accounting for 10 percent, and congenital conditions about 2 percent of all cases.[31] The more frequent causes in terms of numbers disabled are nervous and mental diseases, arthritis, rheumatism, and allied illnesses; tuberculosis, blindness, and cardio-vascular-renal diseases, according to this same source. The impairment may be either physical or mental. It must be of sufficient severity to constitute a substantial handicap to the individual's ability to perform his usual employment. Another factor of eligibility is the definite possibility that the person could benefit from the service to the extent that he would be able to return to gainful employment.

Nature of service

According to regulations governing vocational rehabilitation, the services include: "Any goods and services necessary to render handicapped individuals fit to engage in a remunerative occupation including: (1) diagnostic and related services (including transportation) required for the determination for eligibility for services, and of the nature and scope of the services to be provided; (2) Guidance; (3) Physical restoration services; (4) Training; (5) Books and training materials; (6) Maintenance; (7) Placement; (8) Tools, equipment, initial stocks and supplies; including initial stocks and supplies for vending stands; (9) Acquisition of vending stands or other equipment, initial stocks and supplies for small business enterprises conducted by severely handicapped individuals under the supervision of the state agency; (10) Transportation; (11) Occupational licenses; (12) Establishment of workshops for severely handicapped individuals; (13)

[31] Marjorie E. Moore and Barkev S. Sanders, "Extent of Total Disability in the United States," *Social Security Bulletin* (November, 1950). Also, Theodore D. Woolsey, "Two Surveys of Disabling Illness," *Public Health Reports* (August, 1952).

Establishment of rehabilitation facilities; and (14) Other goods and services necessary to render a handicapped individual to engage in a remunerative occupation."[32]

The first step in the above is medical diagnosis. This is necessary in order to determine whether the individual is handicapped to the degree that he cannot engage in gainful employment and whether there is reasonable hope that with treatment he may be able to return to remunerative employment. It includes "Medical diagnosis to learn the nature and degree of disability and to help determine eligibility for services, the need for additional medical service, and the individual's work capacities."[33]

Treatment, however, must be accompanied by supportive services. Disability is not a phenomenon isolated in the part of the body directly affected. It involves a total personality and the individual's attitude toward himself, his family, and his future. A major illness or injury is a shattering experience. It means reorientation to a life situation. The mental attitudes must be considered in the determination of potential skills or vocational interests. The family must be involved and its aid enlisted in the disabled person's behalf. As Dr. John A. Millet, a psychiatrist, has said, "The shattering of the usual pattern of equilibrium by the disability implies not only the altered equilibrium within the body and mind of the disabled person, but a corresponding disequilibrium in the environment of which he was a dynamic part."[34] This is with reference to the disabled adult.

The disabled child and the adolescent have also their particular problems and stresses in connection with disability. The child deprived of the opportunities for normal participation in play, the adolescent who sees himself handicapped just as the world is opening up to him, need the most careful kind of guidance and counselling.

[32] Office of Vocational Rehabilitation, Department of Health, Education, and Welfare, *Regulations Governing the Vocational Rehabilitation Program* (Sec. 401.1 (w), Pursuant to Public Law 565, 83rd Congress, 2nd Session, Approved August 3, 1954).

[33] *New Hope for the Disabled, op. cit.,* p. 7.

[34] John A. Millet, M.D., "Understanding the Emotional Aspects of Disability," *Social Work,* Vol. 2, No. 4 (October, 1957), p. 17.

Medical treatment and guidance are related closely to training. The point at which training should begin must be determined carefully, considering not only the individual's improvement in the condition which has led to his problem, but also his own attitude and readiness to undertake this task. Physical restoration may require prosthetic appliances which the disabled person must learn how to use. Placement becomes a process which demands the matching of the individual and his personal as well as his vocational capacities to the demands of a particular enterprise. These services all add up to the need for the exercise of a high degree of skill.

This is not the skill of one particular discipline; that is, of medicine or of psychology or of social work. The task of rehabilitation demands coordinated efforts on the part of the doctor, the nurse, the psychologist, the social worker, the rehabilitation counsellor, the occupational therapist, the physical therapist, and others. Treatment, training, and job placement, are parts of an inseparable whole in vocational rehabilitation. The rehabilitation counsellor is a key person in this enterprise. Outside the medical aspects of treatment, he is the one who carries the load of guiding the disabled person, of helping him to select his training facilities, of assisting him to find a job, and of interpreting to the employer what the handicapped person is able to do. In an increasing number of instances in the states, home industries are being acknowledged as legitimate enterprises for the vocationally handicapped. The counsellor may find himself actually in the business of helping supervise such an operation. He must utilize the information provided by the consultant in medicine, in psychology, or in social work, in developing a plan for the client.

As of July 1955, according to Cecile Hillyer of the Office of Vocational Rehabilitation, close to 1200 rehabilitation counsellors were employed in state agencies, with about 85 percent of them coming from the field of education, and the balance from guidance, psychology, and social work.[35]

---

[35] "New Horizons in Rehabilitation," in *The Evolving Concept of Rehabilitation,* Monograph No. 1, American Association of Medical Social Workers, p. 7.

In the fall of 1954, the federal Office of Vocational Rehabilitation initiated its program of direct grants of funds to educational institutions for the training of rehabilitation personnel. The objectives of these grants, according to Miss Hillyer, are "first, to enlarge the supply of trained personnel to meet the serious manpower shortages in the field; second, to assist in improving the knowledge and skills of those already in the rehabilitative services, and third, to develop a better understanding of rehabilitation philosophy and methods on the part of all professional fields which contribute to the rehabilitation process . . ."[36] Grants have been made in the fields of medicine, nursing, occupational therapy, physical therapy, rehabilitation counselling, psychology, prosthetics education, public health, social work, and speech and hearing therapy.

The breadth of this program reflects the conviction that rehabilitation is a total community process, and that the function of the federal program is to strengthen all community services, as well as the agencies immediately responsible for the administration of vocational rehabilitation. This program continues concurrently with the basic services which have been a feature from the outset. Federal grants are made to colleges and universities to assist them in expanding or strengthening their basic teaching programs to better prepare students to work with disabled people. Institutions receiving rehabilitation teaching grants, may also receive traineeship grants enabling them to award grants to individual students to pay part of the living costs and tuition. In summary, funds are provided for basic professional training and for short-term courses or "institutes."

The purpose of teaching grants to universities has been that of encouraging the development or expanding of subject matter in rehabilitation.

Other federal activities in vocational rehabilitation include special project grants. These are grants to state agencies, or to private nonprofit organizations to defray part of the costs of research or demonstration projects, or for the development of special services or facilities. These projects are selected on the basis of the extent

[36] *Ibid.*, p. 11.

to which they promise findings or solutions to problems which are common to all or to several of the states. The only fiscal requirement in this type of grant is that it may pay only a part, not all, of the cost of the project.

Earlier in this volume, some conclusions were offered regarding public subsidization of voluntary agencies to do a public job, and the suggestion was offered to the effect that this is a practice of questionable merit. The special project grant, however, is quite something else. It is designed to assist the receiving agency to perform a service in the public interest, and is not a method of paying the voluntary agency to do the government's own work.

Relation to other public services

The close association of vocational rehabilitation with other public services has already been noted. The fact is that eligibility requirements for the disability benefits under Old Age and Survivors Insurance brings vocational rehabilitation agencies into direct adminstrative relationship with the social insurance measures. Similarly, many public assistance programs require as a condition of eligibility that the individual applicant or recipient accept vocational rehabilitation if he is able to benefit from the service. Training grants to professional personnel in other agencies as well as in the direct administration of this program are designed to enhance the relationship. The recent amendments to the public assistance titles of the Social Security Act stress the importance of working with rehabilitative services to restore the assistance recipient to employment.

The following case, from the actual report of a county welfare office, illustrates a cooperative approach to rehabilitation on the part of a county welfare office, a vocational rehabilitation representative, and the employment service.[37]

The Case

Mr. Y. is a young married man with four small children. He lost a leg in an accident (not industrial) nearly a year ago, and has not worked since. He uses crutches quite efficiently.

---

[37] *Monthly Report,* Contra Costa County (California) Social Service Department, April, 1957, pp. 2-3.

The doctor reported that except for the amputation, Mr. Y. is in good health. However, because of the nature of this amputation, it has not yet been possible to fit him with an artificial limb and further surgical procedures may be necessary.

The social worker's report indicated that Mr. Y's former employment was in heavy labor of an industrial type, and some ranch work. The doctor said that it would probably not be possible for Mr. Y. even after fitted with a limb, to take a job which would require standing on his feet all day. Both the Employer Contact Representative and the Placement Officer reported that it would probably be impossible to place Mr. Y. in heavy industry due to this physical limitation. The same applied to farm labor.

The social worker reported that Mr. Y. had indicated some interest in training in bookkeeping and drafting, that when he was in high school he had taken some preliminary courses in these fields and had gotten good grades. The worker also presented some of the psychological factors in the situation including the fact that Mr. Y's background was not too stable; that there was a history of separations from his wife and family, and that in the past he had considered himself as something of a bad "boy". However, he seems to have adjusted well to his handicap, declares he is ready to settle down and is eager to begin training.

The Team Approach

The representative of the Bureau of Vocational Rehabilitation said that all factors in the case seem to indicate that Mr. Y. would be a good candidate for Bureau services, depending on the results of their testing and the medical factors as evaluated by Bureau of Vocational Rehabilitation physicians. Both of the Employment Office representatives indicated that Mr. Y. had not been previously known to their service, and that there was no record of vocational testing or counselling.

The doctor asked whether, if the Bureau of Vocational Rehabilitation assumed responsibility for Mr. Y's retraining, they would also assume responsibility for his future medical care, including the artificial limb. The Bureau representative indicated they would, provided that testing confirmed the impression that Mr. Y. would be eligible for Vocational Rehabilitation services.

The social worker suggested that in view of Mr. Y's previous history of restlessness and instability a real effort be made to involve him in the vocational planning, and to be sure that it was *his* plan and not one projected on him. She also suggested that if possible, consideration be given to using the private doctor who treated Mr. Y. after the accident if further surgery is necessary, inasmuch as Mr. Y. has tremendous faith in this physician.

The Decision

The decision was that the case of Mr. Y. would be accepted by the Bureau of Vocational Rehabilitation for their testing and vocational counselling procedures, and further medical rehabilitation, if necessary. The social worker will continue to provide casework services in support of the total effort and the Social Service Department will continue financial assistance during the training period.

NOTE: This is not an unusual occurrence. The process is repeated many times during each year. This is presented merely to illustrate one method used by the Department in its continuing attempt to bring about the return of public assistance families to self-support.

In this as in other welfare programs, the approach to the problem is increasingly being recognized as tridimensional: first, the improvement and the administration of the service, and the extension of its scope to meet the needs; second, the enlistment of different disciplines or professions which have a contribution to make in a coordinated approach to the problem, and third, the engaging of the interest of the whole community, including cooperative arrangements with other agencies and services.

MENTAL HEALTH PROGRAMS

It would be difficult if not impossible to present an exact quantitative picture of the incidence and cost of mental illness. It is a staggering figure, which includes the expenses of treatment and care, to say nothing of the loss of productive effort of individuals so afflicted as to be incapable of adequately functioning. Yet even the count of those receiving treatment in hospitals and clinics, or in other treatment facilities, tells only part of the story. Who can calculate the social cost of the individual, perhaps prominently placed and influential, who views society in distorted focus. As an earlier American leader in mental health, Dr. Frankwood Williams, observed some years ago in words that have a contemporary sound:[38]

> The amount of damage that the editor of a great daily can do, socially well placed and influential, economically independent, intellectually keen, and well trained in the best of our universities, but so emotionally handicapped that he can see life, or certain aspects of life, only through lenses that he has had to put on as a matter of personal protection against his own unsolved, or badly solved, or partially solved personal emotional problems—the amount of harm that such an individual, editor, politician . . . , judge, minister or priest, school teacher, industrialist, labor leader, economist, sociologist, psychologist, social worker, psychiatrist, can do, is unlimited, unpredictable . . .

Mental illness is not a precise disease entity, but is rather a complex group of behavior manifestations, difficult to diagnose in many instances, and still more difficult to classify. As has been stated by two authorities, "Even if we were to agree on whom to count, we still have the problem of devising standard methods for case finding and diagnosis needed for separating the population into those who have a mental disorder and those who do not."[39]

The figures on the numbers in mental hospitals, however, are indicative of the magnitude of the problem of mental illness, even though they do not tell the complete story. Dr. Kenneth Appel points out that by present experience, it could be assumed that

38 "Finding a Way in Mental Health," *Annals of the American Academy of Political and Social Science*, May, 1930, p. 10.

39 R. H. Felix, and Morton Kramer, "Extent of the Problem of Mental Disorders," *Annals of the American Academy of Political and Social Science*, March, 1953, p. 5.

one of twelve babies born in this century at some time will enter a mental hospital. With one million persons in mental hospitals throughout the country, and with about half the hospital beds in the nation occupied by mental patients, this seems a reasonable calculation. It includes state and local hospitals, Veterans Administration facilities, and private hospitals. It does not include the neurotic, or others whose impairment is not so severe as to require hospitalization. Appel calls attention to the fact that there are other figures of considerable significance annually, including the fact of 17,000 suicides, 7,000 murders, 3,500,000 problem drinkers including 300,000 severe alcoholics, and those statistics of the numbers of narcotics addicts, criminals, delinquents, and others who manifest serious personality problems.[40] The number of patients in hospitals has increased over the years to the point that, some people believe, one day the bulk of the population might at some time need hospital care for mental illness. It is known that not only the gross number but the proportion of the population in mental hospitals has steadily risen during the century from 1.9 per 1,000 people in 1903 to 3.8 per 1,000 in 1950.[41]

Felix and Kramer suggest, however, that several factors account for this rise, of course including the possibility but not the certainty of a true increase in the incidence of mental illness, but also the effect of the increasing proportion of aged persons—subject to degenerative diseases that may have accompanying problems of mental illness, the increased awareness and knowledge of mental illness, and the greater confidence in mental hospitals today with our consequent increased willingness to use them, and the growth in mental hospital facilities.

All of these factors, including the known numbers of those hospitalized, or those receiving extramural or outpatient care, as well as others whose behavior suggests the need for skilled help, justify the conviction that mental health is certainly one of the most vitally important health and welfare fields.

[40] "Mental Health and Mental Illness," *Social Work Year Book, 1957* (New York, National Association of Social Workers, 1957), pp. 368-369.
[41] Felix and Kramer, *op. cit.,* p. 9.

The term mental health as employed today has a relatively recent origin, as indeed does the accompanying concept of therapy. Mental illness was for centuries a subject which the public regarded with superstitious awe. It has been pointed out, however, that the ancient Greeks had a more enlightened attitude toward mental illness than did western Europe or the United States even in the eighteenth century. The bizarre behavior of the mentally deranged aroused fear on the part of the observer, who in the period during and after the Middle Ages was likely to regard the sufferer as the victim of demoniacal possession, or a purveyor of witchcraft. In a period which featured a strong belief in personal moral responsibility, the mentally-ill person was considered to be suffering the consequences of his own misdoing.

How these ill people were treated reflected this attitude toward them. In Europe, in the seventeenth and eighteenth centuries, special institutions or "asylums" were provided. In addition, many were lodged in jails and workhouses. But no matter where they were lodged, they were accorded the most callous and even cruel treatment. Neglect and indifference were their lot. The term "bedlam" today suggests the horror which was the lot of those incarcerated in such asylums, the term being derived from the name of a real English hospital. While by the end of the nineteenth century such leaders as Pinel in France were beginning to work for more humane treatment, the characteristic lot of the mentally ill or deranged was still a most miserable one until quite recent times.

In this country, the local jail and the almshouse were common abodes for sufferers from mental illness in colonial times and in the first period of our national history. The first general hospitals to accept mentally ill persons were the Pennsylvania Hospital, in 1752, and the New York Hospital, in 1792. The earliest special hospital for mental patients was established at Williamsburg, Virginia, in 1773, and the second was the Friends' Asylum in Frankford, Pennsylvania, in 1797. State institutions were established in six states by 1835.[42]

---

[42] *The Mental Health Programs of the Forty-eight States,* The Council of State Governments, Chicago, 1953, Chap. 1, "History and Background."

Much could be said about the influence of certain pioneers in the development of more humane and understanding care of mental patients in this country. Certainly mention could be made of Dr. Benjamin Rush (a signer of the Declaration of Independence) who really inaugurated the study of psychiatry in this country through his publication of a book on *Medical Inquiries and Diseases of the Mind* early in the nineteenth century. In 1841, Dorothea Dix began a long crusade to improve some, establish and enlarge other institutions for the care of the mentally ill. She found a prevailing and shocking inhumanity in the treatment of the insane—in unclean jails, almshouses, and other institutions which incarcerated all manner of criminal and diseased persons. Treatment in these as well as in so-called asylums included chaining, confinement in strait jackets, flogging, and drugging into stupor. As the result of the efforts of Miss Dix, thirty-two institutions for the care of the mentally ill were founded or enlarged. Another person who made an early and significant contribution to mental health is Clifford Beers, who himself at one time was a patient in a mental hospital. In 1907 he published *A Mind That Found Itself*, which described in detail the sufferings and inadequate treatment he underwent as a patient. He used his experience to bring about better treatment for others. As the result largely of his efforts, the Connecticut Society for Mental Hygiene was formed in 1908, and a year later the National Committee for Mental Hygiene was founded.[43]

Another important bench mark in the development of mental health programs was the establishment of the mental health clinic, "The Juvenile Psychopathic Institute," in 1909 in Cook County (Chicago), Illinois. This clinic was operated in connection with the juvenile court, and was under the direction of Dr. William Healy. Its major contribution was the idea of treating delinquency as a type of disorder amenable to psychiatric treatment.

The growth and improvement in mental health services in the

[43] See Albert Deutsch, *The Mentally Ill in America,* rev. ed. (New York, 1949), for the historical development of mental health programs; also Arthur Fink *et al., The Field of Social Work,* rev. ed. (New York, 1955), Chap. 9, "Psychiatric Social Work."

twentieth century has been made possible by our increasing insight into the nature and possibilities for the treatment of mental illness. While the greater humaneness of the treatment of the mentally ill in institutions, influenced by Dorothea Dix, Beers, and others, was a considerably important expression of a more enlightened attitude toward this affliction, it was still necessary that a concept of treatment be added to that of improved care and custody. It was also important that the less severe disorders receive attention, and that to the function of treatment there be added the ideas of social rehabilitation and of prevention of disorders.

At the beginning of the twentieth century, a far-reaching change, was occurring in the approach to mental illness. Freud, through his studies of hysteria, was evolving an approach based on a dynamic theory of causation—the concept that mental disorders have their roots in early experience, and that the actual onset of illness represents the culmination of a long series of disturbing experiences. The psychosomatic approach to understanding the individual, and to the methods of treatment, was supplanting the older concept that mind and body were separate. To this concept, the psychoanalytic school added that of the importance of personal social experience, particularly with reference to those within the family group, that these experiences are particularly significant as determinants of the future stability of the individual. Other great leaders who further opened the frontiers of understanding mental health include Jung, Adler, Rank, and in this country, Meyer, the Menningers—William and Karl, and many others.

The influence of the two World Wars is frequently cited as having had a profound effect on the development of the treatment of mental illness. The work of the American Psychiatric Association in mobilizing the medical and psychological resources for study and treatment of persons who were cracking under emotional strain in World War I, the so-called "shell shock" cases, led to a more profound realization that all individuals have a maximum tolerance point for strain. World War II "added tremendous impetus to the development of American psychiatry because of the need for psychiatric screening devices in recruitment and effective therapies for combat casualties."[44] The development of out-patient work by the mental hospitals, and the increased emphasis on the study of mental illness and mental health, the development of more effective communication among the biological and social sciences in this study, and the development of such professional services as psychiatry, psychology, social work, psychiatric nursing, all have furthered the development of mental health, both its treatment and preventive aspects. The growth of child psychiatry, and of the child guidance clinic deserve prominent mention as influential factors in the development of mental health.

Few fields provide a better example of the influence of voluntary effort on the growth of a public service than does mental health. The influence of the mental health associations, national, state, and local, has been significant. What Dr. George Stevenson calls "The citizens mental health movement" has provided leadership in the improvement of services throughout this century, and continues to play a significant role in furthering the mental health programs of government, only one of the movement's several functions in the field.[45]

Impetus to the later development of state and local services for mental health was provided by the inclusion in Title VI of the Social Security Act of grants to states for allocation to local health districts for the development and improvement of health services. While this was aimed at general public health services, rather than the particular field of mental health, it paved the way for later legislation in this specific field.

Passage of the National Mental Health Act of 1946 was an important forward step in the improvement of public services in mental health. This measure, which established the National Institute of Mental Health in the federal Public Health Service,

[44] *Training and Research in State Mental Health Programs,* The Council of State Governments, Chicago, 1953, p. 23.

[45] See Dr. George S. Stevenson, "The Citizens Mental Health Movement," Annals of the American Academy of Political and Social Science, Vol. 286 (March, 1953), p. 92.

also provided for grants to states for the improvement of basic services in mental health, and for direct research and training grants to universities, hospitals, and other public and private institutions. The authorization of an amount to be used annually by the states for the establishment and expansion of mental health programs, state and local, has stimulated the growth of community clinics.

State and local response to the federal aid program has been pronounced. As of 1951, 330 community clinics had been established in this country, with 158 started as a direct consequence of the federal grants, and with 172 which had antedated the National Mental Health Act improving their services as the result of federal aid.[46] And since 1951, the development of new clinics has continued.

The mental health clinics, staffed by psychiatrists, social workers, and psychologists, offer treatment to people who need therapy but who do not require custodial care, that is, are able to take care of themselves in their customary surroundings. Some of these clinics are operated in connection with hospitals, but many are not. Clinic personnel also work with the mental hospitals in connection with the admission of patients, and with the rehabilitation of those who may be ready for discharge, to re-enter their homes and communities.

To the important functions of treatment of mental disorders, with attention to the social as well as to the physiological and emotional aspects, and research into the cause and treatment of mental illness, we must add prevention of mental illness. Prevention is receiving considerable attention today, as research is under way to improve scientific knowledge of mental illness. As more is learned of the cause of mental illness, more success is possible in improving home, school, and other conditions which are likely to promote rather than impede healthy development. Actually, some people describe the objective as being not so much that of prevention in the sense of forestalling the onset of disease, as one

[46] George I. Levinrew, *Review of the Proceedings of the Annual Conferences of State Chief Psychiatric Social Workers, 1949-1953*, unpublished manuscript prepared in connection with advanced study at the University of Pittsburgh School of Social Work, Feb. 1955, p. 1.

of promotion of better conditions, of a more favorable climate for mental health.

Public education is necessary, however, to any far-reaching development in mental health. People generally have not entirely extricated themselves from the combination of awe and fear of mental illness as something mysterious, and disgraceful. Bizarre behavior still tends to evoke mixed responses from people, who continue in some degree to demonstrate the statement by two earlier writers on the subject of mental hygiene, that "Mental disease in all its forms has an appeal which both fascinates and terrorizes the untrained."[47] The statement still holds true, although the evidence is conclusive that progress has been made in developing a more enlightened public attitude, as more people are willing to seek help for emotional and mental disorders.

The improvement of facilities for diagnosis, treatment, and rehabilitation of the mentally ill, and efforts to improve public understanding of mental health through the establishment of the community clinic as a focus of leadership in the field are important features of the program. In recent years stress has been laid on the need to integrate mental health services into community life. This means reaching people through the various social institutions through which they meet their manifold needs. It means community-wide planning for services designed to treat and to prevent this most prevalent of human ills. That mental health is a community-wide problem, and should have a program of similar dimension, is stated by Warren Lamson, in these terms:[48]

> This need for integrated service in a community has many interesting aspects. It means that instead of thinking of the several agencies which make the community, it is sounder to think of the community as one comprehensive agency for its people. Then public health, education, social work, public safety, industry, the church, recreation, the court, and other agencies become part of the whole, parts that depend upon each other. No longer, then, can any one of these claim full authority, even

---

[47] Ernest R. Groves, and Phyllis Blanchard, *Introduction to Mental Hygiene,* (New York, 1930), p. 10.

[48] "Integrating Mental Health Services Into the Community Health and Welfare Program," *Journal of Psychiatric Social Work,* September, 1955, p. 244.

within its own sphere. The practical point of this is that mental health planning for a community cannot be restricted to the agencies that are specifically labeled 'mental health'. The mental health of the community is in the hands of the schools, the churches, the courts, the social agencies, and many other organizations.

This method of "permeation" of a community with mental health concepts and purposes offers more hope for the future reduction of mental illness and the promotion of better conditions for mental health than does the case-by-case treatment of the individual after the onset of disturbance.

Another development of importance is the enlargement of an interdisciplinary approach to the problem. The roles of psychiatrist, psychologist, and psychiatric social worker have been acknowledged in the "team" approach to treatment. Increasing involvement of the social scientist, social psychologist, sociologist, and social anthropologist, is resulting from growing recognition of the possibilities in study both of the interplay of social environment and individual experience in the causation of mental disturbance, and of the possibilities for social organization designed to provide better conditions for the healthy functioning of the personality. Some of the most significant discoveries may come from the laboratory of the social situation rather than from that of the clinic or hospital.

Advances have been made in this field. It would be a mistake, however, to assume that there is a lack of serious problems. There are many obstacles to successful achievement of the goals of mental health services which those engaged in this field are the first to acknowledge.

One obstacle is the lack of any precise definition of or general agreement on the term "mental health." The very inclusiveness of meaning which we have just described hampers the precision of thinking needed to mount a carefully designed program in a community. As Lamson points out, "The term has been used to describe any one of several levels of social and individual behavior, depending on the special interest of the professional discipline or the individual using it."[49] A definition that is too broad or general, while increasing the numbers of persons and disciplines who are enlisted in the programs, also has the handicap of making integration into community services more difficult, Lamson adds. The greater the variety of fields engaged in the service, the more complex the problem of coordination of efforts becomes.

Another of the problems is the shortage of personnel. The supply of professional personnel is short, and the efforts, through the training grants, to increase it do not promise to afford sufficient numbers in the foreseeable future to meet the enlarging goals of mental health work. Even the agencies which clinical personnel look to as allies face the same difficulties of staff shortages, whether of teachers, nurses, psychiatrists, psychologists, social workers in schools, family and children's services, or in public welfare.

Mental hospitals, too, are far from ideal. Overcrowded facilities and understaffing remain severe problems. Sufficient money support for services is not always forthcoming in many of the states. Many local communities have no hospital facilities for temporary confinement of persons suffering from severe mental illness. The lack of adequate rehabilitative services in communities, hospital authorities say, results in the continued hospitalization of persons who, if such help were available, might be restored to their home situations.

These and other problems support the conclusion that, although advances have been made in this field, and the public through agencies of government is showing encouraging support of these programs, the situation in mental health provides no reason for complacency. In fact, in some states, conditions in mental hospitals still are shockingly bad.

CORRECTIONAL PROGRAMS

With all the lurid attraction which crime holds for people, and with the space criminal acts receive in the newspapers and the

[49] *Ibid.*, p. 244.

crime programs in the various entertainment media, it may seem strange that we actually do not know how much crime is committed each year. We do not have precise national figures on this subject, although efforts have been under way for some time to develop a nationally uniform system for reporting crimes. The figures in the statistical abstract of the Bureau of the Census are helpful, with their reports of crime rates—both rural and urban— but they are far from complete in coverage, and do not allow for the many existing variations in classification of criminal acts, and in the methods of reporting them. Nevertheless, the figures that are available present a picture of a serious problem, of a crime rate of sufficient magnitude to justify serious public concern.

Few subjects have received more attention in the field of social problems than has juvenile delinquency, yet here, too, information on its incidence is incomplete and inexact. Where there are special courts dealing with juvenile problems, the figures are generally available, but in many places such special courts do not exist.

Juvenile delinquency refers to those acts committed by a juvenile which, if committed by an adult, would be considered criminal. (The range of ages included in the term "juvenile offender" varies in different jurisdictions, as will be discussed below.) This definition is not complete, however, since in some instances, truancy, running away from home, behaving in an ungovernable manner, are classified as delinquent, and are distinctively juvenile acts which do not have counterparts in adult actions. According to the Children's Bureau, "Juvenile delinquency as defined in most juvenile court statutes is the violation of a law or municipal ordinance by persons of juvenile court age, or conduct on the part of such persons so seriously antisocial as to interfere with the rights of others or menace the welfare of the community."[50] According to statistics available from the juvenile courts, delinquency rates have been increasing since 1949, with a rise of 70 percent between 1948 and the end of 1955. As the Children's Bureau points out, the rise in the number of delinquency cases cannot be explained

[50] *Juvenile Court Statistics, 1955,* Children's Bureau, Social Security Administration, 1956, p. 1.

away by population growth. The 70 percent rise in the number of delinquency cases during that period compares with a growth of only 16 percent in the child population, that is, those ten through seventeen years of age.[51]

The administration of criminal law in this country is a complex as well as an extremely important function. Its various aspects include law enforcement, prosecution of the offender, judicial decision, and correction. While these elements are in an administrative sense different tasks, it is becoming increasingly evident that they must be related to each other in practice. Lack of communication and cooperation among these parts of the process of the administration of justice inevitably would have undesirable consequences. If the police officer, the office of the prosecutor, the judge, and the correctional officer do not communicate with each other, justice will not be done.

Turning to the juvenile court, we see a different approach from that which is followed by the regular criminal court. The juvenile court is a civil rather than a criminal court. The establishment of the first such court, in Illinois in 1899, was in effect an extension of the principle long recognized in common law, namely that the child under seven could not be held to have the ability to distinguish between right and wrong, and the child between seven and fourteen could not clearly distinguish between good and evil, and therefore children should be exempt from the criminal law.[52] The juvenile court movement spread rapidly throughout the nation following its beginning in Illinois, until today it is an integral part of the administration of justice throughout the country. While laws from state to state may differ with reference to the age of responsibility for individual acts, they generally recognize a point in the later teens when the child may be considered responsible for his acts.

The nature of corrections work has been defined (by a panel

---

[51] *Ibid*, p. 7. The Children's Bureau points out that the data on this trend are based on reports from 383 courts whose statistics are suitable for comparison. These courts include within their jurisdictions about one-fifth the number of children in the country.

[52] See Grace Abbott, *The Child and the State* (Chicago, 1938), Vol. II, Part II.

studying the role of social work in this field) as the service organization of the administration of criminal justice.[53] It begins after the offender has been apprehended. It includes probation, institutional service, and parole, as well as social work in cooperation with the police and in connection with prosecution and detention. It does not include protective services for children. Without attempting to go exhaustively into the history of this field, it should be noted that corrections represents a change both in purpose and kind of punishment, from those of destruction of the offender to the current effort to maintain or restore him as a part of society.

Since 1800, most important developments have occurred in the administration of justice. These developments have had a profound effect on the whole field of correction work. They have included:[54]

> The implementation of a doctrine of equality regardless of class or economic status.
> The substitution in the penal system of institutional custody and supervision in the community for the punishments of death, mutilation, and banishment.
> The differentiation among offenders on the basis of age for the determination of criminal responsibility and for treatment purposes.
> The provision of probation and parole for those offenders who can remain in the community.
> The provision of various kinds of institutions for the different classes of offenders.
> The attempt to use the institution as an instrument for reform of the individual.

Probation was developed during the last half of the nineteenth century, although the forerunner to this program was the act of a Boston shoemaker, John Augustus, who is credited with beginning the movement in 1841 when he stood as surety for a drunkard who otherwise would have been sent to jail. In 1878, probation was

---

[53] This definition is taken from the minutes of the panel, which met under the aegis of the Committee on Corrections, Council on Social Work Education, 1957.

[54] From an (unpublished) statement prepared for the Committee on Corrections of the Council on Social Work Education, 1957.

officially initiated in Boston, and this was followed by the rapid development of a state-wide movement in Massachusetts. The origin of the juvenile court in 1899 gave impetus to the growing concern for the problems of the juvenile offender, and to the growth of probation for juvenile offenders. As we have seen (see p. 221) the juvenile court gave rise to the mental health clinic for children, the "Juvenile Psychopathic Institute" in Chicago in 1909, for the treatment of delinquency as a mental disorder.

During this century, an increasing knowledge and understanding of human behavior has been influential in the development of a greater emphasis on the rehabilitation of the offender. He has been perceived increasingly as an object of help rather than as a subject for punishment. This is not a universally-held view of the offender, however, nor does it mean that an attitude of understanding of all types of offenders always prevails. People still may have serious reservations about an offender. He has, after all, committed an offense against society. If the crime is one of violence, and particularly if the circumstances are especially shocking, people have considerable difficulty in letting their concern for the offender overcome their revulsion against his crime.

Nevertheless, considerable progress has been made. It has at times been more difficult to achieve than progress in treatment of other kinds of social problems, such as mental illness. The mentally ill are more generally accepted as proper objects of concern. If they have performed acts of violence, their mental condition is considered an extenuating factor. Often the mentally ill person has been harmful chiefly to himself, and so has not aroused the reaction that is likely to follow acts of violence against other people or other people's property.

When we look at the services of correction, we need to realize that they do not cover all people who have committed crimes, or all who are arrested for such crimes. Actually only a part of the offenses committed become correctional service cases. Between the commitment of the offense and the conviction of the offender there are many possibilities which reduce the number of those actually punished. Not all, for example, of the felonies committed result in arrests; among those arrested, many do not get to court for a preliminary charge, but may be released beforehand; of those who do come to court, some are acquitted. The following figures indicate the relationship in numbers between offenses committed and convictions obtained. They are taken from a California report, a state which has a uniform state-wide system of crime reporting.[55]

Felonies reported to police	137,838
Felony arrests	58,211
Felony cases disposed to court for preliminary charge	23,723
Convicted of felony charge	14,238

From these figures, it appears that in California in 1953 about one-tenth of the felonies committed resulted in conviction, and about one-fourth the felony arrests resulted in felony convictions.

Of the three areas of correction, probation, institutional services, and parole, we will look first at the general nature of probation.

If the court decides that the offender, while guilty of the offense, shall be placed on probation, it is deciding to permit him to remain in the community, so long as he meets the conditions which are specified for him. The probation officer's work has two major parts. These are (1) presentence investigation of the offender, and (2) postsentence supervision of him. The former is utilized by the court in deciding whether probation or institutionalization is the best method of dealing with the offender, since the report provides a picture of the family background, the circumstances of the offender's life, and an estimate of the chances for a successful use of the probation experience. Following such an investigation, the probation officer may or may not recommend probation. The decision, of course, is in the hands of the court. This process requires a careful appraisal of the circumstances relating to the offender's prospects for living successfully in the community, and for making a satisfactory adjustment to his problem.

[55] Figures from *Crime in California, 1953,* Dept. of Justice, State of California, 1953, pp. 8, 12, 13, 17; the felonies to which this report refers are: homicide, robbery, assault, burglary, theft except auto theft, "forgery and checks," rape, "sex except rape," and "all other."

Supervision of the offender who is placed on probation requires the exercise of skill in the use of authority. Certain requirements must be met, and rules must be observed. Many of these rules compel the probationer to live a life much more restricted than are the lives of others with whom he associates every day. He may feel the weight of disapproval by people who resent what he has done. While authority is a necessary feature of probation, it must be used by the probation officer in a firm but sensitive manner, designed to foster the capacity of the probationer to adapt to—or get away from—the circumstances of his life situation, and to take responsibility for his own behavior.

The probation office may be attached to the court, or it may be a separate agency to which the court commits the offender. James V. Bennett, Director of the Bureau of Prisons of the United States Department of Justice, states that probation is in effect for juveniles under the laws of all the states, and for adults in most. He notes that about 30 percent of the 3,000 counties have no organized probation service, and that "in many others the proper administration of probation is hampered by an insufficiency in the number of trained probation officers and low salaries."[56]

As Fink *et al.* have noted, "Despite the many enthusiasms for the ideal of probation, neither community opinion nor professional practice has yet succeeded in outmoding the institutional care and treatment of the offender."[57] We still have and need training schools, reformatories, and prisons. There are instances in which the child, or the adult offender requires institutional care and treatment. Both institutions and treatment are or should be organized according to grouping of offenders, that is by age, by sex, by severity of delinquency or criminal history, and by the extent of the security problem.

People who have been sentenced to correctional institutions generally pose problems of safety and of security. This fact in itself has an important influence on the function of personnel, and on the structure of the institution. Much in the institution depends on the emphasis which pervades it in determining the extent to

[56] "Corrections," *Social Work Yearbook, 1957*, p. 203.
[57] Fink *et al., op. cit.,* p. 354.

which treatment is an integral part of institutional administration. Many institutions fall far short of providing ideal conditions conducive to rehabilitation, but there is evidence of a strong movement for the improvement of the methods of custody and treatment.

Both the offender and the community present problems to the corrections officials who seek to render a constructive service. The offender is more than likely to be resentful, and to compound the attitude which got him in trouble by bitterness at being deprived of his liberty. The community, as we have mentioned, does not readily accept the offender as an object of sympathy, and may be reluctant to provide the support in money, materials, and staff necessary to do a good job with these offenders.

Many of the institutions now have reception centers, to which the offender comes for study, diagnosis of his problem, and for a determination of the kinds of treatment he needs. The concept of classification, or individualization of the prisoner, through study of his background, the environmental factors that have influenced his life, and his personality or behavior patterns, has been developing for years, although it is not yet fully developed. The correctional institutions are increasingly being staffed by professional personnel, with psychologists, psychiatrists, social workers, sociologists, and others who contribute to the understanding and treatment of the offender. Education or vocational training are among the features of correctional institutions.

A distinguished leader in corrections, Sanford Bates, points out the change that has taken place in our attitude toward the institutionalized offender, from the days when "Convicted criminals went to prison to be immured, to be forgotten, to be punished, to be cleansed of their sins." He notes the influence of the discovery that punishment did not have the reliability it was thought to have, and that the variety in the human personality meant that what was helpful to one person might be useless or harmful to another. Furthermore, he adds, a significant change in attitude took place when people came to realize that many people were released from the institutions to become a part of community life.[58] This is why it is important that the offender be prepared for life outside the walls, and that attention be given to helping him change to the extent necessary for favorable adjustment in the community.

Parole refers to conditional release from the institution before the term of imprisonment has expired. The parole officer has the task of helping the offender make the difficult transition from a controlled to a free environment. The parolee knows that he is not, like other men, free to live in any way he chooses, but that his behavior, instead, must conform to standards set by other people —by the parole laws of his state. The role of the parole officer is that of supporting the offender in his efforts to re-establish himself. Much of the treatment is similar to that utilized in probation, although the problems which have resulted in criminal behavior may be more deeply ingrained in the personality of the parolee, and may have been aggravated by imprisonment. The parolee is likely to bring to his new status the accumulated resentments, the insecurity about his status, a large measure of hostility, all of which may be further intensified by the difficulty of finding a place in society. The parole officer must work in a skilled and sensitive manner with the parolee, and must utilize community resources effectively to assist the parolee to readjustment.

While probation, institutional custody and treatment, and parole, are separate services, it is important that they be related. Many offenders experience all three stages in the course of one sentence. The information secured by the probation officer regarding the community and family life of the prisoner, his past personal and behavioral history, can be of great assistance to those who are working with the offender in the institution. The way the offender has reacted to the institution and the information gathered there will assist the parole officer in preparing the offender for the next stage, for parole, while he is still in the institution. This will improve his chances for successful re-entry into the community.

[58] *Social Problems of the Prisoner,* pamphlet adapted from an address given by Dr. Bates to the National Conference of Social Work, May 20, 1946.

Another point of communication and a relationship mentioned earlier in this section is that which should exist among all groups engaged in administering the various processes of justice—police, detention workers, sheriffs, jail wardens, prosecuting officers. A good job of screening and referral, and the provision of services early in the offender's experience may make the difference between success and failure in later treatment. Helping the family of the offender through welfare services, work with the employer and other procedures designed to decrease the tension of the experience may have a profound effect on the individual's chances for rehabilitation. All too often personnel in correction work see the offender only after so much has happened to him that successful treatment is doubtful.

Social work is an important part of corrections. The social worker who enters probation, institutional service, or parole must be able to fully utilize his skills. It is fortunate that the profession is resuming its earlier interest in this field and is making serious studies of the role of the professional social worker in an area of service which badly needs his skill.

Correction is an interdisciplinary field. It engages the professional services of the psychologist, the psychiatrist, and the sociologist, among others, as we have noted. Unfortunately, a large number of persons now engaged in correction work have no specific professional preparation for the service. There is great opportunity and need for the development of a strong interprofessional approach to this work, work needing all the understanding and skill which can be mustered.

SERVICES TO VETERANS

From just about every point of comparison, health and welfare services for veterans excel those generally available to the public. The comprehensiveness of benefits and services, their quality, and costs, make these services among the most significant of all those provided in this country. Potentially eligible to receive these benefits are veterans who, with their families, compose about half our whole population. Legislation on certain benefits carries terminal dates, and, although all provisions of course are subject to change through action of Congress, because of the nature of the benefits, and the size of the programs, these services must be considered as important continuing features of the social welfare scene.

Apparent in all legislation for the veteran is the principle that the person who risks his life for his country has earned the nation's gratitude. If he incurs injury or illness in the service of his country, it is considered only right that he be compensated for his loss. In more recent times, interrupted education, deferred careers, loss of opportunity for advancement in civilian life, and other adverse factors attributable to military service have been the subjects of legislation intended to provide redress for any handicap suffered through service.

Actually, this principle is not new. Ever since colonial times some measures have been provided to make up to the veteran for some of the losses and hardships incurred in military service. Each war has brought its program of special legislation. What is recent, however, is the wide scope and liberality of the provisions made since the beginning of World War II.

In a comprehensive study of veterans' programs, a committee headed by General of the Army (ret.) Omar Bradley has offered a brief but comprehensive history of veterans' benefits, along with an analysis of current measures, and recommendations for the future.[59] The Committee divided the development of veterans' benefits into three chronological periods: from the Revolutionary War to 1917, from World War I to World War II, and since the beginning of World War II.

The first period was featured by primary reliance on compensation and pension features, with little provision for readjustment benefits. The Commission calls this a "backward-looking effort," with chief reliance on benefits for service-connected injury, illness or death, and on "gratuitous pension benefits."[60] Some preference

---

[59] "Veterans' Benefits in the United States—Findings and Recommendations," *Report* to the President by the President's Commission on Veterans' Pensions, Washington, April, 1956, Chap. I.

[60] *Ibid.*, p. 41.

to veterans for government jobs, land grants, and mustering-out payments, were the extent of provisions.

World War I and its aftermath resulted in some new benefits for veterans. The new programs included government-financed life insurance and vocational rehabilitation, as well as liberalization of existing benefits. This conflict brought extensive pension benefits, and a bonus for all who served in the armed forces during the war.

The most extensive development in veterans' services has taken place since the beginning of World War II. This is the period in which the concept of help during the period of readjustment from military to civilian life has been developed and one in which the position of the veteran has been advanced to the point that his economic status compares favorably with that of the nonveteran of comparable age. According to the President's Commission, veterans of both world wars are better off today than are their nonveteran contemporaries.[61] This does not mean that they are in such a position solely because of the benefits they have received, but rather it indicates that with help they have successfully overcome whatever handicaps their military service might have imposed on their progress in civil life.

Eligibility

In general, the benefits are or have been available to veterans who have served in a period of armed conflict. Many major benefits for eligible World War II veterans have expired. Under certain conditions, some benefits and services may be provided to veterans of peacetime service if, for example, they have been injured in the performance of their duties under simulated war conditions. The benefits vary somewhat with respect to the different armed conflicts. Each has stimulated the development of particular legislation, although in essential outline, the benefits and services for veterans of World War II and the Korean conflict are similar and in many instances the same. There is a general qualification that discharge from the service must have been under other than dishonorable conditions.

[61] *Ibid.,* p. 8.

Nature and extent of services

The President's Commission has grouped the veterans' benefits into three categories. These are: (1) service-connected benefits for those disabled or suffering an aggravation of an existing disability as the result of military service, or for the dependents of those whose death is the result of service; (2) readjustment benefits, to help the veteran make the transition from military to civilian life; and (3) nonservice connected benefits which are based on a general feeling of obligation to the veteran of wartime service rather than on any specific need or problem attributable to military service. As the Commission suggests, pensions are the chief example of this category. They are also about the most historic.[62]

Under these categories is grouped a large number of benefits and services too detailed for complete description here. Some of the highlights of these services, however, provide a sense of their nature and range. In reviewing these benefits, one cannot help but think how much further the people of this country have gone in their philosophy of governmental responsibility for health and welfare for the veteran than would even remotely be possible for the general public. As the proportion of veterans, servicemen, and families of veterans and servicemen in the total population is 50 percent or more, it is not a relatively small special group.[63]

Among the service-connected disability or death benefits are the following: (1) monthly compensation, with the rate dependent on the degree of disability, for disease or injury which has either been incurred or aggravated in line of duty under wartime conditions; (2) vocational rehabilitation, including special equipment, payment of the costs of training, travel allowances and loans, and monthly allowances to the veteran during this training; (3) assistance with the costs of education to children of a veteran who has died as the result of injury or illness incurred in or aggravated

---

[62] *Ibid.*, pp. 33-34.

[63] For a more detailed summary of veterans programs see Virginia Karl, "Veterans' Benefits and Services," *Social Work Yearbook, 1957* (New York: National Association of Social Workers), pp. 573-584; also *Social Legislation Information Service*, "Federal Benefits Available to Veterans and Their Dependents," Issue No. 76, 84th Congress, Nov. 1, 1956 (a regularly issued bulletin on Congressional Legislation).

by wartime service; (4) special housing for the veteran receiving compensation for permanent and total disability of such a nature as to make him incapable of locomotion without the aid of canes, crutches, braces, or wheelchair; (5) cash indemnity to survivors of a veteran who died in active service after June 27, 1950, and prior to January 1, 1957, or who died during that period within four months following separation from the service; (6) complete care in veterans' hospitals, domiciliary facilities, or elsewhere at government expense if authorized by the Veterans Administration; (7) medical treatment outside a hospital for service-connected disability; (8) prosthetic appliances, seeing-eye dogs, mechanical or electronic equipment for blind (blindness need not be service-connected if the blind veteran has another service-connected disability); (9) automobiles or other types of conveyances for veterans who have loss or total impairment of use of both hands, both feet, or who have suffered a serious loss of vision as the result of service in World War II or the Korean conflict; (10) civil service preference for disabled veteran, his wife, or, if he has died from service-connected cause, his widow. In addition there are substantial compensation and indemnity provisions for the survivors of the veteran whose death is attributable to service-connected injury or illness.

The range of readjustment benefits is considerable, and many of these include income-maintenance provisions. Among the most significant of the readjustment benefits are: (1) grants to the veteran to help him defray the costs of education (for veterans of World War II these benefits under Public Law 346 terminated for the most part on July 25, 1956; for all Korean conflict veterans these benefits under Public Law 550 of the 82nd Congress are to terminate not later than January 31, 1965); (2) loan guaranties for veterans of World War II or of the Korean conflict for the purpose of the purchase, construction, or necessary repairs to homes or business properties, including farms; (3) preference for veterans applying for certain types of farm loans; (4) preference in the rental or purchase of government-sponsored or financed housing; (5) homestead preferences in the acquisition of public lands; (6) job preference in civil service through the allowance of extra points on civil service examinations; waiver of some kinds of job requirements, the right to pass over nonveterans on the register of applicants for jobs, retention rights on jobs during reductions of forces; (7) certain privileges from public employment services in job-counselling and placement.

Veterans of World War II were allowed "readjustment allowances" or unemployment compensation following discharge under other than dishonorable conditions. These benefits, however, are no longer in force, having expired in 1952. Special provisions for veterans under old age and survivors insurance already have been described in another chapter.[64]

Nonservice connected benefits are among the oldest of all the provisions for veterans. These include mustering-out pay, pensions, medical, hospital, and domiciliary care for nonservice connected ailments, provided the veteran stipulates his inability to pay for such care, special life insurance programs, and burial benefits.

Federal programs for the veterans are the responsibility of the Veterans Administration (the V.A.), which operates through a nationwide system of hospitals, domiciliary homes, district offices, area medical offices, and field contact offices located to provide convenient access to veterans throughout the country. These various offices are coordinated in a way that puts the entire facilities of the national administration at the service of the veteran, wherever he may directly apply for service. These installations and offices are set up to provide consultation and other services to the veteran to assist him in any way possible. Service is not just a mechanistic evaluation of rights to benefits. It has been characteristic of this program to look at the veteran as a total personality, and to make every effort to help him improve his capacity as a functioning human being. This has been stressed in the requirements for all V.A. personnel and the coordination of the work of the various professions on V.A. staffs. The quality and standards of medical and hospital care for eligible veterans, for service-

[64] Chap. 4.

connected or nonservice incurred ailments, is very high. These facilities are justly called "second to none."[65] New hospitals throughout the country incorporate the latest in laboratory and treatment facilities. Generally, veterans' hospitals and clinics have attached great importance to teaching, and to research. The quality of professional services has demonstrated again that where there is both learning and teaching, the level of service to patients tends to be higher. A hospital or clinic which is devoted to research and to learning will do a better job in all aspects of its program.

Much of the research completed in medical facilities for veterans is of inestimable value to the total population. New discoveries in medical science have come from these laboratories, and new therapeutic processes are used in the treatment of many diseases. The use of new and enlightened methods also has been characteristic of social and psychological treatment. The close collaboration of highly trained people in various disciplines, in internal medicine, surgery, psychiatry, social work, psychology, nursing, occupational therapy, physical therapy, and others, has demonstrated the potentialities inherent in interdisciplinary "teamwork." It would not be accurate to evaluate these services solely on the basis of what they have done for the veteran.

All of the foregoing benefits and services are provided by the federal government. The states also have programs, of varying content and coverage, for the most part intended to supplement those available from the national government. The state services include the following: A bonus which in many states was paid on the basis of the length of military service; burial allowances and benefits; certain privileges with reference to licensing for trades and professions; free tuition for children of wounded or disabled veterans; employment privileges and preferences; certain tax and license exemptions; homestead preferences; special hospital benefits, and many other special benefits and privileges. All of the states have some form of veterans' legislation. They are not comparable in adequacy with the federal provisions.

These provisions of course vary from state to state. Not all of

---

[65] Virginia Karl, *op. cit.*, p. 575.

the states, for example, have paid a bonus—a highly controversial question in many of them. Only twenty-one states paid such bonuses to veterans of World War II, in addition to Alaska and Hawaii (Hawaii paid it only to disabled veterans), while only eleven states, as of 1956, had made such payments to veterans of the Korean conflict. Where these bonuses are paid, they are usually based on flat amounts per month of service, and are available only to persons who are residents of the state at the time of payment. The other benefits, however, are much more prevalent, specially those relating to employment preferences, homestead rights, and certain types of tax exemptions. Also, many states have established veterans' service offices.

Some states have attempted to establish a special category of public assistance to cover the veterans. In New York, for example, there is a special kind of aid called "Veteran Assistance"; this is a form of home relief or general assistance administered by public welfare officials in local areas to needy war veterans and members of their families.

Veterans also are eligible for the same health and welfare services as the rest of the population is. All of the benefits described in this chapter are in addition to those available to veteran and nonveteran alike. As these other programs continue to improve, it is possible that there will be less need for so many veterans' benefits for matters of a nonservice connected origin. Perhaps it is something of a commentary on the slowness of development of health and welfare programs that a group for which the community has felt some special solicitude has been provided services superior to and beyond those designed for the general population. According to the President's Commission on Veterans' Pensions, an overwhelming proportion of the veterans are opposed to further broad, nonservice connected benefits. The Commission has called attention to the need for modernizing and revising the existing program, which by and large has developed on a piecemeal basis, and also declared its approval of the most generous treatment for service-connected needs, for rehabilitation and reintegration of the disabled into community life.

The Commission also viewed with approval the various readjustment benefits, including those provisions for education and training, job opportunities and preferences, among others. This class of benefits seemed to meet with much greater approval than do those pensions which are unrelated either to service-incurred disability or to readjustment needs.

The general principle which should guide the judgment of the people with reference to legislation for services to veterans, the Commission declared, is that: "Our objective throughout should be to promote not only what is best for the veteran, but also what will best serve the interests of the nation. What best serves the nation in the long run will be in the interest of the veteran."[66]

Summary

Children need the opportunity to grow in the security of the family relationship. But the family is not the only resource for the child; it is re-enforced by such community resources as education, recreation, health protection, and social services.

Even with help, the family may fail the child. Parents may be unwilling or unable to meet the child's needs. The result may be neglect, exploitation, abandonment, or abuse. In such instances, government must exercise the responsibility of protection of the child. The responsibility of government, then, is to support the family's efforts to provide a good environment and a decent opportunity for the child, and to afford protection when the family resource fails.

Governmental responsibility for the care and protection of children rests with the states. Tremendous influence toward the growth of state and local child welfare services was provided by the Social Security Act in 1935, when a program was included for grants to states to assist them in improving their services to children, especially in rural areas, or areas of special needs. Although federal aid has had considerable influence on the development of services, state and local resources have been used extensively to enlarge and extend these services.

---

[66] "Veterans' Benefits in the United States—Findings and Recommendations," in *Ibid.,* pp. 9-13 (a summary of the Commission's findings and recommendations).

Child welfare services include working with the parents and the child in the home to strengthen the family as a resource for the child, placement of the child in an institution or foster home when the natural home fails, acceptance of responsibility for adoptions, establishment of and maintenance of standards for child care in private and public agencies, institutions, community education on the needs of children, studies of special problems of children, and cooperation with schools and other agencies such as health services.

Such services require competent and highly skilled personnel. In recognition of this fact, a large portion of the funds granted to the states by the federal government has been used for the training of personnel—social workers and others whose technical skills are required.

Another important program for children is the one of service to crippled children. This was also one of the measures included in the Social Security Act, which provided grants to states by the Children's Bureau for the purpose of extending services for locating crippled children, and for providing medical care to them.

States vary in their definitions of the crippled child, but generally the definitions specify many kinds of handicap, including orthopedic disabilities, hearing and speech defects, problems of muscle coordination, heart damage, among many others. The maximum age at which a person is eligible for such services in the states is twenty-one.

Services include clinical diagnoses, through clinics staffed by such skilled medical personnel as are required. These clinics are supported by state and federal funds, and do not charge a fee to the individual for the service. Many states, in addition, provide treatment, including corrective, convalescent, or restorative services. The agency may help the family locate such services, or it may assume all or a substantial part of the costs.

Cooperation with other health and welfare agencies, both public and voluntary, work with the schools in the development of an educational program for the handicapped child, and education of the family and the community to their respective responsibilities for the child are among the functions of agencies administering crippled children's services.

The maternal and child health services comprise another important federal-state program, also among those included in the Social Security Act in 1935. This program also provides for federal grants to states through the Children's Bureau.

Actually, this was the first of the federal-state programs for children to be established under the Children's Bureau, and antedated the Social Security Act. The Sheppard-Towner Act passed in 1920 provided for grants to states for maternal and child health services, but the measure was allowed to expire in 1929.

The maternal and child health program is designed to provide or strengthen such services for mothers and children as prenatal care clinics, well-child clinics, health services for school children, dental hygiene and dental care, licensing and inspection of maternity homes, assistance to hospitals through advice on the care of the maternity patient or the newborn child, education in nutrition for the mother and child, and related services. In addition to services for prevention of pre- and post-natal problems, some states also provide medical care facilities.

Considerable emphasis has been placed in this program on the education of physicians, nurses, and nutritionists. Through this program, grants are made for in-service training and special institutes, as well as for postgraduate training for professional personnel.

Vocational rehabilitation is the oldest of the federal-state programs in social welfare. The Vocational Rehabilitation Act of 1920 provided grants to states for training, guidance, and placement of the disabled. This law was enacted for a four-year period, and was successively extended until the inclusion of the program in the Social Security Act in 1935. The Barden-LaFollette Act of 1943 took vocational rehabilitation out of the Social Security Act, and provided separate legislation. The program then remained substantially unchanged until 1954, when the 83rd Congress added some significant amendments, so important that they have been hailed as marking a new era in vocational rehabilitation of handicapped men and women.

This is a state-federal program, with the states carrying responsibility for providing basic services. The federal government, in addition to administering the grants to states, provides technical consultation, and through its various grants stimulates the development of special projects and research.

Eligibility for vocational rehabilitation is established by an impairment of a handicapping nature, physical or mental, caused by disease, injury, or congenital handicap. The impairment must be of sufficient severity to constitute a substantial handicap in ability to perform the usual occupation. Another factor is the definite possibility that the person would benefit sufficiently from the service to be able to return to gainful employment.

The services include medical care, guidance, training, physical restoration, placement, and others as required to restore the person to gainful employment. The need for supportive service, for help in emotional and social adjustment to changed life circumstances may be of great importance to the individual who has suffered a handicapping condition. All features of treatment and restoration require that the skills of the various disciplines be coordinated.

The service requires close association with other public programs. One of these is O. A. S. D. I., which now brings vocational rehabilitation into the program of determining the extent of disability, and restoration to employment. Also, public assistance offers many opportunities for cooperation with vocational rehabilitation, and, as we have seen, great potentialities for cooperating with workmen's compensation administrations are considerable.

Health and welfare services for veterans are among the most comprehensive of all programs in the country. Apparent in all legislation for the veteran is the principle that the person who has risked his life for his country is entitled to the nation's gratitude. Of course this principle is not new. In this country since colonial times, services have been provided to make up to the veteran for some of the losses and hardships incurred in military service in time of war. While each war has brought its crop of special measures, the present scope and liberality of the programs dates from the beginning of World War II. Since then, the concept of service to aid the veteran in readjustment from military to civilian life has developed.

In general, benefits are available to veterans who have served in a period of armed conflict. Many major benefits, as for eligible veterans of World War II, have expired. There is the general requirement that discharge from service must have been under other than dishonorable conditions.

Services are grouped under three categories: service-connected benefits for those disabled, or suffering an aggravation of existing disability, as a result of military service, readjustment benefits to help the veteran make the transition to civilian life, and non-service connected benefits. Medical care, hospital and domiciliary care, cash indemnities, preferences in the civil service, indemnity to survivors of deceased veterans, special conveyances and appliances for physically handicapped, and such readjustment services as loan guaranties, educational assistance, and certain special measures under social insurance are among the benefits which are or have been available.

Mental illness remains one of our leading health and welfare problems. The number of persons in mental hospitals itself tells a grim but not a complete story. It does not take into account the large number who are disabled by illnesses which are not so severe as to require hospitalization, nor does it count the social cost of those who, from influential positions, see life in distorted perspective.

Progress has been great since the days when mental illness was considered a dread and mysterious affliction to be regarded with a mixture of fascination and terror. Increased insight into the nature and the cause of mental illness has resulted in improved methods of treatment, and the mental hospital is no longer the place of horror it once was. The rise of community clinics and earlier diagnosis and treatment have saved many persons from the necessity of being hospitalized.

One of the most important pieces of legislation in this field was the National Mental Health Act of 1946, which established the National Institute of Mental Health as part of the Federal Public

Health Service, and also provided for grants to states for the improvement of basic services in mental health, and for research and training grants to universities, hospitals, and other public and private institutions. State and local response to this measure has been encouraging, as an increasing number of clinics has been established throughout the country.

Modern mental health programs include research and study of mental health with the goal of preventing its onset. Even more than prevention, however, is entailed in the programs of study. The development of a favorable climate for mental health is also an objective. More and more, mental health efforts are directed toward enlisting community agencies on a wide basis to assist in the attainment of the goal of a community life in which conditions are conducive to mental health.

Correction has been defined as the service arm of the administration of justice. It includes probation, institutional service and parole, as well as social work in association with police, prosecution, and detention facilities. Its purpose is the restoration of the offender to a useful and satisfactory adjustment to society. As knowledge of human behavior has increased, the offender has been perceived more as an object of help than as a subject for punishment.

This statement cannot be made without reservation, however, since, after all, the offender violated the law(s) which govern society, and it is sometimes difficult for people to disassociate concern for the offender from revulsion against the offense.

If the court decides that the offender may remain in society, it places him on probation. The offender then may remain in the community so long as he meets the conditions which are prescribed for him. If he violates these conditions, he may forthwith be committed to the custody of an institution. Otherwise, a probation officer is responsible for his supervision. The probation office may be attached to the court, or it may be a separate agency to which the court commits the offenders.

The offender, whether juvenile or adult, may require institutional custody. Training schools, reformatories, or prisons are organized according to the sex and age of the offender. While these institutions vary widely in the services they have available, they are increasingly designed to assist in the rehabilitation of the offender. The services of skilled personnel in psychology, psychiatry, social work, sociology, and other disciplines, emphasis on individualized treatment, and education and training for life after release from custody, are features of the better institutions.

Parole in many of its processes is similar to probation, although the offender may be paroled only after he his attitudes have hardened by a period of custody in an institution. Parole refers to the release of the prisoner from an institution before the term of imprisonment has expired.

Selected References

1. Abbott, Grace, ed., *The Child and the State*. Chicago, University of Chicago Press, 2 v. 1938.
2. Administrator of Veterans Affairs, Annual Reports.
3. American Association of Medical Social Workers, *The Evolving Concept of Rehabilitation*. Monograph 1, Washington, 1955.
4. American Public Welfare Association, *Essentials of Public Child Welfare Services*. Statement Prepared by the Committee on Services to Children.
5. Children's Bureau, Social Security Administration, *Services for Crippled Children*. Children's Bureau Folder No. 38. Washington, Government Printing Office, 1955.
6. ———, *Child Welfare Services, How They Help Children and Parents*. Children's Bureau Publication No. 359, Washington, Government Printing Office, 1957.
7. ———, *Your Children's Bureau in the U. S. Department of Health, Education and Welfare*. Children's Bureau Publication Number 357, Washington, Government Printing Office, 1956.
8. Council of State Governments, *The Mental Health Programs of the Forty-Eight States*. A Report to the Governors Conference, Chicago, 1950.
9. ———, *Training and Research in State Mental Health Programs*. A Report to the Governors Conference, Chicago, 1953.
10. De Francis, Vincent, *The Fundamentals of Child Protection*. Children's Division, American Humane Association, Denver, 1955.

11. Deutsch, Albert, *The Mentally Ill In America*. New York, Columbia University Press, rev. ed., 1949.
12. Eliot, Martha M., "Twenty Years of Progress for Children." *Social Security Bulletin*. Vol. 18, No. 8 (August 1955).
13. Felix, R. H., and Kramer, Morton, "Extent of the Problem of Mental Disorders." Annals of the American Academy of Political and Social Science, Vol. 286, No. 3 (March 1953).
14. Fink, Arthur E., Wilson, Everett E., and Conover, Merrill B., *The Field of Social Work*. New York, Henry Holt and Company, Chap. 11, "The Correctional Services," 1955.
15. Fredericksen, Hazel, *The Child and His Welfare*. San Francisco, W. H. Freeman & Co., 1948.
16. Garrett, James F., ed., *Psychological Aspects of Disability*. Washington, Government Printing Office, 1952.
17. Hagen, Helen R., "Distinctive Aspects of Child Welfare," *Child Welfare*. Vol. XXXVI, No. 7 (July 1957).
18. Karl, Virginia, "Veterans Benefits and Services." *Social Work Year Book, 1957*, New York, National Association of Social Workers, 1957.
19. Keve, Paul W., *Prison, Probation, or Parole*. Minneapolis, University of Minnesota Press, 1954.
20. Kotinsky, Ruth, and Witmer, Helen L., eds., *Community Programs for Mental Health*. Cambridge, Harvard University Press, 1955.
21. Lundberg, Emma Octavia, *Unto the Least of These*. New York, D. Appleton Century, 1947.
22. Millet, John A. P., "Understanding the Emotional Aspects of Disability," *Social Work*. Vol. 2, No. 4 (October 1957).
23. *New Hope for the Disabled*. Office of Vocational Rehabilitation, U. S. Department of Health, Education, and Welfare. Washington, Government Printing Office, 1956.
24. President's Commission on Veterans' Pensions, *Veterans Benefits in the United States, Report to the President*. Washington, Government Printing Office, 1956.
25. Social Legislation Information Service, *Federal Benefits Available to Veterans and Their Dependents*. Issue No. 76, 84th Congress.
26. Tappan, Paul, ed., *Contemporary Correction*. New York, McGraw-Hill Book Co., 1951.
27. Wilson, Everett E., "The Nature of Probation," *The Social Service Review*. Vol. XX (September 1946).

Part III

Organization

In the programs which have been described under Part II, there are many evidences that the character of the services is influenced by the organizations which administer them. In fact, it is not an exaggeration to state that the program is as much an interpretation of policy and purpose by the people who man the organizations and who are in positions of leadership which enable them to make decisions of fundamental importance as it is a direct and literal reflection of the law. After all, the passage of a law is just the beginning of a governmental program of social welfare, and its enactment does not automatically bring a program into being. As quoted in the introduction to Part II, DeSchweinitz stated that the law cannot possibly prescribe a course of action to cover all of the infinite contingencies that may arise in the unpredictable experience of human life.

By this we do not imply that the law is disregarded or circumvented by people in agencies who spend their days trying to outwit the lawmakers. The purpose or intent of the law must be maintained as the basis for decision and action, but in social welfare such intent will best be carried out by people who see in the statute an instrument of service, adaptable within limits to the range of human circumstance encompassed within its purpose.

254

The spirit in which the program is administered may well have as much or more significance to the people who are its intended beneficiaries than does the language of the law.

It is true that in the programs just described, alternatives are present for either a very restrictive or a more broad concept of service. It is not difficult to find examples which illustrate this point. The program depends upon several factors, including the law, public opinion, the money, the staff, and the vision of the agency's leadership. Some agencies are more able, by reason of more adequate resources and less limiting legislation, to take a broader view of services than are others, but the importance of leadership in the organization is common to all services. Child welfare provides an excellent illustration of this point. When the Children's Bureau was given its very general charge under the law which established it, the organization was almost entirely dependent on the vision and insight of its leaders for the selection of matters for investigation and reporting, and for definition of its role in relation to the nation's children. It may be true that the child welfare programs of today are an expression of a changing social and legal philosophy with respect to the rights of children, but it would be a mistake to overlook the influence the leadership of the Children's Bureau has had through the years in encouraging that philosophy.

In the veterans programs, the extent of service is defined by law, which also expresses the nation's attitude toward those who have served their country by military service in armed conflict. But the quality of service in this as in all the programs is the product of the professional personnel on the staffs. Research and interprofessional cooperation are not legislated; they are developed by people who work together in a program given vitality both by the leadership and by an *esprit de corps* within the organization.

Some of the clearest evidences of these kinds of influence are found in public assistance. The differences between these programs and their antecedent, the poor law, are not to be attributed *in toto* to the language of the Social Security Act. It is true that the Act has in it expressions of intent that have made it possible to interpret public assistance as a program designed to safeguard human dignity, and as part of a comprehensive system which stresses human need as arising out of social contingencies rather than personal inadequacy. But this was only the framework for what followed. The rather obscure phrase that the purpose was to provide money payments with respect to needy individuals has led to a carefully developed set of principles respecting the right of the individual who receives the cash to spend it without domination by the agency. The continuing general interpretation of public assistance as a program of social service for the individual and family demonstrates the influence of leadership on the character of a program. This emphasis has received a substantial boost from recent legislation providing for grants of funds to states to enable them to carry out this purpose. But again, that legislation in itself is an outgrowth of the philosophy of the program.

All this is not meant to imply that the law is never more advanced than the administration. There have been examples of laws of a constructive nature which have been enacted out of protest against restrictive or inadequate administration. Nor should it be inferred that the law gives unlimited license to the people who work in the services. There is at least as much danger inherent in a staff which sets no limits on its power to make decisions or policies as there is in one which is too limited in its acceptance of responsibility for leadership. We need scarcely remind ourselves of the importance of the kinds of decisions and action which are taken by agencies in social welfare, and of the impact they have on people's lives. Such responsibility suggests the danger of domination by administrative agencies unless they exercise their function with careful attention to the will of the people. The agency then must respond to both inner and outer direction.

Thus far, we have looked only at the relations between the agencies and the relevant legislation. There is another difficult and important area of relations which unfortunately must be omitted from this volume—the relationship of social welfare to the judicial function. Not only the law's language, but also its interpretation is important, and finding the point at which administrative decisions should stop and judicial interpretations begin is a delicate and complex matter. In certain areas of service, the public social agency and the courts are thrown into a direct relationship, as in adoptions, probation, and certain aspects of other protective services for children.

When a law is enacted establishing a program, machinery must be provided for making the authorized services available, and a structure must be created. This structure may be located in an existing agency, or it may require establishment of a new organization. The outlines of the organization at any rate must be specified in the law. Procedures must be set in motion for the recruitment, selection, and employment of staff. The agency must be organized into divisions, sections, and units, each performing some particular part of the work. In the agency of today, specialization of function is a common feature of organization as the services rendered demand more and more technical skills and processes. The administrative process must be developed to insure the flow of work and the coordination of activities of the organization so that the purposes of the program will be fulfilled. The relationship of boards of advisory or governing committees to the agency executive and to the political authority must develop, as well as that of executive to staff. Personnel policies and procedures must be established, and responsibilities of staff positions clearly delineated.

In each program, the developing administrative policy must set the scope and limits of the service, as well as the procedures for administration. This must be done within an agreed context of objectives. Indeed, one authority on administration has characterized objectives, policy, and procedure as the "why," the "what" and the "how" respectively.[1] The "why" in this case relates to *raison d'être*—the social purpose of the agency. If one administrative group believes that unemployment insurance, for example, is

---

[1] Charles E. Redfield, Lecture to class in "The Administrative Process In Social Welfare," Rutgers, the State University, Graduate School of Social Work, Fall, 1957.

intended to provide for the most limited kind of protection, while another sees the objective as indicating a broad program of income security, the results will be confusion and inconsistency in decisions and in policy. Or if a public assistance agency administration perceives its role as being limited to the provision of financial aid, with services exclusively related to getting people on and off the agency's list of clientele, the result will be quickly and clearly evident. While there is or should be room for individual differences of opinion, there should be what Kidneigh has called "unity of purpose and unity of action,"[2] certainly in the essentials of the programs. The policies should provide a clear guide to what should be done to carry out the objectives, and the procedures should delineate the methods.

Kidneigh has described the administrative process in social welfare as one of "transforming a social policy into a social service."[3] While there are several definitions of the administrative process in this field, Kidneigh's definition has the merit of simplicity, and a comprehensiveness which well denotes the character of the process. The objective is a quality of service, but the policy sets the range and the limits, and provides the base. To make the policy work, a smoothly functioning operation is required. The many techniques and skills involved determine both the availability and the content of the services. Good administration requires the effective mobilization and deployment of resources, the planned participation of staff, the continuous process of gathering and evaluating facts, the proper location of decision-making power, and effective coordination of all parts of the organization.

In the following pages, we shall describe the organizations which administer these various programs. These organizations should be considered against the backdrop of certain problems which are characteristic of public social welfare today. We will look first, then, at some of these problems.

2 John Kidneigh, "Administration of Social Agencies," *Social Work Year Book, 1957*, Russell H. Kurtz, ed. (New York, National Association of Social Workers, 1957), pp. 75-82.
3 *Ibid.*

THE PROBLEM OF INTERGOVERNMENTAL RELATIONS

Social welfare has become predominantly a function shared by federal, state, and local governments. As a result, it is not enough to consider how an agency at one particular level of government works. Social welfare is not so much a divided responsibility as it is a cooperative program of federal, state, and local jurisdictions. The shape and character of administration at each level is profoundly influenced by the characteristics of administration at every other level.

THE PROBLEM OF COORDINATING THE SEVERAL PROGRAMS

A persistent theme of this volume has been the inter-relatedness of the various kinds of service, of social insurances, medical and vocational rehabilitative services, public assistance, child welfare, mental health, and corrections. Repeatedly, attention has been called to the importance of communication among the services, and of cooperation in the interests of treating the individual as a whole person rather than as a collection of handicaps and problems. It is easy to say that all social welfare should be combined into one vast structure, but, as we shall see, such a "solution" would create its own problems. For example, the fact that each of the various programs develops its own impressive body of experience might mean that in one vast structure something of the qualities of the programs might be lost. The question of communication and coordination at each level of government is further complicated by the varying arrangements at the other levels.

THE PROBLEM OF SIZE OF THE ORGANIZATION

This is a problem of excessiveness, of organizations being either too large or too small. In the big organization, we have the threat of bureaucracy, with all the opprobrium which is attached to that term. Bureaucracy, however, may be the product either of public or of private organization. It is not exclusively a problem or product of government.

In its least favorable sense, bureaucracy suggests preoccupation with details of procedure, a love of complication for its own sake, an office where mountains of forms and bales of paper are used. In popular folklore also, staff members or bureaucrats are addicted to the use of a jargon which includes words incomprehensible to the general public supporting and receiving the services. New jargon words, the public believes, are constantly invented, and old familiar words and phrases given special meanings known only to the initiate, the in-group within the administration.

It must be acknowledged that the growth of such a bureaucracy is a clear and ever-present danger in any large organization. Indeed, in a sense, bureaucracy of this sort is largely a product of bigness, rather than of a particular kind of service. Communication may increase in difficulty as an organization grows in size and procedures then are elaborated in an effort to insure a measure of consistency and orderliness. When carried too far this may lead to an overelaboration of method, with too much stress on technical compliance and excessive accountability for acts or methods of individuals or units, with each worker in the organizational hierarchy concerned with the detailed supervision of the worker(s) just below, and so on throughout the structure. When each act must be accounted for in a manner that will provoke no questions, the value of pleasing the supervisor takes precedence over the quality of the service. Or when each division becomes so immersed in its own limited and special functions that it becomes myopic in its view of the total, the worst fears of those who fear bureaucracy may be realized.

Yet despite the danger of excessive bureaucratic concern with its own intricacy, the alternative to method, whether in government or private industry, whether in social welfare or in reclamation of natural resources, would be chaos. We cannot give people even those with a wealth of good intentions, nothing but a general statutory statement of purpose to guide them. There must be both a structure and a process for administration. While it is true that it takes people to make the process work, it is also true that people need the process and must have a structure within which to perform. Smallness, too, however, may create problems of ineffectiveness. The agency or the unit served may be too small to afford the quality and specialized character of service which the program requires. The agency may be so small as to be inefficient, with too few individuals doing too many diversified tasks. This question is relevant to and of some consequence in many of the programs.

THE PROBLEM OF RELATION TO THE PUBLIC

This is purposely phrased as "relation to the public" rather than as "public relations." In one sense this is another way of expressing the importance of avoiding an ingrown bureaucracy. But we are using the expression in another sense, to refer to the need: (a) to be responsive to public needs and public opinion, and (b) to keep in proper perspective the interests of both the general public and the clientele of the agency. These are not conflicting or antithetical interests, by any means. But the need to relate the service to the clientele and the public interest, and to keep the two purposes in essential harmony, is constant.

THE PROBLEM OF STAFF AND FACILITIES

After years of government service, one may become quite fatalistic about the characteristic inadequacy of the available resources to do the job that a conscientious public servant in social welfare may want to do, and sees as needing to be done. Yet there is impressive evidence of growth through the years. When we speak of inadequacies, it is important to keep in mind both quantity and quality. The law and general public policy are not the only conditioning factors. The kinds and numbers of people on the staff will have much to do with decisions about what the agency may or should undertake. Even though planning should make the most of available resources, both human and otherwise in the organization, it still may not be possible to go beyond certain limits in service. It is worth noting, for example, that many of the recent pieces of legislation on improved services have been accompanied by financial provisions for more adequately trained personnel in numbers sufficient to permit realization of the law's intent. There are also instances in which the charge has been given by the legislators, but the wherewithal has not been provided.

With these questions in mind, we now proceed to describe the organizational structure which has been established for the administration of governmental programs in social welfare at the different levels of government. But because of the great importance of intergovernmental participation, we shall look first at that phase of organization, considering both the fiscal and the administrative patterns of cooperation.

7

Intergovernmental Relations in Social Welfare Administration

The proper division of labor and authority between the Nation and the States is the key to maintaining the federal nature of our system of government. The lines of division are not static. They have been controversial from the beginning of our life as an independent country. They remain so today.[1]

With these words a committee appointed by the President to study the question of intergovernmental relations began its report. The characteristics of importance, its controversial nature, and its continuing change are all reasons why this subject receives so much attention.

It is not a subject which lends itself completely to dispassionate, objective analysis. So much is at stake for state and local government that any threat of encroachment is likely to arouse

[1] The Commission on Intergovernmental Relations, *Report* to the President for Transmittal to Congress, June, 1955, p. 9. (Also known as the Kestnbaum Commission.)

263

considerable feeling and opposition. Many people place great value on the maximum preservation of the traditional balance of responsibilities among the levels of government. Frequently, too, there are accompanying issues which are cloaked in the controversy around states' rights, as is exemplified in the recent disputes over civil rights between those who wanted strong federal action, and those whose opposition was largely due to feelings other than those about federal participation *per se*.

This issue has been the subject of an increasing amount of study in recent years. While the Commission quoted above was the first special commission on intergovernmental relations appointed by a President, other groups had given the matter considerable thought and attention. Among the more recent groups is the President's Commission on Organization of the Executive Branch of the Government (the Hoover Commission) which included in its 1949 report several volumes on intergovernmental relations, a report, on Grants-in-Aid issued by the Council of State Governments in 1949, along with numerous studies of particular programs or phases of the problem. On July 20, 1957, President Eisenhower announced the appointment of a seven-man committee to work with ten state governors on the problem of "returning to the States some of the vast powers now exercised by the Federal Government."[2]

More recent evidence of the current concern of the present national administration with the problem of intergovernmental relations is provided by the President's Budget Message to the Congress on January 13, 1958. In his message the President gave several suggestions for reducing the level of federal participation in some of the programs of grants to states for welfare services.

Nor is Congress indifferent to the question. A Subcommittee on Intergovernmental Relations of the House Committee on Government Operations of the 85th Congress has sent questionnaires to selected respondents to secure authoritative opinion on the effect of grants-in-aid on state and local operation, and has solicited opinion on alternatives to the present structure. In addition, the Subcommittee had prepared a series of questions based on the

[2] *The New York Times,* July 21, 1957.

Report of the President's Commission on Intergovernmental Relations, and has now completed a series of regional hearings.

Social welfare is an area of service in which some of the most extensive development in intergovernmental operation has taken place. These programs have done as much as any to set the pattern for what, since the 1930's, has come to be known as "cooperative federalism." An important aspect of this development is the way in which the federal government has entered a field once almost exclusively the property of state and local governments.

This pattern has come about largely through the use of a fiscal device, the grant-in-aid. In general usage, this term refers to sums of money transferred from one government to another for a designated purpose. In their study of the whole complex subject, the Council of State Governments has classified grants under two headings: "regular grants," which they define as "federal grants-in-aid for continuing nonemergency purposes," and "emergency grants" which are "of a temporary nature for relief, war or other extraordinary purposes." Under such a definition, the Council in its report has excluded "(1) shared revenues; (2) payments in lieu of taxes; (3) payments for contractual services rendered for the national government; and (4) cash loans, unless such loans are subsequently converted into grants." Also excluded from the definition are "(1) any expenditure by the national government which is not paid to state and local government; and (2) distribution of commodities or surplus war property to states and localities."[3]

This definition permits inclusion of federal grants both to states and to localities. It does not include subsidies or subventions to private parties including voluntary agencies. While the above definition covers federal grants, it should be noted that states also may make grants-in-aid to local governments. In general, the grants which concern us in the study of organization for the welfare services which we have thus far described are of a regular rather than an emergency nature.

Grants-in-aid for social security and related purposes account

[3] "Federal Grants-In-Aid," *Report* of the Committee on Federal Grants-In-Aid, the Council of State Governments, 1949, pp. 29-30.

for almost three-fifths of the total of almost three and one-half billions of dollars granted by the national government to the states in 1956. This classification includes grants for public assistance, unemployment insurance administration, maternal and child health services, crippled children's services, the various grants from the U. S. Public Health Service, child welfare services, vocational rehabilitation, and such other programs (as the national school lunch program, and the operation of state and territorial homes for disabled soldiers and sailors) which are not included in the scope of this book. The *per capita* expenditure in 1956 for these and other federal grant-in-aid programs was $20.34.[4]

HISTORY OF SOCIAL WELFARE GRANTS-IN-AID

Before examining some of the major fiscal and administrative relationships among the various programs, it will be helpful to review briefly the historical development of grants-in-aid to social welfare, for a background to understanding the contemporary relationships.

The grant-in-aid dates from 1785, according to students of intergovernmental relations, when land was given by the national to the state governments for educational purposes. Congress in that year directed that certain parts of the public domain in the Northwest Territory should be reserved for the maintenance of public schools, and in 1787 further provided for the granting of land to each state for the purpose of establishing a university. In 1862, the Morrill Act provided for a further definition of purposes of the land-grant for education, and for federal supervision of these grants. These were among the earliest of all grants. Others related to the development of agricultural extension work, aid to forestry, to highway construction, for state development and improvement of vocational education (under the Smith-Hughes Act of 1917), especially in agricultural, trade and industrial work, and

[4] Bureau of the Census, *Statistical Abstract of the United States, 1957,* Table 319, p. 261. For a breakdown of federal grants to state and local governments by purpose, for the year 1935 to 1955, see "Annual Statistical Supplement, 1955," Social Security *Bulletin,* p. 10.

home economics; and public health appropriations (under the Chamberlin-Kahn Act of 1918) for the control of venereal disease. The first grant in social welfare, as we have seen, was the Vocational Rehabilitation Act of 1920, followed by the Sheppard-Towner Act in 1921, which provided grants to states for maternal and child health programs.

It was in the 1930's that the grant-in-aid for social welfare came into its own. The Emergency Relief and Construction Act in 1932, which marked the beginning of federal participation in relief, apportioned money to the states for highway construction, although as E. A. Williams has observed, "Recourse was had to the subterfuge of dressing up 'grants' as 'loans' " in order to get the bill passed. This indicates a degree of resistance to federal participation even at that late date.[5] As Mr. Williams observes, opposition to this bill was the last stand of those who opposed any form of federal participation in unemployment relief. He further states that "for the next few years, emphasis shifted to such problems as the amount of administrative authority that should be placed in federal hands; the value of work relief versus direct relief; the conditions which should attach to federal grants for relief, the amount of state matching to be required, and the size of federal appropriations."[6] Measures which followed the enactment of the Emergency Relief and Construction Act were the act creating the Federal Emergency Relief Administration, the creation by executive order of the Civil Works Administration, the establishment of the Civilian Conservation Corps, and the executive order setting up the Works Progress Administration (this name was later changed to Work Projects Administration).[7]

In successive measures, the patterns of federal participation varied. Under the Federal Emergency Relief Act, grants of funds were made to states which generally set up organizations to receive and to administer these funds. Federal grants were made monthly under no specific formula. Financial arrangements be-

[5] E. A. Williams, *Federal Aid for Relief* (New York, 1939), p. 49.
[6] *Ibid.*
[7] For a discussion of the political and social atmosphere which surrounded these developments, see Chapter 3.

tween federal and state governments were quite flexible. The conditions of the grants, by which the federal government matched the sums allotted by the state governments, were : (1) that there be no discrimination in granting of assistance; (2) that public agencies spend public funds, and (3) that personnel, though provided by the states, be approved by the federal agency.

The law gave the federal agency the power to administer federal funds if deemed necessary by the Federal Administrator. In actual practice, this power was invoked in only six instances, and then for a variety of reasons. The urgency of the national problem made the federal government moderate in the use of such power, because the need was so great that the government knew that cutting off funds would mean needy people would not receive aid. The federal government was compelled to participate in a program of unemployment relief. When some states were not making what seemed to be a suitable effort to carry their share of the load, the national government did not choose to abandon the people of that state. At this point the national government acknowledged a primary rather than a secondary responsibility for the welfare of the people in this nation.

The Civil Works Administration, although it existed only a few months—from November 1933, to April 1934—presented still another pattern of intergovernmental relations. This agency was created by executive order to provide work for approximately 4,000,000 unemployed. Essentially, it was a federally-operated program. State and local personnel were appointed by the Federal Civil Works Administrator, and were considered federal employees. Funds were disbursed by federal employees, although state and local governments planned and submitted proposals for the projects on which the funds were spent.

In some respects, federal control was not so great under the Civil Works Administration as it was under some other programs of those years. Mr. Williams notes that states and localities not only exerted considerable influence in the sponsorship of the projects; they also continued to carry considerable responsibility for the management aspects of project operation, including supervision and payment for project materials.[8] This short but rather spectacular operation was significant in the evolution of federal participation in assistance to individuals in need. It demonstrated how far the national government would go toward the direct care to needy persons under the influence of a nation-wide emergency, and provided further evidence of the trend toward accepting unemployment and mass misery as properly a federal concern.

Ostensibly the Work Projects Administration (WPA) was a federally-operated program. Created by executive order in 1935, this program provided a system of work relief for employable persons certified as in need of assistance.[9] It is true that in this program the agency officials were federal employees and that policies were made and enforced by the federal government. Considerable state and local participation was provided, however, both through project sponsorship, as in the earlier Civil Works Administration, and through the use of local and state relief agencies to investigate the eligibility of people for assignment to WPA projects. In most states, written agreements were made between state agencies and the federal administration regarding the responsibility of state and local offices for referring eligible people to WPA jobs.

Other programs in which federal, state, and local agencies shared responsibility were the Civilian Conservation Corps and the National Youth Administration. In all of the emergency programs, whether federally-administered, or state-administered through grants-in-aid, all three levels of government were involved in some degree and in some manner. Existing state agencies were used in some instances. In others, state and local agencies were created for purposes of cooperation with the federal government.

Under the stimulus of federal participation, state and local welfare responsibility grew far beyond its previous proportions. Far from robbing them of their functional importance in this field, federal participation was instrumental in the development of ex-

[8] Williams, *op. cit.,* p. 116.
[9] See Donald S. Howard, *The WPA and Federal Relief Policy* (New York, Russell Sage Foundation, 1942).

panded state and local programs throughout the country in the 1930's.

In the emergency measures of these years, the pattern of federal-state cooperation in social welfare was established through the use of the grant-in-aid device. Federally-aided programs also have had a pronounced effect on local government; that the county, especially, has come into its own is very much due to its welfare responsibility. While not all states have county administration, many do. As late as 1929, the county was referred to as "the dark continent of American politics." These programs, then, have provided an important stimulus to improved state-local, as well as federal-state, relations. They have altered the balance of responsibilities to the point that the local government, while no longer in complete control over a very limited function, has a shared responsibility for a more extensive one.

SOME POLICY QUESTIONS

Why has this kind of relationship developed? When the resources of the states and the localities proved unequal to the task of meeting large-scale welfare needs, why did the national government not take over? Why enter into cooperative arrangements of such size and complexity? If problems are nation-wide, why not meet them with national programs?

These questions and others related to them may be answered from several standpoints. The first is a constitutional consideration. This is a federal, not a unitary system of national government. Under our federal system, as specified in the Tenth Amendment to the Constitution, all powers not delegated to the national government nor prohibited to the states are reserved to the states, or to the people. Throughout our history the question of whether welfare—in such forms as relief to or the establishment of special facilities for certain groups of people—is a legitimate function of national government, has been frequently debated, but the weight of decision and of tradition has placed social welfare among the responsibilities of the states.

Generally speaking, the two parts of the Constitution which have empowered the federal government to enter into such arrangements are Article I, Section 8, which confers on Congress the power "To lay and collect Taxes, Duties, Imposts and Excises, to pay the Debts and provide for the common Defense and general Welfare of the United States," and Article IV, which empowers Congress to make disposition of and control the public lands. It is the interpretation of the clause authorizing the power to tax for the general welfare that has made possible the welfare grants-in-aid. The major court test of the constitutionality of the grant was made with reference to the Sheppard-Towner Act, but the decisions in the two cases which challenged the constitutionality of that Act support rather conclusively the constitutional right of the national government to enter into such arrangements with the states.[10] Generally, however, welfare has remained primarily a state responsibility.

Support to this interpretation has been given historically by the national government through its refusal to enter into social welfare functions. One of the most historic of these decisions was made by President Pierce in 1854, when he vetoed legislation which provided for federal aid to states in the form of land for the construction of facilities for care and treatment of the insane. This measure, which was the result of the untiring efforts of an early leader in the field of mental health, Miss Dorothea Dix, was vetoed on the grounds that it would set a precedent in the care of the indigent mentally-ill which might lead to federal participation in measures for the care of other indigents, and thus, in the language of the President, "to transfer to the Federal Government the charge of the poor in all the States." This, the President feared, would lead to a condition in which "the fountains of charity will be dried up at home and the several states, instead of bestowing their own means on the social wants of their own people, may themselves . . . become humble supplicants for the bounty

---

[10] These two cases were *Massachusetts v. Mellon* and *Frothingham v. Mellon*. In both the complaints were dismissed on the basis of lack of court jurisdiction; see also Council of State Governments, *op. cit.*, Chap. 2, "Legal Background of Federal Aid."

of the Federal Government."[11] This unequivocal interpretation of social welfare as a basic state power and function was reinforced through the years by other chief executives, by Congress, and by the sanction of custom.

Until the depression it was generally unthinkable to people that anyone should ask the national government for direct aid. So deeply ingrained was this idea that President Pierce and others had only to suggest the possibility that an indigent person might go seek aid through the national government, and any proposal of federal aid for welfare would be doomed. It is true that other forms of federal aid to individuals were given, such as homestead rights on public lands, and many aids, direct and indirect to business, but relief of indigency was not considered an appropriate basis for granting funds, except in a few cases of national disaster.

There is a second basis for the interpretation that social welfare is a state and/or local rather than a federal function. This is the belief that government should be kept as close as possible to the people. This of course implies that the national government is the most remote from the people, and that the municipal or county government is the closest. In strictest logic, one might question whether in the great, sprawling metropolis of today, government actually is closer to the people than is the state or national capitol, if one thinks of direct knowledge of problems or of responsiveness to needs. Nevertheless, this belief has been persistent and strong, and has fortified the philosophy of local responsibility for social welfare. For the people in the metropolitan community, the national Senate may be more representative than the state government, because in many states the urban population is insufficiently represented in the state legislature.

A third reason is both political and administrative. It relates to centralization of power and function. In political terms, the dangers of centralization, which were alluded to earlier, cause people to fear any large-scale concentration of power. Administratively, when all decisions are made centrally, a program may become

11 From the *Congressional Globe,* 33rd Congress, 1st session (May, 1854), pp. 1061-63.

cumbersome and unwieldy. Even in a unitary state, as political scientists have pointed out, many functions are performed locally —in the interests of effective service.

But other influences have worked to bring about the present, large-scale pattern of intergovernmental responsibility for social welfare. As the dimensions of the welfare program have grown, and as additional welfare services have been demanded by the people, both local and state resources have proven inadequate. This has brought out an essential anomaly, one requiring some resolution. This anomaly is the fact that the level of government bearing the responsibility for social welfare has not possessed the resources to meet that responsibility, while the level possessing adequate resources has lacked the authority to assume the responsibility.

This fact came out sharply during the depression when, as we have noted, the resources of the state and local governments were strained beyond their capacities by the demands of unemployment relief, and when the exigencies of need demanded that the federal government step in with funds. Other welfare services, however, which engaged federal participation during that period, also evolved out of fiscal facts relating to the needs and resources of the different levels of government. As John A. Perkins, currently Under-Secretary of Health, Education, and Welfare, points out with reference to the health services, states were competing with each other to attract industry. In those that did embark on programs of social legislation, regulation, research, and other activities associated with modern government, according to Secretary Perkins, "industry and citizens found some of their individual and corporate freedom reduced in order to promote the health, safety, and welfare of the people as a whole."[12] He noted further,

Not only that, their taxes were made higher too. Industry and citizens either sought sanctuary, or threatened to do so,

[12] "The Community, the State, and the Nation in Public Health," Speech before Association of State and Territorial Health Officers, Washington, D. C., November 5, 1957.

in other States which had fewer regulations and lower taxes. In the poorer States modern services could be financed only with the greatest difficulty, if at all. Capacity to tax in support of such governmental services on something like an acceptable pattern varied greatly from State to State, depending upon industrial and individual wealth. In general, the tax systems developed by the States are of the regressive variety and employ direct rather than indirect levies, thus heightening citizens' resistance to taxes. Even where there was the wealth and a fairly satisfactory revenue system to do the job, the legislature did not always understand the wishes or requirements of the people. Many of the legislatures were not really representative because they were not properly reapportioned as State population patterns changed. They did not, and sometimes still do not, reflect the predominantly urban culture that has developed in the United States.

Then, too, in many commonwealths, executive authority has been diffused among the governors and a host of other elective State officials. Fixing responsibility for initiation of executive policy—or the failure to initiate it—has been difficult. When laws were passed the same administrative structure, lacking merit systems and without organized and focussed responsibility, sometimes provided less than satisfactory topside administration. It became increasingly evident that the extent and quality of some services of government, such as fighting disease and safeguarding public health, while local by fact of original Federal-State arrangement, were national in their consequences. The Federal Government had to act. The old adage, "money makes the mare go," was recalled. Congress by legislation and appropriation gave incentive to first one, then another function to extend and improve services.

In this country, the grants have been made for special functions rather than for broad general purposes. Thus we have special grants for each of the welfare programs, and in public assistance, separate grants for each of the four categories of aid. Since conditions are attached to these grants, the result is the development of significant federal influence on the programs.

At the federal level, the grant-in-aid is an expression of the philosophy that government has the power to tax for the general welfare in support even of those programs which it cannot itself, under the Constitution, take responsibility for directly administering. In a sense, the federal government, through this device, buys a share of the operation of social welfare programs. Thus the grant-in-aid is designed to permit the use of the resources of a larger unit of government without basically altering the relations among the levels. For the states, the grant-in-aid is a device for helping local governments perform their functions when it is determined to be in the interests of the people to keep the administrative responsibility at a local level. The fundamental constitutional questions which arise in federal-state relations are not inherent in the state-local relationship.

Can any principles be inferred as guiding the decisions of the national government to enter the social welfare field through the use of grants? It seems clear that three conditions must be present: (1) Great need; (2) A problem involving the national interest, and (3) Ways of meeting the problem which exceed the fiscal and administrative capacity of the state and local units of government. While these criteria determine whether or not federal action shall be taken, it should not be inferred that they yield a precise formula. How acute must the problem be? By what standards? What precisely is meant by national interest? Is there a greater national interest in, let us say, aid to the disabled than in the problem of inadequate facilities for education? To keep the question closer to social welfare, is there less national interest in the public provision of good medical care than in the granting of funds for vocational rehabilitation? Such questions suggest that the consideration of national interest is subject to many factors, and determined in the context of the times. Furthermore, wide disparities in fiscal capacity exist among the various states, and among the local units of government within the states. Considerable differences in resources of administrative staff and facilities also may exist, although they are not necessarily related to fiscal capacity so much as to other elements.

On the constitutional question, it should be noted that there are no absolute lines of demarcation between federal and state responsibility. The Tenth Amendment to the Constitution reserves the unenumerated powers to the states or to the people. The people, after all, have representation in the national as well as the state government. They have the power to call on national government for services. More and more, power has been exercised by the legislative branch to choose those services which shall be offered or financed by national government, with less judicial restraint, particularly since the historic Supreme Court decisions of the 1920's and 1930's relating to the right of the national government to participate in social security programs.

The point of concern is the extent to which the spirit of the federal system is violated by increasing national participation in areas once reserved to state and local action. The recent inquiries and studies mentioned in the preceding pages are designed to determine how far the federal government ought to go in the exercise of its powers in this area. Here, too, the people have the final choice. And when there is an acutely felt problem, such as the disturbance over alleged deficiencies in our educational system, or widespread concern over unemployment resulting from the recession which began in the fall of 1957, much of the argument over questions of constitutional theory is likely to be superseded by popular demand for federal action to meet emergencies.

PURPOSES OF GRANTS-IN-AID

Grants-in-aid serve several purposes, of which improving the quality of service is only one. These have been summarized by Byron L. Johnson as follows:[13]

> To encourage or stimulate the States to develop or expand certain services . . .
> To assist the States to finance some kind of "national minimum" in certain public services . . .
> To secure for the Federal Government a measure of leader-

---

[13] "The Principle of Equalization Applied to the Allocation of Grants-in-Aid," *Memo No. 66,* Bureau of Research and Statistics, Social Security Administration, September, 1947, pp. 20-22.

ship with respect to certain State and locally administered functions of national interest and to assure adequate performance of functions involving vital national interest . . .

To combine within a Federal system the virtues of local control over administration of many functions with the superior money-raising powers of the Federal Government . . .

To equalize to a greater or lesser extent service levels and relative tax burdens among the States and among persons in different income classes and different local jurisdictions, thus in effect, also to reduce disparities in income among persons and among areas . . .

To improve the over-all Federal-State-local tax system so that it becomes more progressive and more uniform, by placing more of the cost of government on Federal and State income taxes, less on local property taxes . . .

To aid in approaching full employment, or to counter the business cycle . . .

To an extent at least, grants-in-aid for social welfare serve all of the purposes suggested by Mr. Johnson. Certainly there is plenty of evidence that the states have developed and expanded welfare services. If no clear-cut case can be made that a national minimum of service does exist, it nevertheless is true that the general level of social welfare has been raised through the use of federal grants. Whether federal leadership has actually safeguarded local control is a debatable subject which will be discussed later.

The fifth and sixth points made by Mr. Johnson involve important administrative and fiscal considerations. There is wide variation from state to state in *per capita* income and in over-all wealth. It is harder for the residents of the poorer states to support a program of even minimum adequacy than for people in states where income and wealth are greater to finance a more extensive and generous program. It is also true that the chief source of local funds is still the property tax, and where local support is required, the burden falls upon the least equitable form of taxation. Also, as has been stated elsewhere, wealth is mobile, and to some extent, at least, can escape the burden of supporting such services, when the base for taxation rests with the state and local governments.

The extent to which the purposes of the grant-in-aid are served may vary with the type of grant. There are various types. They may have a single purpose, or a broad general purpose. The latter type includes those in which money is made available for a "block" of programs, as for example, for improving the general level of welfare services. In such grants, the receiving unit of government has the authority to decide how the funds should be allocated among the various kinds of service. This method, some students of intergovernmental relations believe, is the best, but the single-purpose grant is the prevalent one in social welfare today.

The grant may be matched by the receiving authority or it may have no such requirement. The term "matching" refers to the practice of requiring the unit of government to which the grant is made to put up a specified amount in order to secure the funds. This may be required in varying proportions among the various grants. Some programs, as will be seen, are mixtures of the matched and the unmatched grants.

Further variations are found in the extent to which detailed requirements are specified as conditions to be met in order to receive the grant. While no grants-in-aid in social welfare at present are offered free of conditions, some are much more flexible in relation to the uses that may be made of the funds and less detailed in advance requirements than others.

Some people draw an analogy between federal-state and state-local relations. This is not a legitimate analogy. The federal and state governments are considered sovereign in their respective spheres, according to the Constitution. While rigid application of this doctrine has not been possible under the pressures of modern circumstances, it still remains basically true. The counties and municipalities, on the other hand, are subdivisions of the state. Their power derives entirely from state legislation and/or from charters granted by the state. This has definite significance in such welfare programs as public assistance, which within the states depend upon state powers to compel local governments to act. To treat county welfare agencies as if they were parts of a federal system within the state is to misunderstand the nature of the relationship.

There has been more than a casual connection between liberalization of the programs and the shift in intergovernmental responsibility through the grant-in-aid. With the utilization of the resources of the central government, wider financial support has been available. Better standards have resulted as the state and national governments have become involved, administratively and financially. These have been important, in the form of extension of services, greater adequacy in the services which are provided, more liberal standards for qualification, and more humane methods of administration.

FINANCIAL ARRANGEMENTS IN FEDERAL GRANTS

The social welfare grants to the states show considerable state-by-state variation. As the following table indicates, there is little connection between either the wealth or the poverty of the state and the amount of money received in federal grants for social welfare. How account for the fact that New Jersey, which is one of the wealthier states, gets the smallest *per capita* amount in grants of any state, while California, which is also one of the wealthiest, gets one of the higher amounts, and Nevada, which consistently ranks high in *per capita* income, received the highest amount of all states in *per capita* value of grants for social welfare? Mississippi, one of the lowest-income states, on the other hand, received a substantial amount in comparison with other states, while Virginia, another one of the less wealthy states, received one of the lowest amounts *per capita*.[14]

Several factors influence the amount of money a state receives from the national government as grants-in-aid. One is the ability or desire of the state to provide a program which will attract maximum federal participation. Another is the kind of matching pro-

---

[14] Reference to wealth in this connection is based on *per capita* income in the states, although in reality this is only one index of wealth. The difference in *per capita* grants among states with comparable *per capita* income is due to a combination of factors, including strictness or liberality of eligibility requirements, size of the program enacted, and by such conditions as population characteristics, *e. g.*, an industrial state may have more people receiving social insurance benefits, and consequently fewer dependent on assistance.

Federal Grants to State and Local Governments, 1956, by States, and Other Areas

State or Area	Amount (in thousands)	Per Capita	State or Area	Amount (in thousands)	Per Capita
Alabama	94,242	30.30	New Hampshire	11,852	21.43
Arizona	31,405	31.19	New Jersey	57,364	10.77
Arkansas	56,828	31.54	New Mexico	33,432	42.16
California	308,560	23.81			
Colorado	50,884	32.89	New York	245,501	15.32
			North Carolina	85,128	19.60
Connecticut	30,963	14.07	North Dakota	18,867	29.34
Delaware	6,976	17.89	Ohio	122,057	13.65
District of			Oklahoma	95,663	43.29
Columbia	12,807	14.94			
Florida	76,827	21.46	Oregon	34,282	20.35
Georgia	92,378	25.23	Pennsylvania	156,302	14.34
			Rhode Island	20,630	25.25
Idaho	18,769	30.67	South Carolina	46,538	20.18
Illinois	148,404	15.96	South Dakota	21,062	30.84
Indiana	55,980	12.93			
Iowa	54,095	20.25	Tennessee	75,625	22.15
Kansas	51,939	25.21	Texas	189,943	21.71
			Utah	24,770	31.08
Kentucky	71,434	23.72	Vermont	10,352	27.98
Louisiana	107,719	36.71	Virginia	62,135	17.36
Maine	22,259	24.57			
Maryland	41,007	14.94	Washington	66,328	25.44
Massachusetts	89,910	18.84	West Virginia	46,993	23.69
			Wisconsin	57,961	15.66
Michigan	110,950	15.14	Wyoming	14,284	45.78
Minnesota	64,738	20.29			
Mississippi	57,165	26.80	Alaska	9,070	43.40
Missouri	130,496	31.06	Hawaii	13,947	24.91
Montana	21,367	33.97	Puerto Rico	26,712	11.80
			Virgin Islands	838	34.93
Nebraska	34,607	24.83			
Nevada	14,053	59.80	Total	$3,404,389	$20.34

SOURCE: *Statistical Abstract,* U. S. Census Bureau, 1957, Table 319, p. 261.

vision in the federal grant, or whether it favors states with greater or lesser ability to raise money. If the conditions are such that the more money the state spends on a program the more it receives as grants, the wealthier states can receive the lion's share. More and more in the various programs, the federal government has turned to various kinds of equalization formulas in an effort to make the amounts granted to states at least somewhat related to needs. Some grants have special conditions favoring certain groups or types of communities. For example, the amount a state receives for child welfare services is conditioned by the proportion of children living in rural areas.

The grants-in-aid for social welfare are computed by different formulas. Many of them are quite complicated. Yet each has a certain rationale either in the purpose of stimulating a service, equalizing the burden of costs, or some other purpose, and each has been developed in recognition of the special problems involved in the services operated under the different programs. With these considerations in mind, we shall examine the various fiscal formulas.

Grants for public assistance programs

The largest of the federally-aided social welfare programs are those in public assistance. Public assistance is divided into four grants, one for each of the four categories: old age assistance, aid to dependent children, aid to the blind, and aid to the permanently and totally disabled. In 1955 federal funds granted to states for the four categories totalled almost $1.5 billion.

Through the years successive changes in the provisions of the Social Security Act relating to the distribution of costs have increased the federal share, and have tended to relate the amounts granted to the needs of the separate states. In the original Act, under the public assistance titles, the states were required to match dollar-for-dollar the money received from the national government, up to a specified maximum for each individual.

The first break in this rigid pattern was made in 1946, when the federal share was increased, and the maximum limit of individual payments for which the federal government would participate was raised. Under a new type of formula, the federal government paid a larger share of the first part of the grant to the individual, and a lesser share of the remainder, up to the maximum in which participation was permitted. This was the consequence of a long battle for a better way of cost-sharing, one which would permit the federal government to increase its assistance to the poorer states. This was a step toward equalization, *i.e.*, payment on the basis of state need and financial ability, since it was evident that the states with the smallest fiscal capacity and greatest need generally paid the lowest grants. Since the federal portion was greatest for the first part of the grants, the states paying low amounts in grants would receive comparatively more money from the federal government. This was an indirect way of achieving equalization, however, since it was based on the state's performance rather than on a direct measurement of its fiscal capacity.[15]

Raising the ceiling on the amount of payments in which the federal government would participate was intended to liberalize or increase the sums for assistance granted to needy persons. The original maximum for federal aid was $30 per person per month for old age assistance and aid to the blind. For aid to dependent children, it was $18 for the first child in the family, and $12 for each additional child. Successive amendments to the Social Security Act have increased these amounts to $60 in old-age assistance, aid to the blind, and aid to the permanently and totally disabled, and for aid to dependent children $32 is the maximum for any eligible child, and the same amount to the relative with whom the child is living if that relative also is ruled "needy." There are exceptions in Puerto Rico and in the Virgin Islands, where the federal share is one-half the amount paid to any needy individual, up to a maximum of $30.

The formulas for cost-sharing within these maximum amounts are as follows: In three categories—old-age assistance, aid to the blind, and aid to the permanently and totally disabled—the federal share is four-fifths of the first $30 of average monthly payments to individuals, plus one half of the balance of individual payments up to a total of $60. If a state made a monthly grant of $60 to an individual, the federal portion would be $24 of the first $30, plus $15 of the remaining $30, a total of $39 of the $60. In

---

[15] Eveline Burns points out, however, that this practice also benefits the wealthy state which is able but unwilling to pay higher grants; *Social Security and Public Policy* (New York, 1956), p. 243.

effect, the lower the amount of aid, the higher will be the federal share.[16]

In aid to dependent children, the same principle is followed but the amounts differ. Of the matchable maximum, which is $32 each for the first child and one eligible caretaker relative, and $23 for each additional child, the federal share is $14 of the first $17 of the average monthly payment, plus one-half the balance for each individual payment up to the maximum amount which is matchable ($32 and $23 respectively).

Separate provisions govern the sharing of direct payments to vendors for medical care in the public assistance programs. The federal share of such payments in aid to dependent children cases is one-half the cost in any month up to a maximum of $6 for the eligible adult, and one-half the cost up to $3 for a child. In the other categories of aid, the federal share of medical costs is one-half up to $6 for each recipient.

Half the costs of state and local administration of public assistance are paid by the federal government. This, of course, has permitted state and local administration to provide more adequate services to applicants for and recipients of public assistance.

In a number of the states, localities also may participate in the various assistance programs. Under the Social Security Act the states must participate financially in the costs of the program, but they are not precluded from requiring the localities to pay a share of the costs. In many states, the localities bear no part of the burden. Whether or not they should has been a somewhat controversial question in public assistance administration, with some sentiment in favor of local financial participation as a means of insuring a greater degree of responsibility in expenditure of funds, while other sentiment opposes this on the basis of the belief that it is inequitable to place the burden upon local units which vary widely in their capacity to share the costs. These variations in fiscal capacity among localities within a state may be more pro-

---

[16] These provisions do not hold for Puerto Rico and the Virgin Islands, which provide for one-half federal matching up to $30 for assistance to the aged, blind, and disabled, and one-half up to $18 each for the caretaker relative and first child in ADC, and one-half to $12 for each additional child.

nounced than are those among states. In fact, the smaller the units, the greater are the disparities in fiscal strengths. This point was brought out by a special Senate Committee some years ago, which said: "Figures for income and wealth, for assessed wealth and equalized values, all tell the same story. As the size of the local unit decreases, the variation in *per capita* wealth and income increases. All the comparisons of *per capita* wealth in local areas show much greater variations than appear between state values . . ."[17]

Public assistance is unique among federally-aided welfare programs. It serves the largest number of persons, and expends the largest amounts. Only public assistance has the open-end grant feature, which places a maximum on the amount which may be granted on behalf of an individual, but no maximum on the number of individual recipients who may be paid under the program.

In 1955, the federal share of public assistance represented 48.7 percent of the total expended for assistance to individuals. Expenditures from state funds represented 38 percent, and from local, 13.2 percent. The effect of the present system of matching, of providing larger proportions of money for the first part of the grants, is indicated by the following differences in proportions of federal and state funds spent in assistance programs in the states. Mississippi, for example, which ranks consistently near the bottom in average amounts of assistance paid to individuals, had 74.7 percent of its costs defrayed by grants from the federal government. The ten states receiving the highest proportion of federal funds (in proportion to state expenditures) were in the South, where the *per capita* income and the amounts of payments are generally lower.[18]

The two basic factors in equalization are the need for service, and the ability to finance this service. It would be erroneous to

17 Letter from the Acting Secretary of the Treasury transmitted in response to Senate Resolution No. 160, *Special Committee on Intergovernmental Fiscal Relations in the United States,* Doc. No. 69, 1943, p. 191.

18 Social Security *Bulletin,* "Annual Statistical Supplement, 1955," Table 83: "Expenditures for Assistance and Administration: Amount and Percentages Distribution by Program for Each Source of Funds and by Source of Funds for Each State," 1955, p. 61.

make any serious claim that this method of granting public assistance funds to states meets either criterion. While low income states may receive a higher percentage of their expenditures from federal grants as the result of such formulas as those now in effect, high income states which are able to pay up to the federal maximum get the greatest dollar benefit. In the low income states such a method of allocation does not provide any incentive to raise the individual grants of assistance to a level more nearly adequate to meet needs. If anything, states may be influenced to keep the grants at a low level likely to attract the maximum proportion of federal funds, with the result that assistance standards are depressed rather than raised. Other types of formulas, designed for equalization, *i.e.*, for payments related to fiscal capacity, have been consistently advocated by the responsible agencies of administration of public assistance, by the American Public Welfare Association, and lately, by the President's Commission on Intergovernmental Relations. These proposals have been rejected by Congress.

Grants for unemployment insurance programs

Unemployment Insurance has a pattern of federal-state cooperation entirely different from that of public assistance. The federal government offsets 90 percent of all unemployment insurance taxes levied by the states on employers covered under the federal law. Since the payroll tax is 3 percent, the federal share is .3 percent of the taxable amount, or 10 percent of the total 3 percent levy. This means that if the total payroll is $20,000 the payroll tax of 3 percent will amount to $600, and the federal government's share of this will be $60. From the national treasury, funds are made available to the states to cover the costs of administration of employment security when the state programs are approved as meeting federal standards.

Since 1954, the law has stipulated that all unemployment insurance tax collections by the national government must be earmarked for employment security programs, and that any collections exceeding the amounts paid to the states be placed in a loan fund up to a maximum total of $200 million. States may borrow without interest from this fund whenever their benefit reserves are in danger of depletion. After the fund has reached the maximum amount, additional excess collections are distributed among the states in accordance with the relative amount of the payroll covered by the insurance program in the particular state.

There is no allotment formula for determining the amount which each state receives for the administration of employment security, and no matching is required. The funds are appropriated and apportioned on the basis of what the Secretary of Labor deems to be the need of each state for proper and efficient administration.

Grants for services to children

Still different patterns of federal grants are found in services to children. Here, all three federally-aided programs—child welfare services, crippled children's services, and maternal and child health services—express through the methods of fund allocation the purpose of strengthening state measures, without imposing a system of service from the outside.

For child welfare services, the maximum total amount which may be allocated per year to the states now is $12 million. The funds are distributed to the states on the following basis: First, a flat sum of $40,000 is paid to each state which has an approved plan of services. The balance (as provided in section 521 of the Social Security Act) is allocated on the strength of the plans which are presented by the states, in amounts "not to exceed such part of the remainder as the rural population of each state under the age of eighteen bears to the total population of the United States under such age."

The state is not required to match the federal grant. It is expected, however, that the federal money shall provide only a part of the total spent on the child welfare services in the state. Federal funds are not supposed to take the place either of state or local funds, or of services available from voluntary agencies within the states.

With the exception of one year, 1947, the amount appropriated has never equalled the amount authorized. In 1957, although $10 million were authorized, the appropriation was only $8,361,000.

The maximum amount authorized for federal grants to states for Crippled Children's Services is $15 million. This fund presents a combination of matched and unmatched funds. Half of the amount, designated as Fund "A" must be matched dollar for dollar by the state. It is allocated as follows: First, a flat amount is paid to each state with programs of service to crippled children. The balance of Fund "A" is allocated according to the number of children under twenty-one in the State.

The other half of the appropriation, Fund "B" does not have to be matched by the states. It is apportioned as follows: First, 25 percent is required to be used for special projects of regional or national importance. The balance of this fund is apportioned on the basis of the number of children under twenty-one in the state (with children in rural areas counted double) and inversely related to the state's per capita income. In other words, the higher the number of children under twenty-one, especially in rural areas, and the lower the per capita income, the greater will be the state's portion of this Fund. No state may receive less than $25,000 from Fund "B." This is a complicated formula. It seems to represent an attempt to achieve these purposes: (1) to grant a basic amount to all states; (2) to grant additional funds in relation to need as measured by the number of children in the state, particularly those living in rural, and therefore presumably disadvantaged areas from the standpoint of facilities for diagnosis and treatment of crippling conditions; (3) to allow further for differences in state ability to support programs by relating grants inversely to per capita income in the states; and (4) through the use of Fund "B" to encourage the development of special projects designed to improve the quality of services to crippled children.

Like Crippled Children's Services, the Maternal and Child Health program has two funds, designated "A" and "B" respectively. The appropriation is divided equally between the two funds.

Under Fund A, which must be matched dollar for dollar by the state, a grant of $60,000 is made to each state, plus an additional amount based on the proportion of live births in the state to the total live births in the nation.

Fund B is divided into two parts as follows: 75 percent is allotted by formula, based on an index of maternal and child health financial need. The two factors, as in crippled children's services, are the number of children in rural areas, with these children counted double, and *per capita* income in the state, with lower *per capita* incomes receiving larger shares. The remaining 25 percent is designated for special projects, designed to improve or extend services for mothers and children, if such projects are deemed to be in the regional or national interest.

The appropriation for the fiscal year 1958 for child welfare services is $10 million or an increase of more than $1.5 million over the preceding year. Crippled Children's Services have been allotted $15 million, the same as for the preceding year, and Maternal and Child Health Services $16.5 million.

One of the questions which have arisen in connection with this program is whether the time has come to extend federal aid to include children in urban as well as rural areas. The present provision stems from the depression era, when it was assumed that sufficient resources were more likely to be available in the cities. With the population shift to urban from rural areas in the past years, and with the acute problems which seem to be arising among children in the more populated areas, it is maintained that the present distinction favoring rural areas has lost its purpose.

Grants for vocational rehabilitation

Vocational Rehabilitation grants are designed to serve three purposes. These are: (1) to support the basic state services in Vocational Rehabilitation; (2) to assist in the extension and improvement of rehabilitation services; and (3) to support special projects. Most of the funds appropriated for this program are utilized in the support of basic state services. In the fiscal year 1955 of the total of $28.75 million available to the federal office of Vocational Rehabilitation, $24 million was granted to the states for basic support. The states, in turn, matched the federal grants with $14.6 million of their funds.[19]

Basic support grants are divided into two parts. These are: (1) a base allotment, and (2) an additional allotment. The base allotment is the amount granted the state for vocational rehabilitation during fiscal 1954, increased by a percentage which, if applied to the amounts granted all the states, would increase the total of all such allotments to $23 million. The balance, or additional amount, is allotted by use of a formula, which takes into account the population and per capita income of the state. A maximum is placed on the total amount which a state may receive in any single year for basic support. The law also has established a minimum allotment for this purpose. As has been indicated, the states are required to match the basic support grant in accordance with the established formula.

Grants for the purpose of encouraging the states to extend their services and to undertake new activities may pay up to 75 percent of the costs of such projects. The allotment is made according to size of the state's population, although a minimum allotment is specified. The maximum duration of federal financial participation in such a project is three years.

Special project grants may be made to either state agencies, or to private, nonprofit organizations. As we have noted these fall into two general classes: (1) payment of part of the costs for research, demonstration, or development of special services or facilities designed to solve a problem common to all or several states, and (2) grants designed to contribute to the expansion of the program. The federal share of the former is not specified, except for the stipulation that it shall be only for part of the costs. For the second class of grants, the federal share may not be more than two-thirds of the costs.

In addition to the above grants, it will be recalled, the Office of Vocational Rehabilitation provides funds for grants to universities

---

[19] *New Hope for the Disabled,* Office of Vocational Rehabilitation, Washington, D. C., 1956, p. 9.

and other educational institutions for improvement of teaching, for traineeships in the disciplines concerned with the various aspects of vocational rehabilitation, for short-term courses or institutes, and for research fellowships. These are made directly to the institution participating.

Grants for mental health programs

Allotments to states for all public health services (with the exception of grants for venereal disease control) are based on the following factors: (1) population of the state; (2) extent of the health problem, both nationally and within the state; and (3) the financial need of the state. In mental health, 30 percent is based on population, adjusted on the basis of financial need as determined by the five-year average per capita income in the state, and 70 percent on the extent of the problem, *i.e.*, the incidence of psychiatric disorders in proportion to the population. The state must contribute one dollar for each two dollars of federal funds.

All of the health and welfare grants manifest a tendency on the part of the federal government to use funds in a way that takes into account the extent of the problem, the furtherance of the national interest, and the states' fiscal capacity. In recent years, also, the practice of making special project grants, or funds for stimulating research, training, and experimentation has gained momentum. It is quite apparent that the grant-in-aid is being employed with increasing flexibility of purpose.

ADMINISTRATIVE RELATIONS AMONG LEVELS OF GOVERNMENT

How do social welfare agencies operating at the different levels of government work together in administering these various programs? What are the patterns of administrative relations? What methods are used to promote cooperation, to safeguard the purposes of the programs, and to improve their effectiveness? How are the methods of administration employed?

We know that there is more to the arrangements among jointly participating levels of government than merely setting up accounts for receiving and disbursing funds. Actually, the increasing use of the grant-in-aid has given rise to what is essentially a distinct field of administration, one which differs considerably from the pattern of administration within a single organization at one level of government.

We may be quite certain that the success of these various programs depends on how successfully the agencies at federal, state, and local levels work together. The most carefully conceived purpose of a grant-in-aid may be defeated by poor cooperation, or enhanced by successful intergovernmental activity. Let us now look briefly at the factors which determine the nature of administrative relations among agencies at the different levels of government which participate in the administration of social welfare.

The relationship starts with the conditions attached to the grants. These conditions, set forth in the statute authorizing the grant, will vary from program to program in explicitness and amount of detail. As the description of the federal role will show, the conditions attached to some of the federal grants have had a profound effect on the organization and method of state welfare, an influence that extends beyond the program itself. This is notably true of the public assistance grants which, by the nature of their conditions, have influenced the states in the establishment of more comprehensive and unified state and local welfare departments. While not all grants carry the same kinds of conditions, they all involve elements of federal influence on state and local operation.

If the jurisdiction to which the grants are offered does not find the conditions acceptable, it is free in principle to reject them. Or if it decides that conditions once acceptable are no longer so, it may decide to discontinue compliance and the grants will be stopped. On the other hand, if the granting authority finds that conditions are not being met satisfactorily, the grants may be withheld. Disallowances of support for parts of programs may follow disclosure of practices not in accordance with the conditions of the grant.

The foregoing may suggest a pattern of abrupt action, one of clear-cut situations leading to quick decisions. Actually, nothing of the sort happens. The granting authority has every reason to be reluctant to use such a drastic remedy as the withdrawal of financial support for a service which has been deemed sufficiently important to justify the grant. The people most likely to suffer from such action are those receiving the service, and the needy, the physically or mentally handicapped, or the dependent children are not likely to be left without support unless the situation is extremely bad. Not even the threat of withdrawal of support is likely to be made with impunity. Waving the big stick may antagonize those against whom it is brandished, but the experience of people working in intergovernmental programs provides ample evidence that it is not conducive to smooth or effective working relations.

The late David C. Adie, former Commissioner of Social Welfare in New York State, made a significant comment on this point some years ago. "When state, federal, or even local representatives," he said, "worked solely through their own power of financial reimbursement, or their power to issue procedural instructions by fiat, or their power to hand down rules and regulations which have the force of an ultimatum—surely then those practices will rebound, just as they would if we employed them in case work or in individual activity; like a boomerang they will strike us down."[20]

The point is certainly clear. The practice of using force or of invoking authority rather than persuasion works poorly enough in any phase of human relations. In intergovernmental relations however, with all the vested rights which governments feel strongly are theirs, the application of the heavy hand might be especially harmful.

On the other hand, the agency responsible for administering the grant cannot be weak or heedless of its responsibility to safeguard the purposes of the program, and to see that services financed by the grants are administered efficiently and consistently. Some

[20] "Responsibility of the State in the Supervision of Public Welfare Programs," *Social Service Review,* December, 1939, p. 613.

effective means must be found to insure a satisfactory level of operation without arousing the problems which result from the injudicious use of force or direct pressure.

The Commission on Intergovernmental Relations posed the problem in this way with respect to federal-state relations:[21]

> The administrative framework for a grant-in-aid program must reconcile certain conflicts. On the one hand, the desire to achieve a specific program objective points toward fairly stringent conditions and intensive supervision. On the other hand, the concept of the grant as a cooperative device with administration entrusted to the States suggests a minimum of supervision by the National Government.
>
> In brief, the problem is to have enough control and supervision to ensure results—yet not so much that the States virtually become administrative agents of the National Government, applying a uniform National policy.

Legislation establishing the grants and the conditions tends necessarily to be general. This leaves to the agency administering the grant the responsibility for developing rules and regulations which provide greater detail. How detailed and explicit should such regulations be? Here, the Commission on Intergovernmental Relations suggests this as "The Federal Dilemma,"[22] with this discussion.

> Under such conditions the National agency faces a dilemma. If it exercises judgment on individual cases without guidance from detailed regulations, its decisions appear arbitrary. If it tries to cover every condition with a regulation, there is no end to the rules. Regulations that are specific will often be too restrictive. Regulations that are general will permit diverse interpretations by the National agency's own staff and by State authorities.

This is not exclusively a federal-state problem. In state-local relations in social welfare, the same considerations are important.

---

[21] The Commission on Intergovernmental Relations, *A Report to the President for Transmittal to Congress*, p. 136.

[22] *Ibid.*, p. 138.

Wherever the objective is to foster the exercise of responsible judgment and to allow for adaptation of administration to different sets of circumstances, the same need for a combination of firmness and permissiveness may exist. The major objective of intergovernmental administration should be to improve the capacity of people to act responsibly and to function independently, rather than to compel them to behave in a certain way, or to follow orders with robot-like docility. The variability of human circumstances met by social welfare, a subject on which we have commented previously, demands at least a degree of authority to act independently of direct orders or detailed instruction.

Actually, the basic factor is the quality of the relationship developed through cooperation and years of joint participation among those working at the various levels. If the relations between federal and state or state and local agency are marked by coolness and restraint, by mutual distrust and hostility, no administrative device or regulation is likely to alter the situation. Standards should tend to become increasingly matters of agreement, rather than of enforcement. As relations among agencies at the various levels of government mature through years of cooperative experience, legalistic insistence on formal requirements diminishes in importance, and control gives way increasingly to consultation. Policies are not superimposed by central authority; rather they come to bear the mark of experience of all concerned, whether in local, state, or federal office. Communication is fostered, so that the movement of ideas flows both to and from the central agency.

Some years ago, Josephine Brown described the quality of the relationship as it should exist in these words:[23]

> An arbitrary check-up, enforcement of authority or exercise of control are all diametrically opposed to the very essence of the supervisory relationship. Dictation or over persuasion may create dependency or a rule-of-thumb submission or may lead

---

[23] *Field Work with Public Welfare Agencies* (Chicago, American Public Welfare Association, 1938), Part II, "Principles, Content, and Objectives of Supervision," p. 7.

to outward conformity and inward rebellion. In any case they erect a barrier to understanding. This is the kind of barrier which prevents a person who knows he is in the wrong from admitting it, and which is likely to destroy all possibility of helpfulness.

Thus far, the discussion has centered on the obligation of central authority to establish a productive relationship. This is, however, not a unilateral responsibility. Cooperation is a two-way process. Unless the grantee-agency operates satisfactorily and responsibly, and maintains its share of responsibility for communication, the central agency may be compelled to act in a more authoritative manner.

In fact, none of the foregoing discussion of the importance of cooperation should imply that the central agency should abdicate its authority. In view of the public interest in good programs of social welfare and the nature of the laws under which duties and responsibilities are defined, it seems that a floor of performance is necessary. To the extent that mutuality of interest and participation can be obtained, direct use of authority to compel action may be minimized. Still, authority to take action must be present, available for use when necessary. The important consideration is not so much one of whether authority is present as it is one of how it is exercised.

What methods are used in intergovernmental administration, through what mechanisms is joint participation achieved? Following are some of the most important:

1. Written statements of standards, policies, and procedures, generally through the use of manuals or handbooks.

2. Review and approval of plans submitted by the grantee-agency, for both initial and continuing approval.

3. Review and approval of operating budgets, which the grantee-agency may be required to submit periodically, usually annually.

4. Development and enforcement of personnel standards.

5. Fiscal audit of program.

6. Administrative review of operation.

7. Technical consultation and advice.

8. Conferences between central and local officials on the issuance or revision of policy.

9. Requirement of regular and special reports from the grantee-jurisdiction.

10. Decisions on appeals by clientele.

The programs vary in the extent to which the above methods are available to the central authority. Some are more likely to be possible courses of action to state than to federal agencies.

A course of action which is more likely to be employed by the state than by the federal government is the right to take over local administration in extreme instances. There have been cases in public assistance administration in which this has taken place, as a local authority has refused to comply with mandatory standards. In some instances, agencies of state government have won court decisions empowering them to compel local action. Another device which has been used is the public hearing, which through its attendant publicity brings the weight of public opinion to bear on the noncomplying agency. Many of these devices are used only in extreme instances and are more important as potential rather than as operating methods.

Each of the devices which have been mentioned could be the subject for at least a chapter, and in some instances, a book. Although it is not feasible to analyze all the methods in detail, we shall look at some of the more important ones.

In a sense, most of these devices could be classified as mechanisms of: (1) prior and continuing approval of plan; (2) continuing review and inspection of operation; (3) consultation and advice; and (4) reporting.

Let us look first at the use of the manual or handbook. As we have already discussed some of the considerations which govern the detail or brevity of instruction by rule and regulation, we need not go into these considerations again. Information may be communicated through a series of individual directives covering separate phases of operation. Experience has demonstrated the need for a more comprehensive treatment than this, however, and the manual or handbook has been developed as a kind of organic expression of policy and procedure.

In addition to covering those aspects of policy which are mandatory, the manual may also serve to communicate desirable but not required standards and methods. In preparing such manuals, agencies face some difficult problems. The central agency is not in constant, direct relationship to the local unit, always available to answer questions which arise in daily operation. Naturally, there is a strong temptation to try to anticipate all the questions that may arise, and to provide all the answers in advance. Experience has shown, however, that by going to the extreme of including excessive anticipatory detail, the central agency may defeat its purpose and incur the danger of constricting the local agency, and this may lead to excessive dependency on the written word. In a service in which, as we have stated, so much depends on staff competence and judgment, methods which stifle initiative at the point where the program meets the clientele can have seriously damaging consequences.[24]

The course of local administration under the over-explicit and detailed manual becomes one of obedience and conformity rather than of responsible interpretation and intelligent practice directed toward meeting the needs of the individual client. The agency may develop specialists in literal application of written rules, unable to consider how in practice the rule occasionally might have an adverse effect on people.

Nor is existence of the excessively detailed manual necessarily attributable entirely to dominating tendencies on the part of those at headquarters. It may also be a reflection of timorousness on the part of the local administrator who asks for an answer whenever a perplexing problem arises, or a difficult decision is faced. By getting a "policy" from headquarters, he is spared the pain of making a decision, or of arousing antagonism which might be directed at himself.

---

[24] Redfield suggests that there is a distinction between the manual and the handbook, with the latter being much less rigid and more amenable to flexibility of use. For a discussion of this subject see Charles E. Redfield, *Communication in Management* (Chicago, 1953), esp. Chaps. VII, "Manuals," and VIII, "Handbooks."

The manual is potentially a useful, and in today's complex administrative scheme, an almost indispensable document. To serve best, it should include the basic framework of policy, with regulations and procedures designed to stimulate intelligent, consistent, but not stereotyped behavior. The writer of the manual should always be aware of the difficulties of communicating in writing, and must seek language which will evoke the intended actions by the persons to whom the document is directed.

The central agency's review of plans made by the local agencies has been one of the most important of the devices employed in the administration of intergovernmental programs of social welfare. In examining the laws, the administrative interpretations of policy, the description of the organizational pattern of the state or local agency, the budget, and the fiscal base for the program, the central authority has more than one alternative open. Those responsible may be detail-minded, and may look at every phase of operational planning included in the statement with a view to anticipating exactly how it will work in its every phase. Or, the reviewers may take a most limited view of their authority, looking strictly and exclusively at those features which are related to the explicit conditions of the grant which govern the relationship. In practice, the central authority is mindful of how the plan promises to work but relates the written material to knowledge of the local authority's resources, practices, and capabilities. The written plan is part of a broader examination. Concerned also with social welfare as a cooperative undertaking, the central authority may offer suggestions as to what might be desirable as well as mandatory practices. Less preoccupation with the dotting of "i's" and crossing of "t's" and more with the broad outline of how the program will function produce the most effective use of the plan review.

The power of review of the budget is potentially one of the most effective control devices of administrative supervision. The program depends on money, and decisions to reduce or curtail support have the effect of determining what the agency can do. This is a commonly used device, in state-local relations particularly. Like other mechanisms of preliminary review, and perhaps with greater force than most, the possibilities of control this device permits can either be moderate and enabling, or so complete as to verge on the absolute.

The audit or fiscal review, and the administrative review are the two general types of inspection or review of operations common in social welfare. In addition, in some programs there is the personnel review, an examination of personnel practices. Like the plan review, the inspection of operations will depend for its effect on the interpretation of its purpose. If it is seen exclusively as a penalty review, it is likely to create fear and hostility, and to impede working relationships.

It need not be so interpreted, however. The audit or review of fiscal practices should be concerned with adherence to policy, with efficiency of method, and with integrity of administration. Malpractice cannot be disregarded, but the process need not be limited to such considerations. The audit may also include consideration of how fiscal practices may be improved. The term "constructive" audit has come into increasing usage, as this function has become broader in purpose. Under this concept of the role of the auditor, he may be as much a consultant as an inspector.

The administrative review has become an important device.[25] Designed to give an over-all review of administrative organization and practice, it is conducted by persons skilled in the field being reviewed. In child welfare, for example, or in public assistance, the administrative review staff is comprised of persons with professional education and experience in social work, and with particular competence in the field subject to review. Through examination of case records, reports, and other records in the office, through interviews with staff, and through other sources of information available through the local office, the reviewer evaluates the extent to which practice coincides with the approved plan. This device, which relies on basic materials in the office under

[25] For a discussion of the use of the Administrative Review in Social Security programs, see William L. Mitchell, "The Administrative Review in Federal-State Social Security Programs." *Social Security Bulletin,* Vol. 9, No. 7 (July, 1946), p. 11. Also see Kathryn D. Goodwin, "Administrative Review in Public Assistance," *Social Security Bulletin,* Vol. 6, No. 10 (October, 1943).

review, has developed into an important instrument in administrative supervision both by state and federal offices. An important feature of the administrative review which should not be overlooked is its value in the development of policy. It serves, to a significant extent, to disclose gaps or inadequacies in the programs, or to reveal areas of possible improvement of services, quite aside from plan provisions.

Generally, both of these types of review rely on sampling rather than on total coverage of cases. The purpose is not so much to detect individual errors, although this is included, as to determine the total effectiveness of administration. The review is thus more of a diagnostic than a punitive device. At its best, it provides both the local and the state authority with valuable, useful information on what may be done to raise the level of operation.

As has been stated, technical consultation and advice assume larger roles in administrative supervision as the programs mature. Social welfare is a complex operation, and as we again remind ourselves, one which requires the use of many professional disciplines.

Consultation must be related to the service, however, and the special knowledge of the expert must be kept in balance with the other demands of the program. The specialist through his technical knowledge sometimes may become a controlling influence, but most of the time this would be a dangerous relationship, and a threat to the successful operation of a well-balanced program.

The practice of requiring reports may seem rather innocuous, and something which should have little effect on the broad framework of administrative relationships. The kinds of information required, however, and the types of reports demanded give this device in practice potentially significant influence. The agency may be impelled to emphasize and to assess those features which they must report as of great importance simply because they are required features of reports. With increasing sophistication in intergovernmental operation, however, this tendency is minimized, and the report becomes a useful device for understanding and interpreting a service, and for providing basic information needed for such purposes as modifying policy, or preparing recommendations for legislation. It may serve to relate experience in local offices to that of other agencies in the state or national area. There is danger in the report that becomes fixed, and outlives its purpose and usefulness.

Reports and special bulletins are valuable means used by central authorities—state or federal—for conveying certain types of information. They are primarily educational devices, designed to add to the information and skill of staff at the local level, or to call attention to special features of programs. Health information, for example, or material on the discoveries in nutrition, or bulletins describing methods of staff training, or reports of new programs, are useful methods of disseminating general information as well as special knowledge. Research by central authorities has continuing value to local agencies.

Group conferences between central and local authorities are effective ways of enhancing communication and agreement, and of avoiding misunderstanding. The practice of conferring on proposed policy has helped to avoid the kinds of misunderstanding which sometimes occur when a statement of policy or procedural change is received "cold." Such conferences, in addition to promoting better understanding, render valuable service in bringing wide and varied experience to bear on all levels upon a problem.

These methods, plus some of those mentioned in connection with state control over county or municipal administration, demand a structure of organization designed to promote continuous communication. Social welfare agencies of government generally have both "departmental" and "field" organization. The latter is the connecting link between the local and central agency. The field representative maintains a continuing relationship with the local unit, interpreting policy developed by the central office, and serving as a channel of communication for the local office. He goes regularly into the local agency from central office. He is expected to be something of a generalist, since in a real sense he represents the whole state office rather than just a part of it or a specialty within it. He must be able to interpret policy of the state office in a way that will have meaning to the local office which is consistent with the intent of that policy.

All in all, field service deserves a volume in itself. It certainly is in many respects the key to effective administration. In some services the field representative has a line relationship to the local office, with direct administrative authority. In other services, however, this position is not so invested with authority, and the field service worker is more of a liaison person between central and local office, with limited power to make decisions. In either event, the function has some distinctive features, which include combinations of administrative responsibility and the role of a consultant. If, as we have said, administrative supervision should be seen as a device for widening rather than constricting freedom of action by local authority, the use of field service is certainly pivotal, and if continuous communication between central and local authority is necessary to effective intergovernmental relations, the function of the field representative is to foster such communication. In the succeeding chapters dealing more specifically with the structure and function of federal, state, and local agencies in social welfare, the place of field service will be seen to have considerable significance.

Not to be passed over lightly is the importance of control over personnel standards in intergovernmental administration. With the quality of staff as important as it is in public social welfare, control over qualifications of personnel is a quite decisive influence on administration. Through state merit systems, states exercise authority over the qualifications, the examination, selection and appointment of staff, and over conditions of employment by local agencies.

The descriptions of some of the major devices used in intergovernmental administration have been designed to provide an understanding of the relationships among levels of government rather than to afford detailed and technical understanding of their nature and use. This is a developing field, and one which merits thorough study. The problems of relationships, of communication, of developing maximum participation on an interagency basis, and the methods used to solve these problems are subjects of growing interest and importance, as intergovernmental programs increase in numbers and size.

ISSUES IN INTERGOVERNMENTAL RELATIONS IN SOCIAL WELFARE

As was stated earlier, federal-state relations is a subject very much on the public mind at present. It seems to be a subject of constant concern and recurring examination, and the objective seems to be one of returning as many functions as possible to exclusive state and local responsibility and control. Naturally any such moves affect social welfare which, as we have noted, accounts for many of the largest and most significant of the grants-in-aid.

This is really not such a strange phenomenon when viewed against the backdrop of our traditional values which the federal system expresses, and when considered with reference to the many and profound changes which have occurred to alter the balance of federal and state responsibilities. During the past twenty-five years, as the welfare function has grown for all levels of government, it has changed the respective functions of state and federal governments. The decision has been made out of necessity as the public has demanded new and improved services, but as Eveline Burns suggests, "In the carrying out of this decision, responsibilities were often distributed between the various levels of government without reference to any clearly thought-out principle."[26]

The urgency with which this problem has been viewed has been influenced, as Dr. Burns further notes, by the presence in the nation's capital of a philosophy which places great emphasis on local self government and states' rights. The demands of the current international situation have undoubtedly quickened and intensified the desire of the national government to seek to be relieved of some of its present financial burden of aid to states.

[26] "Wanted: More Thought About Grants-in-Aid," *Social Work Journal*, Vol. XXXV, No. 1 (January, 1954), p. 11.

The stated charge given by President Eisenhower to the Joint Federal-State Action Committee is indicative of the extent to which an effort to return functions to the states is in the air. This charge, given to the Committee which, it will be recalled, includes seven high-placed federal officials and ten state governors representing the Governors' Conference, reads as follows:[27]

> One—to designate functions which the States are ready and willing to assume and finance that are now performed or financed wholly or in part by the Federal Government.
>
> Two—to recommend the Federal and State revenue adjustments required to enable the States to assume such functions.
>
> Three—to identify functions and responsibilities likely to require State or Federal attention in the future and to recommend the level of State effort, or Federal effort, or both, that will be needed to assure effective action.

It will be noted that this charge does not seem to foreclose continued federal-state cooperation, or even the possibility of new projects. It does, however, set the tone for critical examination of federal-state programs, current and prospective.

Some highlights of the Committee's approach and recommendations to date are as follows:

The Committee iterates its interest in strong state government, and its belief that diversity of local needs requires action whenever possible at the State and local level. It states that it does not intend to impair existing programs, but rather that its objective is to determine whether certain functions can be assumed at the state and local level and be conducted with greater effectiveness as a result. In such instances, the Committee expresses the belief that the states should and can find the necessary resources to finance the programs.

The Committee is not proposing to undertake research on the subject, but rather to utilize existing research and study such as that completed in 1955 by the President's Commission on Inter-

---

[27] As reported in *Social Legislation Information Service,* No. 41, 85th Cong. (Washington, D .C.), Dec. 16, 1957.

governmental Relations. As its first step, the Committee proposes to recommend action on a limited number of specific functions, and to identify taxes which may be used to support them. It also intends to identify those problems which are likely to require state and federal action in the future, in line with the charge given it by the President. By advance review, it feels, it may afford state and federal government the opportunity to give adequate attention to problems as they arise.

The Committee also has recognized the value of small grants designed to stimulate action to meet emergencies or to further definite and strong national objectives. It states further, however, that these grants shall be used as stimulants, and shall not become permanent fixtures as federal operating responsibilities. It suggests certain guides to be used in determining whether the federal government shall make such "small stimulative grants," including careful selectivity, relation to a clear-cut national interest, and assurance that the action will encourage state and local authorities to continue to carry out their primary functions, and "built-in mechanisms" to prevent the federal government from continuing to carry operating responsibilities in areas of action which are deemed properly state and local. A further principle of considerable significance is that in such grants, the states and localities should have flexibility and control in administration of both the funds and the programs, in keeping with the purpose of the federal legislation.

At this point, the Committee has made certain recommendations for curtailment or reduction of federal support for certain programs. One of these is the Vocational Education program, in which it is recommended that support for the older of the parts of the program be withdrawn, with the governors and the state legislatures being urged to find the money necessary to replace federal support. In this and other programs, the recommendation is based on the assumption that they are proper spheres of state and local action, and that stimulative grants are no longer necessary. Other areas for which recommendations of curtailment or reduction of support are made include natural disaster relief, planning activities for urban renewal, and grants for municipal waste treatment plants.

The Committee is studying the possibilities for additional revenue sources for state and local governments, and the possibilities of tax credits in those instances in which the states levy state taxes on certain sources of revenue now federally taxed. For example, the Committee recommends that the federal government, which imposes a tax of 10 percent on local telephone calls and toll calls above a certain amount, give a 40 percent tax credit to those states which enact a 4 percent telephone tax. In addition, the Committee is examining other sources of tax revenue which might similarly be made available to the states.

None of the larger programs of social welfare is included in the present recommendations, although it is possible that they will be under scrutiny in future months. Whether the result will be any large scale recommendations of federal withdrawal of support is not known. Finding sources of federal revenue which could be relinquished to state and local governments for the support of such large programs as public assistance would be quite another matter.

In his budget message to the Congress on January 13, 1958, President Eisenhower gave considerable evidence of his agreement with the Committee's trend of thinking. He called for the exercise of the utmost restraint in giving new responsibilities to the national government, advocated the transfer of support for some services back to the states and localities, and increased state and local responsibility in three others as suggested by the Committee. Of greatest significance, however, was probably his recommendation that beginning in 1960, federal participation should be reduced in the largest of the welfare grant-in-aid programs, those of public assistance.

Another important current Congressional inquiry into federal-state relations is being undertaken by the Intergovernmental Relations Subcommittee of the House of Representatives Committee on Government Operations. This Committee has conducted a series of regional meetings throughout the country. The questions to which the Committee announced it will address itself were enumerated last summer as follows:[28]

1. (a) What is your appraisal of the impact to date of the recommendations of the Commission on Intergovernmental Relations on:
   (1) The Congress
   (2) The Executive Branch of the Federal Government
   (3) State Legislatures
   (4) The Executive Branch of State Governments
   (b) What approaches can you suggest for achieving better follow-through on Commission recommendations?
2. (a) Do you agree or disagree with the view that the growth of Federal programs in fields traditionally considered State responsibilities has been due in large measure to failure of the States to meet pressing public needs? Please explain.
   (b) If you agree with this view, what are the barriers to effective and responsive State Government and how can they be removed?
3. In relation to existing Federal grant-in-aid programs, is the principle of sharing administrative responsibility with State and local governments sound, or is allocation of complete responsibility for a program to a single level of government preferable?
4. If Federal grants were discontinued with the simultaneous discontinuance of an equal amount of Federal taxation (by vacating certain fields or reducing tax rates), would the States be *able* and *willing* to raise sufficient revenues to support the existing Federally-aided programs?
5. Which, if any, of the present grant programs would you like to see completely a State (and/or local) responsibility in exchange for enlarged taxing capacity?
6. If you favor exclusive State responsibility for some grant programs, which tax areas, or portions thereof, now occu-

---

[28] As reported in *Social Legislation Information Service,* No. 31, August 12, 1957 (Washington).

pied by the Federal Government should be relinquished to the States?

7. Are there any existing programs that the States might terminate if the Federal Government were to stop making grants and vacate certain tax fields?

8. (a) If Federal grants now made directly to local government were terminated (*e.g.*, slum clearance and urban renewal, public housing, airport construction), would State Governments be likely to assume any additional responsibility for these activities?

   (b) Could the municipalities finance these programs alone from local revenue sources now available to them? If not, is it likely that cities would be offered either State aid or enlarged taxing powers to continue these activities in the event that Federal grants as well as some Federal taxes are discontinued?

9. (a) Would you favor some type of tax-sharing arrangement whereby the Federal Government would continue to occupy the major tax fields but turn back to the States some percentage of collections for general governmental purposes?

   (b) If such an arrangement were adopted, should the payment to each State be made strictly in accordance with Federal tax collections within that State or should State fiscal need be taken into account?

   (c) As a practical matter, do you believe that all or most Federal tax collections can be equitably allocated to their State of origin? Please explain.

In 1956 the Subcommittee had sent questionnaires to all the state governors and to the District of Columbia, as well as to a representative sample of cities and counties.[29] The replies to these questionnaires, while showing division of sentiment with reference to the virtue of federal grant-in-aid, did not reveal any overwhelming discontent with the present system. The predominant state view, according to the Committee Report, favored continuation of the partnership arrangement, but suggested that the federal government avoid excessive restriction of state freedom of action, and

[29] Sixth Report of Committee on Government Operations, H. R. 575, 85th Congress, 1st session, 1957.

that it minimize superimposed federal control. Some sentiment was expressed that federal supervision was not flexible enough to take into account differences in capabilities among the states, and suggested that the approach of the national government should vary in relation to the level of administrative competence in each state.

The idea that the federal government should avoid administrative controls based on the lowest level of state performance was an interesting one. It raises some significant questions as to how much a federal administrative agency should vary its approach by exercise of its own evaluation and judgment.

While the dominant state view expressed satisfaction with existing arrangements, the suggestions which were made were quite significant. Some related to the extension of federal grants-in-aid or the liberalization of those now in effect. Other respondents, while a minority, were strongly critical. But in general, it can be observed that this report did not indicate a strong groundswell of popular demand to change drastically the present pattern in social welfare.

In a statement alluded to earlier in this chapter, John A. Perkins, Undersecretary of Health, Education, and Welfare has raised some questions relating to the total effect of grants-in-aid in public health. His comments are interesting also with respect to social welfare. Discussing the whole context of federal-state relations, Mr. Perkins acknowledges the effect of improving the level of services provided by states and localities, and also in maintaining a higher level than would have been possible, or at least likely, without such aid. But he states that this very improvement of service through granted funds or at least of those services of immediate concern to many people has had the effect of providing little incentive to insist on the correction of weaknesses in state and local services that brought about federal aid. He states further that the people who are the most directly affected have to a degree "been removed from the process of decision making." Mr. Perkins says:[30]

---

[30] *Op. cit.*, p. 6 of Mr. Perkins' statement.

The tendency is for the professional people in a certain field to develop a program among themselves and sell it to Congress, which on matters of broad national concern will often lend a more willing ear than will a State legislature or a county board. And besides there is only *one* Congress. Once a Federal program is adopted, it is relatively easy to get legislatures and county officials to take the required action, which usually means putting up matching money. Once a program, like a purchase, is available for half price, the battle is more than half won. The very fact that they come at "bargain rates" makes it possible to set up and operate such programs without the same degree of local interest and support that would be required if the same program were to receive its total support on a strictly local basis. Thus, when it is necessary to withdraw or reduce Federal support, the foundation of *local* interest and support is sorely missed.

Other points raised by Mr. Perkins include: the allegation that the "galaxy of Federal grant programs" results in confusion which makes the local people less aware of the source of funds, and less able or inclined to relate the desirability of the service to the cost; the question of whether adequate safeguards are or can be established to insure the prudent expenditure of money for the purpose for which it is intended; the preoccupation of state officials with carrying out the federal programs to the extent that they have not had the time for the necessary inventiveness and initiative to make the state the laboratory for experimentation; and the distortion of the state budget which results from the tendency on the part of the states to direct their expenditures in such a way as to attract federal funds, leaving too little money for badly needed functions which are entirely dependent on state and local support. Mr. Perkins further suggests that there is a tendency for federal grants to become frozen into the structure of the state's fiscal program, long after the initial purpose of stimulating state activity has been served. While this official did not advocate abandoning the grant-in-aid method, he did suggest that in view of today's realities, including large commitments for defense and for bolstering our international position, consideration should be given to a greater

assumption by the states and localities of the public health burden. All of these suggestions, as we have stated, with but slight
paraphrase could be applied to the whole field of social welfare.

For all of these and other questions which presage some possible change in policy on federal grants-in-aid, there is no overt
expression of any widespread intent to scuttle the device. While the
more recent studies, notably by the President's Commission on
Intergovernmental Relations,[31] and the earlier study by the Council of State Governments, were critical of certain phases of the
grant program, both supported the philosophy of the federal
grant-in-aid for those services which existed in the national interest, and which the states and localities could not maintain adequately without aid.[32]

The Committee on Federal Aid to Welfare of the President's
Commission made a total of twenty-three findings with respect to
is subject. Highlights of the report include:[33]

> While interest in welfare is shared by the National, State, and
> local governments, the primary responsibility for providing an
> adequate welfare program clearly lies with the States and their
> political subdivisions. For that reason there is a strong national
> interest in the maintenance and development of vigorous State
> and local governments in order that they may discharge more
> effectively their responsibilities in the welfare field.
>
> The national interest in welfare extends to all public welfare
> activities to the extent that human needs cannot be met by
> individuals, families, social insurance, State and local govern-
> ments from their own resources, or other resources. More spe-
> cifically the national interest includes the following:
>
> (a) Provision to the following groups of opportunity to receive
>   economic aid needed for maintenance, including aid for
>   medical care:

[31] See President's Commission on Intergovernmental Relations, *op. cit.*, also
Council of State Governments, *Federal Grants-in-Aid, op. cit.*, especially Part II,
"Over-All Aspects of Federal Aid."

[32] *Federal Aid to Welfare*, Study Committee Report Submitted to the Commission on Intergovernmental Relations (Washington, D. C., June, 1955).

[33] *Ibid.*, pp. 5-10.

(1) Jobless employable people.

(2) Children who otherwise would be deprived of parental care and guidance.

(3) Children who are separated from their families.

(4) The disabled, including the blind.

(5) The aged.

(b) Provision to the physically and mentally disabled, who
can reasonably expect to become employable, of opportunity to receive services needed to render them fit for
employment.

(c) Provision to other disabled of opportunity to receive
services needed to make them less dependent upon others
or upon public support, or less likely to become dependent
upon such support.

(d) Provision to all of the opportunity to receive through professional services, the corrective, protective, and preventive advice and assistance which will minimize social
maladjustment and increase individual and family well-
being. The advice and assistance of trained personnel are
essential to the welfare of both children and adults.

The National interest in welfare includes a national responsibility for contributing financial support to States to the extent
necessary to provide an adequate program where such support
cannot be fully provided from State and local resources.

The major purposes of Federal financial assistance therefore
are to equalize among States the fiscal burden of maintaining
an adequate welfare program, and to help support minimum
standards. Assistance should also be extended in such a way as
to stimulate States to assume their reasonable share of an
adequate welfare program.

The affirmation of basic state and local responsibility and the
declaration of federal responsibility to assist states and localities
when necessary are consistently maintained in the statement. Further recommendations relate to the nature of allotments, and to
the respective roles of the levels of government in the administration of programs in which they jointly participate.

Turning to a nonofficial study, that of the Council of State
Governments in 1949, one finds similar support for the continu-

ing use of grants-in-aid in social welfare. The report includes the following observations:[34]

1. The federal government has entered the field of social security permanently . . .
2. State and local governments would find it difficult, if not impossible, to finance the present level of public assistance without federal aid . . .
3. The direct administration of public assistance and emergency relief should be in the hands of state and local governments . . .
4. Grants-in-aid provide the best available device for combining federal participation with state and local administration . . .

Let us now try to sort out some of the major questions on intergovernmental relations, especially as they pertain to social welfare. This is a vast and intricate subject, and one which we can treat only in broadest outline.

Has the grant-in-aid weakened the position of the state and local governments in social welfare? Has it been used to shift authority and control to Washington? The opposite viewpoint has been suggested by George E. Bigge, Special Assistant on Federal-State Relations in the U. S. Department of Health, Education, and Welfare. Mr. Bigge states:[35]

Grants-in-aid are regarded by some as, at best, a necessary evil and, at worst, an insidious device for undermining State and local governments and transferring responsibility for many important functions to Washington. Either interpretation misconceives the nature and misreads the history of grants-in-aid.

Mr. Bigge expresses the opinion that the grant-in-aid is the only device which permits the attainment of certain national objectives, particularly those that relate to the welfare of the individual citizen, without taking from the states some of their most

[34] *Op. cit.*, p. 150.
[35] "Federal Grants-in-Aid: A Bulwark of State Governments," *Social Security Bulletin*, Vol. 13, No. 4 (November, 1950), p. 3.

important functions. While these grants do entail some measure of control or supervision by the granting authority, they are far better than the alternative course, which, in most instances, would be the much less attractive alternatives either of inadequate service or exorbitant state taxes, or direct operation of the program by the federal government. It is the opinion of this authority that the grant-in-aid has "halted rather than promoted a trend toward centralization."[36]

Experience with the federally-aided programs of social welfare supports this statement. In this area of service, as we have already noted, states and localities have much larger and more important functions than ever before, and in a sense, have traded complete control over meager programs of aid for shared authority and control over much larger ones.

The volume of service administered by state and local government would have little meaning in the context of the question of authority, however, if at these levels they are entirely subordinate to federal control.[37] As we have seen, this is one of the most complex of the questions of intergovernmental administration. Any review of the many and almost baffling varieties of state programs of social welfare refutes the charge that they exhibit a stereotyped pattern dictated by national requirements and dominated by federal supervision. On the other hand, changes have taken place in state administration which must be attributed to the influence of federal standards.[38] Merit systems of personnel administration in state health and welfare programs are directly due to federal requirements. Federal insistence on the money payment principle in public assistance certainly accelerated the adoption of this practice by state and local agencies. Standards of state and

---

[36] *Ibid.,* p. 18.

[37] See "The Impact of Federal Grants-in-Aid on the Structure and Functions of State and Local Governments," *A Survey Report* submitted to the Commission on Intergovernmental Relations by the Public Affairs Institute (Washington, June, 1955).

[38] For a discussion of this point, see *ibid.*; the opinions of state officials expressed in the report showed a wide variation with respect to whether federal requirements had distorted state operations. As a whole, however, these opinions indicated that the changes were generally desirable from the standpoint of the states themselves.

local practice in services to children have undoubtedly been influenced by the federal agencies administering the grants and by the conditions which have accompanied them. All in all, however, and notwithstanding these and other factors bearing clearly the imprint of federal influence, the variety of administrative patterns and practices among the states, the growing effectiveness of communication among levels of government, and the increasing use of joint consultation among officials at all levels in the development of policy and practice suggest cooperation rather than domination. This is especially true as their joint experience results in increasing agreement on objectives, and in greater harmony of views among administrative agencies.

It is through the grant-in-aid, William Anderson suggests, that states have attained some check upon national administration. States' administrators now have a voice in national policy in the federally-aided programs, and he says, "political power, like electricity, does not run all in one direction."[39]

Have the grants-in-aid weakened the effort of state and local governments in supporting social welfare measures? In some programs, at least, experience belies this contention. State support for health services to children throughout the nation is far greater than the federal contribution. States which can afford it go beyond the federal matching maximums in their payments to individuals in public assistance. In other programs as well the record of state support is impressive.

Another question is that of whether states are coerced into initiating programs through the fiscal pressures exerted by the national government. It is obvious that the tax offset plan of the unemployment insurance program was intended to compel state action. How free are the states to accept or reject federal grants-in-aid? Nominally, there is nothing compulsory in these grants. As we have stated, if the states do not want the grants, they are free in theory to refuse them, and, in fact, this has been done. Even today some states, for example, have not established pro-

---

[39] *The Nation and the States, Rivals or Partners* (Minneapolis, 1955), p. 204.

grams for the permanently and totally disabled. Experience has
shown, however, that through the years the tendency is certainly
toward increased acceptance of participation, until all states are
or will be participating in the programs. In practical terms, it is
difficult for a state government to refuse for long to accept a federal grant for social welfare. The resident of the state is a federal
taxpayer too, and he sees his taxes going for support of services
not available in his own state. Also, with added demands on state
finances today, the price of independence may well seem prohibi-
tive to the state legislator and governor. On the other hand, it is
true that the programs are developed out of the national interest
and the states share in the national concern. This is another example of cooperative rather than divided federalism.

What of the charge sometimes levelled that federal grants result
in a distortion of the state services, as programs are developed to
secure a maximum of federal aid, even at the price of neglect of
services that do not attract such aid? The fact of such influence
can scarcely be denied. Here again, these programs have arisen
out of a definite need and demand, although it is true that state
action may have been primarily taken in some in response to the
availability of federal funds.

Another of the recurring arguments against the grant-in-aid is
that it is unfair to tax the people of one state to support the residents of another. This question is posed with particular urgency
because some of the states with the highest per capita federal tax
payments do not receive anything like the same proportion of
funds back in grants, while states with lower income may receive
more than they pay on a per capita basis. Again the factor of
national interest may be invoked. These programs are developed
in recognition of the interdependence of all the people of the nation. The effects, for example, of bad health—mental as well as
physical—or of unemployment, cannot be localized, and therefore neither should be the obligation and expense of improving
them.

How important the grants-in-aid for social welfare are to a low
income state is attested to by Dr. Ellen Winston, Commissioner

of the North Carolina State Board of Public Welfare, in these words:[40]

> North Carolina is a low income State. Hence Federal Grants-in-Aid not only are essential to the maintenance of the public welfare program but also are a significant factor in the local economy throughout the State. Current adverse conditions in agriculture, increasing unemployment, a growing population particularly among the young and the aged, the rising cost of providing even minimal care for the sick and the destitute, and the growing recognition of the values, and the necessity, of providing more protective, preventive, and rehabilitative services are all resulting in increased demands upon the State and county public welfare agencies.

Any substantial curtailment of federal aid for welfare in this state certainly would have a damaging effect on welfare services, and also, according to Dr. Winston, on the economy of the state.

Some of the criticisms directed against the grant-in-aid suggest that the states are handicapped in the exercise of functions because the federal government has pre-empted the most productive revenue sources. This leads to the suggestion that functions as well as revenue sources be released to the states, thus making it possible to reduce grants-in-aid. Certainly it would seem necessary that any return of function to the states be accompanied by a release of revenue sources to them by the federal government. This principle has been recommended by the State-Federal joint action committee and by the President in his 1958 Budget message. But this would not take into account the disparities among states in the amount of benefits they would derive from such a move. Mr. Bigge suggests that there are two limitations on such proposals. The first is that the most productive of the national taxes are personal and corporate income taxes, which can be most effectively levied on a national basis. Also, these revenues are national in nature, and are derived from enterprises which are inter-

---

[40] Testimony before the Intergovernmental Relations Subcommittee of the House Committee on Government Operations, Raleigh, North Carolina, December 10-11, 1957. (Dr. Winston is President of the American Public Welfare Association.)

state in the sources of income. Wealth is mobile, and may escape state taxes. Such revenues would be available in only a few states, and these would most likely not be the ones needing support.[41] The maintenance of a level of service consistent with the national interest might thus be jeopardized.

In view of the concentration of certain types of revenue resources in the wealthier states, it certainly is open to question whether the release of tax sources by the national government, in return for greater state and local responsibility for welfare programs, would be an even exchange. There is evidence that some states with higher average incomes might get back in taxes much more than they are currently receiving in grants, while states with lower incomes would suffer a substantial net loss, from the discrepancy between taxes released and the amounts of grants they had been receiving. The effect of any such move will be that of increasing the disparities among the states in their abilities to meet welfare needs, particularly in such large programs as those of public assistance.

The possibility that problems of administrative relations in the states may arise from the programs of grants-in-aid is noted by William Anderson.[42] The governor as the political head of the state government, and the person held responsible for the quality of administration of state services, may find that important parts of the state's program, those that are federally-aided, bypass his authority. "A governor finds that the state department heads (for whom the public holds him responsible) deal directly with their federal counterparts (in highways, social welfare, public health, and education, for example) on federally-aided programs, and also with state legislative committees, instead of clearing everything first through officers who are under the governor's immediate control . . ." This of course could be serious in relation to the total structure of state government, even though in a single program it might be less so. Anderson further suggests, however, that these problems in the federally-aided programs are probably more

---

[41] *Op. cit.*, pp. 3-4.

[42] Anderson, *op. cit.*, p. 207. See also "The Impact of Federal Grants-in-Aid on the Structure and Function of State Government," *op. cit.*

due to various "state-imposed obstacles in the governor's path than to federally-aided programs."[43]

Even those who advocate fiscal and administrative cooperation between the federal government and the states and localities, however, agree that the present pattern of grants-in-aid is far from perfect. The question of equalization, that is, of grants in accordance with a state's need and financial ability continues to occupy an important place in discussion of intergovernmental relations. While efforts have been made to achieve some measure of equalization, it is still far from an accomplished fact. Various formulas have from time to time been suggested, and, as we noted in the descriptions of the grants, to some extent are being used to relate to both need and financial capacity.[44] The so-called variable grant, however, presents many technical problems too involved for analysis here.

Another question relates to the number of special purpose grants. Critics of this approach point to the complexities of administration of so many grants. Eveline Burns calls attention to the existence of nineteen federal grants in the field of social welfare. She calls this "a very unwieldy structure," and one which makes for unnecessary complexity.[45] The alternative is fewer grants for broader purposes.

These are among the questions which are raised by those who believe in the principle of federal aid, but would like to see the methods of granting aid and of administering the grants improved.

Suggestions have also been made for extension of the grants into fields not covered by federal aid. Among the most important of these are the inclusion of general assistance in the federally-aided programs, either as a distinct category or as part of a comprehensive grant for public assistance, and the addition of payments in child welfare on behalf of children in foster homes, a cost which states and localities now bear unaided when the child lives

---

[43] *Ibid.,* p. 208.

[44] See Eveline M. Burns, *Social Security and Public Policy* (New York, 1956), pp. 239-248.

[45] "Wanted: More Thoughts About Grants-in-Aid," *Social Work Journal,* January, 1954, p. 13.

with a family not eligible under aid-to-dependent-children requirements.

In the final analysis, opinions on how extensive or limited
grants-in-aid should be depend on the individual's personal philosophy of governmental responsibility for social welfare. If he
believes that the national government fundamentally shares with
the states the responsibility for an adequate standard of social
welfare, he will favor more extensive federal participation in basic
welfare services on a continuing basis. If, on the other hand, he
believes that federal responsibility is more limited and residual,
and should, at the most, be exercised only when the state is unable
to meet its needs, he will advocate more limited programs of aid.
One fact seems clear, however, with reference to these points of
view. The present standards of social welfare, especially in the
states in which the financial capacity is low and the need is great,
could not be maintained by states and localities unaided. Those
who would curtail the grant-in-aid program in social welfare must
face the virtual certainty that the consequences would be a seriously lower standard of service.

Summary

Many of the major programs of social welfare are intergovernmental, that is, shared responsibilities of federal, state, and local
governments. This is true of the public assistance programs, vocational rehabilitation, unemployment insurance, crippled children's
services, and maternal and child health services. Only veterans'
services and O. A. S. D. I. of the larger welfare programs are federally administered, although it might be noted that these are
just about the largest social welfare programs in the nation. Some
programs are either state-local, or else within the exclusive province of one of these levels of government. Nevertheless, the importance of intergovernmental participation today demands that
careful attention be paid to the kinds of cooperation which are
developing.

The federal government participates in state and local programs
of social welfare through the use of the grant-in-aid. This device

enables the national government to participate in programs which are outside its constitutional powers directly to administer. The grant-in-aid is also used to some extent in state-local programs, although the relationship of state to local unit of government is not the same as that between federal and state levels.

The grants-in-aid entail important fiscal and administrative relationships. Fiscally they are designed, among other purposes, to enlarge the state's capacity to maintain its services, to equalize the burden of support among the states, and to equalize the load on the taxpayers through access to sources of revenue which are based on ability to pay. There are several kinds of grants, but the prevailing form in social welfare is the special purpose grant, rather than the block or general purpose form of aid. Most grants are closed-end, that is limited in the total amount which may be granted for a single purpose, but the largest welfare programs, the public assistance measures, feature open-end grants, which are based on amounts per individual, with no maximum on the aggregate amount the states may receive. Grants follow many patterns or formulas which reflect the nature of the programs, and the several purposes which they may be serving.

Administrative relationships determine the success of the grant-in-aid programs. The conditions which are attached to the funds are important influences. How they are enforced or promoted, and the pattern and quality of administrative relations among the participating levels of government may be equally or more important than the terms of the grants. The objective is cooperation rather than domination, and understanding rather than compulsion. Intergovernmental programs feature certain methods which are generally called those of administrative supervision. These include methods of review, of standard-setting, and of consultation. If employed with skill and in a climate of mutual respect, these devices further the success of the programs. As the programs mature, communication at all phases of policy development and administration furthers understanding, and tends to minimize causes of friction. The key to this is fundamental agreement on objectives.

Another important product of maturing relationships among

agencies at the various levels of government is the release from preoccupation with the details of conforming to written requirements, in favor of more attention to innovation and program improvement. Administrative agencies are able to focus more on research, on special projects, and on methods of service.

Through the years, continuing concern over the alleged disturbance of the balance of power among levels of government has been expressed. Fears that the national power is exercised through its superior fiscal position to encroach on the authority of states comprise a persistent theme. To confirm or confute these fears in social welfare, the evidence is somewhat equivocal. The states and local governments have surrendered their erstwhile complete control over social welfare, and now share this function with the national government. On the other hand, their scope of operation has been considerably enlarged and they are in a stronger position in relation to the kinds of programs and quality of service than they were before the advent of grants-in-aid.

On balance, most studies of intergovernmental relations state that the general method of sharing costs and responsibility through the grant-in-aid is the best that can be devised. Alternatives do not seem to be satisfactory. Criticisms continue to be directed toward some of the methods of cost sharing, however, and general acceptance of the principle does not necessarily indicate complete approval of all of the present methods. It is more than likely that the grant-in-aid will continue to be employed as a method of cooperative federalism in social welfare, and that from time to time changes and adaptations will be made.

Selected References

1. Adie, David C., "Responsibility of the State in the Supervision of Public Welfare Programs," *Social Service Review,* December, 1939, p. 613.
2. Anderson, William, *The Nation and the States, Rivals or Partners?* Minneapolis, University of Minnesota Press, 1955.
3. Bitterman, Henry J., *State and Federal Grants-in-Aid.* New York, Mentzer, Bush and Company, 1938.

4. Burns, Eveline M., *Social Security and Public Policy*. New York, McGraw-Hill, 1956, especially Part Three, "Decisions About the Financing of Social Security Programs," and Part Four, "Decisions Regarding the Structure and Character of Administration."

5. Clark, Jane Perry, *The Rise of a New Federalism: Federal-State Cooperation in the United States*. New York, Columbia University Press, 1938.

6. The Commission on Intergovernmental Relations, *A Report to the President for Transmittal to the Congress*. Washington, June, 1955.

   Special Committee Reports of the Commission:

   A Description of Twenty-five Federal Grant-In-Aid Programs.
   Federal Aid to Welfare.
   The Impact of Federal Grants-In-Aid on the Structure and Functions of State and Local Governments.

7. The Council of State Governments, Federal Grants-in-Aid, *Report of the Committee on Federal Grants-in-Aid*. Chicago, 1949.

8. The Council of State Governments, *State-Local Relations*. Chicago, 1946.

9. Hale, Mark, "The Process of Developing Policy for a Federal-State Grant-in-Aid Program, as Illustrated by the Work of the Social Security Board, 1935-46," *Social Service Review*, September, 1957.

10. Johnson, Claudius O., *American State and Local Government*. New York, Thomas Y. Crowell Company, 1956.

11. Key, V. O., *The Administration of Federal Grants to States*. Chicago, Public Administration Service, 1937.

8

Federal Organization in Social Welfare

The role of the federal government in social welfare, as we have seen, is threefold: (1) To administer certain programs, including old-age and survivors insurance, services to veterans, the various insurances for railroad workers, and services considered the special responsibility of the national government, including services to the American Indians, federal employees, and the management of certain institutions; (2) to assist the states and localities, through grants-in-aid, to provide child welfare services, public assistance, crippled children's services, unemployment insurance, vocational rehabilitation, mental health, etc.; and (3) to take a measure of leadership and initiative in the improvement of welfare services through research or demonstration projects conducted by the national government or encouraged through special grants to states, local governments, educational institutions, or voluntary agencies, or through special subventions to encourage the education and training of professional personnel.

Determination of where these functions belong in the federal government is not always simple. As the welfare programs have developed, it has not always been clear that the administration of them belonged in any particular one of the established departments in the executive branch. During the period of the 1930's when the programs were experiencing their fastest growth, special independent agencies were created for some functions, while others were placed in various existing departments. Through the creation of the Department of Health, Education, and Welfare, however, a considerable degree of integration of administration of social welfare has been accomplished, although several programs, including some of the largest, are either assigned to an independent agency, or are administered by other departments.

While reading this material, the reader might ask himself whether or not the present grouping of functions is in fact the most logical one possible, and whether some programs now in one department might be placed with equal or greater legitimacy in another. Consider, for example, the Bureau of Employment Security, now in the Department of Labor. Formerly, the unemployment insurance function was administered in the Federal Security Agency, the predecessor to the present Department of Health, Education, and Welfare. It could be argued with some cogency that all the social insurances should be a part of the same organization, and that the program of unemployment insurance and the Bureau of Old-Age and Survivors Insurance should be in the same agency. On the other hand, one may argue with comparable cogency that the payment of insurance benefits is so closely related to the placement service that the two belong together, especially because both are concerned with labor. It is possible, instead, to contend that the taxation of employers and the effect on commerce of both these programs might justify a claim that the Department of Commerce should administer these services. The point of all this is that clear lines of demarcation among the various kinds of service are rare.

Another point to consider, and one which has some importance in intergovernmental relations in social welfare, is that different groupings are found among the three levels of government, federal, state, and local. As a result of this situation the same federal agency which includes different kinds of service programs may deal with more than one state agency, and even agencies of different classifications. The Children's Bureau of the Department of Health, Education, and Welfare, may be cooperating with a state social welfare department in child welfare, with a health department in crippled children's services, and perhaps, in its juvenile delinquency service programs, with no central state authority. This fact is noted again as a caution against any assumption that organization of these programs follows a neatly arranged, inevitably consistent pattern.

THE DEPARTMENT OF HEALTH, EDUCATION, AND WELFARE

A cabinet department for welfare was proposed as early as 1920, during the presidential campaign of Warren G. Harding. Later, during Mr. Harding's term as president, a bill was introduced to establish such a department, but it was defeated. Its purpose was to bring under a unified administration such welfare services as were scattered throughout the executive branch of the government.

When the depression forced the national government into large-scale participation in relief, the need for a federal department received more attention and support. The various agencies such as the Federal Emergency Relief Administration, the National Youth Administration, the Civilian Conservation Corps, and others, either were independent organizations or were assigned to various cabinet departments where their affiliation seemed expedient and logical. The Social Security programs featured the same practice. The major insurance and public assistance features were assigned to a newly created independent Social Security Board, and children's services to the United States Children's Bureau, then a part of the Department of Labor.

It was evident, however, as these welfare services at the federal level increased in number and size that some coordination was required. This need was emphasized by a Committee on Administrative Management, which reported to the President in January, 1937. This Committee viewed with some concern the general trend toward what it considered bypassing the regular departments through the growing use of independent agencies, and with respect to social welfare proposed a Federal Department of Public Welfare, to coordinate education, health and welfare responsibilities of the national government, under a secretary who would serve in the cabinet.[1]

A major step in the direction of coordinating federal welfare services was taken with the creation of the Federal Security Agency, under Reorganization Plan I of 1939. This plan brought under one head, the Federal Security Administrator, the following agencies: the Social Security Board, which had been an independent agency, the Office of Education, the United States Employment Service, the Public Health Service, which had been in other departments, and the emergency agencies including the Civilian Conservation Corps, the National Youth Administration, and the Work Projects Administration. (None of these emergency agencies now exists.) Subsequently, accessions to the Federal Security Agency took place as follows: administrative responsibility for the Food and Drug Administration, St. Elizabeth's Hospital, Freedman's Hospital, and Howard University, all in 1940. In July, 1946, under Reorganization Plan No. 2, the Children's Bureau was transferred from the Department of Labor to the Social Security Administration, a component of the Federal Security Agency. In that same plan, the Social Security Board was replaced by the Social Security Administration.

Bills to establish a federal department were proposed but failed to pass until the present Department came into being under Reorganization Plan No. 1 of 1953, effective April 11 under the Act approved April 1, 1953.[2] The Federal Security Agency was abolished and its functions were transferred to the new Department.

---

[1] "Administrative Management in the Government of the United States," Report of the President's Committee on Administrative Management, Washington, 1937.
[2] 67 Stat. 18; 5 U. S. C. 623.

The granting of cabinet status to Health, Education and Welfare has provided convincing evidence that these functions are an integral part of national life. One might well ask why such recognition was so slow in coming. There are several reasons. The first is the fact that by and large these are functions which have been clearly identified as within the province of responsibility of the state and local units of government. The second is that only recently have the programs reached such size and national importance as to build up pressure for such a step. Cabinet status is not something which is lightly granted, and any time such a step is contemplated opposition is likely to arise on the ground that it might remove certain functions from older departments, or might accord status to services which some people are loath to see attain such status.

Another question might be posed regarding the grouping of health, education, and welfare into a single department. As recently as 1949 a task force of the Hoover Commission (on the Organization of the Executive Branch of the Government) had expressed certain doubts of the wisdom of such a unification. Its report raised the point that each of these three major services was in a separate federal department, by and large working with government at the state level, and the *Report* called it improbable that a multifunctional national agency would be able to have a unified program. Each, it was further stated, is a highly technical field, and would tax the leadership of a Department Secretary who would probably be a layman in all three fields. The report observed further that the President could probably get more complete and comprehensive reports from smaller unifunctional agencies than large single multifunctional ones could provide through a cabinet officer who would be sorely taxed to master the technical material that occasionally would be needed. For these and other reasons, the task force stated its judgment that, ". . . it cannot be guaranteed that grouping all these agencies under a single department head would result with certainty in effective coordination."[3]

---

[3] *Task Report on Public Welfare* (Appendix P). Prepared for the Commission on Organization of the Executive Branch of the Government, January, 1949, Washington, pp. 4-22.

People in the major professions engaged in these services can argue strongly that each of the three is important enough to our national life to justify separate cabinet status, and in time such separation might occur. The fact that a generic title cannot be found which would cover—without naming individually—all three is in itself strongly suggestive that this is a grouping dictated as much by expediency as by logic. There is precedent for dividing one cabinet department into two or more. First, is the separation of the Department of Labor from the Department of Commerce and Labor in 1913. More recently, the Department of Defense, merging responsibility over the Army, the Navy, and the Air Force, was created in 1947, replacing the two separate departments—of War, and of the Navy. A major program of Federal Aid to education might precipitate a reorganization, as that function could presumably outgrow its status as part of another organization.

The arrangement is not without basis, however. As R. Clyde White suggests, "Yet there are good philosophical reasons for putting educational, health, and public welfare functions into one major administrative unit of the federal government. The services provided under all of them are concerned with developing, maintaining, or restoring working capacity. They exist to conserve our human capital and by so doing to enhance the creative activities of the people."[4] What Professor White says is true, but the extent of its application to organizational problems is limited. One could find much in common philosophically between the functions of the Department of Labor and of social welfare or health, or education, but any such combination would be unwieldy and, in operation, its internal consistency would be difficult to maintain.

In addition to the criterion of a common philosophy of purpose, two other tests might be applied to the problem of unifunctional versus multifunctional organization at this level. The first is the question of whether there is enough relationship among the actual services themselves to justify the conclusion that cooperation and communication would be fostered by a common organization. The

---

[4] *Administration of Public Welfare* (New York, 2nd ed., 1950), p. 83.

other is whether the size of the functions are such that such a relationship is administratively feasible.

The close relationship of health, education, and welfare services is evident in the character of the services. They overlap, combine, and in many ways touch people's lives in a way that suggests that their common properties exceed their differences. In the descriptions of programs (earlier in the book) there were many instances in which health, welfare and educational services were seen to be concurrently engaged in meeting problems. A crippled child, for example, needs health services. The skills of the health personnel in crippled children's services, of the doctor, nurse, physical therapist, medical social worker, and others, are augmented by the welfare agency which provides needed services to the family. An educational problem may be present, perhaps calling for a home teacher. Certainly, it does not tax the imagination to conceive of many situations in which the local health agency, the welfare department, and the public school might find meeting the needs of an individual or family a joint enterprise.

Sometimes it is difficult to define a service categorically as belonging to one rather than to another of these three classes of functions. Is vocational rehabilitation, for example, primarily a health function, a welfare service, or an educational activity? Certainly it has components of all three. It is concerned with physical and mental restoration and therefore with medical treatment. Therefore it must be basically a health service. But it is also concerned with retraining for a vocation, and therefore must be classified as an educational program. Before we settle for these two possibilities, let us consider the welfare features of rehabilitation, with its income security features, and its concern with social adjustment, or the possibility that the vocational purpose might classify this as a labor program. As we shall see in the chapter on state organization, at the state level wide variations are found in the placement of this service as among the different types of classifications of programs.

Any examination of links between states and the federal government in welfare work will show how much they are joined.

Child welfare grants may be used for the development of educational psychologists, or mental health funds for the training of school social workers. The list could be multiplied, to illustrate further the fact that the various functions do not break down neatly into mutually exclusive categories of function. Their interrelatedness is probably more important than their differences. While, as we have suggested, the magnitude of one or all of these divisions might dictate separation at the federal level at some future time, it is quite clear that pragmatic considerations indicated a combination at this particular time.

The operating units of the Department at present include the following (see Chart 1):

Public Health Service
Office of Education
Social Security Administration
Office of Vocational Rehabilitation
Food and Drug Administration
St. Elizabeth's Hospital

The Department is headed by the Secretary of Health, Education, and Welfare, who, as a cabinet officer, reports directly to the Office of the President. The Secretary is assisted in the over-all administration of the Department by an Under Secretary. As the chart indicates, the Secretary is served by staff units or divisions, which carry special responsibility in relation to the operating offices. These units have the following responsibilities, as listed in the United States Government Organization Manual:[5]

SPECIAL ASSISTANT FOR HEALTH AND MEDICAL AFFAIRS.—The Special Assistant for Health and Medical Affairs reviews the health and medical programs of the Department and advises the Secretary with respect to the improvement of such programs and with respect to necessary legislation in health and medical affairs.

ASSISTANT SECRETARY.—The Assistant Secretary is responsible for directing the Department's field services with

[5] *U. S. Government Organization Manual, 1957-58*, pp. 319-320.

CHART 1. UNITED STATES DEPARTMENT OF HEALTH, EDUCATION, AND WELFARE, AND BRANCHES

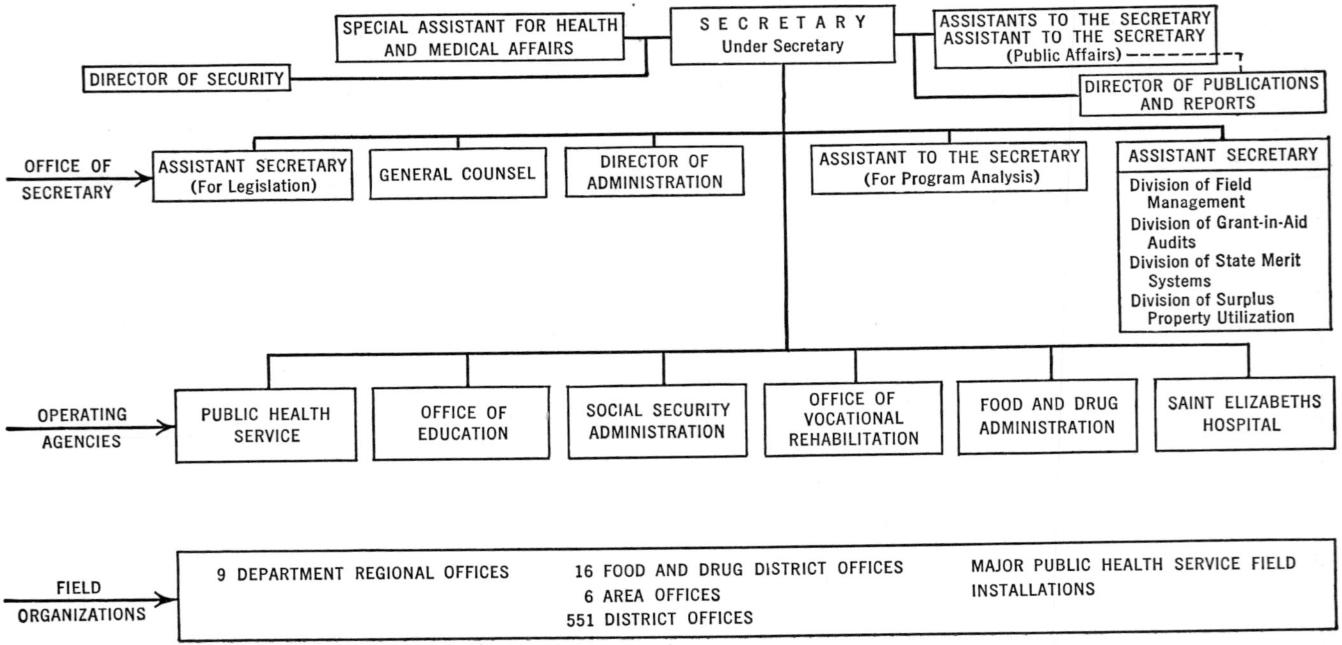

SECRETARY
Under Secretary

DIRECTOR OF SECURITY

ASSISTANTS TO THE SECRETARY
ASSISTANT TO THE SECRETARY
(Public Affairs)

DIRECTOR OF PUBLICATIONS AND REPORTS

OFFICE OF SECRETARY

ASSISTANT SECRETARY
(For Legislation)

SPECIAL ASSISTANT FOR HEALTH AND MEDICAL AFFAIRS

GENERAL COUNSEL

DIRECTOR OF ADMINISTRATION

ASSISTANT TO THE SECRETARY
(For Program Analysis)

ASSISTANT SECRETARY
Division of Field Management
Division of Grant-in-Aid Audits
Division of State Merit Systems
Division of Surplus Property Utilization

OPERATING AGENCIES

PUBLIC HEALTH SERVICE

OFFICE OF EDUCATION

SOCIAL SECURITY ADMINISTRATION

OFFICE OF VOCATIONAL REHABILITATION

FOOD AND DRUG ADMINISTRATION

SAINT ELIZABETHS HOSPITAL

FIELD ORGANIZATIONS

9 DEPARTMENT REGIONAL OFFICES

16 FOOD AND DRUG DISTRICT OFFICES
6 AREA OFFICES
551 DISTRICT OFFICES

MAJOR PUBLIC HEALTH SERVICE FIELD INSTALLATIONS

particular attention to the Federal-State relation aspects of those operations, including supervision of grant-in-aid audits and State merit system activities. He is also responsible for the Department's functions in the disposition of surplus property, program activities related to civil defense, and statutory relationships with the three federally aided corporations.

ASSISTANT SECRETARY (FOR LEGISLATION).—The Assistant Secretary (for Legislation) is responsible for coordination of the development of new programs, draft legislation, and recommendations and data for Presidential messages, and for assistance in the preparation and presentation of testimony on legislation and policy positions for reports on pending bills.

ASSISTANT TO THE SECRETARY (FOR PROGRAM ANALYSIS).—The Assistant to the Secretary (for Program Analysis) is responsible for supervising and directing review of Department programs to identify problems and to develop recommendations for modification; for study of special program problems which cut across Department subject matter interests; and for representing the Secretary in the development of executive branch program policy. He is responsible for continuing efforts toward determining the implications of the increasing aging population on the Department's programs.

DEPARTMENTAL COUNCIL.—The Council consists of the key officials of the Office of the Secretary and the heads of the operating agencies—the Surgeon General, the Commissioner of Education, the Commissioner of Social Security, the Commissioner of Food and Drugs, the Director of Vocational Rehabilitation, and the Superintendent, Saint Elizabeth's Hospital. It assists the Secretary in providing an improved exchange of information and closer coordination of the Department's activities.

OFFICE OF INTERNAL SECURITY.—This Office is responsible for establishing and maintaining an effective internal security program and organization.

OFFICE OF THE GENERAL COUNSEL.—This Office renders legal advice and opinions on questions which arise in connection with administration and operation of programs and participates in the formulation of the Department's legislative program.

OFFICE OF PUBLICATIONS AND REPORTS.—This Office is responsible for the general direction and supervision of all public information activities of the Department.

OFFICE OF ADMINISTRATION.—The Director of Administration serves as special adviser to the Secretary on Department matters involving administrative and financial management. The Office provides coordination, leadership, and guidance within the Department on all administrative and financial management programs and operations. Such programs include budget, fiscal policy and procedures, internal audit, personnel management, organization studies, management improvement efforts, policy guidance and counseling services to operating agencies on major problems in organization, staffing, and control; development of standards where appropriate to secure uniformity, reduce costs, and improve management and service procedures. The Office provides day-to-day administrative and fiscal services for the Office of the Secretary and for related organizations. It represents the Department in its relationships with other central staff agencies of the Federal Government.

The Department has nine regional offices, each headed by a representative of the Secretary of Health, Education and Welfare, and each with regional representatives of the constituent offices of the Department. (See map for boundaries of the regions and locations of offices.) Included are representatives of the General Counsel, Public Health Service, Office of Education, Office of Vocational Rehabilitation, and Social Security Administration. Each regional office has a Director of Field Administration. The purpose of the regional organization is that of decentralizing as much as possible the administration of the various programs by providing for closer access to the operation of the services, and by giving direct services whenever possible. This is an example of the use of field service mentioned earlier in this volume as a means of avoiding overcentralized, cumbersome administration in which all policy, interpretation of policy, and advice would come from a departmental staff.

Yet complete decentralization is a goal difficult to achieve. The regional office can scarcely be considered a miniature of the national or departmental office, with complete autonomy to act on all matters pertaining to the various programs. Each representative in the region has in a real sense a dual accountability: to the head of the regional office, on the one hand, and to the departmental bureau or office which he represents on the other. This may at times make for confusion of authority, or at least it would seem to invite some such confusion. The regional head in effect would seem to be more a coordinator than an administrator, in many respects, although presumably he would have certain powers vested in him by the office of the Secretary to act with authority on matters which cut across lines of responsibility among the representatives, or which are a part of the over-all responsibility of the Department.

It would be a mistake to consider these units of the Department as completely staff and service divisions, if this designation would imply that they were exclusively concerned with facilitating the work of the Secretary's office and with servicing the activities of the program units. Under the Assistant Secretary for Federal-State Relations, for example, the Division of Grant-in-Aid Audits and the Division of State Merit Systems have responsibilities for review and evaluation that reach the heart of the Department's relations with the states in the federally-aided programs. It would also be difficult to justify designating the functions of the General Counsel as strictly staff or as service to the operating units. There are elements of operation inherent in the decision-making that accompanies legal analysis, for example, and the decisions of this part of the Department may have a most important influence on policy and operation. The traditional divisions of administration into "line" and "staff" and "service" are classifications of functions rather than of organizational units.

MAP OF DEPARTMENT OF HEALTH, EDUCATION, AND WELFARE REGIONAL BRANCHES AND OFFICES

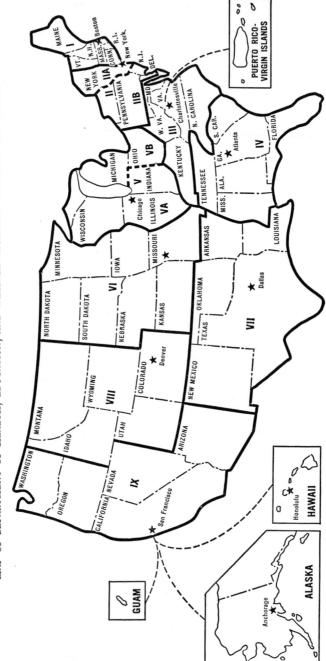

SOURCE: *United States Government Organization Manual, 1957.*

Still, the organizational alignment shown on Chart 1 suggests the designation of six units as operating divisions, with the responsibilities of the other parts of the organization more concerned with over-all activities of the Department. The work of the units "above the line" will continue to have significant influence in the development of the work of the operating units, and on the development of legislative and administrative policy.

In examining the structure of the Department, one might ask the reason why the Public Health office is called Public Health Service, while Education, like Vocational Rehabilitation, is an "Office," Social Security is an "Administration," etc. As White has noted, this does not follow the traditional nomenclature in federal organization, which usually denotes the different levels as "bureaus," "divisions," "sections" and "subsections."[6] As White further notes, these parts of the Department are of varying ages, and their names, which antedate the formation of this Department, have been retained.

At best, this organizational chart (and others which follow) can give a very static picture of administration. It can show in a general way the structural relationships within an organization, but it cannot demonstrate how the structure works. The success of the Department depends largely not only on how well each of these specialized units performs its own task, but also on how effectively the individual performance is related to the central purposes of the entire Department and how the units relate to each other.

Let us now proceed to examine those operating units which are responsible for the welfare programs described in Part II. The Social Security Administration and the Office of Vocational Rehabilitation will be given particular attention, since they are responsible for most of the major programs of the Department which we have classified as social welfare. The relationship of the Institute of Mental Health to the Public Health Service will also be presented, because of its direct and close relationship to many social welfare programs.

[6] White, *op. cit.,* p. 81.

THE SOCIAL SECURITY ADMINISTRATION

In the Social Security Act of 1935, the Social Security Board was created to administer public assistance, old age insurance, and unemployment insurance. This three-member board functioned in effect as a multiple executive with a chairman but no single executive until July 1946, when the Board was abolished, and the Social Security Administration was established under a Commissioner.

Established first as an independent agency, the Social Security Board was made part of the Federal Security Agency when that organization was created by Reorganization Plan I in 1939. In 1946, when the Social Security Board was abolished and the Social Security Administration created, the United States Children's Bureau was transferred to it from the Department of Labor. In 1949 the Bureau of Employment Security, which had shortly before been transferred from the War Manpower Commission to the Social Security Administration of the Federal Security Agency, was again transferred, this time to the Department of Labor. In 1953 the Social Security Administration—as a constituent part of the Federal Security Agency—became a part of the Department of Health, Education and Welfare.

The operating units of the Social Security Administration (see Chart 2) include the following:

> Bureau of Old-Age and Survivors Insurance
> Bureau of Public Assistance
> Children's Bureau
> Bureau of Federal Credit Unions

The organization is headed by a Commissioner and a Deputy Commissioner, who are responsible to the Secretary of Health, Education, and Welfare. The central organization of the office includes a Division of the Actuary, which advises on long-range factors affecting costs and needs under Social Security; the Division of Research and Statistics, which is responsible for the more basic research on features of programs which are broader in scope than the interests of any particular program, and which serves to

CHART 2. SOCIAL SECURITY ADMINISTRATION

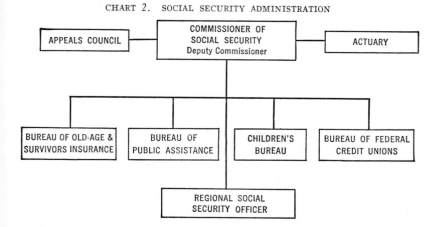

coordinate research undertaken throughout the constituent bureaus; the International Service, which is concerned with providing opportunities for training of foreign students in this country, with cooperation in overseas projects through recruiting technical personnel in the fields of service represented in the Social Security Administration, and cooperates in the international exchange of information and research and in the planning for conferences and meetings. These are central services which have functions of service and of staff assistance to the Commissioner's office on matters which affect the functioning of the total organization. In addition, there is an Appeals Council, which "Holds hearings and renders decisions on disputed old-age and survivors insurance claims and determinations of disability made in relation to 'disability freeze' provisions of Title II of the Social Security Act."[7]

Each regional office has a Regional Social Security Officer who is one of the regional representatives of the operating bureaus of the Social Security Administration, and may serve several bureaus. Thus the regional representative of the Bureau of Old-Age and Survivors Insurance might be serving in such a dual capacity in one region, and the representative of the Children's Bureau or

[7] Organization chart of the Social Security Administration, Appendix A8-000, HEW (2/8/57), courtesy of Mr. William Mitchell, Deputy Commissioner of Social Security (February 8, 1957).

the Bureau of Public Assistance in another. This person, in the language of the organizational chart, "Handles social security matters referred by the Commissioner or the Regional Director; facilitates coordination of technical operations involving inter-relationships between social security bureaus or relationships of such bureaus with other regional office staff.[8]

Let us proceed to review the functions of the operating bureaus, omitting the Bureau of Federal Credit Unions whose program is confined to the administration of a service available to federal employees only and which we are therefore excluding from this book.

BUREAU OF OLD-AGE AND SURVIVORS INSURANCE

More than one hundred million persons with earnings credits, as of 1957, the payment of monthly benefits to more than ten million persons in a given month (July, 1957), certification of benefits to the Treasury Department at the rate of over $600 million a month and more than $7 billion a year; more than 3 million new claims during the fiscal year 1957, and a record of more than 123 million earnings accounts since the start of operations of this program, convey a sense of the size of the job of administering Old-Age, Survivors and Disability Insurance. This operating bureau must offer the public a combination of exactness of records and claims certification, of promptness of action on claims, and of service to a public which inevitably must find the detail of this program complex and difficult to understand.[9]

The job of administration is defined by the Bureau as follows:[10]

> The Bureau of Old-Age and Survivors Insurance is responsible for assigning and identifying account numbers to the individual worker; maintaining his earnings history; accepting his claims for benefits, determining the validity and amounts of benefits due, certifying the amount to the Treasury De-

[8] *Ibid.*

[9] Information on numbers of claims supplied courtesy Office of Commissioner, Social Security Administration.

[10] "The Program and Administration of Old-Age and Survivors Insurance," statement from the Office of the Commissioner, Social Security Administration.

partment (which issues the benefit checks), and of continuously maintaining and modifying the benefit roles as people move or have their benefits suspended, changed in amount, or terminated for various reasons.

The Bureau negotiates agreements with States for inclusion of State and local employees in the program, and administers matters involving contributions for State and local government employees, which are paid by the States to the Federal Reserve Banks.

In connection with the disability insurance program, state agencies through negotiated agreements with the Secretary make determinations of disability for individuals in their states. The Bureau reviews the state determinations of disability and for any class or classes of individuals not included in an agreement, the Bureau makes the disability determinations.

All in all, this is a tremendous undertaking, not only because of the size of the operation itself as expressed in numbers of persons and amounts of money, but also because of the necessity for keeping all the information current. People change jobs, their earning status fluctuates, and many things happen which add to this task. The information must not only be current and exact, but also must be promptly available, so that the certification of claims will not delay payment.

What kind of organization is required for this nation-wide federal operation? Obviously, there must be a combination of centralization of those responsibilities which demand concentration of machinery and technical skill, and decentralization of service to the millions of people who have current or potential rights under the program. The organization must utilize the most modern type of machinery. A visitor to the central office at Baltimore sees an impressive array of the most modern electronic machinery and equipment manned by a highly skilled staff of technicians. Behind their work is a planned system of application and filing of claims, of relating these claims to the rights of the beneficiary, of computing the amount of entitlement, of certification, and of authorization for prompt payment.

CHART 3. BUREAU OF OLD-AGE AND SURVIVORS INSURANCE

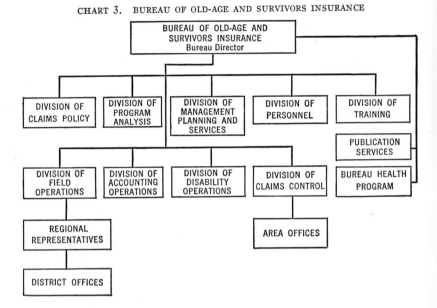

Chart 3 provides a picture of the organization of the Bureau of Old-Age and Survivors Insurance. More than 550 district offices are located in cities throughout the country and territories to help individuals establish their records of earnings, file their applications either for monthly benefits or lump-sum payments, and to establish the evidence necessary to determine their eligibility and the amounts of payments which are due them. Each district has "contact points" in communities other than those in which the district offices are located, for direct services for people throughout the district, or other places in which the district office representative holds scheduled office hours. There are more than 3600 of these "contact points" throughout the country.

The district offices are supervised by eleven regional representatives including one representative for each of the nine regions of the Department of Health, Education, and Welfare, and two subregions. The regional representatives are a part of the Division of Field Operations which in turn is directly responsible to the Bureau Director.

The authorization and certification for payment of claims and for postadjudication is assigned to six area offices under the Division of Claims Control, another one of four operating divisions of the Office of the Bureau Director. The Division reviews all determinations made by the district office, and makes adjustments from time to time. While the Treasury Department is generally responsible throughout the country for the actual disbursement of benefits, in one area office, Birmingham, the payments are made directly by the area office.[11]

The other two operating divisions, in addition to Field Operations and Claims Control, are the Division of Accounting Operations and the Division of Disability Operations. The Division of Accounting Operations has the task of establishing and maintaining records of identity of holders of social security account numbers, number cards, and of receiving reports from employers of wages and of earnings from self-employment. The Division of Disability Operations in addition to responsibility for standards and guides for evaluating of disability, and for the necessary procedures in connection with this process, cooperates with the state in developing agreements for making of disability determination. In a sense this part of the program comes close to being a federal-state program similar to those in some of the other major welfare services, although the actual administrative authority for making decisions on claims remains with the federal agency.

A brief look at the functions of the divisions concerned with the development of policy and of program planning indicates the kinds of services required to back up the work of the operating divisions. As we have already said, the administration of Old-Age and Survivors and Disability Insurance is far from being a cut-and-dried operation. The continuing development and appraisal of policies relating to the claims process, the interpretation of these policies throughout the organization, and the provision of general directions for administration, and for maintenance of effective processes, and coordination of activities, are all parts of the work of the Division of Claims Policy.

The vitality of a program depends in large part on its continu-

---

[11] Area offices are located in Philadelphia, New York, Chicago, Birmingham, Kansas City, and San Francisco.

ing research into and study of its effectiveness in meeting its objectives. Statistical data must be maintained and actuarial estimates provided for the evaluation necessary to legislation and administrative policy. The Division of Program Analysis is responsible for conducting studies and for providing technical and advisory services for legislative proposals relating to coverage extension, benefit structure, proposals for added protection, and for relating Old-Age and Survivors Insurance to the other income security programs.

The Division of Management, Planning, and Services is responsible for the managerial processes within the organization. This division plans, initiates, coordinates, and analyzes over-all management programs, policies, procedures, and actions; develops financial plans and manages Bureau finances; manages the Bureau's work plan and administrative recording system, administers the payroll and is responsible for the detail of property utilization for provision of equipment, supplies, and for the many management services which are a part of any such large organization.[12]

The Division of Personnel is responsible for the coordination of personnel policies, programs and procedures, and for advisory services on the technical aspects of personnel administration. This division offers counselling and other employee relation services and provides classification, recruitment, placing, and testing services. The Division of Training has the staff development function, which is designed to enhance the knowledge and skills of the employees of the organization.

The Bureau maintains a continuing service of general public information. This involves not only preparing material for Bureau publication, but also the development of information for the major communications media, the press, radio, and television. Anyone who has seen the many information stories in newspapers on the Old-Age and Survivors Insurance programs or the scenes

[12] Adapted from the Organization Chart of the Bureau of Old-Age and Survivors Insurance, courtesy of the Bureau administration.

presented on television, must be aware of the painstaking efforts this Bureau makes to acquaint the public with the nature of the program.

As we have already noted, two of the major functions in connection with Old-Age and Survivors Insurance are performed in or by the central office of the Social Security Administration. These are the actuarial services, and the hearings and appeals conducted through the office of the Appeals Counsel.

This is a necessarily brief summary of the organization of the Bureau. Each of the divisions described has its own subdivisions and specialized units, employing a total of 21,260 administrative staff members, as of May 3, 1957.

From the standpoint of the individual who is covered under this program (this means over 90 percent of the total working population) the following points are important: When he begins his working life he is assigned a card containing an account number which will designate the continuing record of his earnings from covered employment. Each month an amount currently $2\frac{1}{4}$ percent of his earnings up to $4200 each year, if he is employed; or $3\frac{3}{8}$ percent if he is self-employed and elects coverage (with exceptions as noted in Chapter 4), is deducted from his salary, and if he is a wage earner a like amount is paid by his employer. This amount is paid in the form of a tax into the Treasury of the United States. Any change in his earning status is promptly reported and the records are adjusted accordingly. If at any time he wishes to discuss this program or if he feels that he may be eligible under the retirement, the disability, or the survivorship features of the program, he may file a claim at the District Office or through one of the contact points from the district office with the help of a staff member of the organization. His claim is then adjudicated and if approved, his right to payment is certified to the Treasury Department by the area office. If he is not satisfied with the decision he may ask for a review by the Bureau and if still not content with the action then taken, he may appeal to the Office of the Appeals Counsel for a hearing.

BUREAU OF PUBLIC ASSISTANCE

This bureau is the unit of the Social Security Administration which is responsible for the administration of grants-in-aid to states for Old-Age Assistance, Aid to Dependent Children, Aid to the Blind, and Aid to the Permanently and Totally Disabled, under Titles I, IV, X, and XIV of the Social Security Act. These grants, as we have seen, are made, subject to certain conditions set forth in the appropriate titles of the Social Security Act. Some of these conditions have already been described (in Chapter 5) as affecting eligibility conditions, treatment of applicants and recipients, and amounts of payments. In addition to these conditions, however, there are others which bear directly on the state organization and administration. They include the following: (1) States are required to participate financially in the payment of assistance; that is, they cannot entirely shift the burden to the localities. (2) The state must administer the program or supervise its administration through a single state agency. (3) The state must operate the plan in all of its political subdivisions; in fact, if there were a single area of the state in which the plan was not operating, federal aid would be subject to withdrawal. (4) The state is required to provide such methods of administration as are considered necessary for the proper and efficient operation of the plan, including a merit system of personnel administration. (5) The federal agency has the power to require reports from the state agencies. In addition, the Bureau of Public Assistance has been responsible during the past few years for such phases of civil defense work as planning programs to provide food, clothing, and shelter. This phase of activity, however, was curtailed as of July 1, 1957, because Congress had reduced the appropriations for federal civil defense program agencies.

In essence, the initiative in developing and maintaining the public assistance program rests with the states, with the federal government's role designed to strengthen the states' own capacity to develop the best possible program within the limits of the states' capacities and resources. In broader terms, under the responsibilities of the assistance legislation, the Bureau perceives as its objectives: ". . . the development, maintenance, and improvement of sound public welfare programs in which States can aid needy people to secure the necessities of life and achieve as much economic and personal independence as possible."[13] According to this same statement, this is seen as requiring that the Bureau discharge its responsibilities by

(1) Assuring itself that federal grants are made in accordance with the Social Security Act; (2) Assisting States in the application of Federal requirements to their programs, and working with them toward improving their particular programs; (3) Securing nation-wide information and data as a basis for reporting and for advising the Department, the Congress, and others on the Public Assistance programs and related programs and problems; and (4) Cooperating with national public and private agencies and organizations with a view towards (a) improving public understanding of the public assistance programs, (b) participating in the coordination of nation-wide public and private social service activities, (c) encouraging local public and private agencies in community planning, (d) exchanging technical knowledge and experience, and (e) encouraging allied groups to provide services needed by public assistance recipients.

It is evident that this interpretation contemplates a role broader than simply assuring that the states are in technical compliance with narrowly interpreted federal requirements. It is noteworthy that much emphasis is given to those functions which involve assisting states in making effective use of the relationship and the even broader functions of cooperating with other national organizations in improving the general level of services to people receiving public assistance. These kinds of activity are examples of what is meant by the acceptance of the responsibility for an important function of leadership in improving the standards of social welfare, a role which depends both on the authorization provided by

[13] "Handbook of Public Assistance Administration," Bureau of Public Assistance, Social Security Administration, Part I, Section 4200, November 29, 1955.

the statute establishing the programs, and the organization and the interpretation of the role by the personnel of the agency itself. A narrower view of its own role would lead a federal agency of this type to content itself with, first, examination of the conditions of the state plans to see whether they were basically in conformity with federal requirements, followed, second, by periodic inspection and review simply to determine whether there was technical compliance with the approved state plan. The assumption of a more constructive participating role with the states seems to be the essence of the relationship. It could be alleged that this more active role infringes upon state freedom to act, and constitutes a kind of interference, however enlightened it might be. It could also be argued that the states would have greater freedom if they were simply left to their own devices to the extent that would be possible if plan review and audit inspection comprised the total of federal participation. Greater freedom, however, would scarcely result from such an interpretation. In effect, the essence of federal participation would be in the nature of imposing penalties for non-compliance. There is every likelihood that such a course of action would lead to a restriction rather than an enlargement of state freedom.

The responsibilities of the Bureau of Public Assistance are carried out through the kinds of devices described in Chapter 7. In relation to this program, the Bureau has enumerated its methods of carrying out its responsibilities as follows:[14]

1. Developing program policies and standards, interpreting the language and intent of the Federal law.
2. Taking action on State plans and amendments.
3. Certifying federal grants to States.
4. Reviewing and evaluating State operations.
5. Providing technical assistance to States.
6. Collecting and interpreting statistical and other data.
7. Furnishing information about the public assistance programs.
8. Participating in a formulation of recommendations to the Congress for desirable changes in federal legislation.

[14] *Ibid.*, Section 4200.

CHART 4. BUREAU OF PUBLIC ASSISTANCE

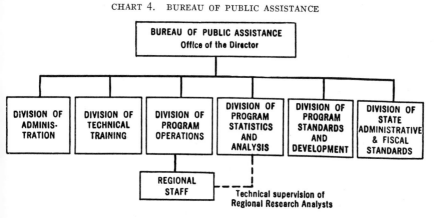

The interpretation of how these functions are performed by the federal agency determines the degree to which the national operation infringes on state authority. If the requirements which are established are interpreted as objectives, with the states by and large free to determine their own methods, except for those methods which are found to be necessary in the strictest sense of conformity, and if requirements imposed on the states are specified clearly and distinguished from those aspects of program which merely are recommended by the federal agency, then the federal role is perceived as one of aiding the states rather than controlling them. (As a matter of fact, these principles are stated in Sec. 4210 of the Federal *Handbook.*)

How is the Bureau of Public Assistance organized to perform these services? As Chart 4 shows, the departmental services are performed through six major divisions. In addition, under the Division of Program Operations, there is in each of the nine regions a regional staff which has the responsibility for maintaining direct relationship with the states in the operation of the plans. The Division of Program Operations is responsible through its departmental and regional staff for field services, for plan review, for reviewing fiscal audits, for recommendations for payments to states, for the continuing review of state and local administration, for keeping the Director of the Bureau advised on whether the state operations meet requirements of the Social Security Act, for

continuing certification of federal funds, and for maintaining a
relationship within the department and with other welfare agencies on matters pertaining to field operations.

Each of the other five special functional divisions, in an agency
administering a program, would be more akin to program planning
and to service operations in the nature of their responsibility than
to line administrative activity. In an organization like the Bureau
of Public Assistance, however, the alignment of responsibilities is
clearly conditioned by the nature of the total organization's function—its responsibility to work with another organization, *i.e.,* the
state, on a collaborative basis, rather than in a direct administrative sense. In a way, then, the entire Bureau is a staff and service
organization, lacking, in a strict technical or legal sense, direct
administrative authority over the states. Formulation of such
policies, standards, and procedures as those relating to organization, management standards, practices of state agencies, fiscal
policies, administrative controls and procedures, costs of administration and technical features of federal matching, are the functions of the Division of State Administrative and Fiscal Standards. It also provides technical assistance to state agencies and to
the regional staff.

The Division of Program Standards and Development is concerned with what is called "substantive content of public assistance programs," such as determination of eligibility and the
amount of assistance, and the development of standards for welfare services and medical care. It also develops guides to standard-setting and may provide technical aid to the regions and to the
states.

The research arm of the Bureau is the Division of Program
Statistics and Analysis. This division conducts the research and
compiles and analyzes statistics on the public assistance programs
and how they relate to social insurance and other welfare activities, and to general social and economic conditions. Such material
is designed for the use of the federal agency in developing administrative policy and recommendations for legislation. In a sense,
this division has a direct line relationship with the regional staff

and responsibility for the technical supervision of a research analyst in each region.

With the growing emphasis on staff development, the Division of Technical Training has an important function. This division develops the policies and the methods in staff development for use by state and local public assistance agencies, and provides technical assistance to regional staff and state public assistance agencies on their staff development programs. The preparation of training material, the recommendation of teaching methods, and the direct conduct of some training activities, are the major functions of this part of the organization. An important task of the Division of Technical Training is that of cooperating with federal and national agencies and educational institutions, particularly schools of social work, on the furtherance of training and other phases of the program to meet personnel needs for public assistance programs.

The Division of Administration has a significant function in the internal management of the Bureau. It assists the Office of Director in coordination of program activities, including work plans and reports; plans and conducts management analyses and appraisal activities and develops methods of operation to implement approved recommendations; prepares administrative budget justifications; coordinates the grant-in-aid estimates; maintains the Bureau accounting system and audits administrative expenses. This Division also conducts the Bureau's own personnel program and performs other administrative management functions.

CHILDREN'S BUREAU

This Bureau, founded in 1912, antedates the Social Security Act by twenty-three years. It was made a part of the Social Security Administration in 1946, and then became known as the Children's Bureau rather than as the U. S. Children's Bureau.

The Children's Bureau today has the following functions: (1) Continuing responsibility for study and for the publication of reports concerning child welfare and child life; (2) The collection

CHART 5.   CHILDREN'S BUREAU

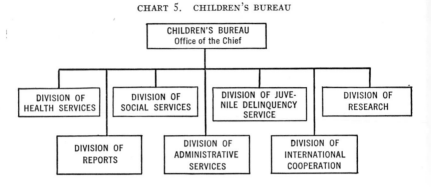

and distribution of information regarding research studies being developed in such facilities as universities, hospitals and clinics, public schools, child welfare agencies, and many other types of public and private health and welfare organizations; (3) The provision of technical assistance in various fields of child life designed to improve the level of services in such areas as juvenile delinquency, health services, mental retardation, and others; (4) The administration of grants-in-aid to the states for programs of crippled children's services, maternal and child health services, and child welfare services; (5) The promotion of better standards of personnel in services to children through the provision of research grants, teaching materials, and educational consultation.

These services are varied and extensive, but it must be remembered that the Children's Bureau, as originally established in 1912, started as an organization with a broad purpose. The fact that since 1935 specific programs of service and care have been added to the Bureau's responsibility has served not to narrow its focus, but rather to provide for activities within a broad area of function.

As Chart 5 indicates, under the Office of the Chief of the Children's Bureau, there are four operating divisions: Health Services, Social Services, Juvenile Delinquency Services, and Research. In addition to these constituent operating units, three divisions of Reports, Administrative Services, and International Cooperation, have over-all functions in the Bureau.

In relation to the states, as with the other bureaus of the Social Security Administration, the Children's Bureau has a regional staff which is responsible for continuing work with the states' child welfare and health services programs. In each region there is a Child Welfare Representative and also a Medical Director, who is responsible for the health care program.

The Division of Health Services, shown on Chart 5, is responsible for grants for maternal and child health services, for crippled children's services, and for various technical and advisory services on the provision of medical care. It is divided into two major branches; administrative methods branch, and program services branch. The former is concerned primarily with administrative and fiscal features of the grant-in-aid program, and with consultation on administrative procedures. It also computes the payment of grant-in-aid funds to state agencies.

The program services branch has responsibility for program development, including plans and policies for operation of health services and for advisory help to regional offices for the development of health programs on a nation-wide basis. Technical consultation in various specialized fields is offered through this branch. It has a nursing section, a medical social work section, and a nutrition section, each concerned with consultation and technical guidance in its respective field. Directly responsible to the head of the Division of Health Services is the regional staff, which administers grant-in-aid programs, approves state plans, and reviews state program operations. The consultation to state and local agencies, both public and voluntary, is provided through the regional staff.

Turning to the Division of Social Services, which has responsibility for Child Welfare Services, we see two major branches. The Social Services branch is responsible for planning and formulating policies and guides in the fields of social work; for providing advisory services, and for the preparation of informational materials, including reports and articles on social services to children. The Field Service branch is responsible for all field activities in Child Welfare Services, including the operation of the grant-in-aid program. It operates through a regional staff which works directly with state agencies on plans for children's services and for the provision of consultative help.

The Division of Juvenile Delinquency Services exists in recognition of the special needs of this persistent and perplexing problem in American life. It has three branches, including technical aid, community services, and training.

The first of these, Technical Aid, deals with the provision of consultation to police, juvenile courts, detention, diagnostic, and reception centers, and various training schools, and helps the states evaluate and develop their own facilities, policies, methods, and standards. The Community Services branch helps the states develop comprehensive plans to cope with juvenile delinquency, and assists with surveys on delinquency and the use of the facilities and resources of public and private agencies and citizen groups. The Training branch provides technical consultation on the preparation of professional and nonprofessional personnel in many areas of service. It is concerned with states, localities, and professional schools in the improvement of training methods and content in relation to juvenile delinquency and with stimulating and encouraging additional training for personnel. This branch of the division, and indeed the work of the division as a whole, will be markedly enhanced if proposed grants for training personnel in the field of juvenile delinquency materialize in the form of legislation and appropriations. This legislation has been proposed persistently in the last two Congresses, but thus far has not been enacted. Under the proposed program, grants would be available for training people in social work, in police work, in criminology, and other areas of services concerned with this particular problem area.

The Division of Research, which in a sense carries the most historic phase of the Children's Bureau's responsibility, has the following branches: Technical Studies, Program Analysis, and Research Interpretation. The Technical Studies branch makes investigations dealing with the fundamental aspects of child life with particular emphasis on the social, economic, and health problems dealt with through the programs of services for children. When requested, it provides research consultation to various organizations which are engaged in or interested in research in these areas of child life and child welfare.

The Program Analysis Branch receives and processes the periodic and special statistics on the various grant-in-aid programs and the other significant fields of child health and welfare. It consults with the states on program reporting and conducts studies which are designed to provide further information on the grant-in-aid programs, and to improve the reporting in relation to the kinds of data and the methods of presentation. This branch also develops the formulae for the apportionment of grant-in-aid funds.

The Research Interpretation branch does the significant and difficult task of translating research findings into usable form, both for technical purposes and for general public utilization. This branch prepares publications and reports on many features of child care and has the function of acting as a clearing house for research related to children.

This organization furnishes an example of how existing services can be effectively used along with new programs. The development of research and interest in community action thus can become a pervasive rather than an isolated and specialized feature of the organization's program. Since such research and community concern can be a pertinent and in many respects a pre-eminently important feature of the action programs in child welfare and health services, the unifying feature of the Children's Bureau responsibility is its over-all concern for child care and development, with the social and economic conditions that affect child life.

One might ask whether Health Services should be a part of the Public Health Service rather than a section of the Children's Bureau. This is not a question to which a conclusively satisfactory answer can be given. There is a logic, of course, in the integration of health services, but there is also a logic in keeping those functions which are performed on behalf of children related directly to each other within an organization. Here, again, is the recurring question of whether it is better to have organization by function, *i.e.*, relating to health, or organization by clientele, *i.e.*, relating to the total needs of children.

OFFICE OF VOCATIONAL REHABILITATION

The Office of Vocational Rehabilitation is responsible for the administration of the three types of grants for this service: grants to states for basic services in vocational rehabilitation, grants to states to encourage them to move into new areas of service, and grants to various types of organizations for research and training of personnel. As noted in the preceding chapters, this is a complex program, since it requires not only the different kinds of relationship under the three purposes, but also demands effective collaboration among several disciplines in the medical, psychological, educational, and social phases of rehabilitation which must accompany the vocational.

The Office was originally part of the Federal Security Agency, and became a part of the Department of Health, Education, and Welfare when this Department was created. In organization, the Office of Vocational Rehabilitation is coordinate with the Social Security Administration, the Office of Education, and the Public Health Service.

The Vocational Rehabilitation Amendments of 1954[15] were intended to strengthen the financial structure of the Vocational Rehabilitation programs, to reach an increasing number of people, and to stimulate and encourage the improvement of methods of treatment and service and the development of additional knowledge. This gave the Secretary of the Department direct responsibility, which in practice he delegates to the Director of the Office of Vocational Rehabilitation, for providing leadership and technical support to the field through the various patterns of cooperative arrangements. This involves relating to other federal Departments, including Labor, Commerce, Health, Education, as well as to state and local agencies and voluntary organizations.

[15] U. S. Code, 1952, Supp. III, title 29, Sections 31-42.

This is not a large agency. There are fewer than two hundred people working in the Office of Vocational Rehabilitation, with about one hundred twenty in the departmental staff in Washington, and thirty in the regional offices.

Grants are made to a total of eighty-eight state and territorial agencies with approved plans for vocational rehabilitation. The administration of grants to states for basic services in rehabilitation is the primary function of the Office. In order to receive a grant for basic services the state must submit a plan with the following features:

1. It must designate a single agency to administer the plan or to supervise its administration in a political subdivision of the state. An exception is made of the agency for the blind which may be designated to administer or to supervise the administration of the portion of the plan relating to vocational services for the blind under the Randolph-Sheppard Act of 1936. The agency designated may either be a vocational education agency or a state rehabilitation agency primarily concerned with vocational rehabilitation.

2. The head of the vocational rehabilitation unit of a state vocational education agency shall be subject to the supervision and direction of such agency or its executive officer.

3. The state must participate financially.

4. The plan for vocational rehabilitation must be in effect throughout all political subdivisions of the state.

5. The plan must show the policies and procedures to be followed under the state program and in the event that services cannot be provided for all physically handicapped individuals who apply for and are eligible for such services, the plan must show the order of selection of those who will be served.

6. The state must provide such methods of administration as are found necessary by the Secretary for the proper and efficient administration of the plan. An exception is made for those methods relating to the establishment and maintenance of personnel standards.

7. The plan must contain provisions relating to the estab-

lishment and maintenance of minimum standards of facilities and personnel. The Secretary is not permitted to exercise any authority over the selection or the tenure of office or compensation of individuals who are employed in accordance with the provisions.

8. Physical restoration services must be provided in addition to training, maintenance, placement, and guidance.

9. The state must make such reports as may be required (by the Secretary).

10. The state agency must show that it is cooperating with whichever state agency administers the public assistance program, with the Federal Bureau of Old-Age and Survivors Insurance, and with other agencies which are related to vocational rehabilitation. This requirement underscores the importance of the coordination of services to the handicapped and the intent of the federal act to promote such coordination.

11. The close relationship of rehabilitation to employment services is recognized in the requirement that provision must be made to enter into cooperative arrangements with the state employment services for the maximum utilization of placement, employment counselling services, and other employment facilities.

12. The state plan must provide, without any kind of discrimination, Vocational Rehabilitation services to any civilian employee of the United States who is disabled in the performance of his duty.

As one of its chief functions, the Office of Vocational Rehabilitation reviews and approves state plans, and all amendments to such plans. In addition, the federal agency reviews budgets and evidences of financial support submitted by states, and certifies grants to the states. In order to determine whether the state agency is operating in a manner consistent with its own approved plan, the federal Office evaluates the administration of state programs, through the audits, through studies of special features of operations, through analysis of reports, and by evaluating standards of performance through case reviews. Technical assistance is given to the states through the preparation of advisory standards,

consultation to agencies by program specialists, and other technical aids. In order to fulfill its responsibility for developing the program, the Office may itself undertake studies and investigations
of special problems, encourage research by others, report to Congress on operations and needs, "and in general keep a watchful
eye on all aspects of extending and improving services to handicapped people."[16] This Office shares with the Public Health Service the responsibility for reviewing and approving state plans for
the construction of rehabilitation facilities and for the approval of
individual projects.

The grants to public or voluntary agencies for special projects,
and the grants to educational institutions for training of personnel,
are administered directly by the Office of Vocational Rehabilitation from Washington.

One of the important functions, according to Cecile Hillyer of
the Office of Vocational Rehabilitation is the following:[17]

> The final function which I might name is the broad, general
> function of exercising national leadership in identifying the
> needs of the disabled and in working out ways that committees
> might help to meet them. It involves a degree of statesmanship
> and ability to work harmoniously with a large number of
> other agencies, many of which have competing interests. In-
> herent in this leadership function, of course, is that of increas-
> ing public understanding and acceptance of rehabilitation as
> a means of both treating and preventing disability.

How is the agency organized to perform these functions? Under
the Director, are four subdivisions of the organization, each
headed by an assistant director. (See Chart 6.) These subdivisions are: (1) Program Planning and Evaluation, (2) Rehabilitation Services, (3) Management Services, and (4) State Administrative Development. The Assistant Director of the last-named
is responsible for the supervision of field staff in the nine regions.

[16] Lecture on functions and organizations, by Cecile Hillyer of the Office of
Vocational Rehabilitation, at the School of Public Health, Harvard University,
March 1957; supplied by courtesy of Office of Vocational Rehabilitation.
[17] *Ibid.*

CHART 6. OFFICE OF VOCATIONAL REHABILITATION

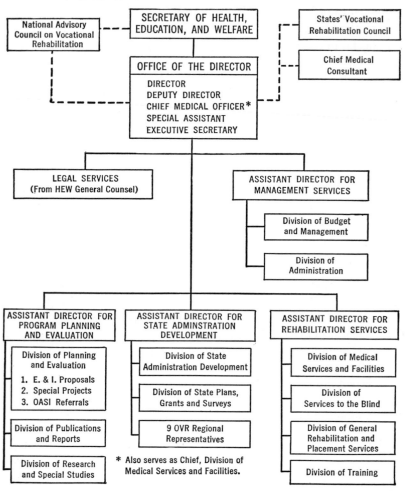

In their combination of administrative with technical functions, it is evident that a high degree of coordination is necessary among these various divisions, and, since the effectiveness is measured in large part by the manner in which other agencies are stimulated, encouraged, and helped to act, communication with regional staff and with state agencies is of paramount importance.

PUBLIC HEALTH SERVICE

We have singled out mental health from the many programs administered by the Public Health Service, because of the particularly close relationship which the mental health program bears to social work. This is especially true in all phases of child and family welfare work. As has been acknowledged, it is somewhat arbitrary to isolate this one service for particular notice. In a sense, there is a close relationship between all health and all welfare programs, and close collaboration is important to the attainment of the objectives of all programs in either area. Nevertheless, to include the whole scope of the Public Health Service's operation would exceed the purpose of this volume, so we shall consider the mental health services only, after a brief outline of the background of the public health services.

Definite impetus to public health services was given by the Social Security Act of 1935. In addition to those health services for children which were assigned to the United States Children's Bureau, other services were supported and strengthened under Title VI of the Act.

The Public Health Service was transferred from the Department of the Treasury to the Federal Security Agency under Reorganization Plan 1 of 1939. Like the other constituent units of the Federal Security Administration, the Health Service became part of the Department of Health, Education, and Welfare in 1953.

The functions of the Public Health Service include: (1) Conducting and supporting research and training in the health field; (2) Helping in the development of the nation's hospitals and related facilities and preventing the introduction of communicable diseases into the country; (3) Assisting the states and local governments in the use of new knowledge relating to disease prevention and control, and improving health services and conditions relating to health.

The four major units of the Public Health Service are the Office of the Surgeon General, the Bureau of Medical Services, the Bureau of State Services, and the National Institutes of Health. The Bureau of Medical Services is responsible for the administration of medical care to those eligible to receive such care from the national government. It also enforces quarantine regulations and has other duties in connection with protecting the people in this country from the introduction of communicable diseases. The Bureau also has a range of technical and consultative responsibilities to the states designed to assist in improvement of hospitals and other treatment and rehabilitation facilities. It also administers grants-in-aid for the conduct of research, experiments, or demonstrations relating to hospital services. This Bureau advises other federal agencies with reference to health care for their employees.

The chief operating bureau of the Public Health Service is the Bureau of State Services. This is responsible for general direction of programs developed to assist states and communities in improving their standards of public health. The Bureau of State Services is responsible for administering grants-in-aid to the states, and for providing technical assistance to the state and local offices. It assists in the training of personnel, and conducts field surveys and demonstrations and various investigations designed to improve health methods. Many other program responsibilities, enforcing interstate regulations, establishing uniform standards for registration of vital statistics, directing the interstate poliomyelitis vaccine program, and other services primarily designed to enhance the quality of state health programs, are within the purview of this unit.

National Institutes of Health primarily devoted to research include the following: National Institutes of Cancer, Heart, Allergy and Infectious Diseases, Arthritis and Metabolic Diseases, Dental Research, Neurological Diseases, Blindness, and, under the National Mental Health Act of 1946, the National Institute of Mental Health.

The National Institute of Mental Health is the part of the federal government primarily concerned with gaining knowledge about the causes of mental illness and with finding more effective methods of treatment and with the improvement of conditions designed to promote good mental health. In order to carry out this responsibility, the Institute gives grants for research in various phases of study of psychoses, neuroses, drug addiction, psychological aspects of aging and in the evaluation of therapy.

The Institute really has two phases of its program; first, its own research into the causes, treatment, and control of mental illness through its own clinical studies, and grants to aid research conducted in clinics and hospitals throughout the country under public and private auspices. In addition, and also throughout the country, the Institute awards funds to help educational institutions to extend their services for training psychiatrists, psychologists, social workers, nurses, physical therapists, occupational therapists, etc. Special grants are given to students in these various fields to defray the costs of education. Technical consultation and services are given to states. The Institute may provide funds to the states for the establishment of mental clinics and for preventive programs in the schools.

While mental health, like social welfare, remains generally a primary responsibility of the states, the federal role has become increasingly important through utilization of the grant-in-aid device and through the extended use of services in aid. Here, as in other programs, the combination is one of federal funds designed to aid the states in strengthening their programs, accompanied by conditions which are considered necessary to assure the federal government that such improvement has taken place. Another feature of mental health which is of special interest is that in this, as in the other classifications of disease represented in the various institutes, the combination of primary research by the Institute and encouragement of such research by other organizations is predominant. This characteristic should not be considered as peculiar to the mental health program, but rather as another strong manifestation of the current tendency of federal health and welfare services toward stimulating research and training. Thus the federal government continues to move away from a basis of minimal support for a floor of standards and in the direction of the promotion of improved methods of care or treatment.

OTHER SOCIAL WELFARE AGENCIES IN THE FEDERAL GOVERNMENT

Although the Department of Health, Education, and Welfare is the cabinet department primarily responsible for the administration of the national government's welfare function, some of the largest and most important programs exist outside this department. The Veterans Administration, as we have seen, is an independent agency of government, and, as we have also noted, has charge of one of the largest of the social welfare and health programs. The Department of Labor has some important welfare functions, including the administration of grants to states for unemployment insurance and for the maintenance of employment services. The Railroad Retirement Board, which administers the retirement, the unemployment, and the disability provisions available to railroad workers, is an independent agency of government. Welfare interests of the Indians are the concern of the Bureau of Indian Affairs of the Department of the Interior.[18] The Department of Justice too, has certain responsibilities which are closely related to social welfare interests, such as those for the administration of prisons and for the immigration and naturalization service.

In a broad sense the work of other agencies, in housing or in agriculture, for example, some of whose functions are related to—but not necessarily a part of—social welfare, could also be included if space permitted. It does not, so we shall limit ourselves to a consideration of the work of some of the important welfare agencies which are currently operating in independent agencies or in departments other than that of Health, Education, and Welfare.

BUREAU OF EMPLOYMENT SECURITY

The Bureau of Employment Security is a part of the Department of Labor. It has been in that Department since 1949, when

[18] See David E. Hailman, "Federal Agencies in Social Work," *Social Work Year Book, 1957*, Russell H. Kurtz, ed. (New York, National Association of Social Workers, 1957).

it was transferred there from the Social Security Administration, part of the Federal Security Agency.

The Bureau reviews and analyzes state laws to determine whether they meet the conditions of the Social Security Act and the Federal Unemployment Tax Act, reviews administration of unemployment insurance to determine whether the state is actually complying with its approved plan for administration, whether individuals are receiving benefits to which the state law entitles them. The Bureau establishes such criteria as are necessary to measure administrative costs, to determine how much money is necessary for administration of unemployment insurance, and furnishes technical assistance to the states on certain administrative and operating problems. It also helps the states by developing legislative recommendations and by analyzing and forecasting trends affecting coverage, contributions, benefits rights, and payments not only by states but throughout the country. This bureau maintains an informational program relating to the operation of unemployment insurance throughout the country, helps the states conduct their own studies of prospective effects of changes in their programs, assists in evaluation of solvency of funds, and the adequacy of financing measures. The Bureau also has special responsibilities in connection with veterans' unemployment insurance under Title IV of the Veterans' Readjustment Assistance Act of 1955, and for federal employees' unemployment insurance under Title XV of the Social Security Act.

To get federal approval of their programs, the states must provide assurance:

(1) That payroll taxes collected for unemployment insurance are used only for the purpose of paying benefits or for refunds;

(2) That benefit funds are safeguarded by deposit in the United States Treasury and investment in United States government securities;

(3) That state administration provides for prompt payment of benefits;

(4) That any claimant for benefits is given an opportunity for a fair hearing when benefits are denied;

(5) That no benefits are denied because of refusals to accept
work in violation of certain labor standards. In connection with this requirement, benefits may not be denied an
individual otherwise eligible who was refused a position
vacant because of a labor dispute, or if the hours or other
conditions of work are less favorable than those which
prevail in the community, or if the individual would be
required to join a company union or prohibited from joining any recognized labor organization.

Administratively, the state is required to include in its law
provisions for such methods of administration as are reasonably
calculated to insure full payment of unemployment compensation.
In addition, the plan must specify the development and maintenance of personnel standards on a merit basis, although, as in
other programs of federal aid with similar provisions, the federal
government does not enter into the selection, tenure of office, or
compensation of any individual who is employed in accordance
with such methods.

Besides its role in unemployment insurance, the Bureau of
Employment Security carries the federal responsibility for the
administration of the public employment service. Under the provisions of the Wagner-Peyser Act as amended, the Bureau is
responsible for "the coordination and guidance of a nation-wide
system of public employment offices operated by State and Territorial agencies affiliated with the United States Employment
Service." These public employment offices throughout the country number about eighteen hundred full time and two thousand
part-time local agencies. The responsibility for this service includes: "checking the individual State plans of operation for conformity with Federal laws; promoting uniform methods for operating employment service offices; maintaining a program for
referring labor from one area to another; giving technical assistance to the States in legislation and administration; assisting in
determining funds necessary for administration of State employment service programs; and maintaining employment service facilities in the District of Columbia."[19]

---

[19] *Federal Labor Laws and Agencies, A Layman's Guide,* Bulletin 123, rev., Bureau of Labor Standards, U. S. Dept. of Labor, pp. 75-76.

The Employment Service performs a wide range of functions, including job placement, designed to bring the employer and employee together; counselling, assisting employers, labor groups, and other organizations by providing information on job requirements and qualifications of workers; assisting in the improved application of new techniques and new uses of materials; providing information on the labor market; and many other services designed to help applicants with special problems and needs. Among the special groups this service is concerned with are veterans, older workers, young people seeking to enter the labor market, the physically handicapped, and minority groups who have difficulties in securing employment.

Other sections of the Department of Labor with functions relating closely to social welfare include the Bureau of Labor Standards, which is a service agency concerned with the promotion of better standards for labor and for industrial safety and health, and with the coordination and enforcement of standards of wage, hour, industrial home work, child labor, and safety and health laws among the states, wherever the states enter into agreements with the federal government. This bureau is also concerned with research, information, and advisory services in the fields of child labor and youth employment, and with the development of standards for child labor regulation under the Fair Labor Standards Act.

The Women's Bureau, which was created in 1918 and made permanent in 1920, has the responsibility for the development of standards for the welfare of wage-earning women, for improving their working conditions, and for increasing their opportunities for profitable employment. The function of this Bureau with relation to promotion of better standards for women is similar to that of the Children's Bureau with reference to the promotion of better standards of child care. The Women's Bureau does not administer any laws but studies the existing laws and administrative procedures which relate to the employment of women.

Actually, in many phases of the work of the Department of Labor, a close relationship to social welfare concerns may be perceived. The work of the Bureau of Veterans' Re-employment Rights, the functions of the Bureau of Labor Standards, which have to do with improved industrial and labor conditions, the Bureau of Statistics, and others have roles which show how closely labor and welfare legislation connect. It emphasizes the importance of effective interdepartmental coordination of activities.

VETERANS ADMINISTRATION

Like the Bureau of O. A. S. I., this independent agency has the responsibility for administering programs of direct service to individuals and families. In this respect it differs from the other federal agencies described in this chapter, which are responsible instead mostly for the administration of aid to states and localities which provide the direct service.

Although the services administered through the Veterans Administration (the V.A.) were described briefly in Chapter 6, a brief summary of the organization's responsibilities will be useful here. The major services may be classified under three headings: (1) medical care and treatment (this includes hospitals, clinics, and homes for veterans); (2) insurance; and (3) financial assistance to veterans and to dependents of deceased veterans, to compensate for earnings loss incurred through service in the military forces, and to aid veterans in rehabilitation to civilian life.

As of June 30, 1956, there were an estimated 22,381,000 veterans in civilian life. Of these, 15,370,000 were veterans of World War II, 4,682,000 were veterans of the Korean conflict, 3,061,000 were World War I veterans, 63,000 of the Spanish-American and earlier wars, and 65,000 were former members of the peacetime Regular Army who were on V.A. compensation rolls.[20] This certainly adds up to a sizable proportion of the population.

The Veterans Administration was created in 1930 by Executive Order 5398 of the President, under statutory authorization of that year.[21] Up to that time veterans benefits had been administered by a number of different offices. The purpose of this Act

---

[20] *Annual Report for the Fiscal Year 1956,* Administrator of Veterans Affairs, p. 15.
[21] 46 Stat. 1016, 38 U. S. C. 11.

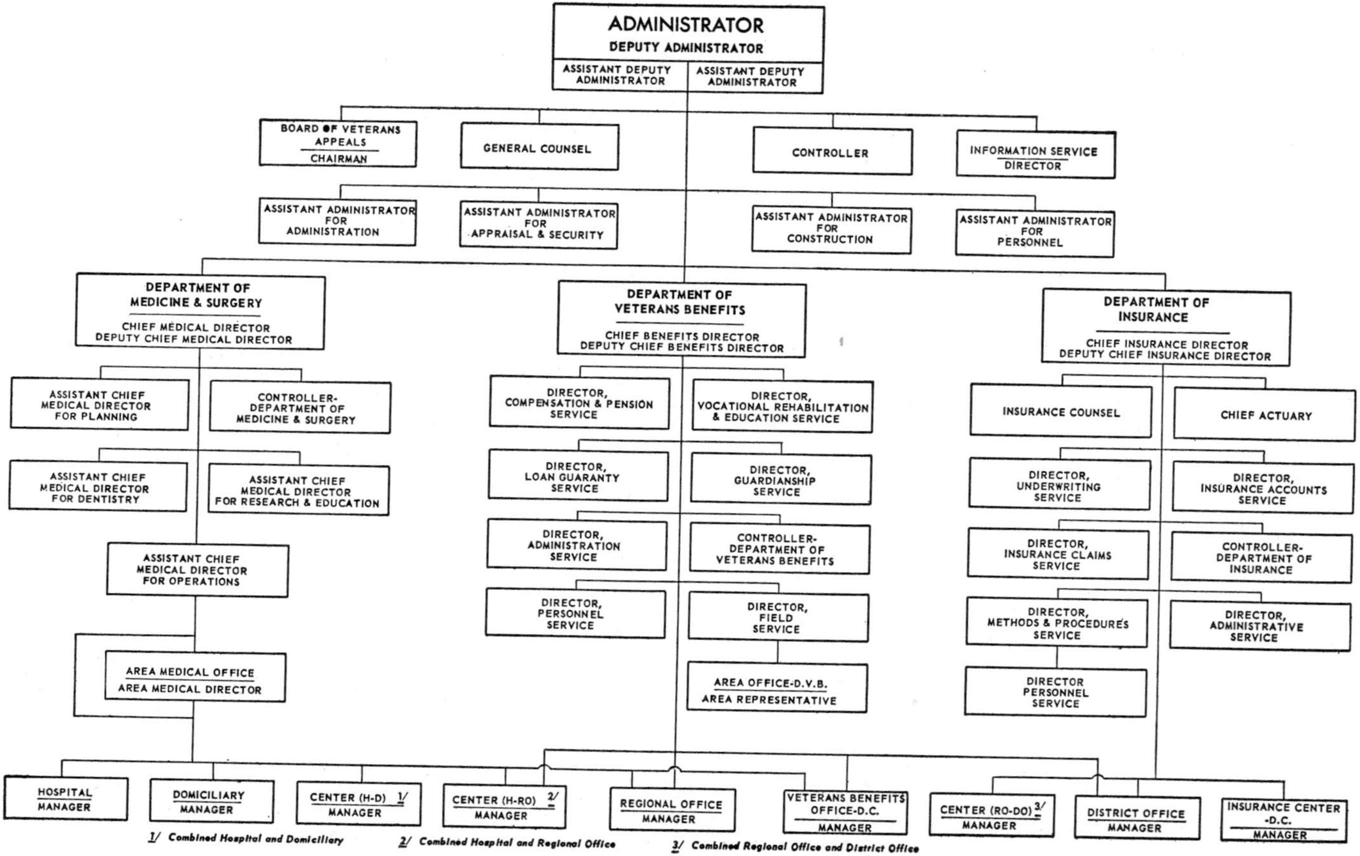

1/ Combined Hospital and Domiciliary *2/ Combined Hospital and Regional Office* *3/ Combined Regional Office and District Office*

SOURCE: Veterans Administration.

was to consolidate these separate services under one central administration, directly accountable to the office of the President.

As Chart 7 indicates, there are three departments in the departmental or central office staff which are responsible for the administration of the programs. These are the Departments of: Medicine and Surgery, of Veterans Benefits, and of Insurance. In addition, there are eight staff units, including the Board of Veterans Appeals, the General Counsel, the Controller, the Information Service, and Assistant Administrators for Administration, for Appraisal and Security, for Construction, and for Personnel. The V.A. provides, as the reader will recall, a very diversified program of service, and one which involves many technical features in all phases of its operation.

There are various types of field installations in the V.A. These include: District Offices, Regional Offices, Hospitals, Centers, Outpatient Clinics, Domiciliaries, Supply Depots, a Forms Depot, a Publications Depot, and V.A. Offices. In addition, there are an Insurance Center and a Veterans Benefit Office located in the District of Columbia. These field offices are subject to orders from the Administrator, the Deputy Administrator, or the Department Directors. Descriptions of the various types of field office, as noted in the United States Government official manual, follow:[22]

> *District Office.* A Veterans Administration district office is a major field organizational element established to render, within an assigned geographic area, services provided by law and under properly constituted authority, to veterans, their dependents and beneficiaries in connection with National Service Life insurance and certain types of death claims (effective June 11, 1956, jurisdiction over all new death claims was assigned to the appropriate regional offices in the continental United States). The office implements established plans, policies, and procedures for National Service Life insurance and death claims programs of the Veterans' Administration, and conducts the auxiliary services essential to the operation of

[22] *United States Government Organizational Manual, 1957-58,* Federal Register Division, National Archives and Records Service, General Services Administration. pp. 513-519.

the district office including finance, personnel, administrative, and supply activities.

Regional Office. A Veterans Administration regional office is a field station which under properly constituted authority grants benefits and services provided by law for veterans, their dependents, and beneficiaries within an assigned territory; furnishes information as to all Veterans Administration benefits and services; procures data regarding applications and claims; rates and adjudicates claims and makes awards for disability compensation and pension; conducts physical and mental examinations for claims purposes; establishes eligibility and need for hospitalization in other Government and private institutions and State-home care; renders outpatient treatment and social service; handles guardianship and fiduciary matters and authorized legal proceedings; aids, guides, and prescribes vocational rehabilitation training and administers educational benefits; guarantees loans for purchase or construction of homes, farms, or business property and, under certain conditions, makes direct home loans; after June 10, 1956, processes all new death claims in those regional offices located within the continental United States; aids and otherwise assists the veteran in exercising his rights to benefits and services; conducts administrative, finance, supply, files, and records activities; and supervises V. A. offices under its jurisdiction.

Hospital. A Veterans Administration hospital is an organizational element established to provide all eligible beneficiaries with medical care at a level comparable with the best civilian institutions treating similar types of illnesses. Hospitals are generally classified as GM & S (General Medical and Surgical), NP (Neuropsychiatric), and TB (Tuberculosis) indicating the major type of treatment. Usually, however, hospitals are equipped to render more than one type of treatment and some hospitals have facilities for highly specialized services such as those for tumors, chest surgery, neuro-surgery, paraplegia, etc.

Center. A Veterans Administration center is an organizational element consisting of a combination of activities of two or more of the following VA field stations under jurisdiction of one manager: district office, regional office, hospital, or domiciliary.

Domiciliary. A Veterans Administration domiciliary is a field station having only domiciliary activities. By domiciliary activities is meant the providing of a program of planned living in a sheltered environment and necessary ambulatory medical treatment to veterans who are unable because of their disabilities to earn a living but who are not in need of nursing service, constant medical supervision, or hospitalization. Domiciliary care is not to be considered as a convalescent service or an adjunct to the hospital for treatment of chronic diseases or as custodial care of incompetent veterans.

VA Office. A VA office is an organizational element under either a manager or an officer-in-charge established to provide contact service and such other services as cannot be conveniently provided to veterans, their dependents and beneficiaries, and others in a given locality by the parent regional office or center.

The total number of employees, full time and part-time, in the Veterans Administration was 176,653 as of June 30, 1956. This number included those classified under civil service and those excepted from such classification.[23] As pointed out earlier, this number includes workers from many occupations and professions. Each of the services, medical care, insurance administration and benefits administration, and readjustment and rehabilitation, demands a combination of many skills and kinds of expertise. And the total organization of such a structure, with its far-flung and diversified operation, requires legal, accounting, administrative, managerial, research, and operational planning services. This is a program which requires continuous planning and adjustment to such changing circumstances as new legislation, expiration of certain types of benefits with terminal dates, legislation in other programs which affects veterans and their families—including O. A. S. D. I., Unemployment Insurance, Vocational Rehabilitation, and others—new treatment procedures and scientific discoveries in the various fields of health, changing age groupings of the veteran population, and many others which affect the lives and the needs of the veterans.

Some of the figures which convey a sense of the size of this

[23] *Annual Report* of the Administrator of Veterans Affairs, 1956, p. 150.

program are the following: a total of approximately 2,737,000 veterans received disability compensation and pension benefits as of June 30, 1956. In the year 1956, 469,000 veterans began training under the vocational rehabilitation, education and training program. More than 600,000 applications were received during the fiscal year 1956 for insurance of loans, almost all of which were for home loans. Nearly 7,000,000 interviews were conducted during fiscal 1956 by contact personnel with veterans, families, and others interested in the problems of veterans. As of June 1956, there were 5,500,000 veterans participating in the national service life insurance program. The patient load in veterans' hospitals in fiscal 1956 was 113,544.[24]

RAILROAD RETIREMENT BOARD

The Railroad Retirement Board is responsible for the administration of railroad retirement, disability and unemployment insurance. The Board consists of three members appointed by the President with the advice and consent of the Senate. One of these members is recommended by representatives of employees and one by representatives of carriers. This is a federally administered program. The functions are performed through a number of field offices which are located in relation to centers of railroad population. There are seven regions within this field organization, each under a regional director who reports directly to the chief executive officer of the Railroad Retirement Board.

Summary

The federal government has three main responsibilities in social welfare; first, to administer certain of the large programs, including Old-Age and Survivors Insurance, Veterans benefits, and those programs of social insurance for railroad workers; second, the administration of grants-in-aid to states designed to strengthen state welfare services; and third, the provision of leadership in research and other activities designed to expand knowledge in

[24] *Ibid.,* pp. 5, 6, 7, 9, 10, 13.

social welfare fields and to improve the level of training, particularly for professional services in social welfare.

The major department of the federal government concerned with social welfare is the Department of Health, Education, and Welfare, which was established in 1953. Previously, most of the functions of this department were assigned to the Federal Security Agency, which was an independent agency of government. The major operating services of the Department of Health, Education, and Welfare are the Public Health Service, the Office of Education, the Social Security Administration, and the Office of Vocational Rehabilitation. In addition, the Food and Drug Administration and St. Elizabeth's Hospital units have administrative responsibilities.

Most of the programs with which we are concerned in social welfare are grouped under the Social Security Administration. To administer these services, the Social Security Administration has three major bureaus: Old-Age and Survivors Insurance, Public Assistance, and the Children's Bureau. In addition, there is the Bureau of Federal Credit Unions which has particular responsibilities affecting federal employees.

The Bureau of Old-Age and Survivors Insurance is the operating bureau of the Social Security Administration, that is, it is responsible for the direct administration of a large program. It is responsible for maintaining records and accounts for individual workers, maintaining workers' earnings histories, processing claims for benefits, and certifying payments. In the disability insurance program, the Bureau negotiates agreements with states for the determination of disability. It operates through a system of regional and field offices throughout the nation in certifying claims to the Treasury for payment.

The Bureau of Public Assistance administers grants to states for the four categories of special assistance, including Old Age Assistance, Aid to Dependent Children, Aid to the Blind, and Aid to the Permanently and Totally Disabled. The Bureau reviews state plans to determine whether they conform to the requirements of the Social Security Act, reviews operations of state agencies under state plans, provides advisory and consultative services on request, and issues standard-setting materials designed to assist the states in improving their level of administration.

The Children's Bureau is responsible for the administration of grants to states for maternal and child health services, crippled children's services, and child welfare services (all under Title V of the Social Security Act). In addition, this Bureau continues its role of "investigating and reporting on all matters pertaining to child life."

Another major unit of administration of welfare services is the Office of Vocational Rehabilitation. This office is responsible for the administration of grants to states for the basic services of vocational rehabilitation, for the special project grants, and for research. This office has been increasingly concerned since 1954 with the promotion of programs for training professional personnel in the rehabilitative services.

The Public Health Service has a long history of responsibility. Currently it operates through medical services and national institutes of health to perform a wide range of functions and to strengthen health services throughout the country; through grants to states to improve the facilities and methods for health procedures and practices; through investigation and demonstration of services, through research, and through grants for special purposes.

Many of the welfare services are outside of the Department of Health, Education, and Welfare, either in other cabinet departments or in independent agencies. Among the most important of the independent agencies are the Veterans' Administration and the Railroad Retirement Board. The Veterans' Administration operates through a system of district offices, regional offices, hospitals, clinical centers and other kinds of installations. The Railroad Retirement Board administers the social insurance programs available to railroad workers through a three-man board which functions through seven regional offices located near major centers of railroad activity.

In the Department of Labor, the Bureau of Employment Security administers grants to states for unemployment insurance in addition to funds for the establishment and maintenance of the state employment services. Through the conditions attached to the grants, this Bureau enforces minimal standards for unemployment insurance, but leaves the states largely free to determine their own programs. In addition to assuring conformity with the federal act, this Bureau provides consultation, advice on current and future unemployment trends, and offers a range of technical services. It is also responsible for the administration of federal functions connected with the work of the Employment Service.

Selected References

1. Administrator of Veterans Affairs, *Annual Reports.*
2. Brookings Institution, *Functions and Activities of the National Government in the Field of Welfare; Report,* Commission on Organization of the Executive Branch of the Government, Washington, 1949.
3. Hailman, David E., "Federal Agencies in Social Work," *Social Work Year Book, 1957,* New York, National Association of Social Workers, 1957.
4. Miles, Arthur P., *An Introduction to Public Welfare.* Boston, D. C. Heath and Company, 1949, esp. Chap. 12, "The Federal Government Becomes Welfare Conscious."
5. Public Health Service, U. S. Department of Health, Education, and Welfare, *The Public Health Service Today.* Washington, Government Printing Office, 1953.
6. Social Security Administration, *Handbook of Public Assistance Administration.* Bureau of Public Assistance, Washington, n.d.
7. Social Security Administration, *Your Children's Bureau in the Department of Health, Education, and Welfare,* Children's Bureau Publication Number 357-1956, Washington, 1956.
8. U. S. Department of Labor, *Federal Labor Laws and Agencies, A Layman's Guide.* Bureau of Labor Standards, Bulletin 123 rev. Washington, Government Printing Office, 1957.
9. U. S. Department of Health, Education, and Welfare, *Annual Reports.*
10. *United States Government Organization Manual 1957-58.* Washington, Government Printing Office.
11. White, R. Clyde, *Administration of Public Welfare,* 2nd ed. New York, American Book Company, 1950.

9

State Organization for Social Welfare

Although the two large public programs of social welfare, Veterans Services and O. A. S. D. I., are federally administered and with due deference to the influence of federal law and fiscal support on other public welfare programs, the state is still regarded as the level of government primarily responsible for the administration of this function. Most social welfare programs are either state-administered, or are operated by county or municipal governments under state supervision.

State control over social welfare was minimal in the early history of the nation. The original responsibility of the state was probably its assumption of care of the "unsettled poor," those who had not established settlement in any local community. Another acceptance of responsibility by the states in our early days was for special classes of the handicapped, as we have previously noted. These handicapped persons, the deaf, the blind, the crippled, were not sufficiently numerous in a local community to justify the building of a special facility for their care, and the costs of doing so would have exceeded the amount the localities would accept.[1]

These institutions generally were placed under boards of managers, appointed by and responsible to the governor and the legislature of the state. As they increased in number, the pressure developed for greater integration of authority and control. The organization of the first State Board of Charities, in Massachusetts in 1863, was a first big step toward state assumption of responsibility for social welfare. While the earlier state boards were limited in their responsibility to visitation, inspection, and reporting on conditions found in the institutions, later some states established central boards of control, with authority over all state institutions.

Marietta Stevenson has described the steps in the development of state agencies as follows: ". . . first, the establishment of a board with limited supervisory functions; then, the replacement of the board or the establishment of another one having administrative functions side by side with it; and finally, the establishment of departments with a combination of both types of functions."[2] The action of Illinois in 1917 in establishing a Department of Public Welfare under its Civil Administrative Code signalized this third stage. Dr. Stevenson states, with reference to the significance of this step, that "With this integration of welfare functions into a department of coordinate rank with finance, agriculture, labor, health, etc., came a recognition of welfare as an important function of government."[3]

The depression of the thirties found the states generally ill equipped to cope with the demands of large-scale relief administration. Few had organizations sufficiently comprehensive and unified to take on the administration of state-wide services, so deeply ingrained had been our tradition of local responsibility for

[1] See Josephine Brown, *Public Relief 1929-39* (New York, 1940), pp. 17-32. For an exceptionally clear historical summary see also Arthur P. Miles, *An Introduction to Public Welfare* (Boston, 1949), esp. Chap. 5, "The Rise of State Agencies," pp. 79-94.

[2] Marietta Stevenson, *Public Welfare Administration* (New York, 1938), p. 11.

[3] *Ibid.,* p. 13.

this function. Seven states, according to Josephine Brown, had made some provision for raising and distributing relief funds prior to the passage of the first of the federal measures, the Emergency Relief and Construction Act of 1932.[4] In the next year, thirty-three additional states, through the influence of the new federal law, made some provision for state-wide relief administration. In thirteen of the forty states with state-wide provision, according to Miss Brown, all or part of the emergency relief function was entrusted to existing state welfare agencies. In the other twenty-seven, emergency agencies were created.

It is quite clear that the greatest impetus to a permanent state structure with primary responsibility for social welfare was given by the provisions of the public assistance sections of the Social Security Act. In order to receive federal aid for any of the categories of aid each state as a condition to receiving funds was required to establish a "single state agency" to administer the program of assistance, or to supervise its administration, and each state was required to have the program in effect in every one of its subdivisions.

Another portion of the Social Security Act, Title V, dealing with child welfare services, has also had considerable influence on the role of the state in social welfare. The requirement that there be a state plan has meant in effect that there must be an agency state-wide in scope to receive and administer the funds, even though this provision did not require operation in all subdivisions. In the unemployment insurance program, in vocational rehabilitation, in crippled children's services, and in the maternal and child health measure, also, the federal government, through its policy of making grants to states, has fostered the concept of the state as the level of government primarily responsible for social welfare.

In a discussion of "Grants-in-Aid and Centralization," William Anderson states that as a result of financial support from federal and state sources, and of being held to high standards by participation in the federally-aided programs, state-administered

[4] *Op. cit.,* p. 177.

services have shown steady growth and improvement. The states have increased their own support of nonfederally-aided functions as well as of those for which federal aid is received, and, as a result, state governments have become more active in the provision of important services, have attracted more qualified people into their service, have increased their staffs, and in general have raised the level of administration.[5]

What Anderson notes with reference to services is very true of public social welfare. The state level of service has improved. The locus of responsibility in this function of government has shifted from the counties and the municipalities to the states. Now the state is the unit which sets the standards for social welfare administration. It either administers or has most administrative control over almost all of the nonfederally-administered major welfare programs. The large dimension of federally-aided social welfare plus the limited resources available to local governments have brought this about.

All the states now have welfare departments. Most of them are called either the department of public welfare or the department of social welfare. This is by no means a stereotype, however, since some use different names. Maine has a Department of Health and Welfare; Missouri, a State Department of Public Health and Welfare; New Jersey, a Department of Institutions and Agencies; Idaho and Washington each have a Department of Public Assistance; Virginia, a State Department of Welfare and Institutions, to name some of the variations of title.

States vary even more in their patterns of organization. Even states of comparable size are unlike in their organization of services, and neighboring states may show little evidence of having influenced each other in this matter. States may be quite unlike each other with respect to: (1) the nature of the agency to which a particular function is assigned, *i.e.*, whether health, welfare or other type of agency; (2) the extent to which the welfare programs have been integrated into large multifunctional agencies rather than assigned separately to special purpose agencies; (3)

5 William Anderson, *The Nation and the States, Rivals or Partners?* (Minneapolis, 1955), p. 183.

how the agencies are organized to perform the service, *i.e.*, the kinds of boards, how the boards are related to the staffs of the agencies, and to political authorities, and the internal structure of the organization; and (4) how the state agencies are related to local welfare units.

One might well ask why there are such variations. Isn't there a single "best" pattern which might be followed? At least couldn't the differences be limited to those necessitated by the variations in area and population of the states? Isn't the nature of the organization important enough to the quality of service to justify some attempt among the states to agree on some rather exact specifications?

No one has yet discovered the one type of state organization guaranteed to yield the best results. Failure to take account of many factors in the states would probably be most unfortunate for the programs. Much of the claim to excellence of a federal system advanced by its proponents rests on variety rather than sameness and on the value of experimentation with different forms of administration which are possible under a decentralized system. To assume that the same system would work in all states would be justified only if conditions in all of them were the same, or similar.

Marietta Stevenson has suggested that to some extent variations in state organization for social welfare may be attributed to differences in social and economic conditions among the states. She notes wide contrasts in per capita wealth and income, in population density, in area, in degree of industrialization and urbanization, and in tax-paying capacity. With reference to the last-named, not only the actual wealth and income of a state must be considered but also the extent to which the wealth and income are available for taxing purposes.[6] States may have provisions in their constitutions or their statutes which limit this power to tax certain kinds of income or wealth. Some states which spend less for social welfare, both in total amount and in per capita outlay, may actually be spending a larger proportion of their wealth and income

[6] *Op cit.*, pp. 61-84.

than are some wealthier states, and the organization of services may reflect this fact.

Only to a limited extent, however, would economic and social conditions seem to account for differences among the states in how they have organized their welfare services. A more likely explanation is the combination of these conditions with the factors of tradition, leadership, and the influence the pattern of other state services has on the character of the social welfare structure. This observation is supported by the fact that states with the most similar characteristics of population density, wealth, and urbanization, may show wide variation in social welfare organization. In some instances the pattern of state welfare organization suggests that the organization was not planned—it just happened.

In general the functions of state welfare agencies are these:[7] (1) administration of certain services, or supervision of local administration of them; (2) licensing and general supervision and standard-setting for voluntary (private) and local public agencies; (3) development of special projects and administration, sponsorship, or encouragement of research designed to develop a more adequate knowledge of welfare needs and services; (4) leadership in educational projects established to strengthen staff competence on both state and local levels of administration; (5) public information to promote a better understanding of the nature and the needs of social welfare within the states; (6) recommendations with respect to legislative and other program changes; (7) development of cooperation with other state agencies in the rendering and improvement of services; and (8) participation with federal agencies in the development of national policy.

Let us now examine the various characteristics of welfare organization among the states.

PATTERNS OF STATE WELFARE ORGANIZATION

As stated in the discussion of the logic of combining health, education, and welfare within a single federal department, it is not

---

[7] The welfare agencies may or may not be responsible for administration or supervision of institutions.

always easy to classify services as belonging predominantly in one rather than in another category. Many of the programs have so many features which seem to fit more than one of these classifications of services that often it is quite difficult to determine what kind of agency should be responsible for a particular program. Of course the prevailing influences may be particular factors within the state rather than anything approaching pure administrative logic. The strength of a given agency, its reputation in the state, its relationship to the political leadership, the way it is regarded by the state legislature at the time the program is enacted may be decisive factors in the determination of where a program is placed among existing agencies. Or sentiment may be strong for the development of a separate agency. The prospective clientele, and their sympathizers may be strong enough to bring about the establishment of a special separate agency in order to further their interests.[8]

Most state welfare agencies have as their core programs public assistance and child welfare. These are the most consistently assigned to state departments of public welfare, although as we shall see, there are a few variations even with respect to where these two kinds of service are assigned. They are less likely, however, to be placed with health or education agencies, or to special commissions than are some of the other services.

Suppose we look at some of the programs with reference to the agency to which they are assigned. As we examine state administration of the programs described in Part 2 of this volume, we see some interesting variations.

Starting with crippled children's services, we see that in thirty-three of the states, the responsibility for administration is carried by state health departments, although there are some in which the service is assigned to a state welfare department and in others to a state department of education. In Iowa, Illinois, Missouri, and Oregon, the crippled children's program is a function of the state university, evidently reflecting the states' belief in the close relationship between clinical teaching and research on the one hand,

---

[8] A good example of this phenomenon is the group supporting services for the blind.

and service on the other. In Maine this program is the responsibility of a combined health and welfare department.

It might seem that crippled children's services clearly is primarily a health rather than a welfare or an educational function.
Still, there are important aspects of special education connected
with the training or retraining of the handicapped child, and certainly needs for social services are likely to be found, as the
handicapped child is helped toward a social adjustment.

Other interesting variations in patterns of administration are
found in vocational rehabilitation. In many states the program is
assigned to departments of education or of public instruction.
However, here also patterns differ. In some states, the programs
are administered by independent commissions or departments. In
others state boards of vocational education administer them. In
two states (New Jersey and Pennsylvania) vocational rehabilitation is one of the functions of a department of labor and industry.
In Utah, the program is assigned to the state health department.
In this program it is interesting to note the separation of administration of vocational rehabilitation services for the blind from
other vocational rehabilitation services in some states. In several
states, vocational rehabilitation for the blind is the responsibility
of a separate commission for the blind or of a division for the blind
in a state welfare agency.

Turning to the field of community services in mental health, we
see further evidence of diversity. In twenty-seven of the states and
in the District of Columbia, Alaska, Hawaii, Puerto Rico, and the
Virgin Islands the program as of 1956 was carried by state departments of health.[9] In twelve states, however, this program is
the responsibility of separate departments of mental health or
mental hygiene. In five states mental health community service is
one of the functions of a state department of welfare.[10]

In many states, unemployment insurance is administered by a
separate commission, but here again there are variations of pat-

[9] This enumeration includes Maine and Missouri, each of which has a combined
department of health and welfare.
[10] This enumeration is based on a map provided by the Community Services
Branch of the National Institute of Mental Health (Washington, November 1956).

terns. In some states, the function is assigned to a state department of labor, or, as in New Jersey, to the Department of Labor and Industry, and in others to a Department of Employment which has more comprehensive functions than that of administering unemployment insurance. Generally, the administration of the employment service and unemployment insurance are combined in one agency.

Nor does the correctional program—the administration of correctional institutions and systems of probation and parole—follow a uniform pattern. In some states there is a separate department of corrections. In others, this responsibility is a part of a large department of welfare, and in one state, corrections and mental health are assigned to the same organization. The picture is further complicated by some separation of the various aspects of corrections, with probation and parole assigned to one unit and the administration of institutions to another. In some states, the Youth Commission has responsibility for probation and parole of young offenders. Minnesota has a somewhat different pattern, with the Corrections Division as part of the Department of Public Welfare, and the Youth Conservation Commission responsible for prevention and parole services, and for diagnosis and treatment of juvenile delinquency and crime.

Much stress has been placed in recent years on the virtues of consolidating welfare agencies into fewer organizations. There has been a trend away from the special commission or agency responsible for a single program and toward the large, comprehensive multifunctional state welfare agency.

In programs of similar natures, such as the several types of public assistance, the logic of consolidation is clear. There seems little justification for having separate administration of one type of assistance, and in fact, at present, only aid to the blind has such separate administration, and that only in a small number of states. In Massachusetts, however, there is an interesting variation. Aid to the blind, along with vocational rehabilitation for the blind and other services, is administered by the Division for the Blind of the State Department of Education. Unless there are very compelling reasons for organization by clientele rather than service, it seems most desirable to combine all types of public assistance under a single administrative agency in each state. Greater efficiency in use of staff and facilities, more comprehensive planning, and a better range of services are possible under a consolidated organization for administration of public assistance. In those instances in which aid to the blind is administered under a commission independent from the agency administering the other public assistance measures, it is evident that the allocation of responsibility has been based on clientele rather than function for the apparent purpose of grouping together all services for the blind. The validity of such separation from other forms of public assistance is certainly open to question.

With one exception, child welfare services and public assistance administration are combined.[11] In Illinois and until recently in Pennsylvania child welfare has been assigned to a welfare department with an identity separate from that of the agency administering public assistance.

The prevailing practice of placing these two important areas of social welfare, public assistance and child welfare, in the same over-all state agency is no accident. It reflects the closeness of the relationship of needs of people for these services, and expresses an intent to strengthen both by placing them in an administrative pattern which facilitates communication and cooperation between them.

In the administration of Workmen's Compensation, there are really only three patterns of assignment. In seventeen states, the law is administered in the labor department, in twenty-six in an independent commission,[12] and in five it is administered in the courts. In Alaska and in the District of Columbia, the law is administered by an independent agency.

[11] In Pennsylvania recent legislation has resulted in combining the two programs.
[12] It should be noted, however, that in two of the states and in Alaska, although the law is administered by an independent commission, the labor department participates in administration through membership on the workmen's compensation agency. *State Workmen's Compensation Laws as of August 1957.* Bulletin 161 rev., Bureau of Labor Standards (Washington, 1957), p. 69.

But the patterns of assignment of programs to state agencies is not the only feature of organization which shows great variation among the states. Another is the extent to which states have consolidated the administration of their programs among fewer agencies. There is considerable sentiment in favor of the large omnibus agency. The multifunctional agency, comprising as many as possible of the state-administered or supervised programs of welfare, or of health and welfare, suggests, among other things, the possibility of improved coordination of planning, better cooperation in the rendering of services, more efficient use of facilitating services such as personnel administration, office management, fiscal planning and control. Such an agency, with a unified accountability for the total program, certainly seems to offer many advantages to the people of the state. It is believed that people will coordinate their activities more effectively if they are parts of the same organizational structure, subject to a unified command, than they are inclined to do when cooperation requires interagency agreement and planning.

These obvious advantages are likely to lead consistently to recommendations to unify or consolidate or integrate. The public is inclined to look with disfavor on scattering of responsibility, and may regard opposition to such consolidation as motivated by a desire to protect vested interests in older organizations on the part of those who work in them. Another factor may be a feeling of public irritation with complexity, which leads to resentment of being unable quickly to comprehend the existing welfare structure, and that it might be simpler as well as more economical to place all under a single organizational roof. Generally we tend to resent that which is difficult to understand, and the person who supports the services and who may need them, wonders why the setup should be so complicated.

Unfortunately, the situation is not so simple that unlimited consolidation of welfare services promises to solve all problems. Bigness creates its own problems, especially when it involves combining a number of different kinds of services. In public administration one considers frequently the problem of determining how extensive an organization can be and yet be manageable.

Another problem which is suggested by combinations of programs under a single administrative canopy was mentioned earlier (in the discussion of the organization of the federal Department of Health, Education and Welfare). This is the desire of the administrative head of any program to have direct access to the Chief Executive of the government, rather than to have to go through an appointed department head. He may feel that his requests will get a better hearing if he has the opportunity to present his program needs separately and by himself, without having them be a part of a larger program. The head of a division of corrections, for example, may wish that his plans would not be subject to competition with child welfare, mental health, and public assistance. Similarly, the head of any one of the other divisions may feel that the interests of his program are in danger of being submerged.

Another sometimes alleged danger, with reference to large, multifunctional agencies, is the possibility of preferential treatment for one service, if the administrator has a pertinent bias. In a department of health and welfare, for example, the administrator is likely to be drawn from one of the two professional fields and, according to those who oppose consolidation, may be inclined to favor that which represents his own specialty. In a department which includes corrections, mental health, child welfare, and public assistance, should the administrator be drawn from any one of these fields? Or should he be a "generalist" with no primary allegiance to any? If the latter, would he have enough program knowledge to enable him to represent effectively the large and complex department for which he is responsible?

It is quite evident that substantial theoretical arguments can be mustered in support of either unifunctional or multifunctional organization of state welfare departments. In a sense the arguments may be dismissed with the statement that that which works best is best, and that any structure can be made to function if those who work in the services are disposed to make the system work. Indeed, Arthur P. Miles suggests that this may be the case, when he states that "Organizational structures are often artificial and not too meaningful in administration," and further, that, "It is, for example, possible that divisions of departments in some states are as independent as departments in other states. Efficiency and consistency in administration are determined not by charts and graphs of the administrative structure, but by the vision, spirit, professional competence, and personal integrity of the employees."[13]

What Dr. Miles says is certainly true in substance. The best of organization will fail unless the employees working within it have the disposition and determination to make it work. Still, the question of structure cannot be dismissed as of no importance. The efforts of staff will be more effective if they work within or from a structure which facilitates their efforts.

The weight of argument today seems to be in favor of greater integration of services. For one thing, government has become so large and complex that a governor and a legislature logically may wish to reduce the numbers of separate appearances before them, and may prefer to have fewer individual requests for support of services. For another, the importance in interservice relationships of a common organizational identity is potentially significant. Furthermore, over-all planning in the interests of public policy is likely to be less narrowly conceived in relation to a single kind of program if it is related in a common organization to other needs.

New Jersey and Wisconsin are generally considered to have gone as far as any states toward a large, comprehensive state welfare organization. In these two states, public assistance, child welfare, mental health, and corrections programs are all assigned to a single department. In these two states also, the responsibility includes both institutional and noninstitutional programs. Another state which has moved far toward consolidation of services in recent years is Minnesota. There, in 1939, a Reorganization Act abolished a Board of Control which had operated state institutions and social service programs, and created a larger Department of Social Security. This department had three divisions: Public

---

[13] *An Introduction to Public Welfare* (Boston, 1949), p. 279.

CHART 8.   ORGANIZATION OF DEPARTMENT OF PUBLIC WELFARE, MINNESOTA

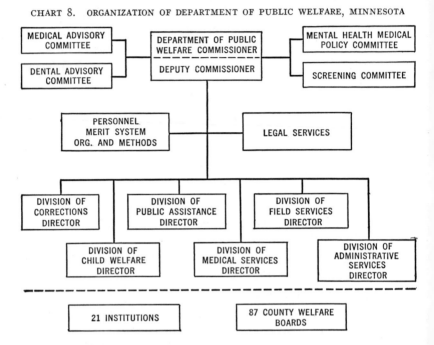

Institutions, Social Welfare, and Employment Security. This proved to be only a nominal consolidation, however, since the divisions actually tended to operate as separate, independent entities. In 1953, two of the Divisions, Public Institutions and Social Welfare, were merged into a single Department of Public Welfare, while the Division of Employment and Security became a separate department. Chart 8 gives a picture of the general organization structure in Minnesota today. It presents an organization not so comprehensive in coverage as Wisconsin's or New Jersey's, especially with reference to corrections. In Minnesota, there is a separate Youth Conservation Commission, and a separate Parole Board, while in the other two states mentioned, these functions are assigned to the over-all consolidated department.

In commenting on the Minnesota structure, Morris Hursh, Commissioner, Department of Public Welfare, has this to say:[14]

[14] Letter to the author, dated September 7, 1956.

To be sure, Corrections and Child Welfare don't have a great deal in common, though there are certain aspects of the work that do respond to close communication between people employed in each of these units. The wife and family of an inmate in our state prison may have need of child welfare services or public assistance, and information about the inmate being readily available within the same department may help the social worker do a better job with his family. I think the chief advantage in having an integrated program of this sort is that the professional services provided are applicable in so many functional areas. For example, all our program divisions (Corrections, Child Welfare, Public Assistance, and Medical Services) utilize and have a need for psychological services, social work services, medical services, and others that may be termed professional in nature. From this standpoint, each division can give a certain amount of help to the others, and I believe that the intercommunication between the personnel involved is beneficial in seeing that others wrestle with similar problems in what is perhaps a different setting; and this, generally, makes for a better program.

Commissioner Hursh adds that work with local welfare agencies tends to be furthered by an integrated department. Cooperation between state institutions and agencies is stimulated by a common approach to the counties.

All this is true of course only if state leadership is exercised to bring about an attitude of cooperation. As Dr. Miles said, lack of communication, failure to cooperate, and confusion of policy may occur in a large, but uncoordinated department, unless the means are found to keep the people in the structure identified with the purposes of the whole agency as well as with their own, individual units.

In states as large as California or New York, consolidation so complete as that in Minnesota, Wisconsin, or New Jersey, would be more difficult because of the very size of the programs which would be affected. The problem of communication increases with the size of the organization, and with the numbers of institutions and agencies which are included. In California and New York there are separate departments of welfare, corrections, and mental health.

Cooperation is no less vital, however, in states with separate organizations for the administration of the various services than in those which are more directly integrated. Social welfare today covers so many related purposes, and is so closely related to such other services as public health, that coordination of effort has become increasingly important.

It is of course necessary that cooperation and coordination take place at the local level of operation, but it is also important that such local activity be encouraged through planning at the state level. Such coordination does not occur automatically, and may come slowly as departments for one reason or other become so immersed in the details of their own programs that they fail to look across the way at other organizations. The slowness with which such cooperation has developed was described not many years ago by the former Surgeon General of the United States, Dr. Leonard Scheele, as follows:[15]

> At any gathering of health or welfare people, the need for a cooperative attack upon inter-related problems is likely to be discussed. Public health people talked about it extensively at the recent American Public Health Association meetings in St. Louis. There is an equal eagerness among social workers. Yet, after the meetings are over, a cold, analytical look at actual operations in local communities and throughout the nation shows that the "trend" toward cooperation is painfully slow. From the standpoint of structure for cooperative action, these organizations seem to be almost as far apart as they were in the days when welfare meant an occasional coal or grocery order, and when public health meant a red placard on the home of a scarlet fever patient.

While spontaneous cooperative activity at the local level may occur, cooperation at both local and state levels will be more

---

[15] As quoted in "Cooperation Between Departments of Health and Welfare," by Jonas M. Muller, M.D., M.P.H., and Pearl Bierman, M.A., in *Public Health Reports,* Reprint No. 3280, Vol. 71, No. 9 (September, 1956), issued by the Public Health Service, U. S. Dept. of Health, Education, and Welfare, p. 845.

assured and effective if it is planned. Turning again to health and welfare as services which need to work closely and continuously together, we see further how the extended scope of services in public assistance has increased the need for effective cooperation with the health services. As stated in a public health publication:[16]

> The current emphasis on extension of welfare department services beyond cash assistance implies a continuing increase in the health responsibilities of welfare agencies: services for unmarried mothers, for dependent and foster children, for the aged, and, in some communities, for families at large; and services directed at the prevention of juvenile delinquency, control of alcoholism, or at the maintenance and improvement of standards of institutional care. In defining the objectives of these programs and in developing ways to attain their goals, welfare and health departments need to pool their knowledge.

ORGANIZATIONAL STRUCTURE AND ADMINISTRATIVE PROCESS

Voluntary social agencies have long recognized the value of the citizen board serving in either an advisory or a policy-making capacity in relation to the staff. In voluntary agencies these boards have been made up of people who serve without compensation. The membership traditionally has consisted of people prominent in community affairs, and interested in social welfare. They have tended to be representative of a cross section of community interests, and have brought to the professional staff of the agency an insight into community needs and public opinion. The boards also generally have been effective in broadening the base of community support, and in serving the agency by interpreting its program to the community.

From the earliest development of the state welfare agency, the board has been a part of state organization. The first state agency, in Massachusetts, had a State Board of Charities, consisting of

[16] *Ibid.*, p. 846.

seven persons appointed by the Governor, and a general agent and a secretary. Other state agencies generally followed the Massachusetts pattern of an unsalaried board, together with a paid secretary.

The state board of public welfare has been important for many of the same reasons that make the board valuable in voluntary agencies. Many of the same considerations apply, namely, the enlistment of popular support for the service, the interpretation of the agency to the public, advice to the agency on the effect of its policy on the general interests of the community, and the judgment of people removed from the closeness of daily association with the programs.

In general, state welfare boards have the following characteristics: they consist of from five to fifteen members appointed by the governor usually with legislative consent; they are unsalaried, although they may receive allowances, generally quite nominal, for expenses incurred by attending board meetings or in the performance of other duties; they are appointed for overlapping terms—that is, so that their terms of appointment expire in different years, in order to allay the danger of "packing" by successive state political administrations; they may or may not be "policy-making" —that is, empowered to make or approve all major policy developed by the state agency. Some boards are only advisory in character.

In many states, these boards have the authority to appoint the welfare director, while in others, the power is vested in the office of the governor of the state. In two states, New Jersey and North Carolina, the state board may appoint the executive, but with the advice and consent of the Governor, although the person so appointed retains his position at the pleasure of the state board. In Nevada, the executive is appointed by the Board with the approval of the Governor, but subject to the merit system, that is to competition through civil service procedures.

In Nebraska, the Board appoints the executive of the Division of Public Welfare, subject to approval by the State Legislature.

Not all states, however, follow the pattern of the unsalaried citizen board. An older pattern was that of full-time salaried boards, or in effect, a multiple executive. An existing example of this type of organization is the Iowa State Board of Social Welfare. In Utah, the Department is operated under a full-time salaried commission. The theory behind this type of organization apparently is that three heads are better than one, if not necessarily three times better, although such an assumption is certainly open to question. Generally, this kind of structure would seem to be less promising in terms of leadership and consistent direction of policy than the single executive and advisory board pattern of organization.

The question of who should have the power to appoint the executive is a controversial one. Proponents of the theory held by students of government, that the chief executive as the general manager of the state should have the power to appoint his program chiefs, would certainly tend to the belief that the governor should select the welfare head. On the other hand, many people believe that the welfare post by its very nature should be removed as far as possible from any suggestion of political influence, and, accordingly, they believe that the executive should be appointed by the nonpolitical state board. It is not easy to assess the relative merits of these two points of view, but one thing seems fairly obvious. That is the fact that as social welfare continues to develop as an integral part of public service, it becomes more and more involved in decisions that vitally affect state policy. Having a welfare executive directly accountable to the elected state administration would tend to reinforce that accountability. This statement is made with full realization that the biennial or quadrennial change in state administrations can be quite damaging to the development of the welfare program, to say nothing of the risk that decisions may be dictated by considerations of political self-preservation on the part of the welfare executive rather than by program interests. But experience has shown the value of continuity of administration, and of a professionally qualified administrator.

This argument is really quite theoretical, in a way. In states in which the appointment is made by the governor, the tradition of social welfare built up in years of conscientious administration may be such that little evidence of "politics" in its worst sense will be evident in the character of administration. Playing politics with the problems of the needy or the handicapped, or with the economic security of the people of the state of course can occur, but it is not widespread. Where a board exists, especially when it establishes policy and is not strictly advisory, it is in a position, through its access to popular opinion, to exert strong influence against the political handling of social welfare.

Over the years the movement in state welfare organization has been definitely away from the salaried, full time board of control. This is perhaps verification through experience of Dr. Marietta Stevenson's opinion, expressed some years ago, that "From an administrative point of view, little that is favorable can be said of the board of control, which gives neither unified control nor protection from political interferences, as the old theory of divided responsibility is not in line with modern theories of governmental efficiency."[17]

Much can be said in favor of a division of responsibility and function in an agency with a board and a single executive which would assign authority to make or approve decisions affecting basic policy to the board, and control over management of the department and over the making of decisions within the range of established policy to the executive. Certainly, little but confusion may be anticipated when a board interferes with the operation of the agency. The behavior of the board, however, as experience has shown, may be a reflection of the strength or weakness of the executive. The latter, if he is not consistently aware of his responsibility in relation to the board, may invite interference through either of the two extremes—by leaning too heavily on a board for decisions which he should make himself, or by not keeping the board sufficiently informed. Administration, like nature, abhors a vacuum, and a failure of executive leadership may create such a vacuum.

[17] *Op. cit.*, p. 159.

CHART 9.   NORTH CAROLINA STATE BOARD OF PUBLIC WELFARE

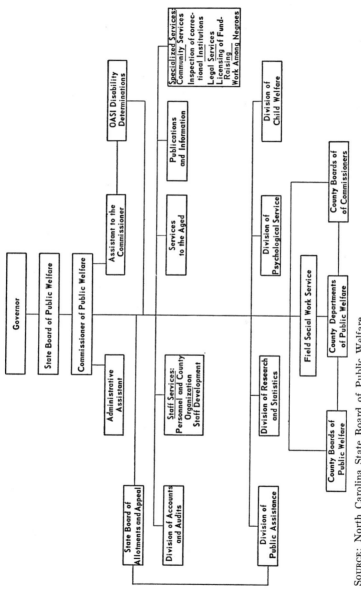

SOURCE: North Carolina State Board of Public Welfare.

In summary, forty-six of the fifty-three jurisdictions have fifty boards of public welfare under various names.[18] In twenty-one the boards may be considered administrative; that is, they have power over organization, personnel, finance, etc. In ten states, the boards are advisory in nature. In eighteen, the boards may be described as policy-making, but with responsibility for management of the department left to the administrator.[19]

INTERNAL STRUCTURE OF STATE WELFARE AGENCIES

The following statement by one authority with reference to business organization applies no less clearly to social welfare administration:[20]

> An essential to that cooperation (so necessary in business organization) is a soundly designed organization structure which gives full release to the energies of each member. The members of a human organization will give their best and co-operate most thoroughly with others when each knows what he is responsible for, to whom he is responsible, and his cooperative relations with others. Indefiniteness in these essentials will obstruct cooperation, encourage the growth of minor and major dictatorships, and lead to loss of effectiveness.

Because of the size and complexity of this structure, necessitated as it is by the numbers of programs and institutions administered by the New Jersey Department, we shall not attempt to describe it in detail, particularly since in these respects it presents an atypical pattern. Organizational Chart 10 shows in general outline the structure of the Department. One feature of the organization, however, which is especially interesting in social welfare is the mixed nature of administration of public assistance within the Department's Division of Welfare. Old age assistance

---

[18] Some of the states have more than one agency with boards.

[19] Charles Schottland, "Public Welfare," in *Social Work Year Book, 1957* (New York, National Association of Social Workers), p. 477.

[20] R. E. Gillmor, *A Practical Manual of Organization,* Book 4 of Reading Course in Executive Technique, Karl Heil, ed. (New York, 1948), p. 2.

CHART 10. NEW JERSEY DEPARTMENT OF INSTITUTIONS AND AGENCIES

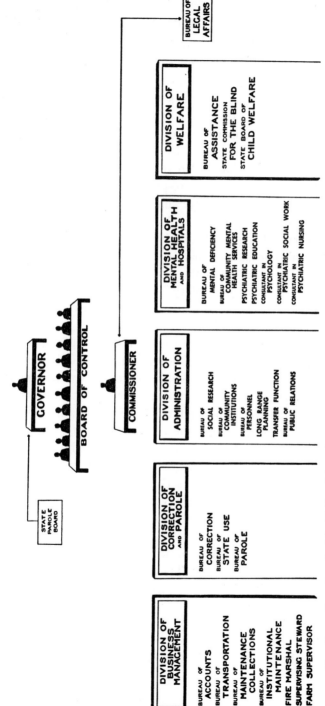

SOURCE: New Jersey Department of Institutional Agencies.

and aid to the permanently and totally disabled are administered by county welfare boards, under the supervision of the Bureau of Assistance. General assistance is administered by the municipalities, and is under the general supervision of the Bureau of Assistance. Aid to the Blind is administered by the county welfare boards under the supervision of the Commission for the Blind, which also carries responsibility for services and vocational rehabilitation for the blind. Aid to dependent children, as well as child welfare services, is the responsibility of the State Board of Child Welfare, which directly administers the assistance program under the name "Home Life Assistance." This combination of state-supervised and state-administered assistance in the same agency is also not a usual pattern, to say the least. An interesting feature in New Jersey is the assignment to the State Board of Child Welfare of responsibility for supervision of children under 14 who are released on parole from the State Home for Boys and the State Home for Girls.

Another unusual feature of the New Jersey agency is the presence of a board and a commission within the Division of Welfare. It is not a common practice to have boards or commissions in state divisions for the administration of noninstitutional services in public assistance or child welfare. The State Board of Child Welfare, for example, is within the Division of Welfare, and operates side by side with the Bureau of Assistance which has no such structure. This is a carry-over from an earlier time. The New Jersey State Board of Children's Guardians, the predecessor to the State Board of Child Welfare, was established by legislative act in 1899, and was incorporated into the structure of the Department of Institutions and Agencies in 1918, when that Department was established. The Board of Managers includes seven members, appointed by the Governor. The Executive Director of the State Board of Child Welfare thus is also in a position of dual accountability, both to the Commissioner of the Department, through the Director of the Division of Welfare, and to the Board of Managers.

In another state, Washington, the State Department of Public

Assistance presents an interesting organizational picture. This Department is far from being as extensive in its program coverage as the New Jersey one, and carries only the public assistance and child welfare programs, and vocational and other services for the blind. (See Chart 11.) As the chart shows, the Department has three major divisions, the Offices of Program Development, Field Operations, and Administration. The Office of Field Operations is the one carrying the line responsibility through its unit for Field Supervision, although the functions of administrative analysis or review, and staff training, while staff functions, are considered so closely related to operations as to be placed in the same part of the organization.

Looking back at the North Carolina chart (Chart 9), one sees a still somewhat different relationship. The field service is directly responsible to the office of the Commissioner, and the lines of communication from the county departments go through the Field Social Work Service. The County Boards, both the elected County Boards of Commissioners and the appointed Board of Public Welfare, however, show a line intersecting at a point above the box denoting the position of the field service. Presumably, then, any point at issue could be taken by the local board directly to the Commissioner's office. The County Department would report through the Field Service, although here too it is quite conceivable that the County Director might take a matter up with the Board of Public Welfare, which in turn could go to the Commissioner, thus in effect bypassing the field service, unless carefully defined administrative procedures prevent this from happening.

North Carolina was the first state to establish the county system of public welfare in anything resembling the form in which it exists today, and was one of the few states with a modern type of state public welfare organization, when the new welfare programs of the 1930's influenced so markedly the pattern and character of state and local welfare organization. It certainly reflects a pattern of state-local relations that places considerable stress on the maintenance of the strength of the local operation through supervision by state leadership rather than rigid or detailed measures

CHART 11. ORGANIZATION OF DEPARTMENT OF PUBLIC ASSISTANCE, WASHINGTON

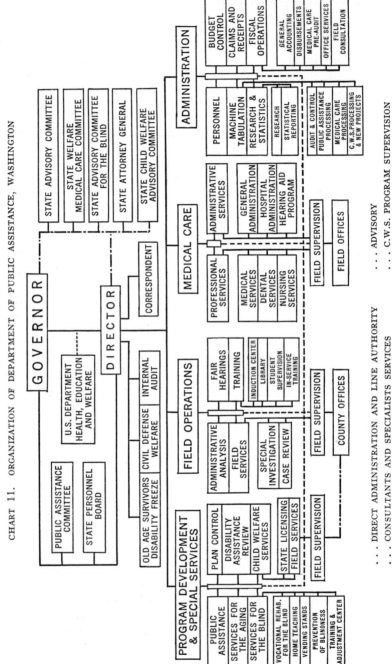

... DIRECT ADMINISTRATION AND LINE AUTHORITY

... CONSULTANTS AND SPECIALISTS SERVICES

... FEDERAL APPROVAL

... ADVISORY

... C.W.S. PROGRAM SUPERVISION

of control. An examination of the chart will reveal a pattern of state organization designed to promote a minimum of fragmentation of responsibility. The staff or program divisions of public assistance and child welfare, as well as the closely related technical division of research and statistics, and that of psychological services, and the over-all general service functions would seem to be in a workable relationship. It is of course true that the North Carolina Department, with its responsibility for only child welfare services, and for public assistance (except for aid to the blind which is vested in the State Commission for the Blind) does not have the problems of complexity that such states as New Jersey, Wisconsin, and Minnesota have with the larger scope of their program responsibilities.

These combinations of skills must be organized whether the agency is responsible for many programs or relatively few. In child welfare services, for example, the social worker is the person most directly responsible for the service to the individual or family. However, the many legal aspects involved in protective services for children make the knowledge of the lawyer indispensable. The psychologist performs the function of testing the child, and of offering technical consultation on psychological needs. Many times health problems are present and demand medical knowledge. Or, in foster care, the boarding home is appraised by the health officer and the fire marshall as a part of the social worker's evaluation of the home.

Income security programs provide other notable examples of the interdisciplinary nature of services. In the federal welfare structure we have already seen how the different technical fields are represented in the various Bureaus and Offices of the Department of Health, Education, and Welfare. In public assistance in the states the social worker who assists the client in the determination of eligibility and to meet other needs certifies the need for payment, but a host of fiscal and management operations are necessary before the actual payment reaches the hands of the eligible person. In income security programs also, there often are legal questions, as situations appear which fall outside the scope of established policy. As Karl DeSchweinitz has stated: "It is to be expected that the lawyer should play an important part in the process through which basic principles and enforceable requirements are derived from the law. In that considerable area in which the interpretation of the acts of the legislature determines decisions and actions, he occupies a major role. He has exercised great influence on the development of the concepts of equity and right which affect every aspect of the administration of social security."[21]

In the state public welfare agency today, one may find the property specialist in connection with the determination of eligibility for public assistance, who makes a technical determination of value of the person's real and personal property holdings, the insurance specialist, who appraises the value of insurance policies as an available resource, the nutritionist or home economist, who offers assistance in determining the amount of money needed to provide a satisfactory diet, and the personnel administrator, who works to develop consistent policies on selection, promotion, classification, and compensation, and who cooperates with the merit system administration or other civil service authority outside the department in establishing personnel policy.

Similarly, in a program such as vocational rehabilitation, with its combination of medical, training, counselling, and job placement functions, it is important not only that the organization comprise various areas of services, but also that the work of all these areas be effectively coordinated so that each person may make optimum use of his energies and skills in furthering the service.

The office of the director is of primary importance to the effectiveness of the organization. The phrase "office of the director" is used, rather than simply "the director" because in modern management of complex programs of any size it is frequently the office, meaning the director and his staff, rather than the person of the executive alone, which carries these responsibilities. Most

---

[21] Karl DeSchweinitz, "The Development of Governmental Responsibility for Human Welfare," in *Social Work as Human Relations,* Anniversary Papers of the New York School of Social Work and the Community Service Society of New York (New York, 1949), p. 83.

such executives have the services of staff people who advise them on technical matters affecting important decisions, and may also have deputies who carry assigned duties in relation to the management of the department.

This is not meant to minimize in any way the role of the individual who is the chief executive of the department. His understanding of the program, his leadership, his vision are still vital, no matter how much of the responsibility is assigned or "delegated" to others. His is still the guiding hand at the helm, and the final responsibility to the board, or the governor, or both, remains his.

Frequently the question is raised as to whether the executive should be a specialist in the field of service which the organization is administering, or whether in the interests of public policy it would be better for him to be disassociated from the particular technical interests of the service. Can he extricate himself from the details sufficiently to enable him to guide agency policy in a way that represents the general public interest? In the national government, the cabinet has consistently been manned by people who have not been specialists or experts in the service for which they have been responsible. Should the same practice prevail with reference to the state welfare executive?

In 1930, a British writer, Harold J. Laski, in an essay on "The Limitations of the Expert" raised the question of the expert in administration. It was his thesis that the expert was hampered in administration by the closeness of his identification with his technical field. Immersed in his specialty, he was considered by Laski to be cut off from communication with the public outside his field, and to be fatally inclined to render his judgment in the light of what would be most likely to produce the most perfect technical product, irrespective of whether its operation was in the public interest. Laski's case against the expert was impressive.[22]

It can be argued with considerable cogency, however, that so

---

[22] For a discussion of the Laski point of view, and others related to it, see Marver H. Bernstein, "Limitations of the Administrative Expert" in the *Proceedings* of the National Conference of Social Work, 1948 (New York, 1949), pp. 440-450.

much of program direction depends upon a knowledge of the service that it is wise to entrust leadership to a person who knows something about it, and who has the security of some identification with the professional point of view represented by the service. According to this point of view, medical programs must be administered by medical doctors, school systems by an executive with preparation in education, social welfare by a social worker, etc. Advantages are perceived in having an executive who can foresee the results in his program which are likely to follow proposed policy, who has substantive knowledge enabling him to gauge the effectiveness of the service under his command, and who can communicate on a professional level with his colleagues in other organizations.

The outcome of this argument does not rest necessarily on a flat determination that the executive should or should not be a specialist. In a program such as that in Minnesota, or in New Jersey or Wisconsin, the question might well be raised as to what expertise should be represented in the person of the executive. With their multiple programs, one would have to determine whether he should be a social worker, a psychiatrist, a criminologist, or perhaps, an administrative generalist. In any program of social welfare, the executive must be able to comprehend the service outcomes of policy if he is to be wise and forceful in his leadership in program development, but he must also be able to communicate with legislators, with various civic and other citizen groups, and to be perceptive and understanding enough to know when or when not to push forcefully for new programs or policies. He must certainly be apt in the maintenance of good public relations.

California has the following statement regarding the qualifications of the executive: "The Director is responsible for administration of the Department's activities; observes and reports to the Governor and Board on conditions of public welfare; evaluates and promotes the program objectives and public understanding of welfare programs; maintains legislative relations and represents the Department before legislative committees; maintains relationships with the public and representatives of national, state, and local agencies; and meets with press, private welfare agencies, and represents the Department before groups at conferences, meetings and hearings. Acts as Secretary of the Social Welfare Board."[23]

It is quite obvious that the duties of the Director are not primarily related to the internal management of the Department, but rather are in large part designed for activities which one might say represent the department in and to the community, and develop support for policies affecting the department. Indeed, the responsibility for internal management in this State agency is largely assigned to a Deputy Director.

It is customary to classify the functions of a welfare organization as being either "line" or "staff," with the former referring to those which are connected directly with the provision of the service, and the latter with facilitating the line function of services. Another distinction similar to this in the classification of function is "program" and "service," which we used earlier with reference to the organization of the Federal Department of Health, Education, and Welfare. Examples of the "line" or program function in the Minnesota Department are the Divisions of Public Welfare, Child Welfare, Corrections, and Medical Services, each of which has the responsibility for direct administration of one or more programs or institutions within the Department. The Division of Administrative Services, on the other hand, is primarily a staff or service unit designed to enhance, through specialized services, the effectiveness of the line or program functions. Not so easy to classify in that state agency would be the Division of Field Services, which seems to have some functions classifiable under each heading.

Actually, the classification should be applied to functions rather than to parts of the structure of the organization. An individual unit in the organization may perform both line and staff functions. A health division in a state welfare department offering medical services may have the authority to make line decisions relating to

[23] "Organizational Handbook of the California State Department of Social Welfare," *Procedure Manual,* Vol. I, Div. I.

eligibility for the service from the standpoint of the medical condition. It may also serve in a consultative capacity with reference to health needs of a recipient of public assistance or child welfare services. Frequently, also, the opinion of the specialist-consultant may have the force of a decision where the decision is one in which his expert knowledge is not subject to question and may be the determinant of whether there is eligibility for a service, or what kind of service is needed.

One of the basic responsibilities of a state welfare agency is that of seeing that there is a reasonable degree of uniformity of application of the program to the people within the state. Under the law, as we have stated, people must be treated equally. This means that policies must be evolved which will meet the major contingencies anticipated under a program throughout the jurisdiction of the department, and also that there be supervisory methods to insure the application of the policy in the intended ways. This means, further, that the agency must have the facilities for testing policy and for communication regarding its effectiveness. In the section on administrative supervision, the field service was described as the part of the organization responsible for maintaining relationships with the local or district office. It is important that there be effective communication between the units of a state organization responsible for the formulation of policy recommendations, and the field service, the unit with the most direct contact with operations. When such communication is absent, the policy may become unrealistic, or the administration of the service may be inconsistent, and in violation of the principle of uniform, or perhaps as it might more aptly be termed, equitable treatment before the law. A policy is no better than its effect, but, on the other hand, it must be so developed as to insure administration by plan rather than by whim.

This is true whether the program is directly administered by the state agency through its subdivisions or districts, or locally administered under state policy and supervision. Both patterns are found among the states. In public assistance, a majority of the states administer their programs through district or county offices which are in effect subdivisions of the state administration. The distinction, however, between state-administered and state-supervised is not always clear. A state agency which is nominally administering a program may have developed a pattern of decentralization which allows a considerable degree of autonomy. On the other hand, the so-called state-supervised but locally administered program can be so thoroughly regulated through extensive and detailed policy and procedure and through closeness of supervisory control as to make any local independence of action more ostensible than real.

Whether the program is administered by offices organized and operating under local auspices, but with state supervision, or by subdivisions of the state central office, policies must be established which are consistent in their application, but which are sufficiently variable in application to take account of the infinite variety of human circumstance. We have seen in our discussion of the various programs how important it is that the application of the provisions of these welfare services permit the administering authority to use them to meet needs in a realistic, consistent, but not stereotyped way. Those units in the state office which are concerned with establishing policy and procedure must have a sense of how these will work, as well as how they sound or read.

The field staff becomes a key to the relations between central and operating offices. Early in the development of these various modern social welfare programs, the importance of this link between central and outlying offices was acknowledged. In the rapidly changing emergency programs of the depression period, the field staff person was needed to keep the outlying staff aware of the policy changes from month to month, or even from week to week.

In fact, under the Federal Emergency Relief Administration, in the 1930's, the field service attained considerable authority and responsibility. E. A. Williams has this to say about that development:[24]

---

[24] *Federal Aid for Relief* (New York, 1939), p. 71.

Certain basic facts led the Federal Emergency Relief Administration to delegate considerable powers to the field representatives. The emergency relief problem had come to a crisis suddenly. State and local organizations were in a constant state of flux, the grant-in-aid relationship for relief was new, and no definite routine for federal-state contacts had been established. Concentration of all control at Washington in this period would not have been successful, for questions were continually arising concerning the interpretation of federal rules, and states far removed from Washington could not wait for authority from the Capital before proceeding to deal with problems that cried for immediate solution.

Mr. Williams goes on to suggest that under a less pressing and dynamic program, the field representatives in this federal operation might not have been given so much power.

In a more stable situation, however, the field staff is still a prime essential. The Bureau of Public Assistance acknowledged this as one of the methods of administration needed to insure the carrying out of the purposes of the program. Since the beginning of the categorical aid programs it has strongly recommended a field staff to carry the burden of the state-local relationship. The Bureau itself, as we have noted, has a field staff of regional personnel.

What is the function of the field service as a part of the state welfare administration? How should it be organized? What should be its relationship to staff and to other line units in the organization? How should it operate in relation to local offices? These are among the more significant questions in relation to this most important part of state welfare organization.

The field representative of the state office is generally concerned with all phases of local operation of the program. As the state representative he is expected to interpret policy, to provide or to make available technical assistance to the local office, to review local operation to determine whether it is in harmony with state standards and policies, and to act as a channel of information and interpretation to the state office on matters relating to the effectiveness of policy and needs for changes. Generally, the field representative is considered responsible for the level of functioning of a whole local or district office rather than with the performance of the executive per se.

The state agency must provide a field service which is related to the kinds of problems the local office has. These will vary to a considerable extent with the size of the local office. The problems of supervision may be quite different for a small rural county office than they are for a great metropolitan office. Noting this problem and its implications, a member of the federal Bureau of Public Assistance commented some years ago:[25]

> . . . . . . Almost every state has one large city which carries a large percentage of the state's caseload. The administrator of such a local agency needs skilled administrative help from the field representative with the addition of consultation in special technical areas. In too many instances the field service to such large units has not provided such help. Probably one of our weakest points is the lack of unity of purpose between the state agency and its large local units. We can see the reason for this, for the large local unit is engrossed with its own particular local problems and not with a state-wide development of services, while, on the other hand, the local unit often sees the state agency developing plans and policies which do not take into consideration the peculiar operating problems of the large center.

At the other extreme, in the small local office, the field representative may be in the position of supervising the executive in a way much more like the function of a case supervisor within an office. The executive may be the only person in the smallest offices, or one of a small staff serving a rural county.

In the local offices in the less populated counties, the director and staff will not have the stimulation of meetings with colleagues in private agencies, or in other public agencies. They do not have the same resources to which to refer their most difficult problems, and are required to be more self-reliant than are their urban coun-

---

[25] Sara H. James, "Field Service—Unilateral or Integrated?" *Proceedings* of the National Conference of Social Work, 1948 (New York, 1949), p. 299.

terparts. The visit of the field representative to the county office can be a signal occasion—one which means much more than the opportunity to discuss the latest state policy. The field representative can provide the local staff a chance to bring up many of their problms—of organization, of case situations, of staff relations, of community developments—in short, of the whole range of concerns of the office. Perhaps this is one of the most important functions of the visitor from the central office—to relieve the loneliness of the local job.

To function in such a variable and exacting role, the field service should have a clearly defined place in the state organization, and an established relationship to the other units, both line and staff, in the department. This is a difficult area of relationship for several reasons. One is the many-sided and technical nature of the programs, which as we know, use the skills of many disciplines. The specialized areas of skill represented in the departmental staff units or divisions may be set up on the premise that a direct line to the operating office is preferable to working through an intermediary staff. Each may consider that it needs to have its own field service to insure an acceptable level of operation in the particular area of skill it represents. A division of research and statistics, for example, may believe that its function of securing continuing information on the basic features of services will be better performed if one of its operatives is dealing directly with the local office. Similarly, the administration may operate on the theory that the accounts and audit material should not be related through a field staff not technically versed in the subject, and may provide separate field services with this technical knowledge.

On the reverse side of the coin, one can perceive problems in multiple supervision. Chief among these is the difficulty of the local office in relating to so many separate supervisors, or representatives, or consultants. Another is the tendency which this difficulty fosters of seeing the program operation not so much as an integrated service, but rather as a collection of technical specialties. The tendency in state welfare programs is increasingly toward the single field representative, at least for each program, with technical consultation arranged through him. The single channel of communication is recognized as possessing many advantages.

There still is some question of the extent to which the field service replicates the entire administration in its relation to the local office. In an organizational plan like that of North Carolina (see Chart 9) the placement of the "Field Social Work Service" in a direct line of responsibility to the Office of the Commissioner indicates representation of the entire range of state authority. In other words, this chart seems to designate the field service as the one channel to the county department of welfare in that state open to the various units and divisions of the State office. In some other states, the field service is a separate bureau or division paralleling in its place in the organization some of the other program units.

States show varying practices in relation to combining the different kinds of programs under an integrated or consolidated field service. In some, child welfare and public assistance each will have its own representative working with the local office. In others they are combined.

One of the big problems in trying to integrate the field function is that of the range of specialty which programs require, a point we have previously called attention to in other connections. Obviously, it would be scarcely possible for a field representative to be a specialist in accounting, law, home economics, personnel administration, medical care, and statistics, as well as social work, to name many of the kinds of competence demanded in the administration of social welfare. The field staff theory does not contemplate that one person should offer technical consultation to cover such a wide range of activity. The chief responsibility is rather that of assisting the local office to maintain a balanced administration, with the role of the field supervisor more that of coordinating the various aspects of service. The field person is generally an expert in one field, and able to give technical help directly in that field. In child welfare and in public assistance, for example, the area of basic competence of the field person would be social work, with competence in assistance planning, in casework services, and supervision, and with the ability to make technical consultation available when needed for special problems.

In some of the larger states, the welfare department has area offices, each of which offers most of the skills available in the central office. These area offices, such as are established in New York and in California, are in effect replicas of the state office. Each has the range of services available in the central office, by and large, and each is in a real sense representative of a regionalization of the service. In general, then, the consolidated or "integrated" field staff possesses the advantage of giving the local office only one person to whom to report, thus relieving the office from the danger of confusion which might be the consequence of reporting to several persons, of giving a comprehensive view to the operation, rather than a fragmentary one, and of offering a consistent, clear channel of relationship between central and local office. Such a responsibility demands people who combine technical competence in their own professional field with the ability to relate to and utilize other fields of expertness, and to see the organization as a total entity, not exclusively as an agency for one particular discipline.

SOME EXAMPLES OF STATE ORGANIZATION

However one tries to generalize on such a diversified topic as welfare organization, with its many patterns among the states, one is confronted by the danger of creating the impression that there are certain "types" or consistent patterns which are amenable to some classification. The many variables among the forty-eight states make any such assumption untenable. Two states which are quite similar in one feature of organization are entirely different in another. They might be quite similar in the kinds of programs for which they are responsible, and very different in internal structure. Or they might seem to be very similar on paper, and operate in a significantly different way. In a sense, a description of the administration of a state social welfare department is much like a "case," with possibilities for limited generalization, but with the necessity for keeping in mind considerable diversity.

Accordingly, it seems desirable at this point to present a few individual "cases" of states, with general descriptions of some, and a more detailed description of one to carry the reader through at least one state's welfare organization. Much of the material has been derived from organizational charts supplied by the courtesy of state welfare offices. In relying upon a chart, we are mindful of a cautionary note sounded with reference to this device by an analyst of organization and management in industry, to wit: "Organizational charts . . . portray a false and frozen structure which, truly as it may have reflected the organization of the company at the time of its drawing, cannot change in pace with the changes which occur within the company, and therefore portray either a past structure or a purely visionary one which the company hopes some day to attain."[26]

What this observer of the business organization says about business is certainly no less true of such a dynamic area of service as social welfare. But, if the reader keeps in mind the fact that an organizational chart is a static picture or "still," and that the various "boxes" are really moving parts which change in their relationships from time to time, he will find the device a helpful one. The chart is a portrait of the organization, which shows its lineaments and contours, but which at best can only capture a mood at a given time.

New Jersey, as we have stated, provides an example of a large multiple program organization. The State Department of Institutions and Agencies is responsible for a wide range of services, ranking with Wisconsin's as perhaps the most comprehensive state welfare agencies in the nation. This Department is responsible for the administration of Corrections, including state homes for juvenile offenders, for reformatories, penitentiaries, and parole services. It has a very unique feature in the Diagnostic Center, which is the psychiatric service for corrections, and gives both

---

[26] Jackson Martindell, *The Scientific Appraisal of Management* (New York, 1950), p. 270.

diagnostic and in-patient service for the division responsible for corrections. The Department's program responsibilities also include mental health, including the administration of mental hospitals and clinics, and the community mental health services. Under its Division of Welfare, the Department is responsible for public assistance and for child welfare services.

Outside its scope of responsibilities are: crippled children's services, which are administered by the State Department of Health; unemployment insurance and temporary disability insurance, which are the responsibility of the Division of Employment Security of the Department of Labor and Industry; Vocational Rehabilitation, which is assigned to the Rehabilitation Commission of the Department of Labor and Industry; and Workmen's Compensation, which is also administered in the Department of Labor and Industry. The services for the hard of hearing and the deaf are administered in the Department of Education.

The agency operates under a Board of Control, consisting of nine members who are appointed by the Governor with the approval of the State Senate. These members serve overlapping terms of eight years each, which means that their terms do not all expire during a single term of office of a Governor. They serve without salary, receiving compensation for expenses.

Each of the institutions has a board of managers, to whom the head of the institution has a definite accountability. This creates confusion in organizational lines, particularly for the Commissioner, who, while held to account for the successful operation of the entire program, is handicapped in the enforcement of policy in institutions by this duality.

The Commissioner, as we have already noted, is appointed by the Board of Control, subject to the approval of the Governor. He serves at the pleasure of the Board. A Deputy Commissioner heads the Division of Administration, and acts for the Commissioner in the latter's absence. The Deputy Commissioner is responsible for public relations, long range planning, research and statistics, through the appropriate units of the organization, and for the supervision of hospital licensing and construction. A Division of Business Management is responsible for over-all operational procedures. The Directors of the three program divisions, Correction and Parole, Welfare, and Mental Health, are directly responsible to the Commissioner.

Missouri is a state with a combined Department of Public Health and Welfare. This Department was established July 1, 1946, as a result of the adoption of the Constitution of the State of Missouri February 27, 1945.[27] This Department's Division of Welfare superseded the State Social Security Commission, which had been established by the 59th General Assembly of the State for the administration of old age assistance, aid to dependent children, and child welfare services. Before that time, the various services had been administered by a variety of agencies, state and local. The present Department was actually created by action of the State's 63rd General Assembly, carrying out the mandate of the State Constitution.

The Department has three major Divisions. These are Welfare, Health, and Mental Diseases. Each Division operates under a Director, appointed, like the Director of the Department, by the Governor with the advice and consent of the Senate. Each division director has the power of appointment and removal of subordinates, subject to the approval of the Director of the Department of Public Health and Welfare, and within the provisions of merit system and other personnel policies.

The Division of Welfare is responsible for administering the laws pertaining to old age assistance, aid to dependent children, aid to the permanently and totally disabled, aid to the blind, general assistance, child welfare services, and pensions for the blind (previously administered by the Missouri Commission for the Blind). It operates through six Bureaus.

The Bureau of Local Welfare Services is organized in a way that shows recognition of the special problems of supervising urban agencies. The Bureau is responsible for supervision of six

[27] *Public Assistance Manual,* Missouri Division of Welfare, Sec. I, p. 1, December 1952.

of these (which are the counties with the largest cities), has classified them as separate administrative units, and has provided for
their direct supervision by an Urban Field Supervisor. The other
counties (there are 109 others) are grouped in fourteen administrative districts. The work is done through district offices, each of
which has a district supervisor of public assistance, and a supervisor of child welfare.

While field service is generally recognized as the channel for
communication between central and local offices, the administrative review is, as was stated in Chapter 7, a supervisory device
established to serve as a basis for more precise evaluation of local
administration. Sometimes this function is carried by the field
service. In Missouri, the County Review Unit is part of the Bureau
of Standards and Procedures.

There are other features of the Missouri pattern of organization
which would be interesting to study. Since we are limiting ourselves to a few "case" examples, however, we cannot go into detail
in our description of these various states, but can only point out
certain particularly illustrative features in each.

To give a good picture of the nature of state welfare organization, however, it seems desirable to describe in some detail one
state welfare office. California has been chosen because of certain
features, including the relationship of its central services to its
field organization.

The organization of this state's welfare office appears in Chart
12.

The program responsibilities are assigned in the departmental
office among several of the divisions. The Division for the Blind
is responsible for program development of aid to the needy blind.
The old-age-security (old age assistance) and the aid-to-needy-
children programs are placed under the Division of Social Security. Under the Division of Child Welfare are placed three
program units, the Bureau of Adoptions, the Bureau of Child Welfare Services, and the Bureau of Boarding Homes and Institutions. Chart 12 shows how the organizational pattern has been
developed within the departmental staff. In the next echelon of

CHART 12. ORGANIZATION OF DEPARTMENT OF SOCIAL WELFARE, CALIFORNIA

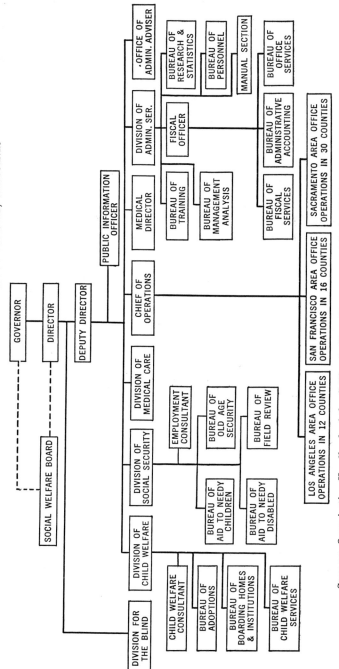

SOURCE: *Organization Handbook* of the California State Department of Social Welfare, October, 1957.

program structure (not appearing in the chart), the Bureaus have subdivisions or sections, if parts of this work are sufficiently specialized and technical to warrant such organization. Thus the Bureau of Adoptions is subdivided into four sections, including the Correspondence and Independent Adoptions Section, and the Adoption of Foreign Born Section. Each has a program specialist assigned to it. While our space does not warrant the complete summarization of all the Bureaus' and sections' activities, we might examine the Adoption Agencies Section, which, according to the *Organization Handbook,*[28]

> Reviews, analyzes, and comments on studies, and reports of field staff; develops policy material; answers memos from field staff. Prepares guides and informational material; develops studies of selected aspects of program; develops and revises forms. Assists in planning workshops and training programs. Acknowledges relinquishments and issues waivers on agency adoptions. Works with research and Statistics, and the Bureau of Financial Administration on yardsticks and budgets.

Each of the other Divisions is similarly divided into sections, so far as the complexity of the organization's tasks demands such subdivision. The Division of Social Security has its special sections and functional assignments. Under the Bureau of Aid to Needy Children, for example, there are special units dealing with foster care, rehabilitation, eligibility, family services, prevention of dependency, and documents and controls. The chart is somewhat misleading here, however. These are not so much sections as they are functional assignments of staff, which are not too rigid or fixed. California provides assistance in this category to over one hundred seventy thousand children in approximately fifty thousand families.

Looking again at the chart for the California Department (p. 419) one sees that many important staff and service functions

---

[28] From the *Organization Handbook* of the California State Department of Social Welfare, "Organization and Functions of the Department, Its Divisions, Bureaus, and Offices, and Detail of Function, Responsibility, and Authority of Key Personnel," Vol. 1, Div. I, January, 1955.

are assigned to the Division of Administrative Services. This Division, according to the *Organization Handbook,* "Directs and coordinates administrative services programs of the Department; develops, maintains, and improves administrative methods; advises the Director."[29] In this Division are a number of key service units dealing with particular phases of administration, including Bureaus of Financial Administration, Personnel, Office Management, Research and Statistics, Training, and Management Analysis. In addition there is a "Manual Section" responsible for developing and keeping up to date the rules and regulations of the Department and its various programs, for preparing reports, and developing and distributing information on proposed legislation.

In the area office itself, a high degree of specialization is maintained. In California there are three such area offices, each under an Area Director. Chart 13 shows the Los Angeles Area Office organization, and gives an idea of the completeness with which the administration of the services are regionalized in this large and growing state. These Area offices are placed administratively under the Division of Field Operations. Each Area Office

> Within an assigned geographical area, administers the department's programs in relation to the counties and agencies under the supervision of the department; directly operates programs in adoptions, boarding homes and institutions; reviews, evaluates and reports to the Central Office on status and conditions of the programs, and matters influencing them; participates in development of department objectives, policies, rules and procedures.

The extent to which the area office replicates the headquarters organization is evident. It is of course true that on occasion the services of specialists in the central office may be utilized in the area office, but by and large a high degree of regionalization is evident in the California office. One reason for regionalization in this state, in addition to the size of the state and its welfare program, is the responsibility the state has for direct administration

29 *Ibid.,* Sec. 1-4602.

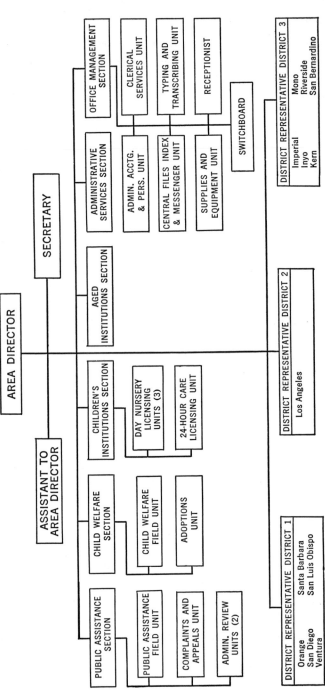

CHART 13. ORGANIZATION OF AREA I OF CALIFORNIA DEPARTMENT OF SOCIAL WELFARE

AREA DIRECTOR

SECRETARY

ASSISTANT TO AREA DIRECTOR

PUBLIC ASSISTANCE SECTION
- PUBLIC ASSISTANCE FIELD UNIT
- COMPLAINTS AND APPEALS UNIT
- ADMIN. REVIEW UNITS (2)

CHILD WELFARE SECTION
- CHILD WELFARE FIELD UNIT
- ADOPTIONS UNIT

CHILDREN'S INSTITUTIONS SECTION
- DAY NURSERY LICENSING UNITS (3)
- 24-HOUR CARE LICENSING UNIT

AGED INSTITUTIONS SECTION

ADMINISTRATIVE SERVICES SECTION
- ADMIN. ACCTG. & PERS. UNIT
- CENTRAL FILES INDEX & MESSENGER UNIT
- SUPPLIES AND EQUIPMENT UNIT

OFFICE MANAGEMENT SECTION
- CLERICAL SERVICES UNIT
- TYPING AND TRANSCRIBING UNIT
- RECEPTIONIST
- SWITCHBOARD

DISTRICT REPRESENTATIVE DISTRICT 1
Orange
San Diego
Ventura
Santa Barbara
San Luis Obispo

DISTRICT REPRESENTATIVE DISTRICT 2
Los Angeles

DISTRICT REPRESENTATIVE DISTRICT 3
Imperial
Inyo
Kern
Mono
Riverside
San Bernardino

of some of the services, such as adoptions, boarding homes and institutions. In a real sense, the county welfare office in California has a dual relationship to the state. In public assistance, the county administers the programs under the supervision of the state office. In the boarding home and adoption programs, the county welfare office is in a position of agent for the state. Such complexity of relationship in addition to the responsibility of the state in relation to voluntary agencies and institutions for children, explains further why a large degree of decentralization is necessary for this state office.

A GENERAL COMMENT

Throughout the foregoing general description of state welfare organization, and the case examples which have been cited, repeated reference has been made to the importance of maintaining channels and methods of communication both laterally in state office, and vertically between central and local offices. One point has not been made sufficiently, however, and because of its vital nature we are taking the liberty of discussing it here. This is the place at which communication should take place. That place or point should be that at which policy is being developed. If communication is limited to a chain of command for the issuance of orders and the interpretation of policies already formulated, one of the richest areas of administrative relations will have been lost.

In recognition of this factor, state offices are increasingly drawing local office executives or other personnel into discussion of proposed policy before it becomes fact, and are directly soliciting suggestions. This in a way seems to bypass the field staff, but actually does not have that effect. The field staff may participate in planning for participation by local offices, and will find communication enhanced both by better understanding of the basis for and meaning of policy, and by a more positive climate for the relationship. Furthermore, the direct experience of the local person provides a vantage point for the evaluation of policy that complements that of the central office. So, the policy conference is becoming an increasingly important and useful feature of both federal-state and state-local relations.

Summary

States show considerable diversity in the administrative organization of their social welfare programs. Indeed so varied are these forms of organization that they scarcely permit classification.

The states vary in the kinds of agencies to which the different programs are assigned. In some states, for example, crippled children's services are the responsibility of a department of public welfare, and in a few they are the responsibility of the state university. The prevalent pattern of assignment is to the state health department.

Similarly, variation is evident in the allocation of responsibility for vocational rehabilitation. In some states there are independent agencies administering this program, in others it is a part of the function of departments of labor and industry, while in others it is considered educational and is placed in the department of education.

Mental health may be assigned either to a state department of health or of welfare, while in some states it is a function of a separate department. Here, too, one sees differences in the interpretation of the primary nature of the service.

Public assistance and child welfare are universally recognized as welfare functions, and are generally placed within the structure of state welfare departments. Here again, however, even in this clearly demarcated field, some variations are found. In a few instances administration of aid to the blind is assigned to separate commissions.

Such variations probably reflect to a considerable extent such local conditions as the strength of a department within the state, the confidence with which it is regarded, and other conditions which have little to do with the pure logic of the allocation of responsibility. Still, there is an important difference in theory to be noted—the contending influences in the direction of assignment by function, or in the direction of assignment by clientele. It also reflects the inter-relatedness of the health, education, and welfare programs in the states.

Another variation among the states is the extent to which the services are consolidated into larger multifunctional agencies. In some states, such services as corrections, mental health, public assistance, and child welfare are combined into a single large department. In a few instances, there are combined departments of health and welfare. In others consolidation has not gone nearly so far. In two states, even public assistance and child welfare are separately administered.

The question of integration or consolidation is a large and sometimes controversial one. In states we find some of the same feeling that was noted with reference to organization at the national level, namely, that the people concerned with a program may want direct access to the chief executive of the state, without having interposed between them some administrative head. Still, there is the feeling that consolidation promotes communication and cooperation, gives people working in related services a feeling of common identity, permits more economical use of central services common to the several fields, and promotes a better public response through lessening the feeling that there is a plethora of agencies administering to people's health and welfare.

Most state welfare agencies operate under boards. These may be policy-making boards with administrative authority, or they may be advisory. With few exceptions, these boards consist of unsalaried people appointed by the governor of the state with legislative consent. In some few instances they may be full-time salaried boards of control, although the tendency has been moving away from that type of board. The board members in the prevailing type are people appointed because of their standing in the community, their qualities of leadership, the geographical area from which they come, and perhaps the group with which they are identified, such as labor, business, etc. They generally serve for overlapping terms, so that no political administration may dominate.

In some few instances the agency is headed by a single executive responsible directly to the state administration. In some cases the executive of the state welfare agency is appointed by the board, and in others by the governor. Also in just a few instances, there are other methods of appointment. Many arguments are cited for and against appointment by the board as against designation by the governor. Some people consider that board appointment promotes freedom from political interference, and continuity of policy. Others argue the opposite view, that in a responsible state administration the governor should have the power to appoint and to remove those who serve in his cabinet, or in the leading administrative posts.

The internal structures of state agencies are no more uniform than are the other features of state welfare organization. The point of assignment of function to special units is important as is the accompanying point of keeping the work of all units integrated with the central purposes of the organization. Generally units are classified as "line," and "staff" or service. The former are the direct operating units, the latter the special parts of the organization established to facilitate the line operation. These classifications are really more of functions than of parts of the structure.

Of key importance to the administration is the field service. This part of the organization is the link between the central and the operating office, whether the program is state-supervised or state-administered, or whether the operating unit is a district, a county, or a municipality. The field service is a two-way channel of communication. It requires personnel with the ability to see performance in terms of a whole agency, rather than only the performance of individuals. It demands personnel competent to offer skilled supervision in the area of the field representative's specialty, and the ability to utilize the special knowledge of experts in other areas of practice. Social welfare demands the practice of many disciplines, and it is important that they be inter-related smoothly and effectively.

States vary in the extent to which they utilize an integrated field service, *i.e.*, a single point of contact with the local or operating office, as compared with a multiple field staff, that is, one which provides for direct channels of supervision from the special units in the departmental staff. The trend in the past several years has been toward increasing use of the integrated field staff. There is also some variation in the extent to which field offices are replicas of the central office in coverage of function and skill.

All in all, the organizational structure and the administrative processes have much to do with the success of a program. While it may be argued that skill, a cooperative spirit, and dedication to the program on the part of the people in the organization can make any structure work, it is also true that their effectiveness will be greatly enhanced if they are working within a soundly planned administrative structure. To deny the importance of structure and to say that only the personnel matters is a bit like maintaining that the make, power, and motor of a vehicle do not matter so long as a skilled driver is at the wheel. The ability of the driver will certainly be employed to better advantage if he operates in a good machine.

Selected References

1. American Public Health Association and American Public Welfare Association, "Strengthening Tax-Supported Health and Welfare Services; The Essentials of Effective Inter-Departmental Relations," *Public Welfare,* Vol. 15, No. 1 (January, 1957).
2. Annual or Biennial Reports of State Welfare Departments.
3. Bernstein, Marver H., "Limitations of the Administrative Expert," *Proceedings* of the National Conference of Social Work, 1948, New York, Columbia University Press, 1949.
4. Breckenridge, Sophonisba P., *Public Welfare Administration, Select Documents.* Chicago, University of Chicago Press, 1927.
5. Brown, Josephine M., *Public Relief, 1929-39.* New York, Henry Holt and Company, 1940.
6. Commission on Intergovernmental Relations, *A Report to the President for Transmittal to the Congress,* June, 1955.
7. The Council of State Governments, *The Book of the States, 1956-57.* Chicago, 1956, Vol. XI.
8. Sara H. James, "Field Staff—Unilateral or Integrated," *Proceedings*

of the National Conference of Social Work, 1948. New York, Columbia University Press, 1949.

9. Leyendecker, Hilary M., *Problems and Policy in Public Assistance.* New York, Harper & Brothers, 1955.

10. Miles, Arthur P., *An Introduction to Public Welfare.* Boston, D. C. Heath, 1949.

11. Schottland, Charles, "Public Welfare Comes of Age," *Public Welfare,* January, 1956.

12. Schottland, Charles, "Public Welfare," in *Social Work Year Book, 1957.* New York, National Association of Social Workers, 1957.

13. Stevenson, Marietta, *Public Welfare Administration.* New York, The Macmillan Company, 1938.

14. White, R. Clyde, *The Administration of Public Welfare.* New York, American Book Company, rev. 1950.

10

Local Organization for Social Welfare

Throughout the preceding chapters, we have emphasized the importance of federal and state policy in the development of welfare services as we know them today. In the course of the discussion of federal and state roles, respectively, we have called attention to deficiencies in the local poor relief provision of the pre-Depression era, and have noted the fact that the growth of state services was largely the result of the inadequacy of local services and resources. It has been made quite clear that the handicaps of local government in the raising of revenue and in the provision of administrative services are considerable, and indeed they indicate that the kinds of social welfare programs in effect today would be quite beyond the fiscal and administrative capacity of most local units of government to provide on their own.

It would be most unfortunate, however, if the impression were left that the local agency has lost its significance in social welfare. It is still at the local level of government that many of the most important and basic of welfare programs meet the people. It is in the local office that all of the planning, the policy development,

429

and the carefully worked out procedure for providing service come to fruition in help to people. How the local agency is organized, what kinds of staff and facilities it affords, how well it relates to the needs of the clientele, how effective it is in community relations, will determine in the last analysis how good the program is, even though it originates in state or federal legislation. So, rather than minimizing the importance of the local welfare agency, we are inclined to call attention to its importance in the final analysis as the key to the welfare program. What the local welfare agency has lost in the exclusiveness of control it had in the earlier days of poor relief administration, prior to the growth of state supervision and later to the influence of the federal laws, has been more than offset by its enhanced responsibilities for larger and more varied services. The local welfare department has a more significant place in community life today than ever before, and there is every indication of continuing development.

Thus it is true that local administration is important to social welfare, and also that social welfare is important to the local community. In fiscal terms, welfare costs rank second to those of education among classes of local government expenditure. The same pattern is indicated in state grants to local government, which in 1955 totalled almost $6 billion. Of this total, education received the largest share, more than $3 billion, but welfare grants were second, even though not a very close second, with over $1 billion.[1]

SIZE AS A FACTOR

The word local generally evokes the image of the home town, the rather intimate association of people who know each other well. It suggests the main street, the town hall, the church, the school, and a pervasive spirit of neighborliness among people who have in common a feeling of pride in their community.

Actually, in government, the word has no precise, single meaning. The local unit of government may be the huge metropolis, or

[1] U. S. Census Bureau, *Statistical Abstract of the United States, 1957,* Table No. 489, p. 407.

the small village. It may be the township, the town, the borough, the county, or any of the vast number of districts organized around some special purpose, such as education, sanitation, highway administration, power, or irrigation.

In 1955, the total number of governmental units in the United States was 102,553, including the federal government and the states.[2] Excluding more than 50,000 school districts, the number of local units was 51,851, including the following classes of local government:

Counties	3,047
Municipalities	17,167
Townships	17,214
Special Districts	14,423

Although this number may seem large, it has decreased during the past decade. Estimates some years ago placed the figures as high as over 160,000 (including all types of local units), but consolidation, particularly of school districts, and to a limited extent of other special districts has resulted in a reduction of the total number—to the still sizable figure of more than 102,000.

Most of the special districts have the power to tax, although some of the special districts are financed in other ways. The source of revenue of all local government is still chiefly the property tax. Of a total of $11,886 million of local tax revenues in 1955, $10,323 million was raised through the property tax. In spite of efforts by localities to find other sources of revenue, this high proportion still poses the problem of finding adequate support for local services.

Local governments, despite the growth of federal and state services, have a larger number of persons in civilian employment than the combined total of those who work at the other levels. As of October 1956, local government employed 3,953,200 persons, as compared with a state total of 1,321,800, and a federal total of civilian employees of 2,195,600.[3]

[2] *Ibid.*, Table No. 480, "Governmental Units, by Type, by States," p. 401.
[3] *Ibid.*, "Governmental Civilian Employment," Table No. 501, p. 419.

Is the large number of local units a problem? Why has there been this drive to reduce the number of local units of government? The nature of the problem was stated some years ago by one student of government in these words:[4]

> Perhaps the most difficult problems of adjustment exist in the field of local government. Here . . . Americans live under layer upon layer of units of local government. While overlapping and waste have been reduced at Federal and state levels, they still flourish unrestrained in large numbers of local units. This multiplicity of dwarf-sized units, struggling under the burden of poor and inefficient management, combines to pose an increasingly heavy burden on the American taxpayers. It seems clear that they cannot, and it is to be hoped that they will not, submit indefinitely to the continuance of this burden.

In their study of State-Local Relations, more than ten years ago, the Council of State Governments had this to say:[5]

> Small, numerous, overlapping local units make it difficult to obtain satisfactory government. Specifically:
>
> 1. They produce inequities in tax burdens which are not in proportion to services rendered.
> 2. They make it difficult, if not impossible, to utilize centralized purchasing, budgeting, and other techniques of modern fiscal administration.
> 3. They dissipate political responsibility and thwart effective citizen control of local institutions.
> 4. They produce an unequal level of services at relatively high cost and forestall community-wide action to meet community-wide problems.

More recently, the Kestnbaum Commission's Report summarized the problem succinctly in these words: "More or less hidden in this picture is a paradox that constantly plagues the States and

[4] Edward R. Gray, "Deficiencies in State and Local Government Data." *Annals of the American Academy of Political and Social Science*, Vol. 207, January, 1940, p. 206.

[5] Council of State Governments, *State-Local Relations, 1946,* Chicago, p. 195.

bars an easy solution of the decentralization of government—too many local governments, not enough local government."[6]

In its report, the Kestnbaum Commission advocated the encouragement of home rule by local government. The Commission stated: "There has been enough experience in such home rule States as Wisconsin, New York, and Texas to demonstrate that as long as the State retains the right by general law to proscribe or supersede local action that might have an adverse effect on other communities, there is much to gain and nothing to lose in leaving a wide range of discretion and initiative to local governments."[7] This was recommended as a means of strengthening state as well as local government. By freeing state legislatures from the detail of acting on matters of only local importance, home rule enables them to concentrate on statewide concerns. It also has the merit of holding local officials accountable for their own acts.[8]

But the superabundance of small overlapping units of government is not the only problem for local administration. The large metropolitan areas present another group of perplexing difficulties. These areas are so rapidly growing that they challenge the inventiveness of the people to cope with their changing problems.[9]

Bigness itself brings with it difficulties of administration which must be faced with all the ingenuity of which the administering authority is capable. Keeping an agency in a huge metropolitan area continually responsive to needs and circumstances in its area presents a formidable challenge. We shall look at this further as we discuss local organization for social welfare.

THE LOCAL UNIT FOR SOCIAL WELFARE

The Social Security Act, the very law that brought the federal government into the welfare picture on a permanent basis, had the

---

[6] "The Commission on Intergovernmental Relations, A Report to the President for Transmittal to the Congress," June 1955, p. 47. See also the report of the Commission's Advisory Committee on Local Government.

[7] *Ibid.*, p. 49.

[8] *Ibid.*, p. 50.

[9] *Ibid.*, p. 51.

effect of strengthening the position in social welfare of local as well as state government. In its public assistance titles, the Act stipulated, as we have noted, that the state, in order to qualify for public assistance grants from the federal government, must have the programs in effect in all its subdivisions, and further that the state plan must be mandatory upon the localities. The states were free to decide what kinds of local units should perform the functions, whether county, city, town, township, or district subdivision of the state office. With the establishment of these organizations for the administration of public assistance, child welfare was generally though not always assigned to the same local unit, thus further strengthening the position of the local unit, especially in rural areas.

What are the local units responsible for social welfare? In number and variety, and in the range of size, they present many of the problems suggested by Mr. Gray,[10] and by the Council of State Governments. This characteristic, of course, will vary from state to state, as is true of virtually all features of administration of social welfare. In public assistance and child welfare, more than three thousand units are engaged in administering the programs. This covers mainly the federally-aided programs of assistance, and does not take into account the municipalities which administer general assistance. All in all, the total number of local units administering social welfare exceeds ten thousand. "Local" in public welfare may mean the town, the township, the county, the city, or, in Louisiana, the parish. It may mean the office manned by a single official, perhaps even on a part-time basis, or the vast, highly organized welfare department serving a city like Los Angeles, or New York, or Chicago, which may employ thousands of people. Or the local office may be a branch of the state organization as in Florida, established on a district basis, each district serving several counties. In general, however, the county is the prevailing local unit for the administration of social welfare.

It may seem logical to ask why the new programs of social welfare failed to establish local administering units in relation to

10 *Op. cit.*

some optimum size and arrangement. Why did this new group of programs with the opportunity for a fresh start, follow the old political boundaries in setting up the units for the administration of social welfare, and why did state legislatures not make a clean sweep when the times were ripe for change? Why did even those states which provided for state administration choose to set up the subdivisions in many instances at the county level, with all their inequalities of size and population, rather than on a regional basis?

For one thing, social welfare, however limited it was, had already been established as a function of local government. As we have seen, this has been the case from colonial times. As Josephine C. Brown stated, with reference to public relief before the 1930's, "The responsibility of local units of government for the relief of the poor is rooted in the common law, supported by state legislation. It is also dealt with in many state constitutions."[11] The colonies and the states in their early history varied with respect to the local unit to which the function of poor relief was assigned. In Virginia in 1641, the function of caring for and training the poor was given to the parish, where it remained until 1785, when the new State of Virginia assigned the responsibility to the overseer of the poor in the county. In New England, the town was the unit of administration of poor relief. On this point, Josephine Brown comments: "Fundamentally the town poor relief system is fairly typical of all New England, because in that area the state is looked upon as the aggregate of the towns and cities, rather than as the basic governmental unit of which the towns and cities are subdivisions."[12]

In the middle west, whether poor relief was a responsibility of the town or township, or of the county, varied from state to state. Further west, and in the South, the pattern was generally one of assignment to the county. The local official might be the overseer of the poor, serving under a county or township board, or in some instances, the local court.

[11] *Public Relief, 1929-39* (New York, 1940), p. 4.
[12] *Ibid.*, p. 5.

By the beginning of the depression when, as we have noted, the modern relationship developed out of federal and state legislation, the county was assuming an important role in social welfare administration. According to Mary Ruth Colby:[13]

> By the beginning of 1932 about one third of the States had developed a county welfare program, although much variation existed in the extent to which such programs had been accepted by individual counties. In only four States (Alabama, California, North Carolina, and New York) had county social workers been employed in a majority of the counties. In the remaining States with a county welfare program counties were wholly unorganized or social services were being carried on by a board of lay members.

Another factor which has been most influential in the decisions by the states to use established local governmental units for the administration of welfare programs, has been the belief that the program should be identified with local government. This has resulted in large measures of local authority even in those states in which the county offices are technically set up as operating units of state-administered programs. The practice of relying on established local political units is an expression of a general tendency to place greater trust in local government and to be suspicious and fearful of central government. Local government, it is argued, is closer to the people, who want their problems settled by a neighbor, rather than by some faceless officialdom operating in a remote capital.

One might question the logic of this argument. How neighborly is a situation in a large urban center, like New York or Philadelphia or Chicago? Indeed, the opposite point of view has been suggested by some, who point to the fact that improved means of communication have brought state and national governments closer to the people, who find the most important issues affecting their lives being settled in the state capital or in Washington rather than in city hall or the county courthouse. As one writer has

[13] *The County as an Administrative Unit for Social Work,* United States Children's Bureau Publication No. 224, 1933, pp. 46-47.

stated, "The Platonic and Aristotelian assumption that democracy could flourish only in direct form and locally within narrow geographical limits, such as the Greek city-state, has been exploded by modern technology."[14] It is true that radio and television have brought national and, to an extent, state government into our living rooms. People may be more familiar with the names, opinions, and the political behavior of office holders in central government than in local.

Does this suggest that the identity of the office as a part of local government is of no importance? Such a conclusion would scarcely be justified. It may be easier for a welfare administrator to cooperate with other agencies administering related services if he is a member of the same official family. Whether entirely logical or not, the feeling people have about the local office may be important in its relationship to the community. And certainly of no little importance is the fact that the state legislator who votes on the welfare programs represents a local constituency and may be more inclined to listen to an official who is one of—and close to—the folks back home than to one who is considered a state employee.

Thus, there is a basis for using the county, an existing political unit, or, in some instances, the municipality, as the unit for the administration of social welfare. This does not preclude the possibility that the unit may not be of a size that offers opportunity for adequate local administration.

Is there an optimum size for welfare administration? The problem of size of the community may be one of excessive bigness as well as of extreme smallness. The bigness of a large metropolitan areas presents difficulties of its own. These include problems of planning, of deployment of staff, of communication, of keeping pace with changing needs, of supervision, and of greater difficulty in relating to community life. In a large city the administrative distance between the administration and the public, especially the clientele, may be as great as though miles separated them. To

[14] Joseph Rosenfarb, *Freedom and the Administrative State* (New York, 1948), pp. 199-200.

keep a program as related to human needs as is welfare close to the people it serves is as important in a big as in a little community; maintenance of this relationship requires the most thorough attention.

It would be difficult to prescribe a population size which would represent the optimum for social welfare organization. It has been suggested that the minimum population for an area to be served adequately in public health is 50,000. Whether the same figure could be applied to social welfare is open to question. The problems that are brought to a welfare office are frequently of such a nature as to demand the technical skill and understanding of a competent trained social worker, who may need to tap the resources of other skills, such as medicine, law, etc. These problems suggest, by their nature, the need for a unit adequate in size to afford the depth and range of skills required.

When we discuss the optimum size, we generally think of population rather than area, although in some of the less populated states including rugged terrain, area might be a factor. Some of the counties in the far west, for example, have mountainous areas so difficult to traverse that distance becomes a factor in administrative planning. Generally, however, in assessing whether a situation favors good administration of social welfare, one would consider the population served by the jurisdiction as a basic factor. It would also be important to take account of such possible variations as type of industry, per capita wealth, cultural background, permanency of the population, and other features which have a bearing on the incidence of need for welfare services. In an industrial municipality or county, for example, the population may include a larger number of younger people of working age, as compared with the population of a rural area containing a larger proportion of retired older people. The people in the industrial area may need more in the way of income security measures, and of supportive family and children's services. Also, a county made up of numbers of people on the move will make particular demands on welfare services, especially as these people face the problems of getting established in a new community.[15] Such factors will influence both the extensiveness and the kinds of welfare services that will be necessary. The relationship of housing to social welfare becomes increasingly apparent, as crowded conditions, unsanitary areas, and other problems of housing, relate to some kinds of welfare problems.

In many ways, the problem of the small local unit in social welfare is not unlike those of some other kinds of community services, such as public schools, or public health. In education, the school district that serves too small a population has difficulty paying for adequately trained teachers in sufficient numbers, or classroom and other facilities, and special education services. Similar comparisons may be made with public health, for the technical and professional services in this field, as in welfare, depend for their local availability generally on a population large enough to support and to make full use of them.

Another problem which could be mentioned is that of costs. The community that is too small may feature an inordinately high per capita cost, from the expenses of establishing and maintaining an office, of hiring personnel who may not always be fully engaged, and of buying and maintaining equipment and supplies. To quote the Council of State Governments again:[16]

> The per capita expenditures of counties actually decrease as the population of the county increases. This is strong corroboration for the fact that increased size means decreased size for similar services because counties, especially within a given state, perform roughly the same services. Some of the increased per capita expenditures of the smallest counties, however, is undoubtedly the result of the fact that these counties (1) have widely scattered populations and (2) contain no sizable incorporated places with which costs may be shared . . .
>
> All of these facts bear upon a single point: small units of government cannot perform functions at an acceptable standard

---

[15] See Wayne Vasey, "Public Welfare in a Rapidly Growing Community," *Proceedings* of the National Conference of Social Work, 1947 (New York, 1948), pp. 183-185.

[16] *Op. cit.*, p. 202.

for low cost. Services in these governments can only be carried on at relatively high cost (which means either high local tax rates or grants from other governments) or at sub-standard levels (which is the more usual procedure).

In some instances, efforts have been made to meet the problem of the small county by combining two or more counties into one welfare unit. This practice has been authorized by law in Idaho and in Washington, for example, and some combinations have been made.

In the larger urban area, decentralization of many aspects of administration to district or area offices may help bring about more effective operation. Much depends, however, on whether the decentralization permits some freedom of action on the part of the district or area offices, or whether tight control over all phases of operation still is retained in the headquarters center.

RELATION OF LOCAL TO STATE WELFARE OFFICE

In public assistance, the largest of the social welfare programs administered through agencies in local governmental units, a distinction is often made between state-administered and state-supervised but locally administered programs. The former refers to those services which are administered through local branches of a state office, whether or not such a branch is a county, a municipality or a district comprising more than one county. In such states, the local personnel are state employees, and policies are made and enforced directly by the state office. In state-supervised programs, however, the county is generally the administrative unit, with the responsibility for adhering to state policy, but working through its own employees, and subject to the local governing body.

Actually, in public assistance, as well as other programs which feature these two types of relationship, the distinction between state-supervised and state-administered may be more nominal than real. The local office carrying on a state-administered program may develop a pattern of independent action, perhaps even with the approval of the state office. The necessity for relating to the various local officials in the carrying out of the program may influence the staff of the agency to think and act like local as much as or more than like state employees. On the other hand, the local staff in the locally-administered programs may become so dependent upon state supervision, and upon detailed approval of administrative acts, or the state administration may be so assertive as to make the control actually strongly state-centered. The nature of state authority over welfare programs is such that the control is potentially as strong as the state wishes it to be or as local tradition will permit, irrespective of the form of the relationship.

The questions of the desirability of a large measure of state control must be weighed against several factors. Through discussion at various times during the past fifteen years (a time span which includes my own experience as a county welfare director), I have noted the following opinions from local welfare officials on the question of the desirability of local versus state oriented social welfare administration. It has been suggested that:

(1) Under a state-operated program, it is easier to establish uniform standards and maintain controls.

(2) The staff members are less subject to personal or political pressures, and have greater security than would be possible under a locally-operated program.

(3) Bias is less likely, and operation according to standards is more likely.

(4) If skill in community organization is exercised by the office, the state-administered program can be more progressive than can the locally-operated program, and with proper leadership the state can furnish ample opportunity for local expression and adaptation.

Contrary opinions have also been offered. Welfare officials favoring a maximum degree of local authority have stated that:

(1) Local administration combines the best standards set up in state law with the virtues of local control over the detail of administration.

(2) A better situation is afforded for good public relations and community support because the people in the areas feel that the program belongs to them.

(3) Progress built up through local or "grass roots" support, while slower, is more durable.

Probably the answer is not to be found in the outcome of any general argument over the relative merits of these two kinds of relationship. It is more likely to be discovered in the quality of the relationship existing between central and local authority.

We would be inclined to agree with the following statement:[17]

> Administrative interrelationships are determined by many factors, such as tradition, the character of the groups in power at the various levels of government, the relative degree of national, state, and local interest involved in a given public service, the types of taxes used to finance the service, the locus of the taxpayer, the desire and capacity for self-government, the relation of the service to the regional or national economy, and many others. Because of the dynamic character of most of these determining factors, administrative interrelationships can be expected to change and constantly do. But whatever intergovernmental arrangement is made in carrying out a given public service, the problem remains: What size and type of unit is best adapted to perform the *local* function?

We would agree with Hansen and Perloff that the question of size and type of local unit remains, but with the further note that social welfare quite obviously requires state standards and methods of insuring their application through adequate state authority. The fate of the general assistance programs in many states is rather telling evidence against any bland assumption that local problems may with confidence be left entirely to local communities.

One of the more difficult problems of state-local relations has been that of determining the extent, if any, of local financial participation in state social welfare programs. In the chapter on

---

[17] Alvin Hansen, and Harvey S. Perloff, *State and Local Finance in the Local Economy* (New York, 1944), p. 72.

Intergovernmental Relations (Chapter 7), we called attention to the disparities in taxable resources among levels of government, and presented a description of the inequalities of resources among the states. There is good evidence that the disparities among localities within the states may be as great or greater than they are among the states. As a special Senate Committee noted some years ago,[18]

> Figures for income and wealth, for taxable income and income tax collections, for assessed values and equalized values, all tell the same story. As the size of the local unit decreases, the variation in per capita wealth and income increases. All the comparisons of per capita wealth in local areas show much greater variations than appear between State values. The smallest local variations are in Massachusetts, which has a larger population in proportion to the number of its local units than any other State and which has a population per town, excluding cities, that is more than twice that of either Illinois or New York. Further, the variation for Illinois townships is far less than the variation for the smaller Illinois school districts.

What the Committee found in 1943 is still true. Local government is handicapped in its search for funds not only by the sources of money available to it, but also by such other factors as constitutional limitations on taxing and borrowing power. The basic and prevailing source of revenue for local government is still the property tax. This form of revenue is relatively inelastic, and is inadequate to meet the demands of an expanding level of service. It tends to fall inequitably upon persons in different parts of the political unit, and among different economic classes in the community. Local government is severely handicapped in its search for other sources of revenue.

In spite of these considerations, many welfare programs require some local financial participation. This may take the form of local

[18] U. S. Senate Special Committee Designated to Conduct a Study on Intergovernmental Fiscal Relations in the United States, report, *Federal, State, and Local Government Fiscal Relations,* Document No. 69, Letter from the Acting Secretary of the Treasury Transmitting in Response to S. Res. 160, 1943, p. 191.

support of the service itself, and local financial responsibility for the costs of administration. It has been alleged by some that local payment of even a small part of a program's costs is desirable in the interests of insuring more responsible behavior on the part of those administering the program. It has been charged that subsidization weakens this sense of responsibility, and encourages carelessness and extravagance. Unless some locally raised money is spent on the program, some people claim that local officials will not care how the funds are spent, since they do not feel the same direct relationship to the tax sources.

On the other side of the picture, when fixed percentages of costs are demanded of the localities, the objective of equal standards throughout the state may be thwarted. The locality unable to raise a sufficient amount may have a less adequate service, even though the need may be greater than in some of the areas better able to raise the necessary amount. This again would seem to be one of those perplexing questions of administration which do not permit definitive answers. With the increasing strain on local resources, however, and with the growing list and increasing standards of welfare services, it seems that the weight of the argument falls on the side of minimizing local financial responsibility for social welfare.

State-supervised or state-administered, county, district or township office, the state's authority over local affairs gives the governing body of the state the power to control local administration of social welfare. Whether this is done with adequate consideration of local sensibilities as well as of economic and social conditions, and whether the relationship shall be positive or restrictive, is a question which was discussed somewhat in the chapter on Intergovernmental Relations. The objective of such supervision should be that of freeing the local office to make decisions which, while consistent with policy, will meet the needs of the individuals who require the services. To this end, a large measure of decentralization is important. Decisions on individual problems made in remote centers will all too rarely reflect the realities of human need as they are met daily by the local welfare office.[19] It is important also, however, that these differences not be so great as to result in inequitable treatment. Local knowledge of community and individual situations will operate to the disadvantage of the welfare program and to the people of the community if the result is a prejudiced attitude. Perhaps one way of stating the objective of state-local relations is to suggest that it should combine the best features of local power to meet individual needs and to work with the community with the consistency and objectivity of state policy guidance and general supervision.

FUNCTIONS OF THE LOCAL WELFARE OFFICE

In sharp contrast to the office of the administrator of the poor law of an earlier day, the modern local welfare office performs services which are many and varied. This is true for two reasons: first, because the welfare programs assigned to it by statute include an extensive range of responsibilities, and second, because the human experiences and needs underlying the problems which bring a person to ask the office for help may be much more complex than the immediate problem he presents. It will be recalled that behind the financial need may be illness, or family disorganization, or disturbances of an intrapsychic nature. Whether the welfare office is or is not equipped to deal with many of such problems will depend both upon the facilities and skills within the agency and available to it, as well as on the complexity of the problem itself. Also, for all the range of social welfare needs, it must be borne in mind that a program based on statutory authorization does not give *carte blanche* to deal with all the problems of the human race, but must perforce be related to its basic purpose. In spite of such limits, there is evidence of pressure from the community itself to extend the range of welfare services, particularly in those areas in which a paucity of other welfare services makes the county welfare office the only place people may turn to

---

[19] See George C. S. Benson, "A Plea for Administrative Decentralization," *Public Administration Review,* Summer, 1947.

in case of trouble demanding outside help. With due regard for the many variables among local welfare agencies, which include the scope of services authorized under state law, the adequacy of staff in terms of numbers and skill, the imaginativeness and leadership of the administrative personnel, and the availability of help from other community services, such as voluntary family and children's services, mental health clinics, etc., we turn to a general summary of the duties and functions of the local welfare department. The wide variation among local agencies in these particulars necessitates a list of functions which can only be descriptive of the different kinds of responsibilities and functions performed by local agencies in the aggregate, rather than a description of a particular pattern which might generally be found.

Among the major functions which may be performed by a county department of public welfare are: (a) administration of public assistance; (b) administration of services to children; (c) administration of assistance for medical care, and responsibility for referral to health agencies; (d) service to the court in probation (although, as we have noted, in many areas the court has its own probation service, and in others probation is administered by a separate organization); (e) licensing of facilities for care of the aged, the chronically ill, and of children; (f) services to the handicapped; (g) participation in emergency programs for meeting needs such as disasters, through cooperation with voluntary agencies, particularly the Red Cross; (h) administration of institutions for children, the aged, and the ill; (i) services to persons discharged or on leave from mental hospitals and correctional institutions, and investigation of home and community conditions at the request of institutions considering such discharge or leave; (j) study of social welfare needs in local communities, and recommendation of possible measures to meet such needs.

Even after such a comprehensive list of the various functions which may be performed by local public welfare offices, one is tempted to append a large "et cetera," for any list of such functions can only be an indication rather than an adequate and complete enumeration. In many places the county welfare department is the only social service office in the community, and, since needs for welfare service are likely to arise in any community, the welfare office may be called on to perform a variety of tasks, making neat classification impossible. But irrespective of such variations as are found in the comprehensiveness of responsibility of the county welfare department, it is now an integral part of community life, just as are the schools, the law enforcement offices, the health department, and other basic local government services. The scope and nature of these services demonstrate the extent to which these local departments of welfare serve all groups in the community. It is not, in its modern development, a service exclusively designed to help a few disadvantaged individuals and families.

As we contemplate the range of welfare services, and the differences in scope of service from state to state, and even from locality to locality, we must also note as an important factor the variations in the extent to which the programs are consolidated within a single administrative structure. From the comprehensive single county welfare department in some states, to the multiplicity of local offices in others, we see many varieties of patterns. If the pattern seems somewhat confusing to the person studying it, think how much more so it must be for the person trying to find out where to go for help.

Let us look first at the patterns in the states which were included in Chapter 9, in the brief descriptions of state welfare organization.[20] We have already mentioned the varied pattern in New Jersey, in which local departments are less consolidated than the state organization, so far as placement of several services within a single organization is concerned. Looking again briefly at New Jersey, we see that aid to dependent children (called home life assistance), is administered by the state through local offices of the state board of child welfare; old age assistance and assistance to the permanently and totally disabled is admin-

[20] For a listing of local agency responsibilities, state by state, see *The Public Welfare Directory,* printed annually by the American Public Welfare Association (Chicago).

istered by county welfare boards under the supervision of the Bureau of Assistance of the State Division of Welfare; aid to the blind is administered through county welfare boards under the supervision of the Commission for the Blind, also in the Division of Welfare; and general assistance is administered by municipal assistance boards, also under the supervision of the Bureau of Assistance of the Division of Welfare. Child welfare services are the responsibility of the State Board of Child Welfare, which, in addition to aid to dependent children, carries the state responsibility for foster home placement and supervision, care and custody, guardianship, special consultation services, and such other matters respecting the care of children as interstate placement of children. All these, as we have stated, are a combination of state-administered and state-supervised but locally-administered services, and are further divided among different types of local units of government.

In Minnesota all the federally-aided programs of public assistance are administered by county welfare boards in all the counties of the state, while general assistance is administered by county welfare boards in most counties, although in some it is the responsibility of the township or the village. Child welfare is carried as a responsibility of the county welfare boards.

In Missouri all of the public assistance programs, including general assistance, and child welfare services, are administered by the State Department of Health and Welfare through its county offices. In addition, the state administers its nonfederally-aided program of pensions for the blind through these county departments.

California and Washington both present pictures of rather comprehensive program coverage by county welfare offices. In California the state supervises county administration of public assistance and child welfare. The same general pattern is found in Washington, as well as in many other western states. This suggests the possibility of greater integration of services in states where there was not a history of welfare organization dating back to colonial and early national history. In the western states generally, there were fewer fixed patterns in existence when the welfare programs developed under the impetus of the Social Security Act.

Many other patterns, showing still further variations in the degree of local integration of local welfare services, could be cited. In Illinois, for example, which we have stated has separate administration of public assistance and child welfare, respectively, county superintendents of welfare are locally responsible for the state-administered programs of public assistance, while child welfare services are administered locally by offices of the Illinois Department of Public Welfare. Indiana is another Midwestern State in which general assistance is administered by townships, while the other types of public assistance are the responsibility of county welfare offices. It is interesting to note that in Indiana, crippled children's services also are administered through the county departments of public welfare.

In Iowa, the county boards of supervisors may elect either to administer general assistance through the county directors of public welfare, who also carry responsibility for other forms of public assistance and for child welfare, or to administer general assistance themselves through a separately appointed director of relief. Iowa has, also, a separate assistance program for honorably discharged veterans of the armed services. This form of aid is administered by County Soldiers and Sailors Relief Commissions.

It should be evident by now that the variations in patterns of administration among the states are more than matched by those to be found in local administration. There is no consistency among these patterns, and many of them could scarcely have been deliberately planned, to say the least.

Is there any point to the consolidation of functions into fewer local welfare agencies? It would seem that there is. The scattering of functions among two or more local welfare offices may constitute a real handicap to the effective administration of services. If there is a problem in too many local units of government in the first place, think how much more difficult the situation is when there are two or more offices administering welfare programs in the same locality.

We have mentioned the confusion which the large number of offices creates among people who need the services. More than one office means that the applicant for service has the problem of figuring out where to seek help, but also there is always the danger in such a situation that the person's needs may be lost somewhere in the separate eligibility requirements which may be set up by law or by administrative regulation. This danger, of being lost among or between the rules, may be acute enough when the same office administers different types of aid. The danger is even greater when the programs are scattered among or between offices.

Another important factor, especially in the smaller localities, is the inefficient use of staff, buildings, equipment and other resources. The separate overhead of several small offices scarcely seems defensible on the grounds of economy. Also, it is more difficult to afford staff of the caliber needed for good service when the programs are so dispersed.

The integrated county welfare office directly responsible for the major welfare services presents some real advantages for cooperation with other programs, such as vocational rehabilitation, mental health and others. One center for the social welfare programs presents more possibilities of community planning for social welfare than do a number of township or town offices, or two or more county departments. All that has been stated regarding the importance of coordinating services designed to help people supports the theory that such coordination should be fostered through integrated administrative organization. But generally, tradition, encrusted by habit, may be a difficult thing to dislodge, and the hodgepodge of local social welfare in its most confused form will find staunch defenders whenever any change toward greater consolidation is suggested.

The local welfare office may or may not be responsible for the administration of hospitals, other medical facilities, and other institutions. It also, in a number of localities, carries the functions of adult or juvenile probation. But irrespective of whether this wider range of service is consolidated, the importance of cooperation and coordination among local services is no less important than it is among state services. Joint planning on projects of common interest and concern among local welfare, educational, health, and correctional offices is something which the public has a right to expect of its officials administering these services. Of no less importance is the participation of public welfare offices in the affairs of community councils of social agencies.

The respective roles played by the board, and by the executive and staff of the local agency are important to the development of the service. Let us now look at the structure and function of the relationships between these two elements in local public welfare administration.

LOCAL BOARDS OF PUBLIC WELFARE

In local administration of public social welfare, the board is an important factor. This board may be either policy-making or advisory. Boards, of both types, are a feature of local public social welfare in a majority of the states, even in those in which the programs are largely state-administered by local branches of state offices. Sometimes they are called committees rather than boards, but in any event, they are a significant force in welfare administration.

The reasons for the widespread use of local boards are in many respects the same reasons that have influenced the establishment of boards in state public welfare departments. It may be said with reference to local boards, as well as to state, that a program as directly involved with the daily lives of people as a social welfare program needs to be sensitive to the will and the desires of the public. However important it is to let the specialist or expert manage the program, the management must be responsive to the popular will. It would be quite serious if the social welfare programs were to "grow away" from the public which they serve.

In a study of citizen participation as reflected in county welfare boards, Helen E. Martz had this to say:[21]

[21] *Citizen Participation in Government, a Study of County Welfare Boards* (Washington, Public Affairs Press, 1948), p. 1.

With the shifting of large areas of responsibility to specialized and highly trained personnel, many social scientists have pointed out the increasing importance of utilizing all possible channels to reflect the opinion of the people in order to keep our government truly democratic. However, the National Resources Planning Board's Committee on Long-Range Work and Relief Policies noted in its intensive study of public aid programs that the general public usually assumes, once performance of certain functions has been assigned to government, that the problem is no longer one with which the individual need be concerned. It seems important, therefore, that government officials utilize those devices effectively which provide for citizen participation in government so they may find out from the people what they want.

In general the members of these boards serve for no pay or for a nominal reimbursement for expenses. One may be prompted to ask why citizens take on such responsibilities. On that point, Dr. Martz states:[22]

In addition to the value which citizen participation has for the administrator, there are also values for the individual in the expression of his citizenship. Participation in community activities makes an individual feel that he is a useful part of something bigger than himself. He may gain a satisfying sense of importance in carrying a public responsibility and in making a contribution to the common good. Through experience in developing his capacities, he may also gain greater maturity as a citizen and thereby come to see his own interest as part of a larger interest, and recognize that his own good cannot be considered apart from the good of others.

Voluntary agencies as well as many public welfare agencies have long recognized the value of participation by the citizen serving as a volunteer in many capacities, including board membership. There is evidence of a growing use of such volunteers in local public welfare. The meaning of volunteers to local welfare

[22] *Ibid.,* p. 2.

programs has been expressed by a national welfare agency in these words:[23]

> Volunteers providing supplementary services join with the staff in extending and enriching the agency services; contribute to the shaping of basic social welfare policy; help in strengthening interagency relationships; and contribute to the public relations program of the agency.

This report goes on to summarize the various capacities in which volunteers may serve, including serving older people through club and leisure time programs, and through friendly visiting services, helping to provide recreation and other services to groups of children and adults in institutions, assisting to secure needed resources for the improvement of welfare services, and in other ways suggested above to bring about a better level of community services.

The local board performs an important role in the administration of social welfare by keeping administration attuned to the public interest. How is this done? What, more precisely, are the functions of the local welfare board?

In about twenty of the states, according to Social Security Commissioner Schottland, the local board appoints the local director.[24] This power of appointment is subject to the provisions of the state merit system, or to a local plan which has been approved by the state authority. In other words, the board must make its selection from a list supplied by the merit system authority.

Generally the board has the power to advise the local director on needs in the community, and on the efficacy and desirability of proposed or operative policy. In many instances, the power includes that of reviewing and approving policy. The board may or may not have been given the power of approval of action on individual cases. It seems highly questionable whether a board should concern itself with the detail of decisions on individual

[23] Bureau of Public Assistance, Social Security Administration, *Citizen Participation in Public Welfare Programs* (Washington, 1956), p. 3.
[24] Charles Schottland, "Public Welfare" in *Social Work Year Book, 1957* (New York, National Association of Social Workers, 1957), p. 478.

cases. It would seem necessary for a body of this kind to concentrate its attention on questions of policy. It would also seem likely that attention to broad considerations of policy would be more effective if the attention of the members were not cluttered by the detail of each individual problem.

In a state with possibly the longest history of county welfare organization as we know it today, North Carolina, the duties of the county board are defined as follows:[25]

> The county welfare boards of the several counties shall have the duty of selecting the county superintendent of public welfare, shall act in advisory capacity to county and municipal authorities in developing policies and plans in dealing with problems of dependency and delinquency, distribution of the poor funds, and with bettering social conditions generally including cooperation with other agencies in placing indigent persons in gainful enterprises, shall prepare the administrative budget for the county welfare department for submission to and approval by the board of county commissioners, and shall have such other powers and duties as may be prescribed by law, particularly those set forth in the laws pertaining to old age assistance and aid to dependent children: Provided, that as to cases requiring immediate action to prevent undue hardship the county welfare board may at its discretion delegate to the superintendent of public welfare authority to consider and process applications under these laws, and to determine eligibility for assistance, amount of such assistance, and date on which it shall begin. The board shall require that any action taken by the superintendent pursuant to such delegated authority be fully reported to the board at its next meeting. The county welfare board shall meet with the superintendent of public welfare and advise with him in regard to problems pertaining to his office, and the superintendent of public welfare shall be the executive officer of the board and shall act as its secretary. The board of public welfare of each county shall at its next monthly meeting accept or reject or modify the action of the county superintendent of public welfare made

[25] North Carolina Welfare Laws, Bulletin No. 24, Revised 1955, North Carolina State Board of Public Welfare, Chapter 108, Article 2, p. 14.

under this Act since the last monthly meeting of the county board of public welfare.

In general, the boards are appointed either by the state authority or by the local governing body. There are, of course, variations in this practice. In North Carolina, the county board is appointed in the following manner: of its three members, one is appointed by the Board of County Commissioners, either from its own membership or not, as it chooses; one by the State Board of Public Welfare; and the third is selected by the two members thus appointed. In some states the official governing board of the county serves as the welfare board. This is true in Nebraska, for example. In Oregon, the county welfare commission of seven members includes four appointed by the Governor, while the other three are members of the county court. The size of the boards varies, but in general they tend to consist of from three to seven members, although in some places they have a much larger membership.

Missouri has an interesting plan for the selection of the county welfare commission, which serves as an advisory board to local agencies. The county welfare commissions consist of four members. They are appointed by the State Director of Health and Welfare from lists submitted by the County Courts. Two members are selected from each of the two major political parties.

In California, the county boards of supervisors are designated by statute as the county welfare departments, with the power to appoint such staff as may be necessary to administer the programs. They are authorized but not required to establish boards of social welfare.

The list of variations could be extended. It may be stated that while the board represents a prevailing practice in local administration of public welfare, the differences in method of selection and the duties of such boards are, like so many other features of local welfare administration, indicative of the varieties of local and state patterns in the administration of these nationwide programs.

A significant statement on the relationship between the board of a local public welfare agency and the executive and staff has been made by a long-time chairman and member of a county welfare board in New York State. He writes:[26]

> I believe that the combination of a citizen board and a professional staff has a lot to offer. The board is a clearing house for testing ideas, and approaches the administration of public welfare in a realistic, practical manner with sympathetic consideration of the problems involved. The membership of a citizen board brings to the department a sensitivity to public reaction and the opportunity to do a job of interpretation.
>
> It is this cooperative effort that brings balance to an organization, with the responsibility for the day to day operation in the hands of the Commissioner and his staff while the responsibility for decisions rests with the Board in the matter of policy and direction. The pooling of ideas and the combined skills of both in their respective capacities makes for efficient administration in a board-staff partnership arrangement, with adequate circulation of the activities of the Board to the agency.

When a board and executive function in a constructive manner, it is a tribute to both. But it is probable that even the best of boards will be limited in effectiveness unless the executive displays skill and leadership in working with the board, and possesses the capacity to keep in balance the respective roles of board and staff in the administration of the programs.

THE EXECUTIVE AND STAFF

The local director has a key role to play in the administration of public social welfare. While this may seem to be a point scarcely requiring elaboration, it should be emphasized for several reasons. In the first place, he is the person who is generally held accountable by the local community for the way a program works. To the extent that he is responsible for programs enacted by the state, and subject to outside policy, he must be able to accept as his own and to interpret to the community the content and purpose of the

[26] J. Craig Roberts, "Relationship of Board and Staff in Policy Determination," *Public Welfare,* Vol. 15, No. 1 (January 1957), pp. 32 and 38.

provisions of the program. He must be skilled in working with the local board. On his leadership will rest the value of the board as a functioning rather than a nominal force. He must also be able to communicate local needs to the state authority. He must be in touch with other public services so that the welfare program is related effectively to such programs as education, health, and law enforcement.

The foregoing suggests the need for a capacity to relate two forces which at times may seem to be counter to each other, namely, the demands of a far-off state office and the immediate pressures of a local situation. What seems of paramount importance to the state office may not appear so to local governing bodies concerned with those activities of most immediate impact on community life. The directive from the state office, or the visit from the field representative with reference to a backlog of reports on the status of old age assistance applications, may coincide with uncomfortable closeness to a series of newspaper reports locally on the condition of an abandoned family on the outskirts of a town, or of a group of migrant laborers and their families, stranded and without employment, or reports of a wave of delinquency or crime among families receiving services from the local department. To meet what so often are contending demands for his attention, and for that of his staff, and to keep the immediate in balance with the long term, ongoing features of his program, require a balance of personal qualities and a rare ability of evaluation.

This, however, is not the limit of his task. He must also have the capacity for organization and leadership of staff, and in the smaller offices—which comprise the majority of local offices in the country—for supervision of the technical work of the staff. In the smallest offices, he may himself carry a case load. This last is true in those offices which are not large enough to afford supervisory positions to cover all of the staff. He must also have ability in business and fiscal management, and must be able to plan for the securing and utilization of office space and equipment.

It is quite obvious that the demands on the local welfare administrator are many and varied. They require a knowledge of the programs, the ability to direct the work of others, skill in public relations, definite capacity for management, and personal qualities which include the strength to face up to pressures which many people would find difficult to endure. One authority has described the administrator in social welfare as one who needs "bifocal vision," *i.e.*, the ability to look at both the immediate and the long range situation, without suffering impairment of sight.[27]

As has been noted, the local welfare executive may be appointed by the local board, subject to civil service (merit system) procedures. In the majority of instances, however, he is appointed by the state department. In New York State, the local commissioner of welfare is elected in some communities, although he may have a deputy appointed by him in accordance with the state merit system for the actual internal administration of the office. In the large city welfare office, the welfare director may be appointed by the mayor.

It would be difficult to overstate the importance of leadership as a required quality of the local director of public welfare. Whether his office is small or large, he is expected to give the program the conviction and force to make it a vital part of community life, and to provide the imagination, the vigor, and the vision necessary to stimulate both staff and community to support a service which is responsive to changing community patterns and needs. In short, the welfare director is responsible for guidance and direction of the program. He should be more than a manager.

According to a study made a few years ago by the Bureau of Public Assistance, about one-sixth of the local public welfare offices administering public assistance were large enough to require the services of a supervisor, although in many of the smaller offices, a caseworker with senior status might supervise the less experienced worker.[28] Generally, in the small office the function of supervision is carried by the director.

Supervision is considered a necessary feature of administration

---

[27] Harleigh Trecker, *The Group Process in Administration* (New York, 1946), p. 27.

[28] Social Security Administration, *Personnel in Local Offices of State Assistance Agencies*, Public Assistance Report No. 12, 1953.

in social welfare. The task of assisting the worker in the development of greater skill, of taking responsibility for making the service effective in line with the purpose of the program, and of carrying responsibility for a part of the agency's total work load are all features of the supervisory role. The supervisor must help new workers learn the job, keep up the work of the unit for which he is responsible, and this work must reflect developments in agency policy. The supervisor, through his direct relationship with the social worker, has access to knowledge of problems which are arising in the actual giving of service, and is expected to keep the administrator informed. The supervisor's job includes teaching, supervision, and administration.

At this point we are attempting to do no more than describe this job. We shall consider the qualifications of it as well as other social work positions in the next chapter. What may be emphasized at this point, however, is that this is a position demanding professional knowledge of social work, technical knowledge of the program, the security which comes from successful experience in social work, the ability to assist the social worker to develop his own capacity for performance, and the administrative capacity to direct the work of a unit.

Much could be said also about the worker in the local welfare office. In general, we may say that the worker is the person responsible directly for service to the clientele.

At best, the worker has a relationship with the individual or family in a fuller sense, for the social worker is a helping person, one to whom the family may turn for counsel and for understanding—within the limits of the function of the agency. But even in those offices in which too many cases assigned to each worker and other factors make such a relationship less possible to maintain, the worker should be one on whom the family can rely consistently for competent help.

The foregoing is certainly an oversimplification of the process of offering service in a local welfare agency. The provision of facilities for interviewing, the division of responsibility in a multiple program among social work staff, the provision of services for recording, the processes of review, supervision, and administrative control, the accounting and audit, the fiscal planning, the maintenance of records, all are essential components of administration in a local welfare department. As is the case in social welfare at the two other levels of government, they require the organization and planned utilization of a number of skills. The organization must be set up to provide for at least minimal assurance of prompt action on applications, consistent policy decisions, alertness to the various service needs of the individual, accuracy of recording and reporting, and in general, organization of effort around the objectives of the agency. It must have facilities for studying conditions which will affect its load of responsibility and for improving its effectiveness in relation to community welfare problems. It must be able to secure information readily for reports, and must have the means to keep the local public, the state office, and other agencies informed as to current and probable future program.

To function effectively the local agency, like the state organization, must have a combination of skills and specialties. The degree of specialization of function, as we have said, will depend upon the size of the load and of the agency. The larger the program, the more complex will be the structure. An agency serving a clientele of one or two hundred people will not justify a number of special units performing the accounting, the reporting, the legal consultation, and other tasks. On the other hand, a large city or county, like that of Los Angeles, or New York, will require considerable organization of tasks, and continuous organizational planning.

Chart 14 presents a picture of a county welfare organization in one metropolitan county, Ramsey County, Minnesota, which includes the city of St. Paul. This office is responsible for the administration of public assistance, child welfare services, and for services to persons discharged from various institutions. It functions under a local board, which has the power to appoint the executive, subject to the provisions of the state merit system.

The line function of the agency is the responsibility of the Division of Public Assistance and Welfare Services, through its two units, the Department of Welfare Services, and the Department

CHART 14. RAMSEY COUNTY (MINN.) WELFARE BOARD

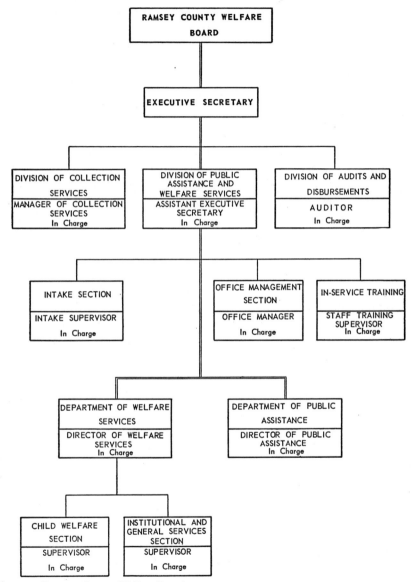

SOURCE: Ramsey County Welfare Board.

of Public Assistance, although the Intake Section also seems to have a line responsibility. The various service functions of accounting, of office management, and of in-service training are other important parts of this agency's operation.

Serving the largest city in the nation, the New York City Department of Welfare had a staff of 8,322, as of January 1, 1957. Of this total, 4,084 were classified as social service workers, 2,933 as clerical, and 1,305 in "other categories.[29] This city department has more employees than do most state departments of public welfare. The Department is responsible for the administration of all types of public assistance, including general assistance, or home relief, as it is called in New York City, child welfare services, employment and rehabilitation and special services.

The Commissioner is appointed by the Mayor. In turn, the Commissioner has the authority to appoint the two Deputy Commissioners.

Chart 15 presents a picture of the general structure of this large agency. As the chart indicates, the noninstitutional direct services to the clientele are made available through the three bureaus which are classified as "Social Services;" these are the Bureaus of Public Assistance, Child Welfare, and Special Services. These Bureaus are under the administrative direction of the First Deputy Commissioner.

The functions of the Bureau of Child Welfare are described as follows:[30]

> This Bureau is responsible for administering child welfare services at public expense for children in need of care away from their own homes, for unmarried mothers in need of prenatal or postnatal shelter care, and for related child welfare services.

These responsibilities are carried out through the Division of Children's Placement Services, the Division of Foster Home Care, the Division of Temporary Child Care, the Children's Center,

---

[29] From *The Welfarer*, official publication of the New York City Department of Welfare, Vol. IX, No. 1 (January 1957), p. 2.
[30] *Ibid.*, p. 6.

CHART 15. NEW YORK CITY DEPARTMENT OF WELFARE

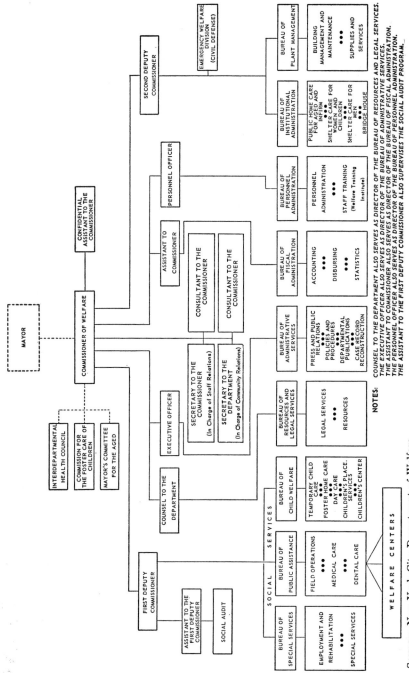

NOTES:

COUNSEL TO THE DEPARTMENT ALSO SERVES AS DIRECTOR OF THE BUREAU OF RESOURCES AND LEGAL SERVICES.
THE EXECUTIVE OFFICER ALSO SERVES AS DIRECTOR OF THE BUREAU OF ADMINISTRATIVE SERVICES.
THE ASSISTANT TO COMMISSIONER ALSO SERVES AS DIRECTOR OF THE BUREAU OF FISCAL ADMINISTRATION.
THE PERSONNEL OFFICER ALSO SERVES AS DIRECTOR OF THE BUREAU OF PERSONNEL ADMINISTRATION.
THE ASSISTANT TO THE FIRST DEPUTY COMMISSIONER ALSO SUPERVISES THE SOCIAL AUDIT PROGRAM.

Source: New York City Department of Welfare.

which provides temporary shelter for dependent and neglected children, and a Division of Day Care, which allocates funds and provides supervision to day care centers operated by nonprofit agencies and community groups. This last-named, it might be noted, is a highly unusual relationship between public and private agencies today.

In the Bureau of Special Services, the Division of Special Services works with agencies providing homes for the aged, with reference to recipients of public assistance who live in such homes. This Division keeps listings of licensed nursing homes for the aged and refers people to them, and lists vacancies for supervised living arrangements which may be offered by boarding homes for adults, certifies such homes for the care of recipients of public assistance, and maintains a day center program for older people, in cooperation with voluntary agencies and community groups.

Other duties of this Bureau include clinics operated in various hospitals throughout the city for the provision of medical care designed to restore the public assistance recipient to employability, a home economics program of technical advice to the Department on standards of assistance and planning for home economic services, a homemaker service to provide homemakers for brief periods to provide partial or complete household management and care of children or ill adults, and a program of training in household and service trades for "selected women in receipt of public assistance."[31]

The Division of Employment and Rehabilitation of this Bureau is responsible for the development of the program of rehabilitation and placement for public assistance recipients, in cooperation with the New York State Employment Service, and various rehabilitation agencies throughout the city.

Under the Second Deputy Commissioner, the Bureau of Institutional Administration is responsible for public home care for the aged and infirm, shelter care, and care and treatment for a limited time of male alcoholics.

This is a large program, and requires an extensive organization

31 *Ibid.,* p. 10.

for fiscal, legal, administrative, personnel, and special services, and for plant management. These services are provided through service Bureaus. Space does not permit detail on the functions of each of these Bureaus, but perhaps a point should be made with reference to them. They are not representative of functions different from those carried in an agency providing a smaller program. Rather, they are indicative of the degree of specialization which can be afforded, and which is necessary in a larger program.

An example of specialization is also provided by the Social Audit, which the reader will note is a separate unit under the Assistant to the First Deputy Commissioner. Usually, one thinks of an audit or administrative review as an activity conducted by one level of government in relation to another. Here, however, we see this function being performed by the same local unit that provides the services. In a smaller office, knowledge of how a program is operating would be more likely to come from the supervisor of the workers, through direct day-by-day familiarity with the operation of the program.

In this large a structure, however, the channels of communication are not so simple and direct, and the city administration has used this method of keeping informed on the operation of the welfare programs.

The Department operates seventeen welfare centers under the Bureau of Public Assistance. These include fourteen centers, located throughout the city, for administration of the five types of public assistance (old age assistance, aid to dependent children, aid to the disabled, assistance to the blind, and home relief), and three special centers, including the Non-Residence Welfare Center for newcomers with less than a year of residence in the State, the Veterans Assistance Welfare Center, for needy veterans and their families, and the Special Services Welfare Center. The Bureau field service visits, coordinates, and helps to maintain practices consistent with Departmental policies and procedures.

Each welfare center is headed by an administrative supervisor, who is assisted by a case supervisor and an office manager. Under the case supervisor are unit supervisors, each responsible for eight social investigators. The number of units depends upon the size of the center's caseload.

In many ways, the relationship between the central office and welfare centers in this large city are like those which exist between state and local offices in many states. Certainly in an organization of this size, the administration has a most formidable task.

SOME PROBLEMS FOR LOCAL ADMINISTRATION

Keeping related to the realities of local needs as well as to state and federal policy would be a challenging task under the most favorable circumstances. Certain features of local welfare administration today, however, make the task more difficult.

The first is the failure of resources in staff and facilities to keep pace with increasing demands for services. With the growing need for cooperation in vocational rehabilitation, for improvement and extension of services in public assistance, for participation in the various health programs, the available resources may not match the need or opportunity for service. One part of the public assistance program, medical care, ushered into the welfare departments in recent years (Social Security Amendments of 1954) alone has opened up whole new types of responsibility, and has demanded what are virtually programs within programs. Too frequently, enthusiasm by the legislature in the state and nation to provide new services is not matched by an intense desire to provide the means.

Another problem comes from the complexity of intergovernmental administration. The kinds of accounting and reporting which are involved in relations between levels of government, the regulation and control that are so likely to be part of the relationship, add to the task of the local office.[32] This, as we have suggested, may be obviated by judicious avoidance of excessively

[32] For an interesting presentation of this point of view, see Robert T. Lansdale, "A Major Problem of Public Welfare: The Growing Complexity of Administering Public Assistance," *Public Welfare,* January 1953.

detailed, procedural regulation, and by reliance on communication through other channels of supervision. Sometimes, however, the regulation or control may be a hardy survivor which long outlives the problem it was designed to solve.

The tendency to retain procedures and regulations which have outlived their usefulness is one that requires careful watching by an administration. Such matters may become habit, and staff members may get so accustomed to observing outmoded procedures that they never think of questioning them. This could well be one of the factors which have produced the mass of detail which is the source of complaint in so many welfare programs.

Within the tenure of any local board, executive and staff member, many changes will take place. A problem of local welfare is the development and maintenance of an attitude of receptivity to change, and of willingness to adapt to altering circumstances and social philosophy. As social welfare becomes more and more an accepted part of community life, new demands will be made upon the local administration for different kinds of service. This will require a combination of imagination and realism, which will not foreclose the growth of responsibility, but which at the same time will avoid overextension beyond the facilities and purpose of the organization.

Summary

Despite all the development of federal and state policy, the local welfare department is still the point at which the welfare program meets the people. What the local welfare agency has lost in the exclusiveness of control it had in the earlier days of poor relief administration has been more than offset by its enhanced responsibilities for larger and more varied services.

Local as a term does not have a single and precise meaning. There were, in 1956, more than 100,000 local units of various classifications in the nation. Questions have been raised more than a few times regarding the problem of the small, overlapping local unit. The small unit has been said to produce inequities in tax burdens, to make it impossible to utilize certain centralized services necessary to efficient operation, to scatter political responsibility, and to produce an unequal level of service at high cost.

But the small unit is not the only problem. The large, urban center of today presents its share of difficulties. In many instances these large urban centers are interstate in nature. Bigness brings with it the problem of keeping the administration responsive to needs and circumstances within an area.

The Social Security Act strengthened the position in social welfare of the local as well as the state government. The Act stipulated that the state plan in each of the public assistance programs must be in effect in all the subdivisions of the state. The states were free to choose their own type of local unit. By and large, the county was made the local unit for administration of social welfare. It had already become established as the unit for this purpose even prior to the Great Depression. Some states have the town or the township as the unit, however. Many of the states which established county or district units for state-aided programs have retained the township or town as the one for the administration of general assistance.

There perhaps is an ideal size of population for the welfare unit, but it has not yet been precisely determined. To find this ideal, factors of population numbers would have to be related to other features of community life.

In some programs, distinctions are evident between state-administered, and locally-administered but state-supervised services. Actually this distinction may be more nominal than real. The extent to which the local program is tightly controlled rests on the quality of the relationship more than on how the relationship is described in law.

Some welfare programs require local financial participation, although most do not. It has been argued that this brings with it a measure of administrative responsibility not so likely to be present when the funds are all state or state and federal. On the other hand, it is probable that this penalizes the locality unable to raise its share, especially unfortunate since that is likely to be the local unit with the greatest need.

The local welfare agency of today has many responsibilities. These are determined by state law, by the pressures of local needs, and by the availability or lack of availability of other welfare services. In many communities the county department of public welfare is the only office providing social service in the community.

Local welfare agencies vary greatly in the extent to which services are consolidated under one agency or scattered among several. There is no pattern that could be cited as characteristic. When there are too many smaller offices rather than one more comprehensive administration, there are certain losses in strength of services, but even more importantly, the clientele may be less adequately served. There may be less efficient use of facilities and services, and the problems of getting adequate personnel may be increased.

The local board is important to local welfare administration. These boards are appointed variously throughout the country, and provide for citizen participation in keeping the services close to the people served and to the interests of the public at large. These boards are generally either advisory or policy-forming. They do not serve as direct participants in the services, although there are areas of service in public welfare in which the volunteer may play an important role.

The executive has a key role in the success of the local program. He must be able to relate both to central office and local demands and policies. He must have skill in management, in leadership, and in keeping related to the public. In many of the smaller offices he may be required to act as case supervisor, and in the smallest, as a case worker too. Another important person is the case supervisor, who must combine the skills of teaching with the ability to direct the work of others, to stimulate the development of the worker, and to function as a part of administration in the development of policy.

To function effectively, the local office must have a combination of skills and specialties available to it. The degree of specialization required varies with the size of the organization. Organizational charts of two urban offices, Ramsey County, Minnesota

(St. Paul), and New York City, are examples of large agency structure.

Local welfare administration has its problems, including the failure of the public to provide increases in staff and facilities that keep pace with growing demands for service, and the complexities of reporting and regulation which seem to accompany intergovernmental administration.

Selected References

1. American Public Welfare Association, *The Public Welfare Directory, 1957*. Chicago, 1957.
2. Brown, Josephine C., *Public Relief, 1929-39*. New York, Henry Holt and Company, 1940.
3. The Council of State Governments, *State-Local Relations, Report of the Committee on State-Local Relations*. Chicago, 1946.
4. Drake, Russell, and Leirfallom, Russell, "Organization and Administration of the Local Public Welfare Program," *Public Welfare*, June, July, August, October, November, 1943.
5. Leyendecker, Hilary M., *Problems and Policy in Public Assistance*. New York, Harper & Brothers, 1955.
6. Martz, Helen E., *Citizen Participation in Government, a Study of County Welfare Boards*. Washington, Public Affairs Press, 1948.
7. Roberts, J. Craig, "Relationship of Board and Staff in Policy Determination." *Public Welfare*, Vol. 15, No. 1, January, 1957.
8. White, R. Clyde, *Administration of Public Welfare*. 2nd ed., New York, American Book Company, 1950.
9. Stevenson, Marietta, *Public Welfare Administration*. New York, The Macmillan Company, 1938.
10. Weller, Evalyn G., and Kilborne, Elizabeth B., *Citizen Participation in Public Welfare Programs*. Social Security Administration, Bureau of Public Assistance, Washington, Government Printing Office, 1956.

11

Services and Personnel

As services are extended in social welfare, and as study and experience in the field provide new insights into human needs and ways of meeting them, the importance of competent, adequately trained personnel increases. The best of legislative intention will become translated into service only if there are people with the ability to provide the service. New knowledge in the social and behavioral sciences can be utilized in social welfare only if there are people with backgrounds which enable them to interpret and apply this knowledge. Modern social welfare has become increasingly a professional service.

In all the programs, it is also an interprofessional service. The various programs have required the collaborative efforts, the skills, and the knowledge, of a number of disciplines, and there is a growing emphasis on the importance of the contribution of each profession or technical field to a common pool of research and practice. It is not necessary to labor the point that a combination of many factors is present among the people who seek the services, but the very fact that many if not most problems have combinations of physical, mental, and social handicap underscores the importance of cooperation among the various professions.

Social work is a basic discipline in social welfare. The social worker has a role in all of the programs described in Part II, and in such fields as public assistance and child welfare has the primary role. This is not to minimize the importance of the social worker in mental health, services to veterans, vocational rehabilitation, and corrections, however. In fact, in corrections the probation officer and the parole officer are generally classified as social workers. In all of these services, the social worker is an integral part of the administration of the service. There is evidence of increasing use of the social worker in the social insurances.

What their qualifications are, what their duties are, how they are selected and appointed, what the possibilities are for a career in social work in governmental welfare services, and the nature of education for social work will be briefly discussed in the rest of this chapter.

THE QUALIFICATIONS

Estimates and enumerations of the total number of social workers in both public and private agencies in the United States have ranged from 75,000 to 100,000. The reason for these differences is the variable way in which the term social worker is used. In a nation-wide study of the number of social workers in 1950, the Bureau of Labor Statistics placed the total number of social workers in the country at 75,000, with public assistance positions accounting for 41 percent, and child welfare staff for 11 percent of that total.[1]

Public assistance personnel as of June 1956 included 36,225 executives and social workers.[2] This figure included directors, caseworkers, supervisors, state field representatives, and others. Of this total, 34,129, were employed in local offices, and 2,536 in state welfare departments. In addition to the executives and so-

---

[1] Bureau of Labor Statistics, *Social Workers in 1950: A Report of the Study of Salaries and Working Conditions in Social Work* (New York, American Association of Social Workers, 1952). For further information on the numbers in child welfare and public assistance see: *Public Social Welfare Personnel,* a study made jointly by the Children's Bureau and the Bureau of Public Assistance (Washington, 1953).

[2] *Public Assistance Personnel, Fiscal Year 1956,* Bureau of Public Assistance, Social Security Administration, March 1957, p. 3.

cial workers, 29,046 other employees in state and local public assistance offices brought the total number of employees in this service to 65,711.

Included in the over-all total are nonsocial work specialists, numbering 2,998. Among the specializations included in this category are home economists, supervising ophthalmologists, legal consultants, insurance consultants, accountants, auditors, social economists, statisticians, and others.[3]

As of June 1956, 5,628 persons were employed as full-time workers in state and local child welfare programs throughout the country. (This figure includes only those child welfare services for which federal funds are received under Title V, Section 3 of the Social Security Act. It excludes those persons who are engaged in child welfare activities, such as public assistance personnel engaged in child welfare, or institutional or court or day care center or children's institution personnel, for which no federal aid is received.)[4] Some interesting facts about the distribution of these workers are that the heaviest concentrations of them are in the eastern half of the country (not including large parts of the South) and in the states of the far west; and that only half of the counties in the country had the services of any full-time workers in child welfare.[5]

Recent figures are not available regarding the total number of people employed in social work positions in the various other governmental programs. There is, however, every indication of an increased demand for social workers in many of these programs, as new mental health clinics are established, as hospitals are constructed and improved, as the field of correction, both institutional and noninstitutional, more and more places emphasis on treatment and rehabilitation of the offender, and as rehabilitation services for the handicapped, all utilize the social worker.

It would be interesting if a profile could be presented, showing the characteristics of social workers in all these services. Since

[3] *Ibid.,* p. 2.
[4] Social Security Administration, *Staff in Public Child Welfare Program, 1956,* Children's Bureau Statistical Series No. 41 (Washington, 1957).
[5] *Ibid.,* p. 4.

this is not possible, we shall content ourselves with some observations of the education and experience of these workers, and some examples of qualifications for positions.

In the study of public social welfare as of 1950, the Children's Bureau and the Bureau of Public Assistance found that almost two-thirds of the public assistance workers, supervisors, and executives had bachelor's degrees, while only 39.1 percent had graduate work in any field of study. It was also found that 34.2 percent did not have bachelor's degrees. The situation possibly has improved since 1950, but it does not seem likely that this improvement is marked enough to alter the essential situation: the disparity between the job to be done and the personnel resources to do that job.

In its statement on "The Public Assistance Worker," the Board of Directors of the American Public Welfare Association in April 1952, set forth an impressive grouping of the content of the public assistance job, the basic knowledge required, and the skills and abilities needed for handling this responsibility.[6] It specified knowledge of the legal and philosophical basis for public assistance, including the law on which the program is based, of the structure of the agency, and of the general structure and function of state government. Also listed were knowledge of social and economic factors affecting public assistance, and of human behavior, including normal growth and development, and deviations from normal behavior. The description of skills and abilities included the ability to plan work, to communicate through writing and speaking, to evaluate eligibility, to discern and to understand reactions, attitudes and relationships of others, and to help the client in a way that conserves his dignity, self-respect, and self-reliance.

In range and depth of knowledge and skills, this list suggests a professional level of operation. Indeed, the American Public Welfare Association acknowledged this fact in the same document, with this statement:[7]

---

[6] American Public Welfare Association, *The Public Assistance Worker,* pamphlet (Chicago, 1952). Statement prepared by the Committee on Social Work Education and Personnel of the American Public Welfare Association.

[7] *Ibid.*

Standards in the field of social work have developed to the extent that it is now generally recognized that education for social work represents a progression from the undergraduate years through two graduate years. It will be some time before all social work positions will be filled by persons who have met this standard. The major source of recruitment for public assistance agencies will for some years be the Liberal Arts colleges.

Further support to making graduation from college a minimum qualification for public welfare, and for graduate education as a desirable standard was given by the conference of State Departments of Public Welfare and Schools of Social Work in the South, in March 1956. This conference, held at the invitation of the Southern Regional Education Board at Atlanta, made the following recommendations:[8]

(a) We recommend, therefore, graduation from an accredited college or university as a minimum educational requirement for induction into social work positions in public welfare.

(b) We recommend further that a minimum of at least one full year of graduate social work education be considered a desirable standard for all social work personnel and that full professional education is essential for certain positions. The compensation plan should reflect the amount of professional education of the social work employee.

The suggestion that certain positions should require full professional education is a reflection of a practice sometimes observed or advocated for optimum use of the limited numbers of professionally trained persons who are available to public assistance programs. It is advocated by some that the best use of these professionally trained personnel would be to assign them to supervisory positions so that they can use their education in the instruction of others. Another way of using them is to assign them to special loads of problem cases, although it is generally quite difficult to predict what cases will develop into the category of special problems.

[8] Ellen Winston, "Sounder Public Welfare Programs through Adequate Staffing," *Public Welfare News,* publication of the North Carolina State Board of Public Welfare, Vol. 20, No. 1 (March, 1957), p. 1.

But the difficulty of securing personnel to meet the needs of the service remains serious in public assistance. The emphasis in the 1956 Social Security Amendments on federal support for the development of state plans for helping recipients of public assistance attain self-support, self-care, and a strengthened family life have served to accentuate the need for more professionally qualified people. But as the present Secretary of Health, Education, and Welfare, Mr. Marion B. Folsom, has commented, only 23 percent of the workers in public assistance agencies have had graduate training, and graduates of schools of social work total less than 2,000 annually. And, we might note, this number includes graduates who enter all areas of social welfare, with only a portion entering public assistance work, specifically.

In child welfare services, the proportion of persons with professional social work education is greater than in public assistance. As of June 1955, 61 percent of the executives and workers had had some graduate education in social work, with 28 percent having completed the full graduate program.[9] Of the 39 percent with no graduate education, only 7 percent lacked a bachelor's degree.

Child welfare has had some distinct advantages as compared with public assistance in the development of a larger proportion of professionally educated personnel. One has been the availability of grants to states for use in paying a substantial part of the costs of education for staff members accepted by schools of social work. While state public assistance agencies have had the authority to use federal funds matched equally by state funds for this purpose, the fact that state expenditures are required has tended to limit the use of these funds. Another factor is the size of the public assistance program. When states accept public assistance funds, they also accept the condition that the plan be in effect in all subdivisions. They cannot wait until a qualified staff is available, but must begin to operate with the resources they can muster. Child welfare grants are not given under any such mandate, so that the state in theory at least may elect not to establish a program until prepared to do so with qualified staff. Even so, the difference has become more one of degree than of kind. State

[9] Social Security Administration, *op. cit.,* p. 11.

child welfare programs have been extended because of community need to the point that available resources of staff are inadequate in many instances to meet the commitments.

The functions of the child welfare worker have already been discussed (in Chap. 6). Such responsibilities as casework for children in their own homes, protective services, adoptions, selection, placement and supervision of children in foster care, work with the delinquent, development of day care facilities, and work with unmarried parents, demand a quality of insight and understanding that again indicates a professional level of practice. In many communities, the child welfare worker in the local office is working without the resources of clinics, court-related services, and others which are available to the worker in the larger urban community. This means that these workers must be resourceful in making the best use of limited facilities, must be able to help develop new resources, and must really act in the community as the spokesman for the disadvantaged child. Skilled services in child welfare can reduce considerably—by forestalling or preventing—the development in the clients of later needs for clinical and hospital treatment, and for other specialized services.

Let us now look at some of the other publicly supported and administered programs which utilize the services of the social worker. In the Veterans Administration, the social worker participates in the program of medical care in VA hospitals, outpatient clinics, and domiciliaries. The general purpose of clinical social work in this service has been defined as follows:[10]

> 1. Clinical social work is an integral part of medical care. Physicians have found that illness is a plight of man often precipitated, intensified, and prolonged by stresses and crises in his personal life and environment. Unless prevented or relieved, these pressures may obstruct or even negate medical treatment; they increase disablement, and cause relapses. In the interest of the individual veteran and good administration of medical treatment and domiciliary care, it is, therefore,

[10] Office of the Chief Medical Director, Veterans Administration, *Program Guide Social Work Service, Standards for Clinical Social Work in VA Hospitals, Outpatient Clinics, and Domiciliaries* (Washington, August 16, 1957), p. 1.

essential to help him modify these unfavorable influences on his health or, if they cannot be relieved, then to support him in his acceptance and endurance of them. Such attention not only enriches the art of medicine; it expedites good medical results and increases their stability and permanency. Most of all it helps the disabled person, whether a patient or a domiciliary member, to increase his peace of mind and harmonize his way of life to the realities not only of his disabilities but also of his remaining capacities.

2. Clinical social work contributes to medical treatment and to domiciliary care a skilled appraisal of the source and significance of the social, emotional, and economic complications of the veterans' disablement and provides a resource for reducing the force of their impact upon him as a sick or disabled individual. Assuring the development of social, psychological, and cultural circumstances as favorable as possible to the patient's or member's sound future health and well-being is expected of clinical social service.

3. The responsibilities of Social Work Service in this health-focused professional activity of collaborating with physicians and others to advance the quality and effectiveness of inpatient, outpatient, and domiciliary care require sound administration of the social service program and a high standard of skilled service to individual veterans.

Positions in clinical social work include those of chief social worker, assistant chief social worker, case supervisor, senior clinical social worker, and clinical social worker. These represent gradations of responsibility, position, and salary, and are based on experience and quality of performance. The minimum qualification in the beginning position in this service is graduation from an accredited graduate school of social work, with the specification that the student must have had supervised field work in social casework in the second year of graduate study, or one year of experience in casework following graduation. Qualifying experience for the more advanced positions may have been secured in hospitals, clinics, or social agencies with acceptable standards of professional service. These are civil service positions in the federal government, and are in the "General Service" classification.

The psychiatric social worker is an essential part of the therapeutic "team" in mental hospitals, clinics, and guidance centers. As psychiatry in its modern form has recognized the importance of fostering the individual's social relations and of considering his social environment in treatment, the role of the social worker has taken on increasing importance in therapy. Yet, the sad fact is that in state and local hospitals, professionally qualified social workers are in short supply. The situation is especially acute in mental hospitals, with the clinics in a more favorable position with respect to numbers of qualified professional social workers.

In the preceding statement of functions for specific clinical positions in the Veterans Administration, the role of the worker in the mental hospital or clinic has been described, in general, as that of providing social, economic, and environmental information to the psychiatrist and other members of the therapeutic team, helping the patient at the time of admission to understand the treatment facilities, assisting the family through the difficult period of adjustment to the patient's illness, maintaining a link between patient and family and community throughout treatment, and helping the patient to re-establish himself in the community and in the family environment. The social worker may find a foster home for the patient at the time of discharge, and may supervise the patient in that period of foster care.[11]

Because of the shortage of qualified personnel, mental health facilities of state and local government have been compelled to recruit many social workers who have had less than the full two years of graduate education in social work and in many instances, no graduate work. This has been particularly true of mental hospitals. Facilities which insist on the minimum professional educational standards may find their budgeted positions unfilled.

In 1951 it was reported that about 6 percent of the state hospitals in the nation were meeting the standards of the American Psychiatric Association for the number of social workers on their

---

[11] The Council of State Governments, *Training and Research in State Mental Health Programs* (Chicago, 1953), p. 79.

staffs. While it is true that the situation may have improved, there is no evidence that such improvement is so marked as to indicate a satisfactory situation respecting social work personnel in these facilities.[12]

In a study conducted in 1950, it was found that in state hospitals reporting, about one-half the social workers had had no professional education, while the other half was evenly divided between those who had completed their training, and those who had partially completed their graduate work. The picture was much more favorable in clinics, and in federal hospitals, but the total picture was one of shortage.[13]

Social work in correctional service is currently a subject of considerable study and concern by national agencies including the National Probation and Parole Association and the Council on Social Work Education. This is a field in which there has been a resurgence of interest in the role of social work during the past few years. The part that social work plays along with the disciplines of psychology, psychiatry, sociology, law, and others, is of increasing interest, as the emphasis in correctional practice features social rehabilitation of the offender.

The personnel situation in social work for this field, however, is far from ideal. The general picture seems to be one of uncertainty as to the minimum qualifications which may be required, and a shortage of professionally prepared people for the positions. In this field, as in others, there is a serious disparity between the defined task and the available personnel resources.

In a report of a study of agency employment practices in the correctional field, the Council on Social Work Education's Committee on Corrections sent questionnaires to 202 correctional agencies in the United States, and received responses from 79. Among the findings reported by the Committee are the following:[14]

Graduate training is preferred for 85 percent of the probation and parole caseworkers and 73 percent of institutional casework-

[12] Council of State Governments, *op. cit.*, p. 80.

[13] See Tessie Berkman, *Practice of Social Workers in Psychiatric Hospitals and Clinics* (Washington, 1953).

[14] Council on Social Work Education, *Youth Wants to Know About Careers in Social Work,* Special Recruitment Issue, April 1957, pp. 18-23.

ers positions, among those reporting on this item. But a bachelor's degree or less is acceptable for 61 percent of these field positions (probation and parole) and 70 percent of the institutional positions. The minimum of graduate training is specified in 23 percent of the field and 29 percent of the institutional positions. In probation and parole, however, the minimum acceptable formal education requirement is a bachelor degree, for "trainee positions."[15] This term has varied meanings, referring in some instances to caseworkers on the job, in others to professional apprentices, and in others to students under special arrangements for combinations of work and study.

The Committee noted trends as follows with respect to the 79 agencies reporting:[16]

1. In an increasing number of agencies graduate training has been accepted as the preferred education for beginning employees. Social work graduate education is increasingly recognized as appropriate for probation, parole, and institutional caseworker positions.
2. Agencies desiring trained personnel have in general not been able to supply their staff needs with trained personnel.
3. Varied diligent efforts have been made by agencies to secure trained staff.
4. Salaries in this field are rising and in many of these agencies are competitive with other social work agencies, if not with private industry.
5. The agencies feel a need for a closer relationship with schools of social work and are willing to work with the schools in enriching curricula. . . .
6. Along with increased salaries there is a strong trend toward establishment of publicly supported student aid programs in order to secure qualified staff.

While this report is based on replies from a limited number of agencies, it nevertheless indicates a growing trend toward utilization of professionally trained social workers in this field.

As we have already mentioned, social workers also are em-

15 *Ibid.*, p. 19.
16 *Ibid.*, p. 23.

ployed in vocational rehabilitation and in the health services, including crippled children's services and maternal and child health services. While we do not have complete information on the numbers so employed at this point, we may offer the general observation that this too is an area of need for professional people, and that in general these social work positions require a specified minimum of graduate study in social work. In vocational rehabilitation, the role of the social worker in relation to the vocational counselors and other disciplines is in the process of clarification and development.[17]

The role of the social worker as a member of the health team in the rehabilitation of the handicapped person—in a hospital, convalescent home, or other facility—has been described as including the provision of information and counseling services, to help the patient to find and to make the best possible use of treatment resources. In the crippled children's program, the medical social worker performs a variety of functions, including those of working directly with the other members of the team in providing and interpreting social information important to treatment, helping patient and family adjust to the demands of care and treatment, developing resources for foster care or special housing when needed, participating in policy decisions and planning for the service, working with other agencies for the improvement of social services for the crippled child, participating in surveys of need, and in other ways helping to augment the quality of treatment available to the handicapped child.[18]

THE MERIT SYSTEM IN PUBLIC WELFARE

Personnel policies and procedures in public programs of social welfare are governed by the principles and practices of the merit system. As might readily be inferred, this term refers to appoint-

[17] See Ruth D. Abrams, and Bess S. Dana, "Social Work in the Process of Rehabilitation," *Social Work,* Vol. 2, No. 4 (October 1957), pp. 10-15.

[18] See Helen M. Wallace, M.D., "The Role of the Social Worker in the Rehabilitation of the Handicapped," *Social Casework,* Vol. XXXVIII, No. 1 January 1957), pp. 19-20.

ment, retention, promotion and compensation of personnel on the basis of merit, rather than on one of personal or political favoritism or other factors having no bearing on the individual's capacity or performance.

Actually, the merit system principle was established years ago with the beginning of civil service systems. In 1883 the Pendleton Act was passed as a reaction to the assassination of President Garfield two years earlier at the hands of a disgruntled office seeker. Revulsion against this act led to determination to abolish the spoils system for nonelective and nonpolicy-making positions in the national government, and to substitute a system based on selection through open competitive examinations.[19] The civil service system was subsequently adopted by some states and municipalities, and in a very few counties.[20]

The term merit system, in public welfare, pertains to the establishment of a system for a department or program or group of programs. It is really, then, a civil service system developed for a particular area of service. It includes the processes of classifying positions, recruiting, examining, certifying successful candidates to the employing agency, and selection by the agency. Through these procedures, positions are established on the basis of the duties and responsibilities they entail, minimum qualifications are established, compensation is determined for each job classification, including maximum and minimum limits or a range for each class, examinations are given to test the capacity of the individual to perform the service, and the candidates with the highest scores are certified for the positions. Scoring is based on a combination of the candidate's performance on the written examination, an oral examination or interview usually by a special board of examiners, and an evaluation of his qualifying education and experience. For some of the professional social work positions the written examination may be waived. An example of this practice is provided in the Veterans Administration's announcement

---

[19] See Arthur Miles, *An Introduction to Public Welfare* (Boston, 1949), Chap. 17: "Personnel Administration," Also Alice Klein, *Civil Service in Public Welfare* (New York, 1940).

[20] *Ibid.*, p. 343.

about the position of clinical social worker, which specifies that candidates will be rated on a scale of 100 on the extent of education and experience relevant to the position, statements on their applications, and additional evidence, which might include references or publications. Other professional positions requiring a high level of education and practice may similarly place less weight on written examination and more on other evidences of ability.

Generally a probationary period of employment ranging from a few months to a year may also be a part of the examination process. During this period, the appointee may be discharged at any time if his performance does not present evidence of prospective ability successfully to discharge the responsibilities of the position. At the conclusion of the period of probation, if the person is appointed, he has tenure—that is, can be discharged only following an established process, which requires that the employer show cause, and that the employee shall have a right to appeal.

Some state and local merit systems have provided for requirements other than education and experience. One of the commonest of these is the stipulation of state or local residence either as a flat requirement or as a preferred qualification. Many systems with such provision, however, specify conditions under which they may be waived. Such residence restrictions on eligibility for candidacy for positions has the effect of limiting the supply of available qualified people, and in that way tends to cheat the service of the opportunity to reach out for the best available people. Another feature of personnel policy is the provision for veterans preference, a practice described in Chapter Six under "Veterans' Services." While a case may be made for this practice on the basis of the obligation to the veteran, it is not a factor related to ability to perform the required work.

For several years, the shortage of qualified people has made it difficult to maintain lists of people who have successfully qualified through examination and are eligible for certification for appointment to social work positions. This shortage is present throughout the various programs and at all levels of government. The result has been a growth of the practice of making provisional appointments, that is, appointments based on the individual's qualifications of education and experience, pending the holding of an examination at a future date.

In the original provisions of the Social Security Act as passed in 1935, the federal agency was authorized to require such methods of administration in public assistance as were found to be "necessary to the efficient operation of the plan" in the federally-aided programs with the exception of those "relating to selection, tenure of office and compensation of personnel." Meanwhile, about nine states had established civil service systems, although as Albert H. Aronson points out, several of these were not functioning effectively.[21]

In 1939 amendments to the Social Security Act included a provision for federal requirement of a merit system in agencies receiving grants-in-aid under the Act. This provision became effective January 1, 1940. Similar requirements were imposed on public health programs by regulation.

By and large, and with only a few exceptions, the states established joint merit systems for these various programs, rather than separate systems for the various services. Programs included in these systems are those receiving grants-in-aid administered by the Children's Bureau, public assistance, vocational rehabilitation, public health services, the employment service and the administration of unemployment insurance. The federal responsibility is assigned in the Department of Health, Education, and Welfare to the office of the Chief of State Merit Systems under the Director of Field Administration. This service cooperates through interdepartmental agreement with the Bureau of Employment Security in the Department of Labor. The federal office serves state merit systems in the maintenance of a pool of examinations, in the development of standards, and in the provision of consultation and other services to states.

State merit systems generally include a board or merit system

21 "Merit System Objectives and Realities," *Social Security Bulletin,* Vol. 13, No. 4 (April 1950), pp. 3-6.

council, which is responsible for the development of policy, and an executive staff.

The influence of federal merit system requirements on state and local personnel standards has been both strong and salutary. In general, as Mr. Aronson says, the evaluations have been very positive, and the contributions to states have been great in relation to general personnel standards as well as to the programs directly affected.[22]

But he also points out some present deficiencies, including an excessive number of provisional appointees, retention of marginal employees because of lack of courage on the part of administration to take the necessary action to separate the incompetent person from employment, and the need to develop better techniques for measuring personal attributes not so amenable to the techniques of evaluation and measurement as are knowledge, skill, and mental ability. In discussing these and other problems, he states that there is need to develop support for the merit system principle, and to help administrators withstand the pressures to hire and retain inadequate personnel.[23]

Like many other administrative techniques and systems, the strength of this one depends largely on how convinced administrators are of its value. Not only the merit system councils and staffs, but the health and welfare agencies as well must have such conviction about it if the merit system is to serve its purpose.

SOCIAL WORK CAREERS IN PUBLIC WELFARE

Facts on staff shortages tell their own story of the availability of professional positions in the public service for people with professional social work training. There are simply more positions than there are trained people, and there is every indication that this situation will continue for an indefinite future. Even if the total output of professional graduate schools of social work were to enter the public service, the needs would be far from met.

[22] *Ibid.*, p. 5.
[23] *Ibid.*, p. 6.

Financial aid for training

Government agencies have tried to solve this problem in part by providing scholarships and fellowships in considerable numbers to enable members of their staffs, or persons interested in joining their staffs, to attend graduate schools of social work. The Children's Bureau has included funds for educational payments in grants to states. While Congress did not implement the provisions in the 1956 amendments to the Social Security Act for grants to states for the purpose of paid educational leave to staff in public assistance, state funds used for that purpose have been matchable as administrative costs (50 percent matching) for years. Many states have provided for staff training under this program. Other federal agencies, including the National Institute for Mental Health and the Office of Vocational Rehabilitation, make direct grants to educational institutions for trainee stipends. The Veterans Administration has encouraged professional education by paying the student in field instruction in VA installations on the basis of an established rate for time spent in such instruction.[24] Generally these grants are established at a rate designed to pay tuition and a large part of living costs.

In short, it would seem that a competent person with a professional degree in social work is certain of employment, and the person who takes a job not requiring the professional degree has an excellent chance to work out a plan for financing graduate study.

Salaries

Consistently, throughout the years, one of the problems in this field has been that of developing salary rates which are related to the ability, the knowledge, and the skill required, and related realistically to the time, expense, and effort entailed in completing professional education. What of the salary rates? The only generalizations that seem supportable are that the amounts of salaries show great variation, that—under the pressure of need—salaries

---

[24] See Council on Social Work Education, *Social Work Fellowships and Scholarships in the U. S. and Canada* (New York, published annually).

are improving throughout the country, and that the outlook is for continued movement toward an improved level. Studies have been made of salaries in social work, but they rapidly become outdated. We will mention one of comparatively recent date, however, since it shows the tremendous range in starting salaries throughout the country.

This study indicated starting salaries in 1956 as low as $182 per month and as high as $361, among the forty-one states included in this survey.[25] Maximum salaries for these positions ranged from $259 per month to $560. These salaries are for social workers and do not include salaries paid to senior workers, supervisors, and executives.

A perusal of listings of jobs in social work, however, tells a somewhat more favorable story. In December 1957, the Social Work Vocational Bureau's listings included a position as a psychiatric social worker in a state hospital, with a salary range of from $4,092 to $4,512 per year, and with the stipulation that the beginning appointment could be made up to the amount of $4,512.[26] Other positions for salaries even higher, in mental health are listed in the same publication with the statement that experience is desirable but not necessary. Positions in the federal service requiring degrees but not experience are established at the GS-7 level, with a minimum of $4,525 and a maximum of $5,335.

Salary figures undoubtedly reflect the diverse qualifications and responsibilities of social workers in the different services. But evidence is accumulating to show that the salary picture for this profession is not nearly so bleak as is commonly supposed. In recent months the Council of Social Work Education, in cooperation with the accredited graduate schools of social work, has made a survey of employment status of former students who were enrolled in accredited graduate schools of social work in the spring semester or quarter of 1957. The following list of median salaries

[25] Mary Lynn Hepburn, *Requirements for Beginning State Social Workers,* as quoted in *Youth Wants to Know About Careers in Social Work,* Council of Social Work Education, April, 1957, p. 11.

[26] Social Work Vocational Bureau, *Jobs in Social Work,* December, 1957 (New York, a monthly).

secured from that survey includes social workers in both governmental and voluntary services.

MEDIAN YEARLY SALARIES OF GRADUATES WHO WERE ENROLLED
IN ACCREDITED GRADUATE SCHOOLS OF SOCIAL WORK DURING
SPRING SEMESTER OR QUARTER OF 1957, AS OF OCTOBER
1957, BY TYPE OF PROGRAM

Type of Program	*Median Annual Salary*	
	Men	*Women*
Public Assistance	$4,915	$6,000
Family Service	4,315	4,395
Child Welfare (non-institutional)	4,650	4,490
Child Welfare (institutional)	4,535	4,545
Juvenile Court	4,835	4,750
School Social Work	4,750	5,250
Mental Health Clinics	4,615	4,515
Mental Hospitals	4,830	4,695
Medical Social Work	4,585	4,440
Rehabilitation	4,750	4,645
Work with Adult Offenders	5,125	4,250
Other Services to Individuals	4,770	4,300
Leisure Time Programs	4,900	4,765
Services to Communities	7,250	5,750

SOURCE: Preliminary report prepared by David G. French, January 1958.

It should be kept in mind that these are former students with prior experience as well as students without experience before attending graduate school. This would possibly account for the rather surprising median salary under public assistance, especially for women. It would not be reasonable to infer from this figure that public assistance salaries are higher than are those for most of the other fields, and even less reasonable to assume that women in this field are paid substantially higher rates than men. It is probable that in this group there were a number of women who held supervisory posts before they enrolled in graduate study.

The survey also compared salaries paid to men and women with masters' degrees and those without these degrees. The report from the same group of graduates and former students revealed a median salary for men with masters' degrees of $4,715 per year, compared with $4,095 for those without degrees, the latter including both those with some graduate work, and those without any. For women, the figures were $4,565 for those with graduate degrees, and $3,905 for those without them.

An important factor in the consideration of social work salaries, however, is compensation for positions beyond the beginning level. Here, the picture is much more favorable. Review of job listings shows considerable increase in amounts payable to persons with professional degrees and experience. It seems only fair to say that social work salaries in the public service, while varying widely by program and by locale, are not universally so bad as frequently believed, and are improving. The chances for advancement in salary and rank for the professionally qualified worker are very good. On the other hand, it seems fair to state that in some areas, the salaries still reflect a depression standard of living.

Professional education

Throughout this chapter, allusion has been made to professional education. Without attempting to present a complete description of the social work curriculum, we shall look briefly at the nature and content of social work education.

There are at present sixty accredited graduate schools of social work in the United States and Canada and ninety undergraduate departments holding membership in the Council on Social Work Education, the national organization which represents the educational interests of the profession of social work. These schools and departments are found both in state universities and in private universities and colleges throughout the country. The graduate professional schools are located in twenty-eight states, and in the District of Columbia, Hawaii, and Puerto Rico.

As was stated earlier in connection with public assistance, the liberal arts colleges are looked to for a large number of personnel. Through preprofessional study, through preparing people for positions not demanding graduate professional study, and through acquainting students with the nature of social welfare as an important factor in American society, these departments render a valuable educational service. The question of the content of the undergraduate curriculum, and consideration of how it relates to the graduate curriculum, are subjects receiving considerable attention in the field. The subject is not one which permits quick and facile answers. There is the large question of reconciling the acknowledged need for a background of a liberal education with the urgent demands and needs of an undermanned field. As part of a comprehensive curriculum study, this area of concern is receiving attention from the Council on Social Work Education. This report, when completed, will undoubtedly be of considerable value in helping to establish a logical and consistent relationship between undergraduate and graduate study for social work, and between each and the field they both serve.

The professional degree in social work requires two years of graduate study in an accredited school of social work. The curriculum is a combination of classroom and field instruction. In other words, the student combines classroom study with educationally supervised experience in a social agency or institution. The field experience extends throughout the two academic years of graduate study. At the end of the period of study, a master's degree is conferred. This is most commonly called a Master of Social Work (although some schools calls it a Master of Arts in Social Work degree and others a Master of Science in Social Work).[27]

No attempt will be made here to describe the content of professional study. The curriculum is designed to help the student to develop the knowledge, and the skills necessary to play a helping role, whether that role is performed in the exercise of responsibility as worker, supervisor, or administrator. In order to insure as far as it is possible to do so that the student who is admitted will be able to develop basic competence as a social worker, the

[27] See Katherine Kendall, "Education for Social Work," *Social Work Year Book, 1957* (New York, National Association of Social Work, 1957), pp. 217-232. See, also, bulletins of schools of social work. These include descriptions of courses, of programs of study, and of field instruction.

schools have selective admissions policies. These generally include requirements of intellectual ability and of personality which are favorable to the mastery of a comprehensive body of knowledge, and to the development of attitudes and skills which an exacting profession demands. As preparation for working with people needing help, many schools specify certain specific areas of study as prerequisites, although not all follow this practice. Most stipulate a minimum average of grades attained during the undergraduate years as acceptable evidence of ability to undertake graduate study. Some have programs of testing to help in the process of predicting chances for succeeding in social work. All provide for a process of application which includes interviews for exploring with the applicant his interests in the field, and possible aptitudes for it. These interviews are a means of assisting the applicant further to assess his interest in the profession, as well as of helping the school in the selection of a candidate for study.

Professional organization

The professional organization in social work is the National Association of Social Workers, which was formed by a merger of seven professional organizations in 1955. The Association had a membership of more than 22,000 in 1956.[28] The groups which joined to form the new organization were the American Association of Social Workers, organized in 1921 as the successor to an earlier organization called the National Social Workers Exchange; the American Association of Medical Social Workers, established in 1918; the National Association of School Social Workers, organized in 1919; the American Association of Psychiatric Social Workers, which became an organization distinct from the American Association of Medical Social Workers in 1926; and three later groups, the American Association of Group Workers (1946); the Association for the Study of Community Organization (1946); and the Social Work Research Group (1949). The last two were study groups rather than professional bodies.

[28] See Nathan E. Cohen, "Social Work as a Profession," *Social Work Year Book, 1957.*

The National Association of Social Workers (NASW) has five sections, which are: Group Work, Medical Social Work, Psychiatric Social Work, School Social Work, and Social Work Research. The professional journal is *Social Work*.

We shall not attempt to describe in detail the purposes and functions of this organization. Its membership is open to graduates of any accredited school of social work. The Association is committed to providing leadership in promoting the quality of social work practice, to establishing and maintaining standards of performance, to working for social legislation and other programs for improvement of social conditions, to helping bring about the best possible working conditions for the profession, to recruitment of people into the profession, and to furtherance of cooperation with other professions. These are some of the major functions. As a professional association it must be concerned with strengthening the capacity of the profession to make the best possible contribution to the public interest.

Public welfare today needs professional personnel competent as practitioners working with individuals and groups, but also able to use the structure of the agency and the administrative process in making help available. Supervisors and administrators are needed, as well as staff members skilled in research, and in organization of community services, and people with qualities of leadership in the development of social policy. Public welfare requires staff whose devotion and skill in helping others are accompanied by the ability to convey to a public sometimes not prepared to see or to listen a clear understanding of the needs of people requiring welfare services.

Summary

Social welfare services of government require professionally qualified personnel. One of the basic professional disciplines is that of social work.

Whether in public assistance, child welfare, mental health, or rehabilitation of the handicapped, the picture now is one of an undermanned field. Many of those holding social work positions have had no professional training. Some of the fields within social work have positions which do not require graduate professional study, but in many of these, such study is preferred even if not required.

Personnel policies and procedures in public programs of social welfare are governed by the principles and practices of the merit system. This term denotes the appointment, retention, promotion, and compensation of staff on the basis of merit rather than on one of political or personal favoritism.

The merit system has been a requirement in grants-in-aid to states for the various programs of health and welfare since January 1, 1940. Programs included are those administered by the Children's Bureau, the public assistance categories, vocational rehabilitation, public health services, the employment service, and the unemployment insurance administration. The merit system has resulted in raised standards for welfare and health personnel in states and localities and has influenced improvement and standards even in those services not directly covered.

There are more positions in social welfare than there are qualified people to fill them. In recognition of this lack of personnel, and in an effort at least partly to overcome it, the various federal and state programs have included provision for paid educational leaves and scholarships to staff members, and to persons who wish to join the services. Salaries vary widely, and, while not generally as high as they should be in relation to the nature of the work and the education and experience required, are improving throughout the country.

There are sixty accredited schools of social work in the United States and Canada and ninety undergraduate departments. The liberal arts colleges are still looked to for a large number of personnel. In order to become a professional social worker, however, a person must complete two graduate years of study in an accredited school of social work. These two years of study include a combination of class and field instruction designed to permit the student to relate theory and practice.

All schools of social work have certain definite entrance qualifications. These include qualities of intellect and personality which hold promise of success in an exacting field of work.

Public welfare today needs professional personnel who are competent practitioners. But also needed are supervisors, administrators, and people at all levels of professional employment who have the qualities of leadership needed to convey a better understanding of human needs.

Selected References

1. American Public Welfare Association, *The Public Assistance Worker*, a Statement Prepared by the Committee on Social Work Education and Personnel, approved by Board of Directors, April 19, 1952.

2. Aronson, Albert H., "Merit System Objectives and Realities," *Social Security Bulletin*, Vol. 13, No. 4 (April, 1950).

3. Berkman, Tessie D., *Practice of Social Workers in Psychiatric Hospitals and Clinics*. New York, American Association of Psychiatric Social Workers, 1953.

4. The Council of State Governments, *Training and Research in State Mental Health Programs*. Chicago, 1953.

5. De Schweinitz, Karl, *People and Process in Social Security*. Washington, American Council on Education, 1948.

6. Hollis, Ernest V., and Taylor, Alice L., *Social Work Education in the United States*. New York, Columbia University Press, 1951.

7. Klein, Alice Campbell, *Civil Service in Public Welfare*. New York, Russell Sage Foundation, 1940.

8. Social Security Administration, *Staff in Public Child Welfare Programs*. Children's Bureau, Statistical Series Number 41, U. S. Government Printing Office, 1957.

9. United States Department of Health, Education, and Welfare, *Public Social Welfare Personnel*. Bureau of Public Assistance, and Children's Bureau, Washington, Government Printing Office, 1953.

10. Wallace, Helen M., M.D., "The Role of the Social Worker in the Rehabilitation of the Handicapped." *Social Casework*, Vol. XXXVIII, No. 1 (January 1957).

11. White, R. Clyde, *Administration of Public Welfare*. New York, American Book Company, rev. 1950, esp. Part Three, "Personnel."

12

Taking Stock

We have come a long way in the development of public programs for social welfare since the tentative beginnings in the early thirties. Some say that we have gone far enough, others that we have some distance yet to travel. The answer to this argument will depend on many factors, some of which, at least, are outside of social welfare.

If we are determined to keep governmental participation in our daily lives to a minimum, no matter how great the need, we are probably going to oppose new or expanded programs, no matter how laudable their purpose. We are likely to argue à priori that any further extension of social welfare is bad, and is dangerously accelerating our progress toward a paternalistic state.

When we respond to a national peril, like the current threat from the Soviet Union's dramatically revealed scientific progress, we are impelled to urge going "all out" to improve our international position. But this costs money, and while we are willing to spend the money, we look for other places to save. Apparently, one of the places to save, in the opinion of some people, is in federal expenditures for social welfare. These programs or at least some of them could be among the early casualties of the national crisis.

496

In the face of mounting unemployment, however, the picture has changed. Literally in the course of weeks, the sentiment has moved from concern over economy to proposals for increased federal spending to counter the decline. Democrats and Republicans in Congress seem to be vying with one another for the leading role as champion of the unemployed. The outlook, at least for the present, is for more, not less, spending by the national government.

But if and when the economy resumes its forward progress, the recurring question of the appropriate limits of federal participation will again be much in people's minds. The problem of state responsibility vis à vis that of the federal government will once more be an issue. The conflicts over this problem of how much social welfare we should support will still be unresolved.

On this question of social welfare expansion or curtailment, the author makes no spurious claim to objectivity. The best he can achieve is some restraint of bias. What follows is presented in that context.

Social welfare is vulnerable to attack because as a people we have not yet resolved our conflicts of philosophy around such large questions as the proper role of government, and our attitude toward dependency. Attacks on unemployment insurance beneficiaries, or on families receiving aid to dependent children, are more readily believed because we are uncertain about the programs and the dependency needs which they meet. An occasional fact becomes compounded many times by rumor. With such uncertain acceptance of these programs, suggestions that we could get along with a little less social welfare have a plausible sound to a receptive ear.

We need to forestall rumor by fact. We need research into the facts about dependency. It is true that experience in individual and family dependency is all around us, and that we should be able to observe the truth for ourselves. For some reason, as human experience has repeatedly demonstrated, we tend to know least about those social phenomena which surround us. The truths imbedded in the complexities of familiar daily experience are the hardest to find. Studies such as those of the Community Research

Associates have revealed some surprising facts about dependency.[1] This study found that in a community, a "hard core" of families with problems required a major part of the social services, and noted significant implications in this for organization of services. This is an example of research which can be of inestimable value.

Meanwhile, from the considerable amount we have learned in the administration of public programs of social welfare, is it possible to develop a rationale which will serve until or unless demonstrated to be false? From national leaders in this field, we have had pronouncements which suggest such a rationale. Mr. Altmeyer, former Commissioner of Social Security, as we noted earlier, has suggested that the role of government is that of affirmatively promoting the well-being of the people.[2] He states that in a country with such economic capacity as ours, the problem is not one of finding new economic resources so much as of developing the social organization to fulfill the promise of our society.

Another of our most prominent leaders in this field, Wilbur Cohen, has stated: "Too frequently, the goals and objectives of our economic, political and social institutions have been evaluated or advertised solely in terms of materialistic accomplishments to our disadvantage both at home and abroad. The goals of maximum employment, production, and purchasing power are means to a larger and more important objective—the promotion of the general welfare and the maximum development of the capacities and creativeness of the individual and strengthening of family life."[3]

The programs of social welfare of today are designed to add to the strength of this society. To treat them solely as expenditures is to deny their contribution to the level of living for all of us. Programs which help to sustain purchasing power, which restore

---

[1] See Bradley Buell and Associates, *Community Planning for Human Services* (New York, 1952).

[2] Arthur Altmeyer, "The People and Their Government," in *New Directions in Social Work,* Cora Kasius ed. (New York, 1954).

[3] Wilbur J. Cohen, "Health, Education and Welfare Policies and Expenditures for Economic Growth and the General Welfare." Summary of Testimony Presented to the Joint Economic Committee Subcommittee on Fiscal Policy, November 26, 1957, Washington, D. C. (Statement provided by courtesy of Mr. Cohen.)

handicapped people to production, reduce the staggering costs of mental illness, contribute to the reduction of crime and delinquency, help children to have a decent chance to grow up to be productive members of society, and lighten the heavy burden of insecurity on the American family add to the real wealth of the country.

These programs, if competently administered, should not create dependency. Instead, they should decrease the need to depend on others. The whole rationale for social welfare in the programs which we have covered in this book has been that of strengthening the capacity of the individual to meet his and his family's needs, not to take the responsibility for this from him.

In a real sense, these programs, by assisting the physically, mentally, and socially handicapped, express a fundamental purpose of a democracy, the equalization of opportunity. We have recognized the social injustice of compelling the handicapped person to fend for himself, without any help that might enable him to function in a competitive society. We have said that he must have the chance to make the most of his capacity for self-care and self-direction.

Can the burden of care of those unable to provide their own maintenance become insupportable? Are we approaching a peril point of taxation for social welfare which will threaten our solvency? This is a question that is difficult to answer.[4] Thus far, our national product has increased at a faster proportionate rate than our welfare expenditures. The problem of how much social welfare we can afford is, as Dr. William Haber says, not one which permits simple solutions.[5]

Many commitments to governmental support for social welfare are already made. We can scarcely turn our backs now on the responsibilities already assumed. Such factors as the increasing size of the population, the general level of prosperity, the make-up of the population, *i.e.*, the proportions of the aged and the very

[4] See Dr. William Haber, "Why Financial Need in an Expanding Economy?" *Public Welfare*, Vol. 15, No. 1 (January 1957).

[5] *Ibid.*, p. 10.

young, changes in the methods of production and their effect on the labor force, and other factors of a general social and economic nature will have much to do with the future of social welfare.

But so will our social goals. If our objective is a fuller life for all, then we cannot be satisfied with the programs of today. The many gaps which have been mentioned throughout these chapters need to be filled. The deficiencies in social insurance, public assistance, child welfare, and other services are formidable. As we have seen, the provision which they do make is generally considerably short of the goal of adequacy.

Continuation of the present pattern of cooperative federalism in which the levels of government share in the support and development of social welfare is of paramount importance. Intensification of the federal government's role in stimulating research and the improvement of personnel standards is badly needed if the programs which are enacted are to live up to their promise. But this function of stimulating and encouraging the development of a better understanding of social welfare problems should be in addition to, not in place of, federal support for the basic costs of social welfare administration and service.

The same forces which have impelled us thus far to continue the development of social welfare will work for the extension and improvement of welfare services, irrespective of any temporary curtailments. This is true because social welfare has evolved out of a changed pattern of economic and social conditions, and in response to a developing social philosophy of interdependence. The programs have not created the problems which have come with changing conditions. They are a response to them. Aid to dependent children is necessary for some families because fathers leave home, not vice versa. The income security programs for the aged do not create the problem of dependent old age. They are developed to prevent such dependency, or to meet the condition when it occurs. Certainly, failure to recognize the impending social problems is not going to prevent their occurrence. Out of our frustration over the fact that these conditions are beyond the scope of individual control, and because of their complexity, we are often inclined to want to eliminate them because of the unpleasant realities they suggest. But we do not cure illness by throwing away the medicine.

When we come to recognize the fact that dependency itself is to a degree the lot of all of us, and that the important matter is how it is met rather than whether it exists, we shall be in a position to deal rationally with it. Then, instead of denying dependency, we may look at the best way of meeting it. The choice of what social institutions we shall use for dealing with dependency is ours in a democracy. Whether we elect to leave the responsibility with the individual, assign it to voluntary organizations, or allocate the function to government, the decision still is ours.

The rapidity of events denies us the opportunity to stand still in social welfare. New patterns may develop in response to changing conditions in the future. As a people, we need to be ready to adapt our social institutions to changes which take place in all phases of life. The social welfare of the future may be quite different from that of today. But its value to society will be increased, if it is regarded as a positive factor in social and economic progress, not as a drag on the economy. An affirmative program of social welfare is an expression of the promise of a democracy to all its people, not just to those who are strong.

Index